# Lecture Notes in Computer Science

Edited by G. Goos and J. Hartmanis

## 221

# Logic Programming '85
Proceedings of the 4th Conference
Tokyo, Japan, July 1–3, 1985

Edited by Eiiti Wada

Springer-Verlag
Berlin Heidelberg New York Tokyo

**Editorial Board**
D. Barstow  W. Brauer  P. Brinch Hansen  D. Gries  D. Luckham
C. Moler  A. Pnueli  G. Seegmüller  J. Stoer  N. Wirth

**Editor**

Eiiti Wada
Department of Mathematical Engineering and Instrumentation Physics
Faculty of Engineering, University of Tokyo
3-1, Hongo 7-chome, Bunkyo-ku
Tokyo 113, Japan

CR Subject Classifications (1985): C.1.2, D.1.3, D.3.4, I.2.4, I.2.5, I.2.8

ISBN 3-540-16479-0 Springer-Verlag Berlin Heidelberg New York Tokyo
ISBN 0-387-16479-0 Springer-Verlag New York Heidelberg Berlin Tokyo

This work is subject to copyright. All rights are reserved, whether the whole or part of the material is concerned, specifically those of translation, reprinting, re-use of illustrations, broadcasting, reproduction by photocopying machine or similar means, and storage in data banks. Under § 54 of the German Copyright Law where copies are made for other than private use, a fee is payable to "Verwertungsgesellschaft Wort", Munich.

© by Springer-Verlag Berlin Heidelberg 1986
Printed in Germany

Printing and binding: Beltz Offsetdruck, Hemsbach/Bergstr.
2145/3140-543210

# Foreword

This volume of the Springer Lecture Notes in Computer Science contains most of the papers submitted, accepted for, and presented at the fourth Logic Programming Conference which took place on July 1 to 3, 1985 in Tokyo.

The first conference was held in March, 1982 in Tsukuba Science City, one month prior to the foundation of the Institute for New Generation Computer Technology (ICOT) which sponsored the later conferences. It was felt at that time that since the interests in Prolog were apparently so prevalent and research work had already been widely conducted in various institutions throughout Japan, time had come to organize the Prolog Conference.

For the subsequent years, the name of the conference was changed to "The Logic Programming Conference '8x", its site was moved to Tokyo, and the annual conferences themselves attracted many high quality papers and active audiences.

The conferences were announced and papers were called for only in Japan. The original proceedings contained both papers in Japanese and those in English.

Now, for the fourth conference, the papers written in Japanese were translated into English and all papers published in the present volume were refined.

The last word is my gratitude to authors who contributed their papers for this English version of the proceedings with additional endeavour and to each member of the program committee who spent much of his precious time to organize the conference.

Eiiti Wada
The University of Tokyo

# Program Committee / Editorial Board

| | |
|---|---|
| Eiiti Wada(Chief) | The University of Tokyo |
| Hitoshi Aida | The University of Tokyo |
| Kazuhiro Fuchi | ICOT |
| Koichi Furukawa | ICOT |
| Susumu Kunifuji | ICOT |
| Fumio Mizoguchi | Science University of Tokyo |
| Tohru Moto-oka | The University of Tokyo |
| Katsumi Nitta | ETL |
| Hidetoshi Shirai | Tamagawa University |
| Hozumi Tanaka | Tokyo Institute of Technology |
| Satoru Tomura | ETL |
| Akinori Yonezawa | Tokyo Institute of Technology |

# Referees

H. Aida, T. Fujita, K. Futatsugi, A. Goto, S. Goto,
M. Hagiya, K. Handa, S. Hayashi, K. Hirata, A. Ishii,
M. Ishikawa, H: Kondou, S. Kunifuji, T. Kurita, F. Maruyama,
T. Maruyama, H. Matsuda, T. Miyachi, T. Miyaji, T. Miyazaki,
H. Miyoshi, F. Mizoguchi, F. Motoyosi, K. Mukai, M. Nakagawa,
H. Nakashima, K. Nitta, M. Ohki, R. Onai, K. Sakai,
T. Sato, E. Shibayama, K. Shibayama, H. Shirai, A. Takeuchi,
T. Takewaki, T. Takizuka, H. Tanaka, J. Tanaka, Y. Tanaka,
S. Tomita, S. Tomura, O. Watanabe, H. Yasukawa, H. Yokota,
K. Yokota, H. Yokouchi, A. Yonezawa, K. Yuasa, M. Yuhara

# Table of Contents

Rikio ONAI, Hajime SHIMIZU, Kanae MASUDA,
Akira MATSUMOTO and Moritoshi ASO
Architecture and Evaluation of a Reduction-based Parallel Inference Machine: *PIM-R* ... 1

M. SUGIE, M. YONEYAMA, T. SAKABE, M. IWASAKI,
S. YOSHIZUMI, M. ASO, H. SHIMIZU and R. ONAI
Hardware Simulator of Reduction-based Parallel Inference Machine: *PIM-R* ... 13

T. MARUYAMA, K. HIRATA, H. TANAKA and T. MOTO-OKA
A Note on the Elementary Execution Unit in a Parallel Inference Machine ... 25

H. MATSUDA, M. KOHATA, T. MASUO, Y. KANEDA and S. MAEKAWA
Parallel Prolog Machine *PARK*: Its Hardware Structure and Prolog System ... 35

Etsuo ITOH and Hiroshi NAKAGAWA
Heuristics Applied in Tree Manipulation Algorithm Synthesis ... 44

Makoto HARAGUCHI
Analogical Reasoning using Transformations of Rules ... 56

T. HISANO and M. SUWA
Synchronization and Communication in The '*SUBJECT*' ... 66

H. ITO and H. UENO
*ZERO* : Frame + Prolog ... 78

Hidehisa TAKAHASHI and Etsuya SHIBAYAMA
*PRESET* - A Debugging Environment for Prolog ... 90

M. NUMAO and H. MARUYAMA
*PROEDIT* - A Screen Oriented Prolog Programming Environment ... 100

Shinichi HONIDEN, Naoshi UCHIHIRA and Toshiaki KASUYA
Software Prototyping with *MENDEL* ... 108

H. YOSHIDA, H. KATO and M. SUGIMOTO
Retrieval of Software Module Functions Using First-order Predicate Logical Formulae ... 117

T. AOYAGI, M. FUJITA and T. MOTO-OKA
Temporal Logic Programming Language *Tokio* - Programming in *Tokio*   128

S. KONO, T. AOYAGI, M. FUJITA and H. TANAKA
Implementation of Temporal Logic Programming Language *Tokio*   138

K. NAKAMURA
Heuristic Prolog: Logic Program Execution by Heuristic Search   148

Jiro TANAKA, Takashi YOKOMORI and Makoto KISHISHITA
AND-OR Queuing in Extended Concurrent Prolog   156

Kazunori UEDA
Guarded Horn Clauses   168

Satoru TOMURA
TDProlog : An Extended Prolog with Term Description   180

M. KISHIMOTO, T. SHINOGI, Y. KIMURA and A. HATTORI
Design and Evaluation of a Prolog Compiler   192

Akira YAMAMOTO, Masaki MITSUI, Hiroyuki YOSHIDA,
Minoru YOKOTA and Katsuto NAKAJIMA
The Program Characteristics in Logic Programming Language *ESP*   204

Kuniaki UEHARA, Takashi KAKIUCHI,
Osamu MIKAMI and Jun'ichi TOYODA
Extended Prolog and its Application to an Integrated Parser for Text Understanding   214

H. SUZUKI, M. KIYONO, S. KOUGO,
M. TAKAHASHI, S. MOTOIKE and T. NIKI
A Travel Consultation System : Towards a Smooth Conversation in Japanese   226

J.M. CHOI, M.S. SONG, K.J. JEONG, H.C. KWON, S.Y. HAN and Y.T. KIM
A Prolog-based Korean-English Machine Translation System and its Efficient Method of Dictionary Management   236

Masahiro FUJITA, Makoto ISHISONE, Hiroshi NAKAMURA,
Hidehiko TANAKA and Tohru MOTO-OKA
Using the Temporal Logic Programming Language *Tokio* for Algorithm
Description and Automatic CMOS Gate Array Synthesis     246

Yasunori NODA, Tetsuo KINOSHITA, Akira OKUMURA,
Tatsuro HIRANO and Tadashi HIRUTA
A Parallel Logic Simulator based on Concurrent Prolog     256

I. NAGASAWA
A Method of Representing Processes in a Constraint Solver     266

Katsumi NITTA and Juntaro NAGAO
*KRIP*: A Knowledge Representation System for Laws relating to Industrial
Property     276

Yasushi MATSUMURA, Takashi MATSUNAGA, Yusuke MAEDA,
Shusaku TSUMOTO, Hiroshi MATSUMURA and Michio KIMURA
Consultation System for Diagnosis of Headache and Facial Pain: '*RHINOS*'     287

Isao SUGIYAI and Keiko ISHIKAWA
Knowledge Realization and Transformation in *KRISP*     299

# Architecture and Evaluation of a Reduction-Based Parallel Inference Machine : PIM-R

Rikio ONAI [1], Hajime SHIMIZU, Kanae MASUDA [2], Akira MATSUMOTO and Moritoshi ASO

Institute for New Generation Computer Technology
Mita Kokusai Bldg. 21F, 4-28, Mita 1-Chome, Minato-ku, Tokyo 108, Japan

## ABSTRACT

This paper proposes a Reduction-based Parallel Inference Machine : PIM-R and describes the architecture and its evaluation using two kinds of software simulators. Target languages of PIM-R are Prolog and Concurrent Prolog. PIM-R executes Prolog programs in OR parallel and Concurrent Prolog programs in AND parallel. The simulation results show that PIM-R is able to exploit the parallelism in Prolog and Concurrent Prolog programs.

## 1 INTRODUCTION

Currently there are several proposals for parallel inference machine architecture (Moto-oka 84 ; Ito 84) and predicate logic languages (Shapiro 83 ; Clark 84 ; Pereira 84). We have chosen Prolog and Concurrent Prolog (Shapiro 83) as the target languages of PIM-R. These have been selected by ICOT as the base languages for its Kernel Language version 1 (KL1(84)). The basic operation of PIM-R consists of parallel generation of new resolvents. PIM-R executes Prolog programs in OR parallel and Concurrent Prolog programs in AND parallel. In PIM-R, if a process has multiple goals (the multiple goals, as a whole, are called the parent process), only the reducible goals, specified by various operators, are copied and reduced. Each resolvent generated contains a pointer to its parent process; the solution obtained is returned to the parent process using the pointer. That is, PIM-R executes Prolog and Concurrent Prolog programs by expanding and reducing a process tree. When the processing ends, the tree is logically deleted.

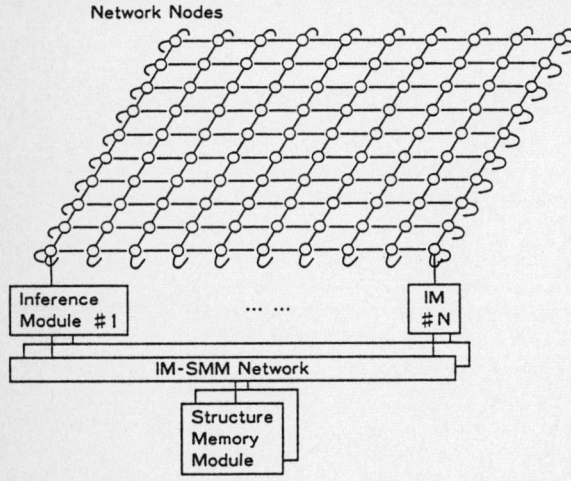

Fig. 1 Conceptual configuration of PIM-R

---

Present Address :
1.NTT Basic Research Laboratories, 3-9-11 Midori-cho Musashino-shi Tokyo 180 Japan
2.Mitsubishi Electric Corporation, Computer Works, New Product Development Dept.
  325 Kamimachiya Kamakura-shi Kanagawa 247 Japan

## 2 PIM-R ARCHITECTURE

PIM-R uses the structure-copy method to increase the independence of individual processes and decrease the network traffic due to structure sharing. It also uses the only reducible goal copy method and a unique process-structuring method to decrease the amount of copying, and the number of packets passing through the network. PIM-R architecture features include the distributed shared memory for Concurrent Prolog, network nodes for efficient packet distribution, and a structure memory to store a part of the structured data to reduce copying overhead. As shown in Figure 1, PIM-R basically consists of two types of modules, an Inference Module and a Structure Memory Module, besides networks connecting these modules.

### 2.1 Inference Module (IM)

The Inference Module (Fig. 2) consists of two units: the Unification Unit (UU) and the Process Pool Unit (PPU).

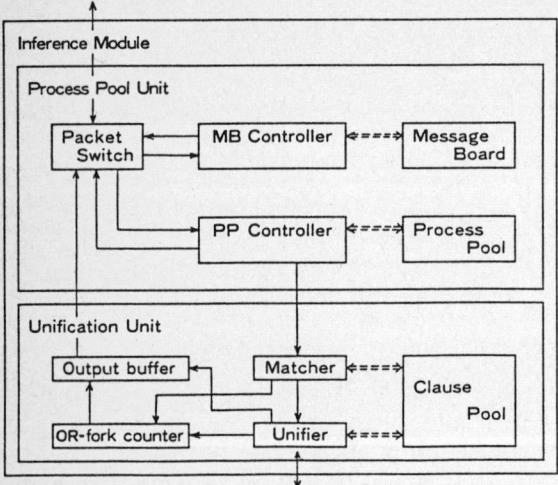

Fig. 2 Inference Module Configuration

#### 2.1.1 Unification Unit (UU)

(1) Clause Pool (CP)

The Clause Pool (CP) in each IM stores the same clauses (each word in CP is 32 bits). The Clause Pool consists of a Clause Definition Group Management Block and a Clause Definition Block. The Clause Definition Group Management Block stores the number of clauses in OR-relation, a pointer to the Clause Definition Block where each clause is stored, and the data type of the first argument of the head literal of a clause. The Clause Definition Block stores the definition of a clause and consists of a header, a variable area, a literal header, a literal area, and a structure area (Fig. 3).

(2) Matcher and Unifier

The Matcher chooses candidate clauses according to the data type of the first argument of the goal passed from the Process Pool Unit. The Unifier stores the goal sent from the Matcher in the goal memory and a clause copied from the CP in the clause memory, unifies the goal with the clause, generates the final result in the goal memory, and passes it to the output buffer. Also the Unifier executes built-in predicates.

| | | |
|---|---|---|
| #0 | Int  Clause length<br>Int  Head address of structure area<br>Int  Head address of literal header | Header |
| | Int  Number of variables<br>: | Variable area |
| | Int   Literal count<br>Type  Head literal<br>Type  Body literal N<br>:<br>Type  Body literal 1 | Literal header |
| | : | Literal area |
| | : | Structure area |

Fig. 3 The configuration of the Clause Definition Block (Type is either Poi,Lit,Sym, or Para)

## 2.1.2 Process Pool Unit (PPU)

The Process Pool Unit (PPU) consists of two types of memories (Process Pool and Message Board) and two types of controllers (Process Pool Controller and Message Board Controller).

(1) Process Pool and Process Pool Controller

The Process Pool (PP) is a memory for storing processes (32 bits/word, the same as the Clause Pool). PIM-R employs a process configuration method capable of minimizing communications between IMs. A process consists of Process Control Blocks (PCB) for storing control information of a goal sequence, a Process Life Block (PLB) to manage the number of Process Control Blocks, and Process Template Blocks (PTB; a PTB and a PCB makes a pair) to hold the template of a goal sequence. These blocks are assigned to an IM as a set.

The PLB is the top level block in a process and contains the commit tag, the number of PCBs under the PLB, and other information. At Concurrent Prolog execution, the commit tag is turned on by the PCB in the process that first succeeds in executing its guard part.

The PCB contains the state of a goal sequence (reducible (ready), run (unification is under way), wait (waiting for a solution to be sent from a child process), dead, or suspend (consumer process is waiting for a shared variable to be connected with a value)), reduction level, number of OR forks (when an OR-parallel Prolog program is executed) or AND forks (when a Concurrent Prolog program is executed), number of returns (i.e., return from forked processes), a pointer used to connect to the Ready Process Queue, etc. The reduction level means the relative depth of each process, assuming that the depth of the process which corresponds to the root of the process tree is 1. When under a PCB, a PTB has the same internal format as clauses in the Clause Pool (CP) except for the clause length. Simply put, a reducible goal in a PTB is sent to the UU, and when its solution is returned to a PCB, the goal sequence in the corresponding PTB is copied, the binding environment is assigned, and a new goal sequence (a PCB-PTB pair) is generated under the same PLB.

Process Pool Controller (PPC) is responsible for process creation, renewal, and deletion. When a new resolvent is returned from the UU, PPC creates a new process which consists of a PLB and a PCB-PTB pair. Process renewal is the updating of the fork count and return count and the creation of a new PCB-PTB pair. When a PCB enters the dead state (i.e., fork count = return count), the PPC sets the PCB state dead and increments the PCB return count in the corresponding PLB by 1.

(2) Message Board (MB) and Message Board Controller (MBC)

Each IM has a distributed shared memory called Message Board to store variables used as channels (these variables are called simply channels). The MBC is designed to reduce the load of PPC processing. The MB consists of channel cells, value cells, and a suspend process list. Channel cells consist of four words and contain a write tag, a suspend tag, a pointer to a value cell, the suspend process count, and the head address of the suspend process list. In Concurrent Prolog, when a consumer process suspends the PPC requires the MBC to check whether a producer process has already sent a message to that MB containing the cell of the channel causing the suspension. If a message has arrived, the MBC sends the message to the PPC to activate the consumer process; otherwise, the MBC writes the PP address of the consumer process in the suspend process list.

A channel can be described with two "channel information" words stored in the structure area in a PTB. Given a goal sequence "p(X), c(X?)", p(X), which is placed in the PP of an IM as a result of an AND fork, has a PTB in Fig. 4. ChIR is a data type which stores a pointer to channel information. The first word of Channel Information is usually a pointer to an appropriate channel on the MB. The second word stores local data. When unification on a guard succeeds and the commit operation is performed, this local data is written into the appropriate channel cell on the MB.

| | PTB | length |
|---|---|---|
| | Head address of structure area | |
| | Head address of literal area | |
| | Int | 1 |
| #X | ChIR | |
| | Int | 1 |
| | Lit | 2 |
| | Int | 2 |
| | Poi | p |
| | UChR | #X |
| | Poiter to MB | |
| | Var1 | (local data area) |

Channel Information

Fig. 4 Process Template Block of p(X).

## 2.2 Structure Memory Module

We have introduced the structure memory concept to reduce the copying overhead. The Structure Memory Module stores only a large structured data, such as large combined lists and vectors. Each Structure Memory Module (SMM) is connected to several Inference Modules (IM) via the IM-SMM Network and a part of the structured data is accessed by the Unification Unit (UU) in the IM on a unification-demand basis. Our SMM has the following characteristics.

(1) Ground instance sharing method

We have chosen the most basic method: that of sharing only ground instances which do not include any unbound variables. This sharing method can maintain highly parallel environments among processes.

(2) Combined representation of structured data

We use a combined representation scheme, which includes the list-based representation with pointers and the record-based representation storing data in successive memory cells.

(3) Lazy unification between arguments

For unification requiring the structured data stored in the SMM, PIM-R uses a lazy unification between arguments to avoid unnecessary unifications and accesses to the SMM. If there is an argument referring to the SMM in either the reducible goal or the unifiable clause, then this unification will be delayed and the other unifications between arguments not referring to the SMM will be executed with higher priorities.

## 2.3 Network

At execution of Prolog or Concurrent Prolog programs on PIM-R, when a goal succeeds in unification with a rule, a child process (new resolvent) is generated. However, even if a goal succeeds in unification with a fact, the result is only returned to the PCB in a parent process and a child process is not generated. Our previous report (Onai 84) shows that the average OR-relation number is about 2 or 3 in Prolog programs that consist mainly of rules. Thus it is possible to map an average process tree onto a cyclic mesh structure.

In programs of logic languages such as Prolog, when there are several solutions, locations (depth) of each solution in the AND-OR tree are usually different and children forked simultaneously rarely return solutions to a parent process at the same time. Thus, the mesh-type network node, onto which the upper part of a process tree is mapped, only rarely gets overloaded by concentration of solutions returned to a parent process. Also all accesses except for those to the MB at Concurrent Prolog execution are between neighbor nodes. For these reasons, we chose mesh type structure for the inter-IM network (Fig. 1). In the inter-IM network, nodes are located at mesh points and an IM is connected to each node. The network between IMs and the SMM, the IM-SMM network, is of the equal distance type and at present is expected to be implemented with a shared bus.

## 3 BASIC SOFTWARE SIMULATION

The basic simulator is developed to confirm fundamental validity of PIM-R mechanisms and written in Prolog/C-Prolog, and runs on DEC2060 or VAX-11.

### 3.1 Simulation conditions

Simulation is performed under the following conditions:

(1) A network is ideal, excluding packet conflict.

(2) Each unit has a buffer of sufficient size.

(3) The performance of PPUs (process creation, renewal, and deletion) and UUs is determined by the number of steps required when they are written in an ordinary assembly language. (Moto-oka 84), who adopted the all goals copy method, shows that the average time of a unification and size reduction in a 6-Queens program is about $42 \mu sec$. Since PIM-R uses the only reducible goal copy method and the amount of copying for this method is less than that for the all goals copy method, we assume that UU in PIM-R is able to execute a unification and produce the packet to send to PPU in $100 \mu sec$ at worst. (We think that UU is able to execute those operations in under $50 \mu sec$ if special hardware for the UU is implemented.) Since the average packet length through networks of 4-Queens is about 20 words (about 600 bits), we assume that network speed is 10 Mbps and average network delay is $60 \mu sec$.

(4) When unification with a unit clause succeeds in OR-parallel Prolog processing, the unification result is returned to the parent process in PP and no child process is created. On the other hand, when unification with a clause other than a unit clause succeeds, the new resolvent (new child process) is distributed. In Concurrent Prolog, goals in AND relation are distributed as different processes. This simulation adopts the following static and cyclic distribution strategy: IM concerned, East IM, South IM, IM concerned,... and so on. In simulations with two IMs, new processes are distributed to the IMs according to the following strategy: the first process is distributed to the IM concerned, the second to the neighboring IM, the third to the IM concerned,... and so on.

## 3.2 Simulation results

### 3.2.1 Prolog program

The 4-Queens program was run to collect the necessary data.

(1) Effect of number of Inference Modules (Fig. 5)

The 4-Queens program increases in performance as the number of Inference Modules (IM) increases. Processing time decreases as more Inference Modules are used up to seven or eight units. Then it levels off. This trends roughly corresponds to the average level of OR parallelism, about 6, resulting from a dynamic analysis (Onai 84). The results show that PIM-R is able to exploit the parallelism in the Prolog program.

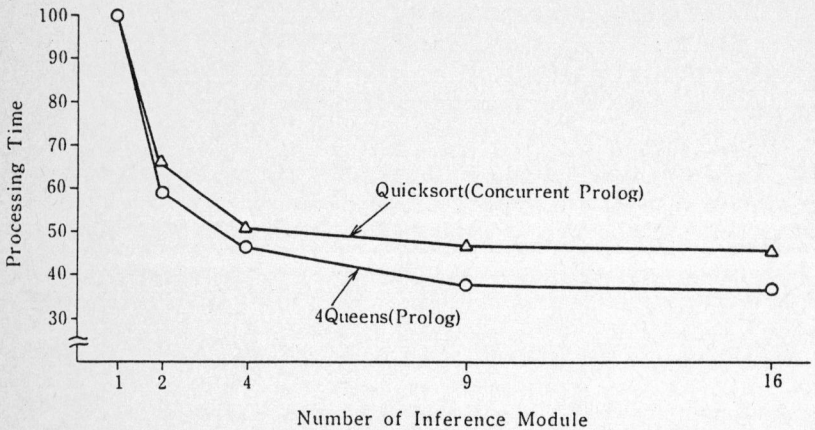

Fig. 5 Effect of Number of Inference Modules

(2) Halting dead child processing

The number of packets passing through the network is shown by their types in Table 1.

Table 1    Packet Number (through the network)

|  | 2IMs | 4IMs |
|---|---|---|
| Total number of packets | 151 | 207 |
| Number of true return packets | 31 | 47 |
| Number of OR-fork packets | 60 | 80 |
| Number of fork-down packets | 60 | 80 |

The fork-down packet is used by a child process to inform its parent process that it has entered the dead state. It is concerned with garbage collection and is not directly related to the solution-obtaining processing. Therefore, if the PP has sufficient space, lower priorities can be given to dead child processing and the generation and transfer of fork-down packets in the PPC. Higher priorities are given to first executing processing required to obtain solutions and to transfer the respective packets. This can reduce the number of packets passing through the network by about 40% for two and four IMs. Also it alleviates processing load in the PPC, resulting in about 8% and 15% reductions in processing time to obtain the first and second solutions for four IMs respectively.

(3) Local execution control using reduction level

Local pseudo depth-first execution was tried giving higher priorities to Ready PCBs with deeper reduction levels and to processing of true-return packets from child processes. At the same time, lower priority is given to fork-down packet processing. The result was that 12% and 17% reductions in processing time to obtain the first and second solutions for four IMs respectively were achieved.

(4) Network load average and network speed

The load average of each link is about 10% for two IMs and 6% for four IMs. (There are 2 links for two IMs and 8 links for four IMs.) The more IMs the less load average. Simulation condition (1) is appropriate. The maximum input buffer length of the Packet Switch is 15 for two IMs and 14 for four IMs. If we speed up the network from 10Mbps to 60Mbps, we get about 10% reduction in processing time for four IMs.

(5) PPU load average and dynamic process distribution

When 60Mbps network speed for four IMs is achieved, the PPC in each IM recorded load averages of 42%, 55%, 54%, and 80%. Relatively wide discrepancies exist among these figures, because the child process distributing strategy at OR fork was fixed. In this case, the average input buffer lengths of the packet switches are 0.46, 0.69, 0.49, and 4.5 units. These results correlate with the load averages of the PPC. When network nodes are used to dynamically distribute child processes to the IM whose packet switch has the shortest input buffer length, the processing time necessary for obtaining the first and second solutions can be decreased further by 10% and 14% for four IMs; then the PPC in each IM has balanced load averages of 69%, 72%, 62%, and 65%.

### 3.2.2 Concurrent Prolog program

The Quicksort (ten elements) program was run to collect various data items.

(1) Effect of number of Inference Modules (Fig. 5)

The Quicksort program increases in performance as the number of IMs increases. Processing time decreases as more Inference Modules are used up to five or six units. Then it levels off. Since this example has a parallelism of about 4, the results show that PIM-R is able to exploit the parallelism in the Concurrent Prolog program.

(2) Halting dead child processing

Table 2 shows the number of reductions and other data at the execution of Quicksort.

Table 3 shows the number of packets passing through the network during Quicksort execution by their types.

Table 2  Reduction Number

| | |
|---|---|
| Number of reduction | 284 |
| Number of successes | 196 |
| Number of failuers | 19 |
| Number of suspended reduction | 69 |

**Table 3  Packet number**

|  | 2IM | 4IM |
|---|---|---|
| Total number of packets | 141 | 211 |
| Number of true return pakets | 17 | 19 |
| Number of AND-fork packets | 21 | 26 |
| Number of fork down packets | 21 | 26 |
| Number of MB-related packets | 82 | 140 |

These tables show that, while 284 reductions occurred and 196 of them succeeded, 141 packets passed through the network for two IMs and 211 packets for four IMs. In other words, a packet passed through the network each time about 1.3 or 2 reductions occurred. Unlike the Prolog program, the MB-related packets account for 58% of the total for two IMs and 66% for four IMs, as shown in Table 3. This means that halting dead child processing and generation and transfer of fork-down packets, an effective approach in the Prolog program, could reduce the number of packets passing through the network by only 15% for two IMs and 12% for four IMs. Unlike the fork down packets, these MB-related packets cannot have a lower transfer priority attached; if they do, no solution will be obtained. Therefore, faster packet transfer is more critical for Concurrent Prolog.

(3) Effect of Message Board Controller (MBC)

A channel cell is allocated on the MB when unification succeeds in the UU, a new child process is returned to the PPU, and there is a new channel. At execution of Quicksort, 88 channels are stored on the MB and, as Table 2 shows, successful unifications are total 196. This requires the cell for a channel to be allocated on the MB every time about 2.2 unifications succeed. Thus the speed of allocating a channel cell on the MB influences PIM-R processing speed. This problem can be eliminated by introducing a MBC to handle MB-related processing. If the MB-related processing were handled by the PPC, instead of the MBC, processing time would increase by 13% for one IM and by 10% for four IMs.

(4) AND-OR parallel execution

When Concurrent Prolog programs are executed in AND-OR parallel, child processes distributed in the different IMs from the parent process have to check the commit tag in the parent process through networks when guard execution is successful. Child processes have to wait for the return packet from the parent process. This increases network traffic. In the case of four IMs at execution of Quicksort, since the number of commit tag check packets and return packets is 22, the total packet number increases about 10%. As a result, the processing time for AND-OR-parallel execution increases about 13% over that of AND-parallel execution. OR-parallel execution is not suitable for Concurrent Prolog programs.

## 4 DETAILED SOFTWARE SIMULATION

Detailed software simulators have been developed using Occam (INMOS 84), a language capable of describing multiple processes running concurrently and message communications between processes. The major emphasis is on simulation which precisely reflects the detailed structure of PIM-R, such as internal data formats, and which involves 16 to 64 or more IMs. The simulators are currently running on the VAX 11 to collect various pieces of data.

### 4.1 Simulation Conditions

(1) Dead process processing is not halted in PPC.

(2) If the PTB does not get longer at compaction (ONAI 85) when a solution to a built-in predicate is returned, direct overwriting to the process template is possible.

(3) The PPC attaches new Ready PCBs to the tail of the RPQ and transfers the head Ready PCB to the UU.

(4) Simulation clock is not introduced yet.

(5) Process distribution is the same as that of basic software simulation.

## 4.2 Simulation Results

### 4.2.1 Message Board (MB) - related packets

Packets passed through the inter-IM network include AND-fork packets and packets indicating successful/ failed unification of child processes. They also include MB-related packets such as the channel-value write/ read packets that are passed when Concurrent Prolog channel variables are not stored on the MB of the IM concerned and the activation packets are returned to suspended processes. Table 4 shows how the number of packets and the total length of the packets (in words) changes with the number of IMs for Quicksort (50 elements) simulation. Table 4 suggests that the MB-related packets, each consisting of a small number of data words, account for most of the packets transferred between IMs. Therefore, fust transfer of MB-related packets is important.

Table 4   Packet number and word length

| IM number | 1 | 2 | 4 | 9 | 16 |
|---|---|---|---|---|---|
| packets in IM | 8106[PKT] 166258[W] | 6773 161267 | 6127 158849 | 5694 157162 | 5683 157123 |
| inter IM packets | 0 0 | 1535 11110 | 2247 15709 | 2674 17261 | 2681 17106 |
| MB-related packets in inter IM packets | 0 - 0 - | 1333 (87%) 4991 (45%) | 1979 (88%) 7409 (47%) | 2412 (90%) 9096 (53%) | 2423 (90%) 9135 (53%) |

### 4.2.2 Effect of shared Clause Pool (CP)

The software simulator involving two IMs ran 6Queens written in Prolog and Quicksort (50 elements) in Concurrent Prolog to collect data on the PTB and packets. The results are shown in Table 5 and Table 6 bellow ("literal length" = literal header length + literal area length).

Table 5   Effect of shered Clause Pool (in Prolog)

| 6Queens | Average total length in word(A) | Average literal length in word(L) | L/A(%) |
|---|---|---|---|
| PTB | 44.8 | 21.7 | 48.4 |
| OR-fork packets | 43.7 | 23.4 | 53.5 |
| true return packets | 30.9 | 9.9 | 32.0 |

Table 6   Effect of shered Clause Pool (in Concurrent Prolog)

| Quicksort | Average total length in word(A) | Average literal length in word(L) | L/A(%) |
|---|---|---|---|
| PTB | 37.7 | 11.0 | 29.3 |
| AND-fork packets | 36.2 | 4.5 | 12.4 |
| true return packets | 24.3 | 5.5 | 22.5 |

If the PPC can access the CP, the length of the PTB can be shortened by about 30 to 50% by removing the literal header and literal area from the PTB. This results in a decrease in the amount of processes generated and renewed copying in the PPU as well as the amount of unification-related copying in the UU. In addition, OR-fork and true-return packets in 6Queens can be reduced in length by 54% and 32%, respectively, and AND-fork and true-return packets in Quicksort by 12% and 23%, respectively. This in turn leads to reduction in network traffic.

### 4.2.3 Effect of Structure Memory Module (SMM)

Various data items are being collected by running evaluation programs, such as the morphological analysis program, DCG program, a formula simplification program (Equiv2), and Quicksort (50 elements), on the prolog software simulator. The data obtained is used to examine the effect of the SMM on the structured area and the effect of lazy unification in particular.

(1) Reducing effect of structure area

As shown in Table 7, the use of the SMM for program 1 to 3 reduced the PTB length by 20 to 30% when the CP was not shared (A/B) and by 30 to 45% when it was shared (C/D). The SMM was also able to shorten (in words) the OR-fork and true-return packets by 10 to 45 percent for the non-shared CP (A/B) and by 20 to 50% for the shared CP (C/D). The combined effect of sharing the CP and the use of SMM (C/B) resulted in about a 50 to 60% decrease in length for the PTB and about a 50 to 60% decrease for OR-fork and true-return packets. Since the structure area generally accounts for a larger portion in true-return packets than in OR-fork packets, the introduction of the SMM was slightly more effective for true-return packets. Also, the simulation leads to the conclusion that the SMM will have a significant effect on programs, such as the morphological analysis, DCG, and formula simplification programs, which perform various processing operations on structured data bound with ground instances without changing the data, but an insignificant effect on programs like Quicksort which successively create new lists.

Table 7  Reducing effect of structure area

| | test programs | | Average length in words (Clause Pool not shared) | | | Average length in words (Clause Pool shared) | | |
|---|---|---|---|---|---|---|---|---|
| | | | SMM used:A | SMM not used:B | A/B (%) | SMM used:C | SMM not used:D | C/D (%) |
| 1. | Morphological analysis | PTB | 44.2 | 64.2 | 68.8 | 23.6 | 43.7 | 54.1 |
| | | OR-fork | 35.8 | 47.4 | 75.5 | 17.9 | 29.7 | 60.2 |
| | | true return | 32.3 | 52.6 | 61.4 | 24.0 | 44.3 | 54.2 |
| 2. | DCG | PTB | 29.3 | 37.9 | 77.3 | 14.5 | 23.1 | 62.9 |
| | | OR-fork | 28.3 | 34.6 | 81.3 | 13.2 | 19.7 | 66.8 |
| | | true return | 51.3 | 86.0 | 59.7 | 42.8 | 77.4 | 55.3 |
| 3. | Formula simplificaton | PTB | 35.3 | 43.4 | 81.3 | 20.4 | 28.5 | 71.5 |
| | | OR-fork | 35.9 | 40.8 | 88.0 | 20.5 | 25.4 | 80.9 |
| | | true return | 54.5 | 98.5 | 55.3 | 46.9 | 90.9 | 51.6 |
| 4. | Quicksort | PTB | 85.7 | 94.2 | 91.0 | 61.7 | 74.2 | 83.1 |
| | | OR-fork | 63.3 | 73.0 | 86.7 | 42.7 | 52.4 | 81.6 |
| | | true return | 132.7 | 144.5 | 91.8 | 122.7 | 134.5 | 91.2 |

(2) Effect of lazy unification

As Table 8 suggests, the use of lazy unification could lower the number of SMM read requests and the total length of SMM read returns by about 10% for the morphological analysis program. Lazy unification, however, cannot work effectively for some programs like the DCG program.

Table 8  Effect of lazy unification

| Morphological analysis | lazy(L) | nomal(N) | (N-L)/N (%) |
|---|---|---|---|
| Number of SMM read requests | 822 | 908 | 9.5 |
| Total length of SMM read returns | 2772 | 2956 | 6.2 |

### 4.2.4 Effect of writing programs in GHC and GHC-supporting data types

In programs written in GHC (Ueda 85), the base language of KL1(85), PTBs need not to have a local environment for a channel. The following table shows goals-related data (not built-in predicates) which were passed from the PPU to UU when 50-element Quicksort in Concurrent Prolog ran on the two-IMs. Table 9 suggests that the packet length can be reduced by 25% by writing programs in GHC (a pointer to the MB can be stored in the ChIR-type word in the variable area). Note that, when a predicate is called in GHC, binding which can be observed from the caller cannot be generated while the guard in a clause is being executed. Therefore, such a binding (unification) must be moved to the body of the clause.

Table 9  Effect of writing programs in GHC

| | |
|---|---|
| Average goal length in words | 35.4 |
| Average structure area length in words | 18.0 |
| Average channel information (a pointer to the MB and local enviroment) length in words | 8.8 |

For example, a clause "qsort([],[]):- true | true." in Quicksort in Concurrent Prolog is expressed in GHC as follows:
    qsort([],X):- true | X=[].

This causes the variable area to increase by one word for the new variable X and the literal area by four words because the internal format of "X=[]" is four words in length. These increases in the variable and literal areas in GHC over Concurrent Prolog require the CP to be accessed from the PC as well. This is also necessary to benefit from the GHC's ability to eliminate local environments (if the CP can be accessed from the PPC, the literal area can be removed from the PTB). Also, the introduction of three new GHC-supporting data types - TopCh (channel in the goal in the first calling process), WritableCh (channel capable of undergoing binding), and NestedCh (channel called from a guard directly or indirectly) - seems to make it possible to write programs in GHC without changing the Concurrent Prolog execution mechanism in PIM-R.

## 5  CONCLUSION

This paper described the architecture and evaluations using software simulatiors of PIM-R, a reduction-based parallel inference machine. The introduction of the PLB into a process can make it unnecessary to report each generation or deletion of a goal sequence to its parent process, irrespective of how many goal sequences are generated or deleted in that process. Therefore the use of such process-structuring methods permits a decrease in the number of packets passing through the inter-IM network.

As for architecture, PIM-R uses a Message Board to handle Prolog and Concurrent Prolog programs equally. It was confirmed that the MB permits PIM-R to execute Concurrent Prolog functions including back communication and finite-length buffer communications. The evaluation using PIM-R software simulators demonstrated that PIM-R is able to exploit parallelism in Prolog and Concurrent Prolog programs. In other words, the number of Inference Modules does affect the performance of parallel processing. It was also confirmed that the dynamic distribution of child processes by network nodes, introduction of the MBC, halting of dead child processing, stopping the generation and transfer of fork-down packets in the PPC, local pseudo-depth-first execution using reduction level, introduction of the SMM, and shared Clause Pool are all effective measures.

At Concurrent Prolog execution, over half the packets sent through networks are related to MB access. Therefore, we think that it is not sufficient to increase packet transfer speed. It is also necessary to decrease the relative number of MB-related packets to other packets. It is a way of introducing modularity into the language to enlarge grain size of AND-parallel processing of Concurrent Prolog. Since a channel in Concurrent Prolog is a logical variable, a producer and a consumer have to execute unification for sending and receiving a message respectively. It causes a reduction in speed of message transfer. Clearly, research into the implementation problem of communication and synchronization in logic-type languages not using logical variables is necessary.

At present we are developing a hardware simulation system consisting of sixteen MC68000s (Sugie 85). We plan to conduct various detailed simulations of many programs, with these tools to validate and enhance PIM-R.

ACKNOWLEDGMENTS

Finally, thanks are due to Director Kazuhiro Fuchi and Dr. Shunichi Uchida at ICOT for providing the opportunity to pursue this research. The discussion with and comments of Dr. Mamoru Sugie, Mitsugu Yoneyama and Masa-aki Iwasaki of the Central Research Laboratory Hitachi, Ltd. were of great benefit.

REFERENCES

Clark KL, Gregory S (1984) PARLOG:Parallel Programming in Logic, Research Report DOC 84/4, Dept. of Computing, Imperial College, London

INMOS Limited (1984) Occam Programming Manual, Prentice-Hall International Series in Computer Science

Ito N, Masuda K (1984) Parallel Inference Machine Based on the Data Flow Model, Proc. of the International Workshop on High Level Computer Architecture 84, Los Angeles

Moto-oka T, Tanaka H, et al (1984) The Architecture of a Parallel Inference Engine-PIE-, Proc. of Int. Conf. on Fifth Generation Computer Systems 1984, ICOT, Tokyo

Onai R, Shimizu H, Masuda K, Aso M (1984) Analysis of Sequential Prolog Programs, ICOT TR-048

Onai R, Aso M, Shimizu H, Masuda K, Matsumoto A (1985) Architecture of a Reduction-based Parallel Inference Machine:PIM-R, New Generation Computing, vol 3/2, Ohmsha, Springer-Verlag, p 197-228

Pereira LM, Nasr R (1984) DELTA-PROLOG: A Distributed Logic Language, Proc. of Int. Conf. on Fifth Generation Computer Systems 1984, ICOT, Tokyo

Shapiro EY (1983) A subset of Concurrent Prolog and Its Interpreter, ICOT TR-003

Sugie M, et.al. (1985) Hardware Simulator Implementation of PIM-R, Logic Programming Conference '85, Tokyo

Ueda K (1985) Guarded Horn Clauses, ICOT TR-103

Hardware Simulator of Reduction-Based Parallel Inference Machine PIM-R

* M. Sugie, M. Yoneyama, T. Sakabe, M. Iwasaki, S. Yoshizumi
** M. Aso, H. Shimizu, R. Onai

* Central Research Laboratory, Hitachi, Ltd., Kokubunji, Tokyo 185, Japan
** ICOT, Mita, Minato-ku, Tokyo 108, Japan

## ABSTRACT

A hardware simulator of PIM-R (Reduction-Based Parallel Inference Machine) has been developed. Eight MC68000 single board computers and shared storage operate as the inference modules and the network, respectively. In order to realize high simulation rate, an event-driven method is introduced. "Queens" program and "Quicksort" program were executed on the simulator. The results show that a PIM-R architecture can effectivity utilize the parallelism in Prolog/Concurrent Prolog programs.

## INTRODUCTION

As a result of research carried out under the auspices of the Fifth Generation Computer Project, knowledge/information processing system based on a predicate logic programing language has been developed. The system hardware of that system has been dubbed an "Inference Machine", since the principle of predicate logic is inference. Since inference can be carried out in parallel, the machine's operation is based on parallel action. Several ideas concerning parallel inference processing and predicate logic programming language, have recently been reported [1],[2],[3],[9], and the authors have proposed a parallel inference machine based on the reduction concept which was given the name "Reduction-Based Parallel Inference Machine" (PIM-R) [4],[5],[6],[7],[10].
As the first step of verification of PIM-R architecture, software simulator (written in Prolog) was developed. As a result, it was confirmed that PIM-R can extract the parallelism which exists in Prolog and Concurrent Prolog programs, that introduction of a special purpose controller for Message Board is effective, and that dynamic dispatch of subprocesses through network nodes is effective, etc. [8].
However, it was difficult to simulate PIM-R accurately and in detail for the data structure, etc., since the objective of this software simulator was to confirm the basic principle of PIM-R. Also, it was too slow for detailed simulation. Therefore, in order to achieve ① simulation of detailed structure of PIM-R, ② increase in simulation speed, ③ expansion of memory space, and ④ simulation in a parallel environment, we decided to develop a hardware simulator. In particular, parallel environment simulation was selected as the main objective of the hardware simulator. The reason for this is that it is difficult on a sequential machine to collect data on typical problems (deadlock etc.) and software utilities in parallel environment.
In developing the hardware simulator, flexibility was a major consideration. The hardware simulator must be flexible in order to shorten the cycle time of data collection/ evaluation /improvement in the architecture design of PIM-R. Since the principle of PIM-R is confirmed by the software simulator, it is appropriate to work on the evaluation of the detailed structure of PIM-R as soon as possible. In order to realize flexibility and quick development, we have decided to implement the Inference Module of PIM-R by a single board microcomputer (abbreviated as SBC) using the MC68000. All modules of PIM-R were implemented by software for easy updat-

ing and modification. A VAX11/780 was used as the supervisor of the hardware simulator. This paper presents the details of the PIM-R hardware simulator and the results of simulation on Prolog and Concurrent Prolog programs.

HARDWARE SIMULATOR

System Organization

functional organization

The conceptual structure of the hardware simulator is shown in Fig. 1. In accordance with the architecture of PIM-R, it consists of three modules, IM (Inference Module), NSM (Network and Structure Memory Module), and CM (Control Module).
The following are the main features of these modules. CM consists of a System Manager which compiles programs, drives IMs, and outputs results. NSM provides data buffers and storage for long structured data. The CM buffer and the IM buffer are used to transfer data between CM and IM, and IM and IM, respectively. The IM consists of five modules and three storage buffers. The functions of the IM are as follows :

  (a) Nucleus
  ①Processes interrupts generated by commands from CM. (commands from CM are described in the following section.)
  ②Activates PPU (Process Pool Unit).
  (b) PPU
  ①Creates and deletes processes, and controls the transition between ready, wait and suspend status.
  ②Picks up goals from queueing ready processes, and sends these goals to UU (Unification Unit).
  ③Sends packets to NET.
  (c) UU
  ① Unifies goals and corresponding clauses for carrying out reduction.
  ②Calls SMU (Structure Memory Unit) for unifying long structured data.
  (d) NET
  ①Writes packets to the IM buffer for data transfer.
  ②Manages the wait queue for packets in the IM buffer.

  (e) SMU
  ①Unifies long structured data.
  (f) Process Pool
  ①Stores process information. Process status, originating process and variables are included in this information.
  (g) Clause Pool
  ①Stores source programs.
  (h) Message Board
  ①Stores data on channels for concurrent process synchronization.

hardware organization

Fig.2 shows the hardware organization of the hardware simulator. An IM consists of an SBC board and a local storage connected to the SBC bus. NSM is simulated by a shared

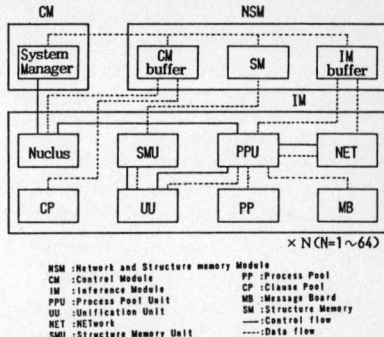

Fig. 1. Conceptual block diagram of the hardware simulator

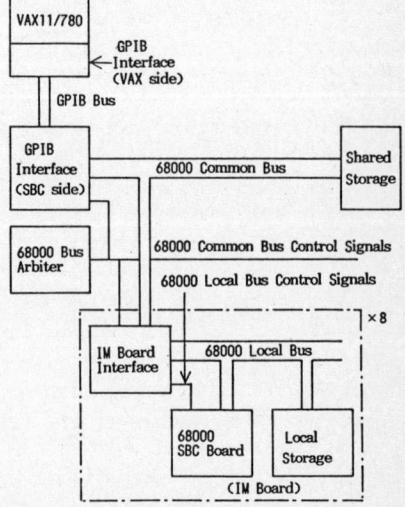

Fig. 2. Hardware block diagram of the simulator

storage, which can be accessed by 8 SBCs. The VAX11/780 is used as the CM. The shared storage is connected to a common bus, to which the GPIB Interface, 8 IM Board Interfaces and the shared storage are connected. The GPIB Interface handles the communications between VAX11/780 and the shared storage. On the other hand, the IM Board Interfaces handle the communication between SBCs and the shared storage. VAX11/780 accesses to the shared storage through the GPIB Interface, and sends commands to the destined SBC. Every SBC accesses the shared storage through the IM Board Interface. The Bus Arbiter enables 8 SBCs and VAX11/780 to access shared storage by controlling the ownership of the common bus. The IM Board Interface is introduced in order to enable every SBC to have its own local storage. The local storage and the shared storage are distinguished by address area. SBC buses are connected to the common bus when shared storage address area is accessed.

The address map of the SBC is shown in Fig.3. The storage capacity can be up to 10MB for every local storage, and 4MB for the shared storage. On the hardware simulator, 2MB of shared storage and 30MB (2MB~6MB/SBC) of local storage were installed in total.

We have decided to avoid the special network hardware and use the shared storage as the NSM so that we can simulate several types of networks.

### system operation

The outline of the hardware simulator operation is as follows : First of all , the CM resets all IMs, after which it reads the program, simulation parameters and query from user files, broadcasts program and parameters to all IM local storages, and writes the query into the IM buffer for IM#0. After these transactions are completed, the CM activates all IMs. In an IM, Nucleus is activated by a power-on-reset or reset command from the CM. After initializing the head address of the Clause Pool, the head address and the current pointer of the Process Pool, and the Message Board etc., the Nucleus starts waiting for activation by the CM. When the IM is activated by the CM, Nucleus gives control to the PPU. The PPU then examines language selection parameters and calls either the Prolog routine or the Concurrent Prolog routine. The Prolog routine and Concurrent Prolog routine call the PPU-packet handling routine, which starts execution of reduction. The PPU-packet handling routine and the ready process handling routine execute unification by calling UU when there exist goals to be reduced. The UU-packet handling routine dispatches goals to IMs according to a predetermined strategy, and calls NET to send packets to other IMs in the event the goals are to be sent to those IMs.

### method for communication

Communication between CM and NSM takes the form of data transfer. After initializing the DMA controller by sending commands to the IM through GPIB, VAX11/780 sends and receives data through GPIB. There are two types of communication between CM and IM. One is command transfer and the other is data transfer. Data transfer between CM and IM is executed via the CM buffer in NSM. For data transfer from CM to IM, VAX11/780 writes data to the CM buffer, sends commands to SBCs, and instructs SBCs to receive data in the CM buffer. For data transfer from IM to CM, VAX11/780 sends commands to SBCs and instructs them to write data to the CM buffer, and after receiving completion signals, reads data from the CM buffer. All commands are sent through GPIB. Communication between IM and IM takes the form of data packet transfer via NSM. In NSM, there are IM buffers corresponding to each IM, and data packets are written to the IM buffer

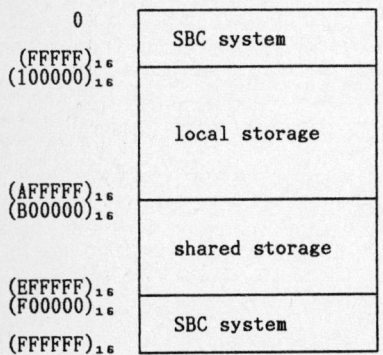

Fig. 3. SBC address map

which corresponds to the destined IM. The IM which is to receive the packet extracts data packets. Every IM searches the arrival of data packets, and reads them when they arrive.

Hardware

interface

Four methods are designed for the interface. These are shown in Table 1.
(1) Command transfer from VAX11/780 to SBCs are executed by interrupts from VAX11/780 to SBCs.
(2) Transaction requests from SBCs to VAX11/780 are executed by status monitoring by VAX11/780.

(3) Data transfers between VAX11/780 and SBCs are executed by DMA method. DMA transfer is controlled by a DMA control LSI (Hitachi HM68450).
(4) Data transfesr between SBCs are executed by the PIO method.

The interface between VAX11/780 and SBC is realized by data read/write to registers. Register specifications are shown in Table 2. CDTR1 is used to transfer data between VAX11/780 and SBCs. CDTR2 is used to inform SBCs of DMA transfer byte counts and DMA transfer destination/source addresses, which are used for data transfer between VAX11/780

Table 1. Interface

| Item | Interface |
|---|---|
| Command transfer from VAX11/780 to SBC68K | Interrupt from VAX11/780 to SBC68K |
| Request transfer from SBC68K to VAX11/780 | Status Monitoring by VAX11/780 |
| Data transfer between VAX11/780 and SBCs | DMA |
| Data transfer between SBCs | PIO |

Table 2. Register specifications

| Register Name (abbreviated name) | bit length | Specification |
|---|---|---|
| Data Register 1 (CDTR1) | 8 | used to transfer data |
| Data Register 2 (CDTR2) | 8 | used to transfer DMA control data |
| Status Register 1 (CSTR1) | 8 | used to inform status of SBC68K |
| Status Register 2 (CSTR2) | 8 | used to distinguish which SBC requests data transfer |
| Status Register 3 (CSTR3) | 8 | used to detect the completion of transaction by SBC |
| Control Register (CCTR) | 8 | used to specify which SBC VAX11/780 send command to |
| Command Register (CCMR) | 8 | used to specify commands |

Table 3. VAX11/780→SBC interface commands

| Command | specification |
|---|---|
| shared storage write | command to transfer data from VAX11/780 to shared storage |
| shared storage read | command to transfer data from shared storage to VAX11/780 |
| local storage set | command to transmfer data from shared storage to local storage of SBC |
| shared storage set | command to transfer data from local storage of SBC to shared storage |
| analysys data request | command to transfer statical data from local storage of SBC to shared storage |
| local storage dump request | command to transfer data from local storage of SBC to shared storage |
| initialize request | command to initialize tables in SBC |
| abort request | command to stop reduction operation immediately |

and SBC by the DMA method. CSTR1 is used to inform VAX11/780 of the completion of DMA transfer preparation and completion of data transfer. CSTR2 is used to distinguish which SBC requests data transfer. CSTR3 is used to detect the completion of a transaction by SBC, for the commands to SBCs except shared storage read/write ones. CCTR is used to specify which SBC VAX11/780 sends command to. CCMR is used to specify commands from VAX11/780 to SBCs.

command

We designed 8 types of interface commands between VAX11/780 and SBC. These are shown in Table 3. "Shared storage write" is a command to transfer data from VAX11/780 to the shared storage. "Shared storage read" is a command to transfer data from the shared storage to VAX11/780. "Local storage set" is a command to transfer data from the shared storage to the SBC local storage. "Shared storage set" is a command to transfer data from the SBC local storage to the shared storage. "Analysis data request" is a command to transfer statistical data from the SBC local storage to the shared storage to analyze the architecture. "Local storage dump request" is a command to transfer data from the SBC local storage to the shared storage. "Initialize request" is a command to initialize SBC tables. "Abort request" is a command to request SBCs to stop their reduction operations immediately.

implementation

The only types of special hardware are the GPIB interface and the IM board interface ( shown in Fig. 2). These are implemented by 4 different types of boards. The rest of the system is assembled by using commercially available components. Table 4 shows the main components of the special hardware which has been designed and implemented.
The GPIBIF1 board includes 4 registers ( CDTR1, CSTR1, CCTR, CCMR) and their control logic. The GPIBIF2 board has 2 registers ( CSTR2 and CSTR3), their control logic, a DMA control logic, and a bus arbitration control logic. The CONECT board holds the driver ICs, which transfer the signals between the motherboard on which the shared storage is installed and the motherboard on which SBCs are installed. The ISMBDIF board incorporates interrupt logic to SBCs, the acceess control logic to the shared storage, and the SBC bus arbitration logic.

Software

Each IM function is realized by software. The PPU module consists of a Prolog routine and a Concurrent Prolog routine. Each routine consists of the following routines .
(1) PPU-packet handling routine (PPKT)
(2) UU-packet handling routine (PUPKT)
(3) Ready Process handling routine (PRDPR)
(4) Concurrent process synchronization routine (Concurrent Prolog system only)

Table 4. Main components of boards

| Board | Number of ICs | Main Logic |
|---|---|---|
| GPIBIF1 | 58 | CDTR1<br>CSTR1<br>CCTR<br>CCMR |
| GPIBIF2 | 63 | CSTR2<br>CSTR3<br>DMA controller |
| CONNECT | 14 | Bus Drivers |
| ISMBDIF | 56 | Interrupt control logics |

| relative address | Tag Field | Data Field |
|---|---|---|
| 0 | INT | Packet Length |
| 1~2 | | Simulation Clock |
| 3 | INT | IM number which sends packet |
| 4 | INT | Flags of Packet Types |
| 5~n | TAG | one of the following informations<br>• subprocess creation request<br>• subprocess success response<br>• subprocess failure response<br>• Message Board read request<br>• Message Board write request<br>• activate request<br>• reduction request |

Fig. 4. Data structure of the packets between PPUs

| 0 | 7 | 8 | 31 |
|---|---|---|---|
| Tag Field | | Data Field | |

Fig. 5. Word structure

The PPU-packet handling routine accepts packets sent from other IMs through out the network. Fig. 4 shows the types of packets transferred between PPUs. Fig. 5 shows the basic structure of the word which constructs a packet. The word length is 32 bits, with the first 8 bits for the tag field and the other 24 bits for the data field. The packet types of the Prolog system are subprocess creation requests, subprocess success responses and subprocess failure responses. On the other hand, the packet types of the Concurrent Prolog system are reduction requests, subprocess success responses, subprocess failure responses, Message Board read requests, Message Board write requests, and activation requests.

The UU-packet handling routine accepts unification result packets which are sent from UU in the same IM. Packets between UU and PPU are not sent by means of NET, because they are in the same IM. In the Prolog system, unification success packets are dispatched to other IMs as subprocess creation packets by the UU-packet handling routine. In the Concurrent Prolog system, all unification success packets are registered to a ready process queue in the same IMs where reductions are executed. This process dispatch method prevents the communication traffic between IMs from increasing for commit operations.

The Ready Process handling routine picks up AND literals as goals from processes, which are registered in the ready process queue, and calls UU in order to execute unification. In the Concurrent Prolog system, a plurality of parallel AND literals are dispatched to other IMs according to a predetermined dispatch strategy.

Table 5. shows the measured results of dynamic steps of implememted modules (corresponding to MC68000 machine language) on a bench mark program (4-queens). When implementing these modules, we concentrated on the design of the simulation machine, and did not take the efficiency into consideration. Consequently, about 10,000 steps per reduction were needed. For the next step, our plan is to improve the performance by adjusting data structure and transaction algorithm, and other factors.

SIMULATION METHOD

Time Control

The purpose of this hardware simulator is to evaluate the architecture of PIM-R by large scale bench marks, so an increase in simulation speed is essential. In this hardware simulator, the event-driven method is employed so as to eliminate idling time during simulation.

Concerning the timer, the simulator does not have a TOD (Time of Day Clock), which uniformly manages time over the whole system, but it does have a software timer in each IM. The timer count is renewed by adding a certain value (predetermined in the simulation parameters), every time a transaction of any one of several functions is executed. When packets are sent to other IMs, network

Table 5. Prolog system load

| level 1 | | | level 2 | | | level 3 | | |
|---|---|---|---|---|---|---|---|---|
| module | steps | weight | module | steps | weight | transaction | steps | weight |
| PPROLG | 9743 | 1 | PPKT1 | 3146 | 1 | child process creation | 2526 | 0.46 |
| | | | | | | True | 6248 | 0.25 |
| | | | | | | Fail | 1386 | 0.29 |
| | | | PRDPR1 | 4461 | 1 | UU-packet creation | 859 | 1 |
| | | | | | | unification | 3582 | 1 |
| | | | PUPKT1 | 2136 | 1 | child process creation in own IM | 1750 | 0.08 |
| | | | | | | child process creation in other IM | 2075 | 0.33 |
| | | | | | | True | 2302 | 0.5 |
| | | | | | | Fail | 1556 | 0.09 |

delay time, which is also predetermined, is added to the timer count, and this value is attached to the sent packet to indicate arrival time. The IM which receives the packet controls the timer count by comparing this arrival time and its own timer when it accepts the packet.

The packets in the IM buffer are queue-controlled. The packet queue is arranged according to the descendant order of the arrival time. This queue control is carried out by the IM which sends the packets.

Fig. 6 shows the flow chart of timer count control. As long as the timer count in the IM is smaller than the arrival time of the head packet in the packet queue, the ready processes are transacted continuously. This means that packets which will arrive in the future will not be accepted. In the event that there is no ready process, and the arrival time of the head packet is greater than the timer count, the IM sets the packet arrival time to its own timer, accepts the packet, and continues the transaction. In this case, the difference between the timer count and the arrival time of packet is the IM idling time.

Execution Sequence

In the event-driven method in this hardware simulator, a problem exists in that the execution sequence can not be observed. The time when the packet transfer is really executed depends on the physical execution time of the hardware simulator. A packet which has an earlier simulation time sometimes arrives physically later, since packet arrival time in simulation is determined independently from physical execution time and since a plurality of IMs send packets to the same IM. In the event that packets with a later arrival time still exist in the packet queue, the correct transaction sequence can be maintained by queue control, but in the event that it has already transacted, the sequence according to simulation clock can no longer be observed. Some processes will be transacted in the same IM. The sequence between transaction of these processes and transaction of the processes from other IMs can not be observed for the similar reason.

This hardware simulator takes the above-mentioned problem into account as it collects evaluation data. Evaluation results were compared with those obtained with a software simulator written in Prolog[8] (using the clock-driven method), and very good coincidence was confirmed for program execution performance by the bench mark program of quick sort (10 elements) written in Concurrent Prolog.

RESULTS

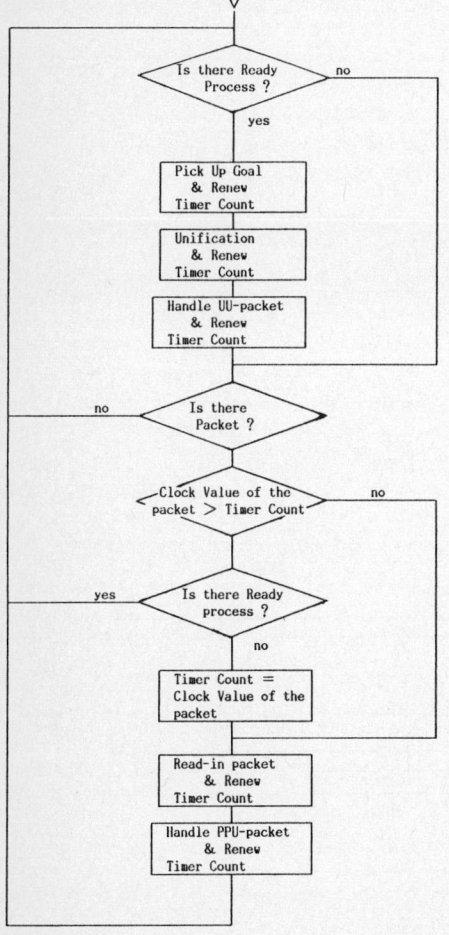

Fig. 6. Simulation clock control flow

Some test programs were executed on the hardware simulator, and data on execution time as a function of the number of processor elements, etc. was collected. In a parallel inference machine, process dispatch is important. In simulation, our examination was focused on the network architecture and the process dispatch strategy. We examined the effects of network structure, network throughput and process dispatch strategy on the execution time as a function of the number of processor elements and the activity of those elements. We also collected statistical data on packets passing through network, aiming at the reducing the number of communication packets between processor elements.

## Simulation Conditions

(1) Collision free networks are assumed for packet transfer.
(2) Sufficiently large input/output buffer is assumed for every IM, and the waiting time which is due to the overflow of input/output buffer is not taken into account.
(3) A new subprocess is dispatched to IMs when unification is successfully done with a rule in Prolog or when an AND-fork occurs in Concurrent Prolog. We selected the following dispatch strategy for two types of networks.
chain structure network : own IM→right IM→left IM→own IM→······
mesh structure network [7] : own IM→east IM →south IM→west IM→north IM→own IM→······

## Simulation Result

### Prolog

Prolog system was examined on Queens programs (4-queens, 6-queens, 7-queens).

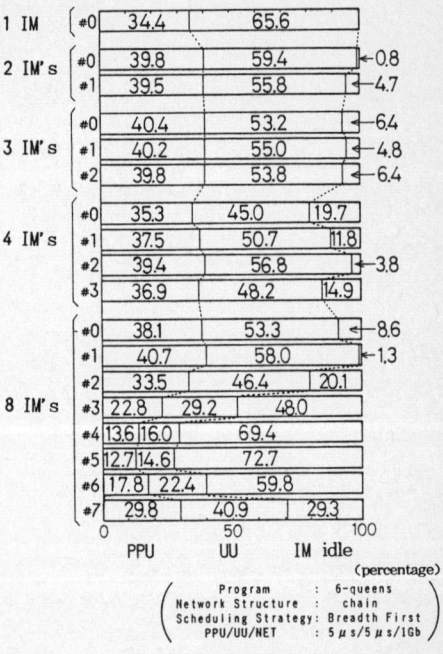

Fig. 8. IM activity

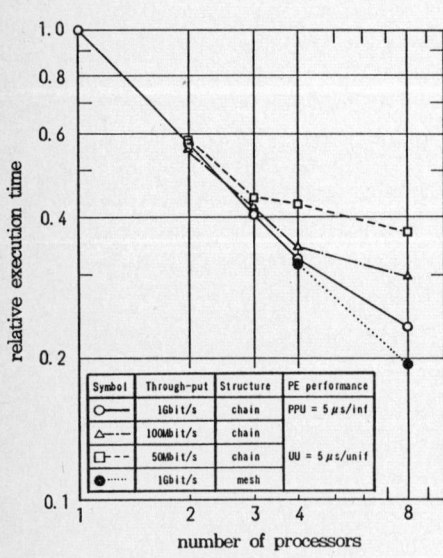

Fig. 7. Execution time as a function of the number of processor elements

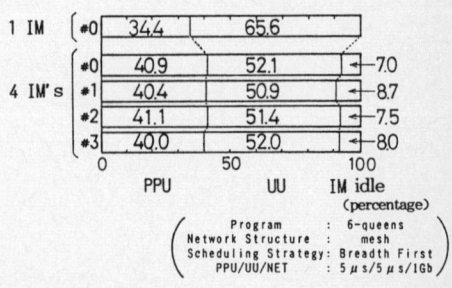

Fig. 9. IM activity

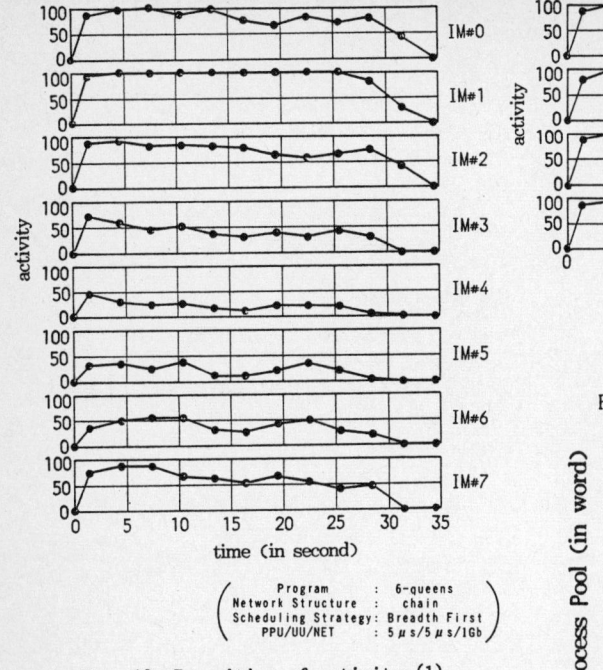

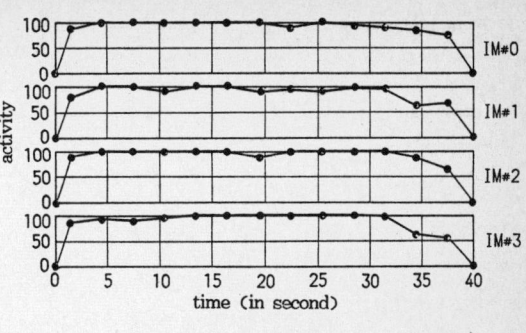

Fig. 11. Transition of activity (2)

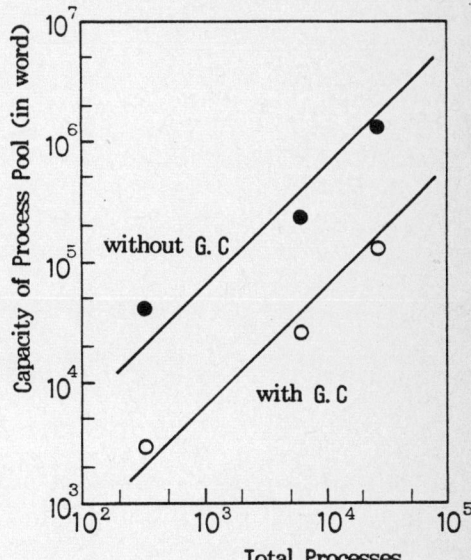

Fig. 10. Transition of activity (1)

Fig. 12. Required process pool capacity

Table 6. Data on sending packets

( program : 6-queens, throughput =1,000 Mbit/sec, network structure = chain, scheduling strategy = depth first )

| IMs | IM # | total packet counts | total packet length(W)*1 | subprocess packet counts *2 | subprocess packet length (W) | success packet counts | success packet length (W) | fail packet counts | fail packet length (W) |
|---|---|---|---|---|---|---|---|---|---|
| 2 | 0 | 1,754 | 56,392 | 801 | 36,205 | 516 | 16,691 | 437 | 3,496 |
|   | 1 | 1,758 | 56,946 | 821 | 36,856 | 514 | 16,706 | 423 | 3,384 |
| 3 | 0 | 1,169 | 37,277 | 513 | 23,289 | 357 | 11,596 | 299 | 2,392 |
|   | 1 | 1,164 | 37,977 | 545 | 24,686 | 339 | 11,051 | 280 | 2,240 |
|   | 2 | 1,169 | 37,596 | 564 | 25,379 | 302 | 9,793 | 303 | 2,424 |
| 4 | 0 | 805 | 25,207 | 354 | 16,140 | 230 | 7,299 | 221 | 1,768 |
|   | 1 | 929 | 30,862 | 460 | 20,599 | 266 | 8,639 | 203 | 1,624 |
|   | 2 | 935 | 30,933 | 460 | 20,694 | 262 | 8,535 | 213 | 1,704 |
|   | 3 | 821 | 25,498 | 348 | 15,798 | 244 | 7,868 | 229 | 1,832 |
| 8 | 0 | 651 | 21,394 | 326 | 14,610 | 169 | 5,536 | 156 | 1,248 |
|   | 1 | 687 | 22,378 | 330 | 14,851 | 189 | 6,181 | 168 | 1,344 |
|   | 2 | 595 | 19,370 | 290 | 12,833 | 165 | 5,417 | 140 | 1,120 |
|   | 3 | 378 | 12,040 | 160 | 7,235 | 125 | 4,061 | 93 | 744 |
|   | 4 | 213 | 6,624 | 81 | 3,742 | 77 | 2,442 | 55 | 440 |
|   | 5 | 190 | 5,913 | 74 | 3,453 | 64 | 2,044 | 52 | 416 |
|   | 6 | 305 | 9,752 | 130 | 6,029 | 96 | 3,091 | 79 | 632 |
|   | 7 | 495 | 15,890 | 230 | 10,302 | 140 | 4,588 | 125 | 1,000 |

*1 : 1W=4 bytes
*2 : subprocess packet = subprocess creation packet

Figures 7,8,9,10,11 show the execution time as a function of the number of IMs, IM activity, and transition of IM activity for 6-queen program. Fig. 7 shows that, by using mesh structure network, the execution time is improved in proportion to the number of IMs in the event that the number is less than or equal to 8. This result shows that PIM-R can utilize the parallelism which exists in Prolog programs. The figure 7 also shows that, for a chain structure network, improvement in execution time reaches a maximum when there are 5~6 IMs. The reason for this is that the activity of every IM, drops as is shown in Fig. 8. On the other hand, for a mesh structure, the average IM activity level is high, and the deviation is small, as is shown in Fig. 9. The drop mechanism for the IM activity in a chain structure network can be thought to be as follows. As Fig. 10 shows, the initial activity of IMs that are far from IM#0, which transacts goals from CM, is low. In other words, it takes an excessive amount of time to distribute goals. For the present simulation, the dispatch strategy mentioned in the previous section (simulation condition) was selected. In this case, one-third of the goals are dispatched to left-hand IMs even if the activity of the right-hand IMs is low. Therefore, high-activity IMs create many processes, and as a result, they receives process creation packets from the right- and left-hand IMs, and maintain high activity.

Thus, the dispatch strategy which is chosen on the present simulator, has the problem of low process propagation speed. Such improvement as IMs located on the right-hand of IM#0 dispatch processes to the right will be needed. It is shown in Fig. 8 that the 4 IMs, IM#0, #1, #2, #7 have high activity. From this result, it can be assumed that process distribution can be homogenized in a chain structure network composed of ~4 IM chains. This is because the improved execution time can be obtained on 2×2 and 4×4 mesh structures.

Table 6 shows the numbers and lengths corresponding to packet types passing through a chain structure network for 6-queens. Packet transfer occurs about once per 1.8 reductions, since 6-queen program execution includes 6,353 reductions.

Fig. 12 shows the relationship between the Process Pool capacity and total number of processes. This figure shows that, for the Process Pool, 63 words per process are needed when garbage collection is not executed, and 6.3 words per process are needed when garbage collection is executed.

Concurrent Prolog

In the Concurrent Prolog system, we selected the Quick-sort program as a bench mark. Fig. 13 shows the source list of the Quick-sort program. Figures 14 and 15 show the execution time as a function of the number of IMs and IM activity of on the Quick-sort program. Table 7 shows the numbers and lengths corresponding to packet types passing through a chain structure network.

As the source program in Fig. 13 shows, on the Quick-sort program, an AND-fork occurs only in the body of the first clause of 'qsort' and, the second and the third literal are suspended until they are activated by the first literal, 'partition', and the fourth literal is suspended until it is activated by the second and the third

```
go :- quicksort([27,74,17,33,···,59,8])//
      screen(S?).
screen([ ]) :- display([ ]) | true.
screen([E|F]) :- display(E) | screen(F?).
quicksort(U,S) :- true | qsort(U,S).
qsort([X|Un],S) :- true | partition(Un?,
         X,Smaller,Larger) // qsort
         (Smaller?,S1) //qsort(Larger?,S2)
         // lappend(S1?,[X|S2?],S).
qsort([ ],[ ]).
partition([X|Xs],A,S,[X|L]) :- A < X |
         partition(Xs?,A,S,L).
partition([X|Xs],A,[X|S],L) :- A ≥ X |
         partition(Xs?,A,S,L).
partition([ ],_,[ ],[ ]).
lappend([W|X],Y,[W|Z]) :- lappend(X?,Y,Z).
lappend([ ],X,X).
```

　　Fig. 13. Quick-sort program source
　　　　　list

literals. Thus the parallelism of the Quick-sort program is low, (only about 4, it is thought). The distribution of activity in Fig. 15 shows that processes are distributed to only 4 IMs, for the most part, although there are 8 IMs in all. The reason the improvement in execution time in Fig. 14 is lower than that in the 6-queen program in Fig. 7, is the low parallelism of the Quick-sort program.

Table. 7 shows that packets which passes through the network increase as the number of IMs increases. This is due to the increase in the number of packets related the Message Board. The Quick-sort program shown in Fig. 13 includes 1,387 reductions. Packet transfer occurs about once per 0.6 reduction

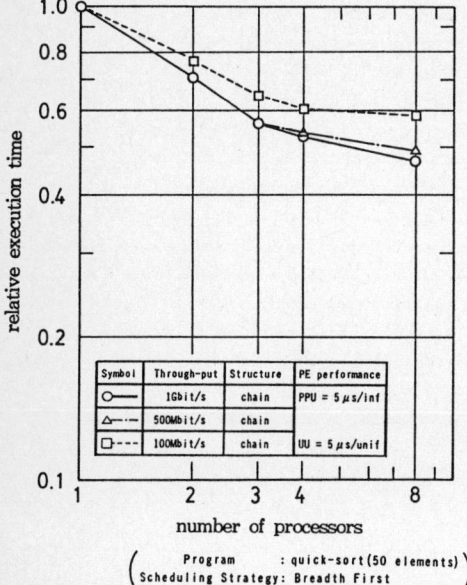

Fig. 14. Execution time as a function of the number of processor elements

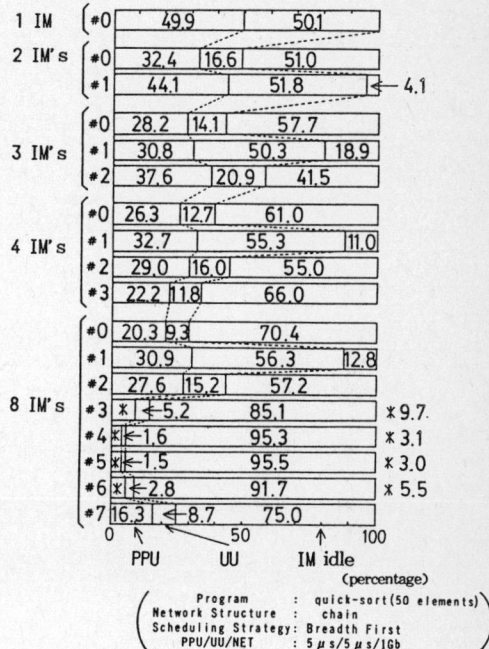

Fig. 15. IM activity

Table 7. Data on sending packets

(program :Quick-sort, throughput = 1 Gbit/sec, network structure = chain, scheduling strategy = depth first)

| IM's | I M # | total packet counts | total packet length(W)* | success packet counts | success packet length(W) | goal packet counts | goal packet length(W) | MB read packet counts | MB read packet length(W) | MB write packet counts | MB write packet length(W) | activate packet counts | activate packet length(W) |
|---|---|---|---|---|---|---|---|---|---|---|---|---|---|
| 2 | 0 | 910 | 15,559 | 69 | 3,350 | 65 | 3,181 | 423 | 3,807 | 65 | 883 | 288 | 4,338 |
|   | 1 | 905 | 16,863 | 65 | 3,254 | 69 | 3,490 | 288 | 2,592 | 60 | 799 | 423 | 6,728 |
| 3 | 0 | 645 | 10,833 | 42 | 2,098 | 49 | 2,417 | 310 | 2,790 | 38 | 518 | 206 | 3,010 |
|   | 1 | 652 | 12,407 | 42 | 2,211 | 50 | 2,582 | 184 | 1,656 | 41 | 582 | 335 | 5,376 |
|   | 2 | 749 | 12,211 | 49 | 2,514 | 34 | 1,622 | 330 | 2,970 | 53 | 733 | 283 | 4,572 |
| 4 | 0 | 592 | 9,712 | 36 | 1,799 | 41 | 2,035 | 295 | 2,655 | 31 | 421 | 189 | 2,802 |
|   | 1 | 678 | 12,140 | 31 | 1,669 | 42 | 2,200 | 208 | 1,872 | 28 | 379 | 369 | 6,020 |
|   | 2 | 590 | 9,307 | 35 | 1,679 | 21 | 1,002 | 268 | 2,412 | 37 | 492 | 229 | 3,722 |
|   | 3 | 509 | 8,383 | 31 | 1,535 | 29 | 1,384 | 217 | 1,953 | 31 | 449 | 201 | 3,062 |
| 8 | 0 | 431 | 6,918 | 26 | 1,238 | 30 | 1,509 | 228 | 2,052 | 23 | 309 | 124 | 1,810 |
|   | 1 | 601 | 10,841 | 24 | 1,342 | 37 | 1,962 | 175 | 1,575 | 22 | 314 | 343 | 5,648 |
|   | 2 | 523 | 8,155 | 25 | 1,544 | 18 | 858 | 239 | 2,151 | 25 | 342 | 216 | 3,560 |
|   | 3 | 188 | 3,140 | 10 | 538 | 13 | 620 | 77 | 693 | 9 | 129 | 79 | 1,160 |
|   | 4 | 81 | 1,293 | 9 | 422 | 2 | 94 | 38 | 342 | 11 | 141 | 21 | 294 |
|   | 5 | 77 | 1,269 | 6 | 272 | 5 | 238 | 32 | 288 | 6 | 83 | 28 | 388 |
|   | 6 | 137 | 2,349 | 11 | 480 | 10 | 476 | 56 | 504 | 11 | 139 | 49 | 750 |
|   | 7 | 400 | 6,221 | 20 | 1,001 | 16 | 764 | 179 | 1,611 | 21 | 311 | 164 | 2,534 |

* : 1W = 4 bytes

when there are 8 IMs, and almost 90 % of the communication packets are related to the Message Board. This result shows that, in a Concurrent Prolog system, it is important to arrange enough network throughput to ensure Message Board access.

The above-mentioned consideration is restricted to 6-queen and Quick-sort programs. In the event other programs are examined, a different conclusion may be obtained. For the next step, our plan is to increase the number of bench marks to obtain a more realistic evaluation of PIM-R.

CONCLUSIONS

A hardware simulator for the Parallel Inference Machine PIM-R based on the reduction concept was implemented, and data on the execution time as a function of the number of processor elements etc., were collected. From these data, it is confirmed that PIM-R can utilize the parallelism which exists in programs, and that process dispatch strategy with high speed process propagation is important to speed up transactions.

For the next step, our plan is to improve the architecture for PIM-R with 100 processor elements by designing the network structure and dynamic dispatch technique of subprocesses on the network node. By improving the data structure and by introducing a shared storage etc., into the processor element, we hope to obtain significantly improved performance. We are also planning to collect data to implement parallel inference machine software utilities by utilizing the actual parallel environment.

ACKNOWLEDGEMENTS

The authors would like to thank Dr. Hisashi Horikosi, former head of the 8th department of Hitachi Central Research Laboratory, Mr. Tsuneyo Chiba, present head of the 8th department of Hitachi Central Research Laboratory, Dr. Kunio Murakami, former chief of the 1st ICOT Laboratory, and Dr. Shun'ichi Uchida, chief of the 4th ICOT Laboratory, for their guidance and support.

REFERENCES

1) Clark KL et al. (1984) PARLOG : Parallel Programming in Logic. Research Report DOC 84/4, Dept. of Computing, Imperial College London
2) Ito N et al. (1984) Parallel Inference Machine Based on the Data Flow Model. Proc. of the International Workshop on High Level Computer Architecture 84 : 4.31-4.40
3) Motooka T et al. (1984) The Architecture of a Parallel Inference Engine -PIE-. Proc. of International Conf. on Fifth Generation Computer Systems 1984, ICOT : 479-488
4) Masuda Y et al. (1985) Implementation of Structured Memory of Parallel Inference Machine PIM-R. 30th National Conf., Information Processing Society of Japan : 6c-5 (in Japanese)
5) Onai R et al. (1985) The Architecture of Parallel Inference Machine PIM-R. 30th National Conf., Information Processing Society of Japan : 6c-6 (in Japanese)
6) Onai R et al. (1985) Architecture of a Reduction-Based Parallel Inference Machine : PIM-R. New Generation Computing, vol. 3
7) Onai R et al. (1985) The Architecture of Reduction-Based Parallel Inference Machine. Logic Programming Conference '85 : 2.1
8) Onai R et al. Software Simulation of Parallel Inference Machine PIM-R. 30th national Conf., Information Processing Society of Japan : 6c-9 (in Japanese)
9) Shapiro EY (1983) A Subset of Concurrent Prolog and Its Interpreter. ICOT Technical Report TR-003
10) Shimizu H et al. (1985) Internal Process Expression on Parallel Inference Machine PIM-R. 30th National Conf., Information Processing Society of Japan : 6c-7 (in Japanese)

A NOTE ON THE ELEMENTARY EXECUTION UNIT IN A PARALLEL INFERENCE MACHINE

T.Maruyama, K.Hirata, H.Tanaka and T.Moto-oka

Department of Electrical Engineering, The University of Tokyo

Bunkyoku, Tokyo 113, JAPAN

Abstract

When we design a parallel inference machine which executes logic programs, there are some important problems that greatly influence the machine performance. The most important problem is how to decide the elementary execution unit (granule). The less the size of the elementary execution unit is, the less is the overhead of copying and transferring, but the control among the units becomes more complicated.

Until now, a few models of parallel inference machines have been proposed. However, we think that this problem is not discussed enough in these models. In this paper, we discuss the problem in detail.

1.  Introduction

When we design a parallel inference machine, there are some important problems that greatly influence the machine performance. The most important problem is how to decide the elementary execution units that will be executed in parallel (we call this unit simply a goal). The less the size of the goal is, the less is the overhead of copying and transferring the goals, but the control among the goals becomes more complicated and may decrease the machine performance.

Until now, a few models of parallel inference machines have been proposed (Haridi 83; Ito 84; Onai 85). However, we think that the problem is not discussed enough in these models. We discuss the problem in detail, according to the research work on a highly parallel inference engine - PIE - (Moto-oka 84; Yuhara 84).

2.  Data Sharing in a Parallel Inference Machine

In general, there are two kinds of data sharing in a parallel inference machine. One is the sharing of the structure data which compose the goals. This sharing aims to decrease the goal size and the overhead of copying and transferring the goals by storing structures in the shared memory, and sharing them among the descendant goals. This sharing further aims to decrease the amount of memory to store goals. However, if we try to share too many structures, the overhead of separating them from the goals and the access conflict on the shared memory may decrease the performance against our will. Structure memory will be needed to implement this sharing method efficiently.

The other is the sharing of the goal itself. In a parallel inference machine, a goal may be shared among its descendant goals produced as the result of OR-parallelism, according to the level of the goal (elementary execution unit). For example, if a goal is composed of a literal, a goal is unified with several definitions, and a few descendant goals are produced, then the parent goal (which was unified) is shared among the descendant goals. In this case, the unifications of descendant goals may change the values of the parent goal variables. The parent goal has to be copied, or only the variables whose values change have to be copied at this time. If the level (granularity) of the goal is too low, this goal sharing may cause access conflict and load concentration. This sharing is tightly related to the granularity of the goals. If the goal has all environments that will be needed for its further unifications, the sharing of goals like this will not happen.

## 3. Elementary Execution Unit

There are two important points when we decide the elementary execution units (goals).
 (1) the granularity of the goal
 (2) copying/sharing the skeletons of
     the literals and structures
The first point is how to decide the granularity of the goal. The lower the granularity (the less the size) is, the less is the overhead of copying and transferring the goals. However, the access conflict and load concentration caused by the sharing may decrease machine performance. The second point is how to represent the goal in a parallel inference machine. Sharing of literal/structure skeletons decreases goal size, but the access conflict to the memory that stores the environments may decrease the performance.

The parallelisms that will be mainly realized in a parallel inference machine are
 (1) inter-argument parallelism,
 (2) AND parallelism,
 (3) OR parallelism,
and
 (4) inter-goal (elementary execution units) parallelism.
We think that stream parallelism is one form of inter-goal parallelism. We mainly discuss how to decide the granularity and internal representations of goals which are suitable for parallelism 2, 3 and 4.

## 3.1. Level of the Goals

In a sequential inference machine, OR parallelism is replaced by backtracking. If we try to make a parallel inference machine by slightly modifying a sequential inference machine, we can think of a model that regards parts of a stack as a goal, and transfer the goals among the sequential machines. In this case, parts of a stack in a machine may be shared by the goals distributed to the other machines. For example, if three goals are generated by unification of their parent goal, these goals share the parent goal environment (parts of a stack). These descendant goals may change the values of the parent goal environment one after another. The parent goal environment must be copied on every change of the values. The access conflict to the memory that stores the parent environment becomes a problem. In a parallel inference machine, the granularity of a goal decides the independency among the goals. The lower the goal granularity is, the smaller is its size, and the less independent are the goals. It is difficult to decide the granularity of the goal.

In general, we can consider four kinds of goal granularity as follows.
 (1) argument
 (2) literal
 (3) clause body
 (4) the environment from the initial goal

According to the increase of the item number, the granularity becomes higher. No sharing of goals occurs in 4. In 1 ~ 3, we can regard several arguments, several literals and several clause bodies as a goal. For example, if we regard several literals as a goal, and the number of literals in the goal is the same as the number of literals in the clause body, this goal is equal to the one in 3. This kind of enlargement of goals is taken for the increase of the machine performance. We think that our classification above is adequate for the discussion below.

We show the execution phases of each goal level (granularity) in Fig. 1 ~ 4. Though each figure is simply an example of the execution of each goal level, we think each figure represents the features well. Consistency check becomes necessary in Fig.1 because the arguments which are AND-related are unified in parallel. To avoid the overhead of it, we can dynamically cluster the arguments, but this is also rather heavy. This inter-argument parallelism can be combined with the executions of the other parallelisms.

In fig.2, each goal puts back the values of the bound variables into the parent goals (Fig.2a) and the next literal of the clause is separated from the clause as a new goal (Fig.2b).

The example shown in Fig.3 is almost same as the one in Fig.2. But there is no need to separate new goals explicitly as shown in Fig. 2 because the level of the goal corresponds to the clause body. The timing to put back the

?-app([1,2],[3],X),print(X).
app([H|A],B,[H|C]):-app(A,B,C).

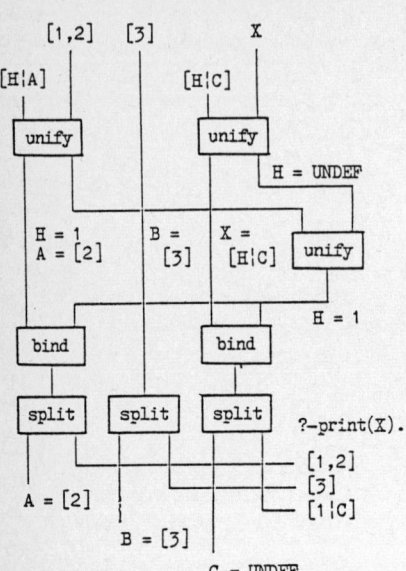

Fig. 1   An Example of
         a Data Flow Graph

?-f(X,Y),g(Y,Z).
f(X,a) :- p(X), q(X).
f(X,b) :- r(X), s(X).

p(a).   q(a).   r(a).   s(a).
p(b).   q(b).   r(b).   s(b).

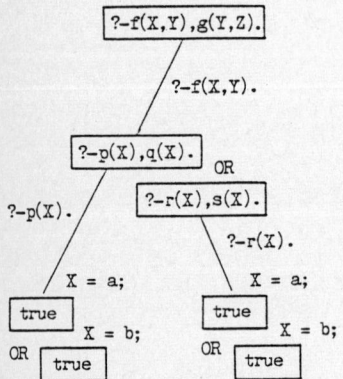

Fig. 2a   An Example of
          the Execution
          of Literal Level

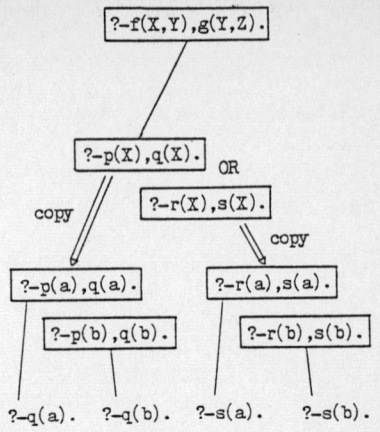

Fig. 2b   An Example of the Execution
          of Literal Level
          (the generation of new goals)

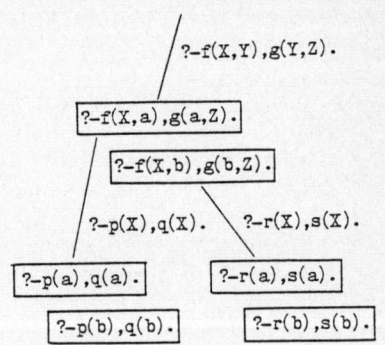

Fig. 3a   An Example of the Execution
          of Clause Body Level

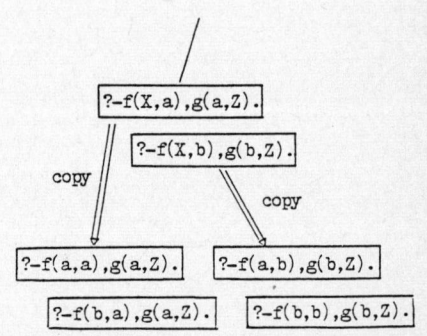

Fig. 3b   An Example of the Execution
          of Clause Body Level
          (the generation of new goals)

values of the bound variables also differs from the one in Fig.2. The size of the goal in Fig.2 is usually smaller than the size in Fig.3, but the overhead of separating the next literal as a new goal becomes necessary.

In Fig.4, because all environments needed for further unifications are included in each goal, there is no need to put back the values of the bound variables into the parent goal. The control among the goals greatly differs from the one in Fig. 2 and 3.

## 3.2. Skeleton Sharing / Copying

In sequential inference machines or in systems written on sequential machines, skeletons of literals are shared in most cases. The overhead of literal skeleton copying is too heavy in a sequential machine, but if we consider the overhead of copying in a parallel inference machine, it may become negligible through pipeline execution of copying and unification. If it becomes negligible, we can find a few advantages in literal skeleton copying. Dereferences during the unification becomes fewer, and the initialization of the variable area becomes unnecessary, and so on. We can think of four kinds of the internal representations of the goal for each goal level (granularity).
 (1) literal skeleton sharing / structure skeleton sharing
 (2) literal skeleton sharing / structure skeleton copying
 (3) literal skeleton copying / structure skeleton sharing
 (4) literal skeleton copying / structure skeleton copying
In these combinations, 3 is obviously inefficient and we will not discuss it. We regard the execution of the argument level as included in 2 (or 1), because it is natural to

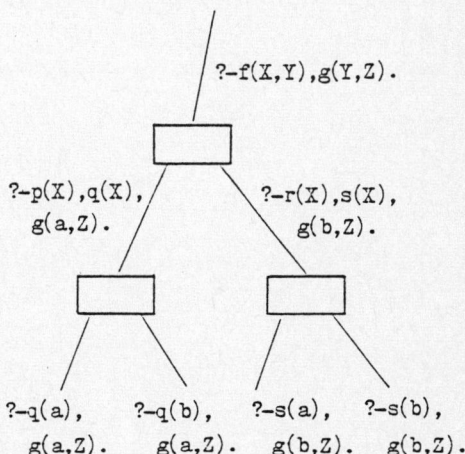

Fig. 4  AN Example of the Execution when the Goals has all Environments Needed for Further Unifications

think that each literal is preprocessed into data flow graphs and that literal skeletons will not be copied. The examples of the internal representations of the clause body level goals are shown in Fig.5.

In combination 1, a molecule will be constructed when a variable is bound to a structure, and changing of the values of the parent goal variables by the descendant goals will happen if the descendant goals don't have all environments needed for their unifications. We can think of two methods for changing the values of the parent goal variables: The first method is that the variable area (only the variables whose values will change) is copied during the unification if the environment pointer (Env) of the molecule points to the parent goal variable area, while during the unification the values of the parent goal variables are referred to; The other method is that the part of the parent variable area that will be needed for further unifications is copied, to avoid the overhead of the reference to the parent goal.

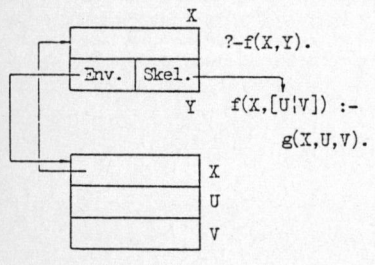

(a) Literal Share / Structure Share

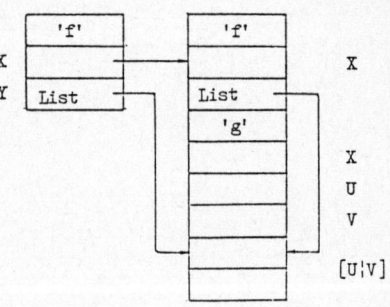

(c) Literal Copy / Structure Copy

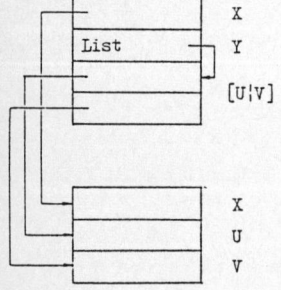

(b) Literal Share / Structure Copy

Fig. 5  An Example of Internal Representation of the Goal

Anyway, both methods are inefficient. In the first method, the access conflict to the memory that manages the parent goals seems to become too heavy. In the second method, the number of the variable is used to access variables through the molecule, and the difficulty of renumbering of the variables tends to copy all the structures that were once referred to and will not be referred to any more.

In the combination 2 and 4, we can think of the same methods as in the 3. But in these cases, only the structures needed for further unifications can be copied easily, because the variables are accessed not using the skeleton of the structures (the value of each variable in the copied structure is changed to 'ref' etc). The size of the goals in 4 becomes larger than the size in 2.

## 4. Internal Representation of the Goals

In chapter 3, we discuss the granularity of a goal and sharing/copying of skeletons. In this chapter, we discuss the combination of them. We can think of the internal representations of the goals as shown in Table 1. When we try to evaluate each representation, there are some important points, as follows:

(1) size of the goal
   The less goal size is better, as far as the dependency among the goals caused by the less size (lower granularity) does not decrease the performance.

(2) independency among the goals
   The dependency among the goals strongly depends on the granularity of the goal. Higher independency makes the load distribution easier.

(3) faster unification
   The elementary operation of the inference machine is unification. The representation that makes unification faster and also makes deterministic unification faster is better.

In the following sections, we discuss the internal representations shown in Table 1 from the aspects above.

### 4.1. Inter-argument Parallelism

We can take two approaches for inter-argument parallelism. One is the approach that aims to exhibit maximum parallelism. This approach seems to be suitable for data flow machines. The overhead of consistency check (or dynamic clustering of the arguments) and the fact that the input/output of a variable will be decided dynamically become problems. The other approach aims only to execute the arguments in a literal in parallel. This approach can be combined with the other level parallelism, but the degree of parallelism in a literal is small and the effect of this approach is not evident. It is necessary to study dedicated hardware to realize the inter-argument parallelism.

## 4.2. Literal Sharing / Structure Sharing

In 2 and 3 in Table 1, the environment pointer (Env) of the molecule may point to the environments of the other goals. As mentioned above, it is inefficient to refer to the parent goal during the unification and it is also inefficient to copy the structures needed for further unifications because it is difficult to copy only the structures that will be needed. Therefore, the methods 1 and 2 seem to be less efficient than methods 6 and 7. If we consider the size of stacks of sequential inference machines, the method that copies all the data like 4 is not acceptable.

Anyway, the sharing of structure skeletons in parallel inference machines is inefficient unless we aim to execute only a few degree of the parallelism.

## 4.3. Skeleton Copying

In 6, 7, 9 and 10 in Table 1, we can consider two methods like 2 and 3. The method that changes the values of the parent goal variables does not suit parallel processing, but the method that copies the structures needed for further unifications is efficient in this case (Fig. 6).

First, we compare 7 and 10. The goal size of 10 is generally larger than the size of 7. But in 10, the unification may be faster if the machine executes the unification in a interpretive manner (if definitions are compiled, there is no difference). The merit of 10 compared with 7 is

Table 1   The Elementary Execution Units

|                  |                  |   | argument | literal | clause-body | Env. |
|------------------|------------------|---|----------|---------|-------------|------|
| structure share  | literal share    |   |          | 2       | 3           | 4    |
|                  |                  | 1 |          |         |             |      |
|                  | literal copy     |   |          | x       | x           | x    |
| structure copy   | literal share    |   |          | 6       | 7           | 8    |
|                  |                  | 5 |          |         |             |      |
|                  | literal copy     |   |          | 9       | 10          | 11   |

Env. is the environments from the initial goal.

that we can execute deterministic unification faster by regarding the goal as a part of a stack of a sequential inference machine.

Next, we compare 6 and 7, 9 and 10 respectively. In 6 and 9, the goal size is smaller, and the overhead of copying and transferring is less. But the overhead of extracting literals from the clauses as new goals and the overhead of changing values of the parent goal variables become necessary. If we can find a fast algorithm for them, 6 and 9 may be efficient methods, but it is a subtle problem. 6 and 9 are different with respect to copying/sharing of literals but really have very similar form. In 6, the arguments for unification will be copied like the arguments of a subroutine call. In 6 and 9, it is difficult to execute deterministic unifications fast, owing to the rather complicated control among the goals (literals).

It may seem that the goal size of 11 is larger than the size of 8, but in fact, in 8, it is difficult to discard the unnecessary data because the variables are referred to through the variable number in literals. In the worst case, the size of the goal amounts to the size of the stacks of the sequential inference machine. Therefore, the goal size of 8 and 11 strongly depends on the application programs.

The goal size of 8 and 11 is larger than the size of 7 and 10. However, if we can cover the overhead through pipeline execution, 8 and 11 becomes more efficient than 7 and 10. No operation is needed to put back the values of the bound variables into the parent goal in 8 and 11, but the goal size may become too large.

To realize AND parallelism, we must basically lower the level of the goal to the literal level. If we can neglect the overhead of copying, we don't have to lower the level. In 7 and 10, the size of the goals seems to be not so much larger than the size in 6 and 9, but in 8 and 11 maybe the size becomes too large.

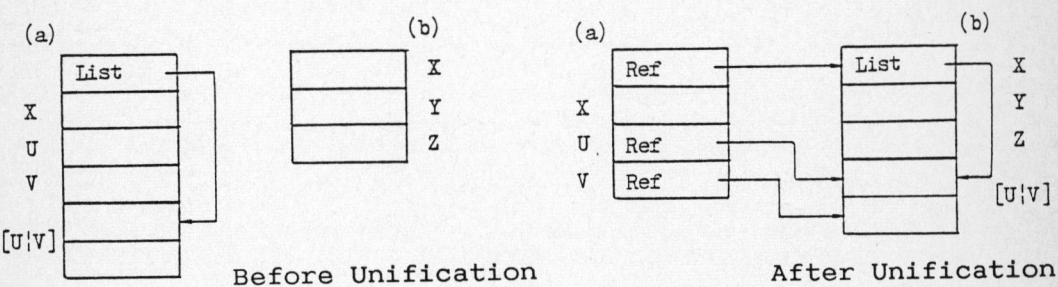

Fig. 6  An Example of the Structure Copying

## 4.4. Multi Sequential Inference Machines

The methods mentioned above intend to construct highly parallel inference machines. To construct a parallel inference machine, we can think different approach that we connect sequential inference machines. In this model, it becomes most important to enhance the working rate of each sequential machine. If the all machines are executing their jobs, there is no need to distribute goals to other machines. So, the distribution of the goals doesn't happen so many. It is not so important to decrease the overhead of the goal distribution. 3 and 7 in Table 1 may seem to be good goal representations for these machines, but the amount of unifications caused by the goals of 3 and 7 is not so many. 4 and 8 are suitable for this machine. At this time, it is better to distribute the alternatives that is near to the root of the search tree as goals.

## 5. Summary

In this paper, the internal representation of the goals in a parallel inference machine is discussed. The selection of the representation is the trade off problem between the overhead of the copy and transfer of the goals and overhead of the complicated control among the goals. We think that a combination of methods like 7 and 8 in Table 1 that is changed dynamically according to the size of the goals and to the load of the system is the best method.

The evaluation of each overhead mentioned above through simulation is future work.

## References

Haridi,S. and Ciepielewski,A., An OR-parallel Token Machine, Logic Programming Workshop 83, 1983.

Ito,N. and Masuda,K., Parallel Inference Machine Based on the Data Flow Model, Proc. of International Workshop on Highlevel Computer Architecture 84, 1984.

Moto-oka,T.,Tanaka,T. et al, The Architecture of a Parallel Inference Engine - PIE -, FGCS'84, ICOT, 1984.

Onai,R. et al, The Architecture and Software Simulation of the Parallel Inference Machine PIM-R , ICOT Technical Report TR-077, 1985 (in Japanese).

Yuhara,M. et al, A Unify Processor Pilot Machine for PIE, Proc. of the Logic Programming Conference '84, Tokyo, 1984.

Parallel Prolog Machine PARK: Its Hardware Structure and Prolog System

H. Matsuda[*], M. Kohata[**], T. Masuo[***], Y. Kaneda[***], S. Maekawa[***]

[*] The Graduate School of Science and Technology, Kobe University, Rokkodai, Nada, Kobe 657, Japan.
[**] Faculty of Science, Okayama University of Science, Ridaicho, Okayama 700, Japan.
[***] Faculty of Engineering, Kobe University, Rokkodai, Nada, Kobe 657, Japan.

ABSTRACT

In this paper we describe the hardware structure of PARK (is short for a PARallel processing system of Kobe university) and a parallel Prolog system, called PARK-Prolog, which will be implemented on this machine. PARK is a multi-microprocessor machine connected with a common bus. PARK is divided into one host processor and several (currently 3) slave processors. Each processor is composed of a 16 bit microprocessor (Motorola MC68000), a local memory, an address translation unit, and a common memory (the slave processor only). A broadcast operation can be performed on the common memory. The execution in PARK-Prolog exhibits AND parallelism, OR parallelism, and the combination both of them. PARK-Prolog equips a concurrent AND constructor and a parallel AND constructor for AND parallelism and a mode declaration for OR parallelism. The communication among processes is performed with a special built-in predicate through a communication channel.


INTRODUCTION

We are currently constructing a parallel Prolog machine PARK (is short for a PARallel processing system of Kobe university). In this paper we present its hardware structure and a parallel Prolog system which will be implemented on this machine. The PARK machine is a multiprocessor system which is consisted of one host processor and several slave processors (currently three slave processors, we will extend to fifteen in the future). All processors are connected with a common bus. The host processor is mainly in charge of I/O processing and the slave processors execute Prolog programs in parallel. Each processor is composed of a 16 bit microprocessor (Motorola MC68000, clock 8MHz), a local memory (host 256K Bytes and slave 128K Bytes), and an address translation unit. In addition each slave processor has a common memory (512K Bytes). A processor can read from its own common memory and write to it at any time, can read form the other common memory and write to it if the common bus not used, and can multiply write to the all common memories (a broadcast operation) if the bus not used.

A parallel Prolog system on the PARK machine can be executed by the methods of AND parallelism and OR parallelism. The system does not automatically divide a Prolog program into the parts which can be executed in parallel. A user must point out the parts in the program. The system executes them as concurrent or parallel processes. The consistency checks of shared variables in AND parallelism is performed by inter-process communications. The communication is done not with shared variables such as Concurrent Prolog (Shapiro 1983) but with communication channels such as Delta-Prolog (Pereira and Nasr 1984).


HARDWARE

Hardware Design Principles

We designed PARK as a machine to execute Prolog programs in parallel. We took the following considerations in designing this machine.

(1) Prolog is the interactive language executed mostly by an interpreter. For this point of view we especially designed a host processor which plays the part of interactive processing. The rest of processors are slave processors to execute Prolog programs in parallel.
(2) All processors are tightly connected with a common bus. In this structure all processors are equal against the bus. It is therefore relatively easy how to balance the loads into each processor.
(3) An execution in Prolog consumes a large amount of memory space and its size dynamically changes in executing. We selected MC68000 which has 16M Byte linear address space for this reason. PARK has a large common memory which can be shared with all processors. The common memory is divided into segments. Each segment is attached to each slave processor to reduce memory racings on the common memory.

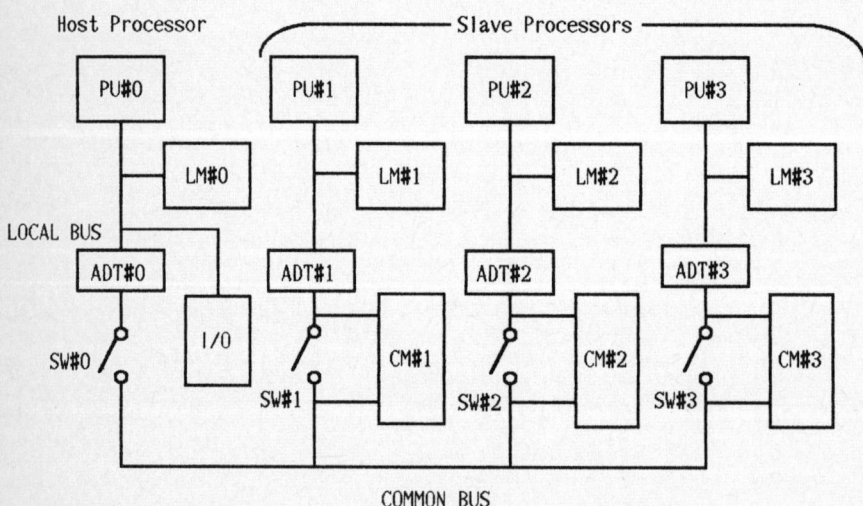

Fig. 1. Hardware structure of PARK
PU: processing unit (MC68000, 8MHz), LM: local memory (host 256KB, slave 128KB), CM: common memory (512KB) ADT: address translation unit, SW: bus switch.

## Hardware Structure

The hardware structure of PARK is shown in Fig. 1. A processing unit (PU) is consisted of MC68000. A local memory (LM) stores programs and private data in the processor. This memory can be accessed only by its owner processor through a local bus. A common memory (CM) can be accessed by all processors through a common bus. This memory has two ports for the local bus and the common bus. An address translation unit (ADT) is in each local bus. The ADT translates an address signal which is sent to the common memory. We describe about this unit in the latter. Bus switches (SW) connect all local buses with the common bus. At most one of the switches is closed if a processor uses the common bus and all switches are open otherwise.

## Access Methods to Common Memory

The access methods to a common memory is the most significant in the hardware configuration of PARK. The common memory segments are allocated to a successive address space (see Fig. 2). Each common memory can be identified with its address. All common memories are also allocated to a broadcast area in a pile. The access methods is as follows:
(1) local access: The access method is performed when a processor reads from a common memory which is attached to the processor and writes to it through a local bus.
(2) bus access: The access method is performed when a processor reads from a common memory which is attached to the other processor and writes to it through a common bus.
(3) broadcast access: The access method is performed when a processor can write to all common memories through a common bus.

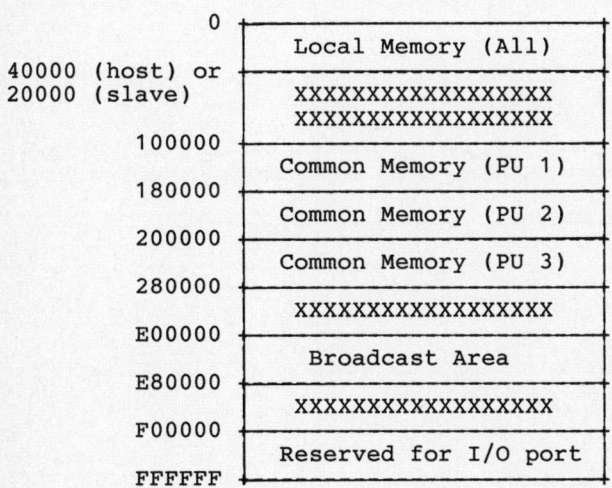

Fig. 2. Memory map in PARK. Strings of "X" denote free areas.

A bus racing occurs when several processors do (2) or (3) at the same time since the common bus is only one. A bus arbitration unit solves the bus racing. As the result only one processor obtains the bus. The other processors wait while the bus is used. The common bus is locked while only one memory access is performed. A function of bus lock is therefore provided. The function is necessary to operate semaphore for mutual exclusion among parallel processes. By this function the bus can be locked during several successive memory accesses to a same address (for example TAS: Test-And-Set command in MC68000). The bus lock is provided such a function as lock-prefix in Intel i8086.

Address Translation

An address in a common bus is not a direct address from MC68000 but is translated by an address translation unit (ADT). The ADT is composed of high speed static RAMs (INMOS IMS1420P-55, access time 55ns). In the ADT there exists an address translation table. Each entry in this table is as shown in Fig. 3. One entry is 16 bit long. A physical address part are a bit pattern which indicates a translated address. The ADT requires address signals A23 - A13 and a read-write control signal R/W as input. The minimum size to be translated (page) is 8K Bytes. The tables for reading and writing are different and they can be set independently. The function of write-protect can be easily implemented. The bits in a control part such as LOCAL, BUS, LOCK are used to control the common memory accesses previously described. A control bit CT is used for an evaluation for this machine, for example counting the references to the specified pages.

PROLOG SYSTEM

The parallel execution methods in Prolog has been proposed recently. They are AND parallelism, OR parallelism, stream parallelism, etc. We implemented a parallel Prolog system called "K-Prolog" (Matsuda et. al. 1985) on a machine which uses Intel i8086 as CPU. Two sorts of interpreters are created. They are based on pipelining parallelism and OR parallelism respectively. In this implementation, for example, the OR parallel version of the interpreter executes all AND parts as a pipeline and all OR parts simultaneously in program. For this reason so many processes are created more than necessary and the switching times of these processes are bottleneck in high speed execution. In PARK-Prolog which we will implement from now we take the following design principles to improve them.

```
 15           11   10                                    0
+-----------------+---------------------------------------+
| *  C  L  B  L   | P  P  P  P  P  P  P  P  P  P  P       |
|    T  O  U  O   | A  A  A  A  A  A  A  A  A  A  A       |
|    C  S  C      | 2  2  2  2  1  1  1  1  1  1  1       |
|    A     K      | 3  2  1  0  9  8  7  6  5  4  3       |
|    L            |                                       |
+-----------------+---------------------------------------+
   Control Part         Physical Address Part
```

Fig. 3. Address translation table. A "*" denotes an unused bit.

(1) It will be based on AND parallelism, OR parallelism, and their combination.
(2) The parts to execute sequentialy can be described with a sequential AND and a sequential OR. They are executed as a single process. It reduce the numbers of processes.
(3) The programmer should decide the parts which can be executed in parallel and describe this explicitly. A concurrent AND constructor and a parallel AND constructor and a parallel OR mode declaration are provides for this description.
(4) A communication among the processes is performed by sending to a channel for communication and receiving from it. These functions are implemented as built-in predicates.

## Description of Parallel Execution

The following constructors, which are operaters between goal literals, and the mode declaration are used to describe the parts to be executed in parallel.
(C1)   concurrent AND constructor: "&"
(C2)   parallel AND constructor: "//"
(M1)   parallel OR mode declaration: "%mode par"

The constructor and the mode declaration to describe sequential execution is as follows:
(C3)   sequential AND constructor: ","
(C4)   sequential OR constructor: ";"
(M2)   sequential OR mode declaration: "%mode seq"

Since the sequential OR mode is default, the clauses which are not declared their mode become implicitly sequential OR mode.

## Creation of Process and its Allocation to Processor

The parts to execute sequentially is considered as a process in this system. The program only contained sequential constructors and mode declarations is therefore executed as single process.

A concurrent AND constructor creates two processes which correspond to left side goal and right side goal of this operator in the program. But these processes are allocated to only a processor. Only one of these processes can be therefore executed simaltaneously. It is principally a following order in program which process is executed first. But the second process is executed when the first process suspended and the second one is ready.

A parallel AND and a parallel OR also create processes. These processes are allocated to as other processors as possible respectively and can be executed simaltaneously.

## Binding Environment

In sequential AND, all goals are executed as one process and therefore have the same environment. In concurrent AND, all goals are executed as other processes but allocated to one processor and also have the same environment. In parallel AND, all goals are executed as other processes and allocated other processors and therefore have other independent environments. The shared variables between two goals become different after the parallel AND was executed.

In both sequential OR and parallel OR, the environment of each goal is different. In sequential OR mode only one of the environments can exist at the same time. But in parallel OR mode all of the environments can exist simultaneously.

Execution Models

Five execution models can be organized with the combination among the constructors and the mode declarations. The models are as follows:

```
        AND           OR
(1) sequential   sequential  ... sequential type    (ex. DEC-10 Prolog)
(2) concurrent   sequential  ... coroutine type     (ex. IC-Prolog)
(3) parallel     sequential  ... AND parallel type  (ex. Delta-Prolog)
(4) sequential   parallel    ... OR parallel type   (ex. K-Prolog)
(5) parallel     parallel    ... AND/OR parallel type
```

the combination of concurrent AND and parallel OR does not exist because it is contradiction that concurrent AND requires an allocation to single processor and parallel OR is allocated to as many processors as possible.

Inter-Process Communication

In AND parallelism, the consistency check is required for the shared variables among several processes. PARK-Prolog is provided a method to communicate among the processes as built-in predicates. The functions of the predicates are sending to / receiving from a channel for communication such as Occam (Inmos 1984) or Delta-Prolog (Pereira and Nasr 1984). But unlike these languages, communication channel is dynamically created in executing. This is useful for recursive calls.

There are two communication method in this system. One is a method called single send-receive. It is used for one-to-one communication. Another is multiple send-receive. It is used for many-to-many communication. In OR parallelism, a process is copied and splited to many processes. The multiple send-receive is useful for the multiple communication among such splited processes.

The built-in predicates are presented as follows:
(1) make channels: "mkchan"
This creates new communication channels. It is necessary to indicate whether it is used for single send-receive or multiple send-receive.

ex. :- mkchan([C1/s,C2/m])
Two channels are created. C1 is a channel pointer used for single send-receive and C2 for multiple. These are treated as variables but the contents of these are pointers to channels.

(2) single send-receive operators: "!", "?"
These perform single sending/receiving. These require at least two arguments. One is the channel pointer which created with mkchan predicate and another is a communication pattern. The pattern is an arbitrary term in Prolog. If two patterns of sending and receiving can be unified, the communication succeeds. Otherwise, the communication fails and one of these processes backtracks. Two auxiliary conditions can be optionally provided. One is a matching condition which is tested after the pattern match succeeded. If this condition is not

satisfied, the communication fails. Another is a retry condition which
is tested after the communication succeeded and the the control
reached here with backtracking. If this condition is satisfied, the
communication is tried again. Otherwise, the system only backtracks
next choice point. Any predicate but not to need resatisfy can be used
as these conditions. Furthermore the following special predicates can
be used.
* reject    force to fail both of the partner process and itself
* retry     force to fail the partner process and communicate again
* restart   force to fail the partner process until its start point and
communicate again

ex. :- mkchan([C/s]), (C!1 // C?X:X>0).
Two processes are created. One process sends 1 thorough a channel C.
Another process receives it into a variable X and then it is tested
whether it is greater than 0.

(3) multiple send-receive operator: "!+", "!-"
These perform multiple sending/receiving. The arguments are the same
as the single send-receive except the retry condition is omitted.

ex. %mode par p(-).
    p(C) :- C !+ 1.
    p(C) :- C !+ 2.
    q(C) :- C !- X: X>0.
    :- mkchan([C/m]), (p(C) // q(C)).
The situation which is executing this example are shown in Fig. 4.
Since two process p send to C, process q is copied and two process q
receive from C.

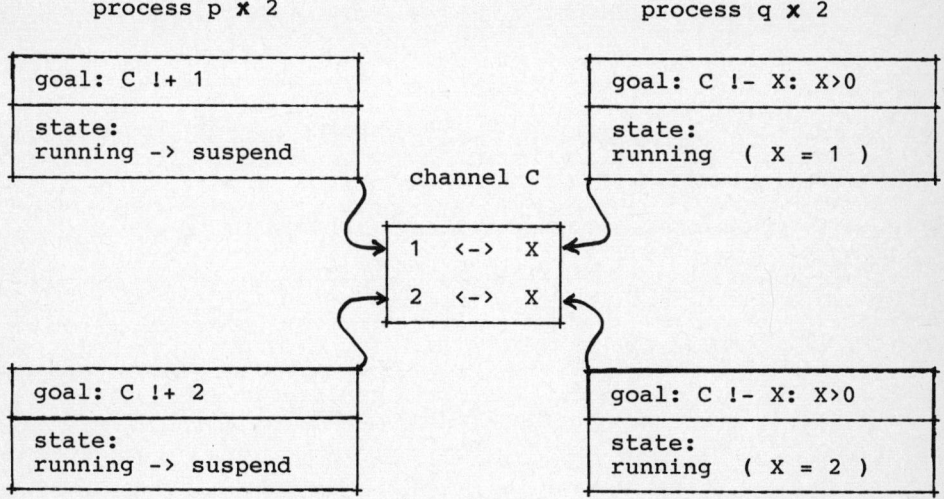

Fig. 4. Situation of multiple send-receive. Two processes p suspend
while the partner processes q test the matching conditions.

## EXAMPLES

Several examples are shown in Fig. 5. In Fig. 5, the examples (1), (2), (3) correspond to the execution model (2), (3), (5) respectively. Example (1) is modified Kowalsky's program (Kowalsky 1974) to execute with coroutine. Example (2) is the program of N-Queen problem. In (2), "fork" is a built-in predicate which creates new process. Example (3) is a program to execute the join operation between two tables such as in relational database. The precedence of the operators is high in the following order: ",", "&", "//", ";". "\:" denotes the prefix of a retry condition in single send-receive.

```
sort(X, Y) :- mkchan([C/s]), (perm(X, Y), C!Y & C?Y: ord(Y)).
perm([], []).
perm(Z, [X|Y]) :- perm(Z1, Y), delete(X, Z, Z1).
delete(X, [X|Y], Y).
delete(X, [Y|Z], [Y|Z1]) :- delete(X, Z, Z1).
ord([]).
ord([X]).
ord(X,Y|Z]) :- X<=Y, ord([Y|Z]).
```

(1) sorting.

```
queens([], Y, Y).
queens([X1|X2], Y, Z) :- mkchan([C1/s,C2/s,C3/s]),
   (select(C1, [X1|X2], C2) // check(C1, Y, C3)),
   (C2?V \: retry & C3?U \: restart), queens(V, [U|Y], Z).
select(C1, [X|Y], C2) :- C1!X, C2!Y ;
   mkchan([C4/s]), fork(select(C1, Y, C4)),
   C4?V \: retry, C2![X|V].
select(C1, [], _) :- C1!_: reject.
select(_, _, C2) :- C2!_:reject.
check(C1, Q, C3) :- C1?U: safe(U,Q, 1), C3!U ; C3!_: reject.
safe(U, [], W).
safe(U, [P|Q], N) :- nodiag(U, P, N), M is N+1, safe(U, Q, M).
nodiag(U, P, N) :- T1 is P+N, T2 is P-N, U \= T1, U \= T2.
```

(2) N Queen

```
%mode par r(+, +).
r(a1, b1).
r(a1, b2).
r(a2, b1).
r(a2, b3).
%mode par s(+, +).
s(b1, c1).
s(b1, c2).
s(b2, c3).
s(b2, c4).
rr(C) :- r(X, Y), C !+ [X,Y].
ss(C, J) :- s(Y, Z), C !- [X,Y], J !+ [X,Y,Z].
join_rs :- mkchan([C/m,J/m]), (rr(C) // ss(C, J)),
   J !- [X,Y,Z], write([X,Y,Z]).
```

(3) Join of relations

Fig. 5. Sample programs.

SUMMARY

This paper has described the hardware configuration of PARK. PARK is a multiprocessor machine which is tightly connected with single common bus. On this machine the Prolog system called PARK-Prolog is being implemented. This system has five execution models which are created by the combination of constructors or mode declarations. AND parallelism, OR parallelism, and AND/OR parallelism are included in the models. The communication among parallel processes is implemented with special built-in predicates which uses a communication channels in the operation.


REFERENCES

Inmos Limited (1984) Occam programming manual, Prentice Hall, London
Kowalski R (1974) Predicate logic as programming language, IFIP '74:569-574
Matsuda H, Tamura N, Kohata M, Kaneda Y, Maekawa S (1985) Implementing parallel prolog system "K-Prolog", Transactions of information processing society of Japan, vol 26/2:296-303 (in Japanese)
Pereira LM, Nasr R (1984) Delta-Prolog: a distributed logic programming language, Proc. of the international conference on FGCS:283-291
Shapiro E (1983) A subset of concurrent Prolog and its interpreter, ICOT technical report TR-003

# HEURISTICS APPLIED IN TREE MANIPULATION ALGORITHM SYNTHESIS

Etsuo ITOH and Hiroshi NAKAGAWA

Dept. of Computer Eng. Faculty of Eng. Yokohama Nat. Univ.
156, Tokiwadai, Hodogayaku, Yokohama 240, Japan

## ABSTRACT

PROLOG program transformation is a hopeful method for derivation of algorithm. We apply this method to tree manipulation algorithm. In this case, besides Unfold/Fold transformation, some heuristic knowledge is necessary, for example avoiding re-execution of the same pattern of transformations. In this paper, we describe these heuristic knowledge in transformation. We also present B-tree insertion algorithm synthesis as a fair size example.

## 1. INTRODUCTION

In PROLOG programming, declarative-style programs are easy to write and understand, but they are possibly inefficient. On the other hand, a procedural-style PROLOG program is efficient but complicated and hard to understand. The notion of PROLOG program transformation is a programming paradigm that gives one solution for this situation. Under this paradigm, one writes a clear, declarative though possibly inefficient program, and transforms it into a program which is more efficient and algorithmic although probably less clear.

In general, relevant works on the program transformation can be divided into three categories. The first is about derivation from a specification that is usually expressed in the first order predicate logic, to computable predicates of Horn logic (Hogger 1981; Sato 1984). The second is about transformation from an inefficient, declarative-style, logical program to an efficient, procedural-style program (Nakamura 1984; Tamaki 1984; Tarlund 1982). The last is about transformation of functional (Burstall 1977; Darlington 1981).

Though there are a lot of works, transformations of programs which manipulate data-structures are quite few but works of manipulating a d-list structure (Darlington 1981; Nakamura 1984), and they have not obtained excellent results. In this paper, we present a different strategy to synthesis of efficient and procedural tree insertion programs by transformation from declarative programs of tree insertion. Both kinds of program are in PROLOG because we are able to write programs both declaratively and procedurally in PROLOG.

The definition of an ordered binary tree which is "any node's value in its right subtree is greater than the value of its root and any node's value in its left subtree is less than the value of its root" does not determine a unique structure of a tree. By a procedural tree insertion program a structure of tree depends upon the order of inserted elements. But why? A tree insertion program written in procedural language contains some other information besides an original definition of an ordered binary tree. This additional information is one of the important origin of a procedural programs. Our final aim is to make clear what this additional information is. In order to approach the aim, we study a process of PROLOG program transformation above described. If we transform only in an equivalency preserving manner, although the result is correct, we can find only a very limited class of the additional information. In this paper, we adopt a different approach. We search and use useful but possibly non equivalency preserving heuristic knowledge to attain a procedural program. This is a constructive approach, but we think it to be one of hopeful approach at a state of the art of this area now.

In section 2, our basic approach is described by a transformation of an ordered binary tree insertion algorithm. Section 3 is for transformation process of a balanced tree, and section 4 for B-tree. In section 5, we categorize some heuristic knowledge found in transformations of previous section.

## 2. A PRINCIPLE OF TREE MANIPULATION ALGORITHM SYNTHESIS

In this section, in order to clarify our approach, we show a simple example, i.e. a transformation from a declarative ordered binary tree insertion program into a procedural one. A declarative tree insertion program in PROLOG consists of two parts. The first part is a predicate that expands a tree into a list, and inserts an element into the list. The second part is a predicate that transforms the list into a tree. When we write a program that inserts an element *a into a suitable place in a given ordered tree t(*l,*x,*r), we usually use a well-known algorithm 'binary search'. In PROLOG, a predicate that inserts an element *a into a suitable place of the expanded list using the binary search algorithm is defined as:

```
        tins(*a,[],[*a]).                                          (1.1)
        tins(*a,t(*l,*x,*r),*y) :- *a<*x,
                        tins(*a,*l,*ly),
                        traverse(*r,*ry),
                        append(*ly,[*x|*ry],*y).                   (1.2)
        tins(*a,t(*l.*x,*r),*y) :- *a>=*x,
                        traverse(*l,*ly),
                        tins(*a,*r,*ry),
                        append(*ly,[*x|*ry],*y).                   (1.3)
```

where '*x','*l', etc. denote variables. The first clause (1.1) is for insertion of *a into a null tree. The binary search algorithm is expressed in (1.2) and (1.3). 'Traverse' is defined as follows.

```
        traverse([],[]).                                           (2.1)
        traverse(t(*l,*x,*r),*list) :-
                        traverse(*l,*ll),
                        traverse(*r,*lr),
                        append(*ll,[*x|*lr],*list).                (2.2)
```

Next we are going to define a predicate which makes up a tree from a given list. A list-to-tree predicate 'bltree' is defined as:

```
        bltree([],[]).                                             (3.1)
        bltree(*y,t(*l,*x,*r)) :- append(*ly,[*x|*ry],*y),
                        bltree(*ly,*l),
                        bltree(*lr,*r).                            (3.2)
```

The 'append' in (3.2) generates lists *ly and *ry, and atom *x from the given list *y. We use the predicate 'bltree' as a prototype to make up a tree from a list.

Using the predicates 'tins' and 'bltree', a tree insertion predicates 'ins' that inserts an element *a into a tree *t is defined as follows:

```
        ins(*a,*t,*ta) :- tins(*a,*t,*l),bltree(*l,*ta).           (4)
```

The variable *ta is the result tree. The predicate 'ins' is the declarative version of the tree insertion program that uses a list as an intermediate representation. A procedural tree insertion program generates a result tree whose structure is the same as the original tree except for the inserted *a. But this inserted tree will be generated by program (1.1)-(4) after times of backtracking.

Next we will transform (4). In the whole course of transformation, we mainly use unfolding and folding and sometimes introduce a new predicate (Sato 1983). Besides these methods, we introduce a heuristic called 'H1' based on human information processing.

At the first step of transformation, the 'tins' in the body of the predicate 'ins' is unfolded and the result is:

```
ins(*a,[],*ta) :- bltree([*a],*ta).                              (5.1)
ins(*a,t(*l,*x,*r),*ta) :- *a<*x,
                          tins(*a,*l,*ll),
                          traverse(*r,*lr),
                          append(*ll,[*x|*lr],*lis),
                          bltree(*lis,*ta).                       (5.2)
ins(*a,t(*l,*x,*r),*ta) :- *a>=*x,
                          traverse(*l,*ll),
                          tins(*a,*r,*lr),
                          append(*ll,[*x|*lr],*lis),
                          bltree(*lis,*ta).                       (5.3)
```

From the clause (5.1), by unfolding 'bltree' we derive a terminating-condition as follows:

```
ins(*a,[],t([],*a,[])).                                           (6)
```

(5.2) and (5.3) will be transformed into a program to manipulate trees directly.

If unfolding is applied to 'bltree' of clause (5.2), the result is the next one:

```
ins(*a,t(*l,*x,*r),t(*tl,*nx,*tr)) :-
              *a<*x,
              tins(*a,*l,*ll),
              traverse(*r,*lr),
              append(*ll,[*x|*lr],*lis),
              append(*nl,[*nx|*nr],*lis),
              bltree(*nl,*tl),
              bltree(*nr,*tr).                                    (7)
```

The first 'append' appends *ll and [*x|*lr] and gives the result *lis. On the other hand, the second 'append' generates *nl, *nr and *nx from *lis. Here we introduce a heuristic as next stated:

H1: If after a goal (called g1) execution, next goal (called g2) execution is a syntactically inversion of the previous goal(g1), then rename every variable of the goal g2 to be the same as corresponding variable of the goal g1. After this renaming, eliminate both g1 and g2.

Although this heuristic may not preserve equivalency of transformation, it introduces an important information to synthesize a procedural program, which avoids the same execution. If we apply H1 to the unfolded clause (7), each instance bound to every variable in the second 'append' for a generator is forced to be the same as the instance bound to the corresponding variable in the first 'append'. By this transformation, we pick up a special solution in which *nl, *nr and *nx correspond *ll, *lr and *x respectively. By this operation, we lose the equivalence of programs. But on the other hand, we get an efficient algorithm. In (7), renaming of

*ll <- *nl, *lr <- *nr and *x <- *nx          (8)

is applied to whole clause including the variables in the head. After this renaming, two 'append's are the same and have no effect in this clause, therefore we eliminate these two 'append's by H1. The result is:

```
ins(*a,t(*l,*x,*r),t(*tl,*x,*tr)) :-
            *a<*x,
            tins(*a,*l,*ll),
            traverse(*r,*lr),
            bltree(*ll,*tl),
            bltree(*lr,*tr).                  (9)
```

Next, we consider the mode declaration. As for the first 'bltree', it has '*ll' as an input variable, and '*tl' as an output variable. Since all the input variables are given before the 'tins', the 'bltree' can move to the place direct after the 'tins'. Then by folding a pair of 'tins' and 'bltree' with 'ins', (9) is transformed into:

```
ins(*a,t(*l,*x,*r),t(*tl,*x,*tr)) :-
            *a<*x,
            ins(*a,*l,*tl),
            traverse(*r,*lr),
            bltree(*lr,*tr).                  (10)
```

Now, we use H1 again. Since in (10) the constructing a tree (which is the work of 'bltree') is the inversion of the operation expanding a tree by 'traverse', the structure of the tree does not change. By its virtue, we can make *tr to be equal to *r. So we rename *tr to *r, and eliminate a pair of 'traverse' and 'bltree'. The final result is:

```
ins(*a,t(*l,*x,*r),t(*tl,*x,*r)) :-
            *a<*x,
            ins(*a,*l,*tl).                   (11)
```

If we imitate the same course of program transformation for clause (5.3), the result is:

```
ins(*a,t(*l,*x,*r),t(*l,*x,*tr)) :-
            *a>=*x,
            ins(*a,*r,*tr).                   (12)
```

The final program resulting from the above described transformation (6), (11), and (12) is a procedural program of direct tree insertion.

Clearly, by using H1, we have lost equivalency preserving feature of transformation. On the other hand, we find some insights into the human mental process for algorithm synthesis.

How about an order of computation? The order of computation of the declarative program, i.e. (1.1)-(4) is $4^n * n^{3/2}$ (Knuth 1977), on the other hand, the order of computation of the procedural program, i.e. (6), (11) and (12) is log n. This improvement comes from the heuristic H1.

## 3. APPLICATION TO BALANCED TREES

There are many kinds of tree satisfying a special property, for example a condition on number of nodes of subtrees, etc. They have been given names such as perfect balanced trees, etc. So, we apply the principle in section 2 to perfect balanced trees. In this case, we need rebalanced method, whose algorithm is "if the test of whether or not a constructed tree is balanced fails, then backtracking occurs and finally we get a balanced tree". And after transformation, we get a balanced tree not after backtrackings but as the first solution. So we will explain what kind of knowledge is necessary to synthesize a balanced tree insertion program. In this section, we manipulate only perfect balanced trees and every subtree has number of nodes in itself as additional information in order to be easy to test whether or not the subtree is balanced.

The declarative program is as follows:

```
instree(*a,*ot,*nt,*n) :- tins(*a,*ot,*1),
                         mktree(*1,*nt,*n).                    (13)
```

Here the 'tins' is the almost same as 'tins' of section 2 except that number of nodes in a tree is contained. We make 'mktree' by adding to the 'bltree' a test goal that checks a condition of being balanced, and it returns number of nodes of the tree. The meaning of (13) is that if *a is inserted into *ot, then the result is get *nt and the number of its nodes is *n.

After unfolding of 'tins' and 'mktree' in (13), we split it into two cases. One is a case which need no re-balancing operations. In this case we can transform it by imitating the transformations of section 2. Another is a case which needs re-balancing operations. We well trace the transformation in this case. One of clauses which must include re-balancing operations is as follows:

```
instree(*a,t(*1,*x,*r,*n),t(*tl,*nx,*tr,*b),*b) :-
               *a<*x,
               tins(*a,*1,*1y),
               traverse(*r,*ry),
               append(*1y,[*x|*ry],*lis),
               append(*11,[*nx|*lr],*lis),
               mktree(*11,*tl,*c),
               mktree(*lr,*tr,*d),
               balanced(*c,*d,*b).                             (14)
```

The method to re-construct a balanced tree from an unbalanced tree is called here 'one element shift'. It is that when a tree has not been balanced any more by an insertion of an element into a right (or left) subtree, then an element of the root node is inserted into another subtree, and the root node is replaced by the minimum (maximum) element of the right (or left) subtree. By the application of the 'one element shift' to 'append's in (14), we can eliminate '*lis', and also eliminate 'append's, so we get next clause.

```
instree(*a,t(*1,*x,*r,*n),t(*tl,*nx,*tr,*b),*b) :-
               *a<*x,
               tins(*a,*1,*1y),
               traverse(*r,*ry),
               append(*11,[*nx],*1y),
               mktree(*11,*tl,*c),
               mktree([*x|*ry],*tr,*d),
               balanced(*c,*d,*b).                             (15)
```

Now, we apply an equivalency relation 'E1' to 'tins' in (15).

E1: 'tins' is equivalent to a pair of 'traverse' and 'insert'. ('insert' is a predicate which inserts an element into a linear list.)

The result is

```
        instree(*a,t(*l,*x,*r,*n),t(*tl,*nx,*tr,*b),*b) :-
                    *a<*x,
                    traverse(*r,*ry),
                    traverse(*l,*la),
                    insert(*a,*la,*ly),
                    append(*ll,[*nx],*ly),
                    mktree(*ll,*tl,*c),
                    mktree([*x|*ry],*tr,*d),
                    balanced(*c,*d,*b).                              (16)
```

The equivalency relation is based on the following heuristic.

H2: If the effect of a predicate is equivalent to other pair of goals that are not a definition of the predicate itself, the goal can be replaced with the predicate.

If we want to apply the heuristic automatically, we must examine whether or not the equivalency relation holds anywhere at any time.
   Next, we introduce 'E2'.

E2: Consider about next two pairs of goals:
(A)     insert(*a,*c,*d),append(*e,[*b],*d)
(B)     append(*f,[*b],*c),insert(*a,*f,*e)
If *a is not equal to *b, the effect of (A) is the same as the effect of (B), and we get same *e in both case.

This equivalency relation is based on H2 extended to plural predicates. After applying E2 to 'insert' and 'append' pair in (16), the result is split into two cases; one is a case of *a<*b, another is *a>=*b. The result is

```
        instree(*a,t(*l,*x,*r,*n),t(*tl,*nx,*tr,*b),*b) :-
                    *a<*x,
                    traverse(*r,*ry),
                    traverse(*l,*la),
                    insert(*a,*la,*ly),
                    append(*ll,[*nx],*ly),
                    *a>=*nx,
                    mktree(*ll,*tl,*c),
                    mktree([*x|*ry],*tr,*d),
                    balanced(*c,*d,*b).                              (17.1)
        instree(*a,t(*l,*x,*r,*n),t(*tl,*nx,*tr,*b),*b) :-
                    *a<*x,
                    traverse(*r,*ry),
                    traverse(*l,*la),
                    append(*mid,[*nx],*la),
                    insert(*a,*mid,*ll),
                    *a<*nx,
                    mktree(*ll,*tl,*c),
                    mktree([*x|*ry],*tr,*d),
                    balanced(*c,*d,*b).                              (17.2)
```

   Next, we get H3 by expanding H2 to a case of no side effect.

H3: When goals having no side effect are inserted into a clause body, a behavior of the clause is invariant.

Here we insert the following goals between the 'append' and the 'insert' of (17.2), in order to separate 'insertion an element' from 'one element shift'.

```
        mktree(*mid,*tree,*h),traverse(*tree,*mid)                   (18)
```

These goals expand the tree constructed by themselves, so they have no
side effect and the meaning of the clause is invariant. After applying
H3 and moving '*a<*nx' to the place direct after the first 'mktree', we
get the following clause.

```
instree(*a,t(*l,*x,*r,*n),t(*tl,*nx,*tr,*b),*b) :-
                *a<*x,
                traverse(*r,*ry),
                traverse(*l,*la),
                append(*mid,[*nx],*la),
                mktree(*mid,*tree,*h),
                *a<*nx,
                traverse(*tree,*mid),
                insert(*a,*mid,*ll),
                mktree(*ll,*tl,*c),
                mktree([*x|*ry],*tr,*d),
                balanced(*c,*d,*b).                            (19)
```

In (19), an operation of the five first goals is the 'insertion an
element' and an operation of the rest goals is the 'one element shift'.
Please pay attention to a pair of traverse(*tree,*mid) and
insert(*a,*mid,*ll) in (19). By E1 the pair of the goals is transformed
into tins(*a,*tree,*ll). Then we can fold this 'tins' and
mktree(*ll,*tl,*c) of with 'instree'.
    Next, we make a new predicate 'dell' from 'traverse', 'append' and
'mktree' of (19).

```
dell(*l,*tree,*nx) :- traverse(*l,*la),
                     append(*mid,[*nx],*la),
                     mktree(*mid,*tree,*h).                    (20)
```

It expands a tree, picks up the maximum element and constructs a
balanced tree. It can be transformed by the same way of the
transformations of section 2. As the result of transformation, we get a
predicate which does not expand a tree to a list. After we fold
'traverse', 'append' and 'mktree' with the 'dell', and transform it in
the same manner of the transformation of section 2, we get (21) which
doesn't expand a tree to a list on the way of insertion.

```
instree(*a,t(*l,*x,*r,*n),t(*tl,*a,*tr,*nn),*nn) :-
                *a<*x,
                instree(*x,*r,*tr,*nr),
                dell(*l,*c,*nx),
                *a>=*nx,
                instree(*nx,*c,*tl,*nl),
                balanced(*nl,*nr,*nn).                         (21.1)
instree(*a,t(*l,*x,*r,*n),t(*tl,*nx,*tr,*nn),*nn) :-
                *a<*x,
                instree(*x,*r,*tr,*nr),
                dell(*l,*c,*nx),
                *a<*nx,
                instree(*a,*c,*tl,*nl),
                balanced(*nl,*nr,*nn).                         (21.2)
```

## 4. APPLICATION TO B-TREE

In this section, we apply the strategy to a 'B-tree'. The declarative
program for an element insertion to B-tree is

```
b-tree(*a,*old,*new) :- btins(*a,*old,*lis),
                       bltree(*lis,*new).                      (22)
```

The predicate 'btins' is a predicate for expanding a B-tree and an element insertion. The predicate 'bltree' is a predicate for constructing a B-tree. By the way a B-tree has a next property that if n is given, every page contains at least n and less than or equal to 2n nodes. So, by (22) the result may not be a B-tree at first. But after some backtrackings, we get a 'B-tree' by (22). Here, we treat a case of n=2.

Because in the top page of a B-tree the number of nodes may be less than n, we must prepare a 'bltree' as the top level predicate and a predicate 'bltree1' for other cases. And in this section, we represent a B-tree as a linear list, where 2i+1 th (i=0,1,..) elements are subtree, and 2i th (i=1,2,..) elements are node of the page. Appendix 1 is a precise definition of (22).

Because a B-tree is also a kind of balanced trees, we need a re-balancing operation. The knowledge for the synthesis of the re-balancing algorithm is called 'separation of pages'. So through the transformation of a B-tree, we split the program into the following three cases.

1) The first case is that the balance of a subtree is not lost by an insertion.
2) The second case is that although the balance of the subtree is lost by an insertion, the effect can be absorbed in the page.
3) The last case is that the balance of the subtree is lost by an insertion and the effect cannot be absorbed in the page. In this case the page must be split.

By unfolding of 'btins' and 'bltree', we get clauses which correspond to each case of 1),2),3). In the first case, we can transform it in the same cause as section 2. So we will trace the case 2) and 3).

At first we manipulate the case of insertion into the left most subtree. In the case of 2), we have next clause.

```
b-tree(*a,[*s,*r|*1],[*t1,*b|*tr]):-
        *a<*r,
        btins(*a,*s,*a1),
        btra(*1,*a2),
        append(*a1,[*r|*a2],*lis),
        append([*c,*d|*e],[*b,*lr1|*lrr],*lis),
        bltree1([*c,*d|*e],*t1,*flag),
        bltree([*lr1|*lrr],*tr),
        count(*tr,*cn),
        add(*cn,1,*n),
        *n<=4.                                        (23)
```

When the balance of the left most subtree is lost, the page is split. Since the subtree must be the type of [*n1,*nx,*nr], we replace *t1 to [*n1,*nx,*nr] and change the structure of the third argument of head to [*n1,*nx,*nr,*b|*tr] in order to include this new subtree in the page of the argument. After this operation, we can transform it in the same course as before, and the result is shown in (27.5).

In the case of 3), we have the following clause.

```
b-tree(*a,[*s,*r|*1],[*t1,*b,*tr]) :-
        *a<*r,
        btins(*a,*s,*a1),
        btra(*1,*a2),
        append(*a1,[*r|*a2],*lis),
        append([*c,*d|*e],[*b,*lr1,*lrr|*lr],*lis),
        bltree1([*c,*d|*e],*t1,*flag1),
        bltree1([*lr1,*lrr|*lr],*tr,*flag2).           (24)
```

In this case, we must get an element which is included into upper page. We replace *1 to [*s1,*r1|*1], *t1 to [*ta,*tb,*tc,*td,*te], and the first 'bltree1' to the following goals.

```
append(*la,[*td|*lc],[*c,*d|*e]),
bltreel(*la,[*ta,*tb,*tc],F),
bltreel(*lc,*te,*flag),                                          (25)
```

After this operation, the input tree and the corresponding output tree is as following:

```
the input tree  [        *s,        *r,*s1,*r1|*1]
                         :         :   :
the output tree [[*ta,*tb,*tc,*td,*te],*b,*tr]                  (26)
```

So we can transform it with 'append elimination'(H1 heuristic), and the result is (27.6).

Next we consider the case of an element insertion into subtrees except the left most subtree. If the balance is kept, we use recursion as (27.7). Otherwise if the balance is lost, we replace the third argument of the head as (27.8).

In the way of transformation, there appears a pair of 'btins' and 'bltree1' except for the top page, we make a new predicate of them, and transform it in the same manner as before. The final result is:

```
b-tree(*a,[],[[],*a,[]]).                                       (27.1)
b-tree(*a,[[]],[[],*a,[]]).                                     (27.2)
b-tree(*a,[[*s,*r|*rest]],*t) :-
       b-tree(*a,[*s,*r|*rest],*t).                             (27.3)
b-tree(*a,[*s,*r|*rest],[*t1,*r|*rest]) :-
       *a<*r,
       bb$2(*a,*s,*t1),
       count([*t1,*r|*rest],*cn),
       *cn<=4.                                                  (27.4)
b-tree(*a,[*s,*r|*rest],[*s1,*sx,*sr,*r|*rest]) :-
       *a<*r,
       bb$1(*a,*s,[*s1,*sx,*sr]),
       count([*s1,*sx,*sr,*r|*rest],*cn),
       *cn<=4.                                                  (27.5)
b-tree(*a,[*s1,*r1,*s2,*r2|*rest],
          [[*s1,*sx,*sr,*r1,*s2],*r2,*rest]) :-
       *a<*r1,
       bb$1(*a,*s1,[*s1,*sx,*sr]).                              (27.6)
b-tree(*a,[*s,*r|*rest],[*s,*r|tr]) :-
       *a>=*r,
       b-tree(*a,*rest,*tr),
       count([*s,*r|*tr],*cn),
       *cn<=4.                                                  (27.7)
b-tree(*a,[*s,*r|*rest],[[*s,*r,*s1,*r1,*s2],*r2,*sr]) :-
       *a>=*r,
       bb$3(*a,*rest,[*s1,*r1,*s2,*r2|*sr]).                    (27.8)
```

In this program, 'bb$1', 'bb$2' and 'bb$3' are new predicates made of 'btins' and 'bltree1'. The 'bb$1' is used for a case of the balance is lost, the 'bb$2' is used for a case of balance is kept, and the 'bb$3' is used only for (27.8). We show these programs precisely in appendix 2.

## 5. STUDY OF HEURISTICS

We have transformed a program which inserts an element into a tree, and in the transformations we keep the structure of tree as invariant as possible. In the way of transformation, we have introduced some heuristics, such as H1, H2 and H3. Besides them, we have introduced the following knowledge other than the definition of tree.

1) The heuristics for transformation.
   H4: Moving goals based on the information of the mode declaration.
   H5: Applying the 'case split'.
2) The knowledge for keeping the structure of tree to be as invariant as possible.
   H6: Introduction of the 'one element shift'.
   H7: Changing structure of variables to make the result of transformation to be B-tree.

Although these knowledge is very naive, they are important because of the ease of the transformation of programs which manipulate tree structure.

Now we must pay attention to the nature of heuristics used in transformation. We consider that the heuristics can be classified into some categories. We think that this classification depends on the difficulty of applying the heuristic automatically, in other words similarity to human mental process of finding algorithm. So, we divide heuristics into three levels.

LEVEL 1) Heuristics which can be applied if we have the data base of rules other than unfold/fold in the transformation system.
LEVEL 2) In order to determine whether or not applying this category of heuristics is effective, we must continue transformation far and far.
LEVEL 3) Heuristics of this level is when, what and how heuristics of LEVEL 1) and 2) must be applied. So, this is a meta-level heuristics.

Examples of the heuristics of level 3) is finding the method of re-balance such as 'one element shift'. We think heuristics of level 1) or 2) is the method to realize the heuristics of level 3). Heuristics that makes the judgment when and where the heuristics must be introduced belongs to this level. Therefore, we can regard the level 3) as the meta-level, so the only heuristics of this level can be called 'heuristic' in a narrow sense.

The heuristics of level 1) consists of various equivalency relations. So, the heuristics of this level can be applied easily if the level 3) heuristics has found out the usefulness of the level 1) heuristics.

There is level 2) between level 1) and 3). The examples of heuristics of level 2) are as follows; what is re-calculation in H1, where and what goals are inserted to in H3, what structure is given in H7, etc. Their special feature is a very large search space being necessary, so their realization requires amounts of development of the method of reasoning and hardware. But since they are not meta-level, there is some possibility of applying them in transformation automatically.

Since it is very difficult to apply level 3) heuristics automatically, we think our short range aim is a transformation system that can apply level 1) and 2) heuristics automatically.

## 6. CONCLUSIONS

We have described transformation of the certain kind of tree manipulate-programs. As result, we can transform a declarative style program to a procedural style program by adding some intuitional ideas

which depend on avoiding re-calculation, and they are very easy.
   In general, for algorithm synthesis, it is important what knowledge is added to declarative expressions. So in this paper, we suggest clearing up knowledge of tree manipulation and method of transformation in a mechanical way. Although the study described in this paper is not general, we think we take a step forward to our aim which is an integration of declarative knowledge and knowledge for algorithm synthesis.


REFERENCE

Burstall R.M., Darlington J. (1977) A Transformation System for Developing Recursive Programs. JACM 24: 44-67
Darlington J. (1981) An Experimental Program Transformation and Synthesis System. Artificial Intelligence 16.
Hogger C.J. (1982) Derivation of Logic Programs. JACM 28: 372-392
Knuth D.E. (1981) The Art of Computer Programing, Vol 1. Addison-Wesley.
Nakamura N., Nakagawa H. (1984) Transformation of Prolog Program with Heuristics. Proc. of the Logic Programming Conference '84.
Sato T. (1984) Transformational Logic Program Synthesis. Proc. of FGCS '84.
Sato T., Tamaki H. (1983) Transformation in Prolog. Proc. of Logic Programming Conference '83.
Tamaki H., Sato T. (1984) Unfold/Fold Transformation of Logic Programs. Proc. of the 2nd International Logic Programming Conference.
Tarlund S.A., Hasson A. (1982) Program Transformation by Data Structure Mapping. LOGIC PROGRAMMING. Academic-Press.


APPENDIX 1:The Declarative Program of 'B-TREE'

```
    b-tree(*a,*t,*ta) :- btins(*a,*t,*1), bltree(*1,*ta).

    btins(*a,[],[*a]).
    btins(*a,[[]],[*a]).
    btins(*a,[[*r|*1]],*lis) :- btins(*a,[*r|*1],*lis).
    btins(*a,[*s,*r|*1],*lis) :-
        *a<*r,
        btins(*a,*s,*s1),
        btra(*1,*11),
        append(*s1,[*r|*11],*lis).
    btins(*a,[*s,*r|*1],*lis) :-
        *a>=*r,
        btra(*s,*s1),
        btins(*a,*1,*11),
        append(*s1,[*r|*11],*lis).

    btra([],[]).
    btra([*a],*b):-btra(*a,*b).
    btra([*s,*r|*lis],*ans) :-
        btra(*s,*1),
        btra(*lis,*a),
        append(*1,[*r|*a],*ans).

    bltree([*a],[[],*a,[]]).
    bltree([*a,*b],[[],*a,[],*b[]]).
    bltree([*a,*b,*c],[[],*a,[],*b,[],*c,[]]).
    bltree([*a,*b,*c,*d],[[],*a,[],*b,[],*c,[],*d,[]]).
    bltree(*lis,[*t1,*r,*tr]) :-
        append([*11,*12|*1],[*r,*r1,*r2|*rr],*lis),
```

```
                bltree1([*l1,*l2|*l],*tl,flag1),
                bltree1([*r1,*r2|*rr],*tr,flag2).
    bltree(*lis,[*tl,*r|*tr]) :-
                append([*a,*b|*c],[*r,*r1,*r2,*r3,*r4,*r5|*1],*lis),
                bltree1([*a,*b|*c],*tl,*flag),
                bltree([*r1,*r2,*r3,*r4,*r5|*1],*tr),
                count([*tl,*r|*tr),
                *n<=4.

    bltree1([*a,*b],[[],*a,[],*b,[]],B).
    bltree1([*a,*b,*c],[[],*a,[],*b,[],*c,[]],B).
    bltree1([*a,*b,*c,*d],[[],*a,[],*b,[],*c,[],*d,[]],B).
    bltree1(*lis,[*tl,*r|*tr],B) :-
                append([*a,*b|*c],[*r,*r1,*r2,*r3,*r4,*r5|*1],*lis),
                bltree1([*a,*b|*c],*tl,B),
                bltree([*r1,*r2,*r3,*r4,*r5|*1],*tr),
                count(*tl,*r|*tr],*n),
                test(*n,B).

    count([*a],0).
    count([*a,*b|*c],*n):- count(*c,*cn),add(*cn,1,*n).

    test(*n,E) :- *n<2.
    test(*n,F) :- *n>4.
    test(*n,B) :- *n>=2,*n<=4.


APPENDIX 2:The Program of BB$1, BB$2 and BB$3.

    bb$1(*a,[[*1,*x|*r]],*tr) :- bb$1(*a,[*1,*x|*r],*tr).
    bb$1(*a,[*s1,*r1,*s2,*r2|*tr],[[*1,*x,*r,*r1,*s2],*r2,*tr]):-
                *a<*r1,
                bb$1(*a,*s1,[*1,*x,*r]).
    bb$1(*a,[*1,*x,|*r],[[*1,*x,*s1,*r1,*s2],*r2,*s3]) :-
                *a>=*c,
                b-tree(*a,*r,[*s1,*r1,*s2,*r2,*s3]).

    bb$2(*a,[[*1,*x|*r]],*tr) :- bb$2(*a,[*1,*x,*r],*tr).
    bb$2(*a,[*1,*x,|*r],[*n1,*n|*r]) :-
                *a<*x,
                bb$2(*a,*1,*n1),
                count([*n1,*n|*r],*n),
                test(*f,B).
    bb$2(*a,[*1,*x|*r],[*n1,*nx,*nr,*x|*r]) :-
                *a<*x,
                bb$1(*a,*1,[*n1,*nx,*nr]),
                count([*n1,*nx,*nr,*x|*r],*n),
                test(*n,B).
    bb$2(*a,[*1,*x|*r],[*1,*x|*nr]) :-
                *a>=*x,
                b-tree(*a,*r,*nr),
                count([*1,*x|*nr],*n),
                test(*n,B).

    bb$3(*a,[[],*r|*tr],[[],*a,[],*r|*tr]) :- *a<*r.
    bb$3(*a,[*s,*r|*tr],[*n1,*nx,*nr,*r|*tr]) :-
                *a<*r,
                bb$1(*a,*s,[*n1,*nx,*nr]).
    bb$3(*a,[*s,*r|*tr],[*s,*r|*nt]) :-
                *a>=*r,
                b-tree(*a,*tr,*nt).
```

# Analogical Reasoning using Transformations of Rules

Makoto Haraguchi
Research Institute of Fundamental Information Science,
Kyushu University, Fukuoka, Japan

### Abstract

Regarding analogical reasoning as a deduction with a function of transforming logical rules, this paper presents a formalism of analogical reasoning in terms of deduction. This paper also presents a method, which is an extension of Prolog interpreter, to realize the analogical reasoning in logic programming system.

## 1. Introduction

Analogical reasoning is an important reasoning method in our problem solving activities. Based on some analogy between two domains, we often transform knowledges of one domain into those of another, and make use of the transformed knowledges to solve the problem or to reason some unknown facts. Generally the reasoned facts are not true, however, the analogy under which the facts are reasoned gives an evidence showing that the facts may be true. The purpose of this paper is to present a formalism of analogical reasoning and a system which reasons the unknown facts by analogy. Since the knowledges are generally represented by formulas, it is natural to consider the domains as axiom systems. However, in the present paper, we assume that the knowledges are simply facts about individuals in the domains and that the domains consist of such facts. We leave the problem of analogy between axiom systems in the future.

In order to formalize the analogical reasoning, we need,

first of all, the definition of analogy. Since deduction is of importance to the analogical reasoning, it is desired that one language can describe them. From this viewpoint, Haraguchi [1] has defined the analogy in terms of first order language. We briefly review the definition of analogy in Section 2. Secondly we need to show a system which performs the analogical reasoning. We consider in this paper Winston's analogy-based reasoning [5] which makes use of causal structures of facts. Regarding causal structures as logical rules, we view the analogy-based reasoning as a deduction with a function of transforming rules. The transformation of rules is the key notion introduced in this paper, and is defined in Section 3. Then we give a formalism of analogical reasoning by which facts reasoned by analogy are precisely determined. In Section 4, we show a backward reasoning method which derives the facts reasoned by analogy. The method is easily realized by an extension of Prolog interpreter which tries to derive some facts by finding possible transformations of rules.

## 2. Analogy as a partial identity

We start with reviewing some necessary definition, stated in [1], to precisely discuss the analogical reasoning. The analogy we consider is based on Polya's clarified analogy [3]:

"Two systems are analogous if they agree in
clearly definable relations of their respective part."

Here each system consists of a set of parts and a set of relations between the parts. Thus when we say that some systems are analogous each other, they have at least one pair of relations, one from each, which agree under a correspondence of parts.

Each relation in the system can be represented as a ground atom, and the system is described by a set of ground atoms. For example, a family is a system of relations such as parent(a,b) and father(b,c), where "parent" and "father" are predicate symbols, and a, b and c are constant symbols to denote the

members of family as system parts. Now consider two analogous systems $S_1$ and $S_2$:
$$S_1 = \{A_1,\ldots,A_n\},$$
$$S_2 = \{B_1,\ldots,B_m\},$$
where $A_i$ and $B_j$ are ground atoms representing relations in the systems.

Since $S_1$ and $S_2$ are analogous, there exists a pair
$$\langle A_i, B_j \rangle \in S_1 \times S_2$$
of relations which agree with each other. We say that two relations agree if they have the same relation name (i.e. predicate symbol). Thus the pair $\langle A_i, B_j \rangle$ is written as
$$\langle p(t_1,\ldots,t_k), p(t'_1,\ldots,t'_k) \rangle,$$
where the pairing $\{\langle t_i, t'_i \rangle\}$ of terms is the correspondence under which $A_i$ and $B_j$ agree. We also say that these ground atoms are identified under the pairing of terms. Generally there may exist several pairs of atoms identified under a pairing of terms. These pairs of identified atoms form a set
$$\{\langle p_1(t_{11},\ldots,t_{1n(1)}), p_1(t'_{11},\ldots,t'_{1n(1)}) \rangle,$$
$$\cdot$$
$$\cdot$$
$$\langle p_k(t_{k1},\ldots,t_{kn(k)}), p_k(t'_{k1},\ldots,t'_{kn(k)}) \rangle\}$$
with a pairing of terms
$$\{\langle t_{ij}, t'_{ij} \rangle : 1 \leq j \leq n(i),\ 1 \leq i \leq k\}.$$
Introducing a variable $X_{ij}$ for each pair $\langle t_{ij}, t'_{ij} \rangle$, we represent this set by the following set W of atoms and pair $u = \langle u_1, u_2 \rangle$ of substitutions.
$$W = \{p_1(X_{11},\ldots,X_{1n(1)}),\ldots,p_k(X_{k1},\ldots,X_{kn(k)})\},$$
$$u_1 = \{X_{ij} \leftarrow t_{ij} : 1 \leq j \leq n(i),\ 1 \leq i \leq k\},$$
$$u_2 = \{X_{ij} \leftarrow t'_{ij} : 1 \leq j \leq n(i),\ 1 \leq i \leq k\}.$$
The variable $X_{ij}$ represents the pair
$$X_{ij} = \langle X_{ij} u_1, X_{ij} u_2 \rangle = \langle t_{ij}, t'_{ij} \rangle.$$
We sometimes write the pair of substitutions as $X_{ij} - \langle t_{ij}, t'_{ij} \rangle$. Moreover each atom A in W represents the pair $Au = \langle Au_1, Au_2 \rangle$. Hence $Var(W)u = \{Xu : X \in Var(W)\}$ is the pairing of terms, and $Wu = \{Au : A \in W\}$ is the set of identified atoms, where $Var(W)$ denotes the set of all variables in W. We require that both

Var(W)u and Wu are one-to-one. Now we can give the definition of formal analogy.

**Definition 1.** Let $S_1$ and $S_2$ be finite sets of ground atoms with no common individual constants, and let u be a pair $\langle u_1, u_2 \rangle$ of substitutions. Then we say that u satisfies the partial identity condition for a set W of atoms, if $Wu \subseteq S_1 \times S_2$, and both Wu and Var(W)u are one-to-one relations. In this case, we call (W,u) an analogy between $S_1$ and $S_2$.

We have defined an analogy between two sets of ground atoms. Each ground atom represents a relation between system parts. Definition 1 still stands to define an analogy concerning more complex relations, such as relations about relations. (For details, see [1].)

## 3. Transformation of rules based on analogy

As mentioned in the introduction, we consider Winston's analogy-based reasoning [5]. Since the power of analogy-based reasoning essentially depends on the ability of deduction, and since the underlying priciple of analogy-based reasoning can be viewed as the rule transformation defined in this section, we propose to deal with analogical reasoning in a deductive system with the function of transforming rules.

Winston [4,5] has asserted that causal relations enables a common-sense reasoning that reasons some relations in a system from a relation in another system, provided that the two systems are analogous. His assertion is based on the principle that it seems reasonable for the common reasons to lead to a common effect. The principle is depicted in Fig.1, where the relation $r_1(a,b)$ and $r_1(a',b')$ are identified by an analogy

$$(W,u) = (\{r_1(X,Y)\}, \{X - \langle a,a' \rangle, Y - \langle b,b' \rangle\}),$$

and the cause relation

$$r_1(a,b) \Longrightarrow r_2(c,d)$$

shows that $r_1(a,b)$ works as a reason for $r_2(c,d)$ to hold. For the system $S_2$, $r_1(a',b')$ holds. We regard $r_1(a,b)$ and $r_1(a',b')$ as a common reason, since they are identified by the analogy

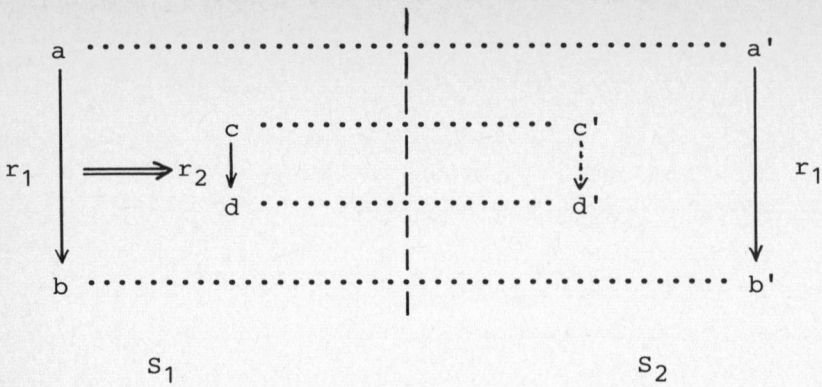

Fig. 1  The principle of analogical reasoning

($W,u$). Then the principle suggests that a common effect corresponding to $r_2(c,d)$ may hold in $S_2$. The common effect should be identified with $r_2(c,d)$ by ($W,u$). Hence it must be $r_2(c',d')$ which is a missing relation in $S_2$.

Here we should notice that the cause relation works just like a logical rule. In order to reason the missing relation $r_2(c',d')$, we may just apply the logical rule

$$R' : r_2(c',d') \leftarrow r_1(a',b'),$$

which is equal to

$$R : r_2(c,d) \leftarrow r_1(a,b)$$

except for the pairing $Var(W)u$, to the relation $r_1(a',b')$ which already holds in $S_2$. In other words, the principle of analogical reasoning can be realized in a deductive system with the function of transforming rule $R$ to $R'$, because the missing relation $r_2(c',d')$ is deduced by applying modus ponens to $R'$ and $r_1(a',b')$.

The transformation is now formally defined in terms of Definition 1. In what follows, we assume that each cause relation of the reasons $A_1,...,A_k$ and the effect $B$ is encoded to a definite clause $B \leftarrow A_1,...,A_k$, and we simply call it a rule.

**Definition 2.** Let ($W,u$) and $C_1 : A \leftarrow A_1,...,A_k$ ($k>0$) be an analogy and a ground rule, respectively. Then we say that a ground rule $C_2 : B \leftarrow B_1,...,B_k$ is a $C_1$-analogue under ($W,u$), if there exists a definite clause $C : D \leftarrow D_1,...,D_k$ such that $Cu_i =$

$C_i$ (i=1,2) and $\{D,D_1,...,D_k\} \subseteq W$ hold.

We call the conversion from $C_1$ to $C_2$ a transformation under (W,u). The clause C in Definition 2 is called a generalization of $C_1$ and $C_2$ ([2]). In what follows, we represent the transformation by the following schema:

$$\frac{C_1 : A \leftarrow A_1,...,A_k}{C_2 : B \leftarrow B_1,...,B_k}$$

According to Definition 2, the principle of analogical reasoning is now written as the following schema:

$$\frac{\dfrac{A \leftarrow A_1,...,A_k}{B \leftarrow B_1,...,B_k} \quad B_1,...,B_k}{B} \quad ,$$

where the premises $A_1,...,A_k$ of the upper rule are assumed to hold, and the real line shows modus ponens. Thus the analogical reasoning is a combination of the usual deduction and the rule transformation. We call this schema the fundamental one of analogical reasoning.

Generally reasoning is a process of applying inference rules. Hence it is natural to consider a process in which the rule transformation and modus ponens are applied consecutively. For instance, consider the following derivation of facts, where $A_i$ and $B_j$ are facts in $S_1$ and $S_2$, respectively.

$$\frac{\dfrac{A_1 \leftarrow A_2}{B_1 \leftarrow B_2} \quad \dfrac{\dfrac{A_2 \leftarrow A_3}{B_2 \leftarrow B_3} \quad B_3}{B_2}}{B_1}$$

It should be noticed that the premise $B_2$ to conclude $B_1$ is derived by the fundamental schema. Hence we derive the fact $B_1$ by applying the fundamental schema two times.

In the derivation above, we transform rules in $S_1$ into those in $S_2$. It is also natural to transform rules in $S_2$ to derive some facts in $S_1$. For instance, we allow a derivation shown in the following:

$$\frac{\dfrac{B_1 \leftarrow B_2}{A_1 \leftarrow A_2} \quad A_2}{A_1} \quad ,$$

where the premise $B_2$ of the rule $B_1 \leftarrow B_2$ is logically true or is derived by transforming rules as in the former derivation.

To precisely state the analogical reasoning, we now give a formalism of analogical reasoning.

**Definition 3.** Let $S_i$ be a set of ground definite clauses for $i=1,2$. Then we define the set $S_i^+$ of facts (ground atoms) as follows:

$$S_i^+ = \cup\ S_i^n,$$
$$S_i^0 = \{\ A : S_i \vdash A\ \},$$
$$S_i^{n+1} = S_i^n \cup \{\ A : S_i^n \cup R_i^n \vdash A\ \},$$
$$R_i^n = \{\ C : B \leftarrow B_1,\ldots,B_k\ (k>0):$$
$$\text{for a rule } C' : A \leftarrow A_1,\ldots,A_k \text{ in } S_j\ (i \neq j),\ C$$
$$\text{is a } C'\text{-analogue},\ A_m \in S_j^n \text{ and } B_m \in S_i^n \text{ for all } m\}.$$

The facts in $S_i^+$ are said to be reasoned by analogy.

Note that $S_i^n$ is the set of ground atoms which are derived by transforming rules at most n times.

## 4. Backward reasoning method

In this section, we present a "proof procedure" reason which is a Prolog program with the following properties.

(1) A fact B is in $S_i^+$ if reason(B) succeeds.

(2) A fact B is not in $S_i^+$ if reason(B) finitely fails.

By the definition of $S_i^+$, it is clear that a fact A is reasoned by analogy iff A is derived by a finite application of modus ponens and the rule transformations. Prolog interpreter realizes the application of modus ponens. Hence, first of all, reason is designed to be an extension of Prolog interpreter. First three clauses of reason interprets pure-Prolog clauses:

(C1)    reason(true) :- !.
(C2)    reason((Goal,Goals)) :- !, reason(Goal), reason(Goals).
(C3)    reason(Goal) :- clause(Goal,Goals), reason(Goals).

Since the definitions of $S_1^+$ and $S_2^+$ depend each other, reason has goals of the forms

$$\text{fact A in } S_1^+ \text{ and } \text{fact B in } S_2^+,$$

and we represent these goals by

fact1(A) and fact2(B),
respectively. We also represent a rule $A \leftarrow A_1,\ldots,A_k$ in $S_1$ by a clause
fact1(A) ← fact1($A_1$),...,fact1($A_k$).
For rules in $S_2$, the similar representation is assumed.

Now we show a method to realize the function of transforming rules. For this purpose, we exemplify how reason transforms rules. Let $S_i$ be the following set of ground definite clauses:

$S_1$ = { g(a,c), f(a,d), p(d,c),
 p(d,c) ← f(a,d), g(a,c) },
$S_2$ = { f(a',d'), g(a',c'),
 r(c',d') ← p(d',c') }.

To show r(c,d) in $S_1^+$, we set up the following goal:
← reason(fact1(r(c,d))).

This goal never succeeds as long as we use C1, C2 and C3, since r(c,d) $\notin S_1$. So we must try to transform some rule in $S_2$. The new clause C4 performs the act of transforming rule, and is applied when C1, C2 and C3 fails to apply.

(C4) reason(Goal) :-
 prematch(Goal,Tgoal,Tgoals),
 transform(Goal,Tgoal,Tgoals,Fgoals,Agoal)
 reason(Tgoals),
 reason(Fgoals),
 call(Agoal).

"prematch" tries to find a possible rule in $S_j$ to be transformed, given goal in $S_i$ (i≠j), and returns a rule in $S_j$ whose head and body are Tgoal and Tgoals, respectively. For the goal reason(fact1(r(c,d))), prematch succeeds and we have the rule fact2(r(c',d')) ← fact2(p(d',c')) to be transformed.

"transform" tries to transform this rule for fact1(r(c,d)):

$$\frac{\text{fact2(r(c',d'))} \leftarrow \text{fact2(p(d',c'))}}{\text{fact1(r(c ,d ))} \leftarrow \text{Fgoals}}$$

Firstly transform generalizes the heads of these rules and obtains a pairing {<c,c'>, <d,d'>}. Then, using this pairing, transform applies the pairing to the body fact2(p(d',c')). Since c' and d' are paired with c and d, respectively, transform obtains fact1(p(d,c)) as Fgoals. From the Definition 3, we must verify both $p(d,c) \in S_1^+$ and $p(d',c') \in S_2^+$. Hence we derive the new goal

← reason(fact2(p(d',c'))),reason(fact1(p(d,c))).

Since $p(d',c') \notin S_2^0$, we try to transform

fact1(p(d,c)) ← fact1(f(a,d)),fact1(g(a,c))

for fact2(p(d',c')). Generalizing fact1(p(d,c)) and fact2(p(d',c')), we have the pairing {<c,c'>,<d,d'>}. However, some term to be paired with a is not defined by this pairing. Hence, introducing new variable $X_a$ for a, we consider the following rule transformation:

fact1(p(d,c))  ←  fact1(f(a,d)),fact1(g(a,c))
------------------------------------------------
fact2(p(d',c')) ← fact2(f($X_a$,d')),fact2(g($X_a$,c'))

Then we derive the new goal by this transformation:

← reason(fact1(f(a,d))),reason(fact1(g(a,c))),
  reason(fact2(f($X_a$,d'))),reason(fact2(g($X_a$,c'))).

It should be noticed that the value substituted to the variable $X_a$ must not violate the partial identity condition (Definition 1), since we define the rule transformation under some analogy (Definition 2). In other words, we must verify that the pairing {<c,c'>,<d,d'>,<a,$X_a$>} is one-to-one. For this purpose, transform returns the predicate instance

Agoal : analogy([[c,c'],[d,d'],[a,$X_a$]]),

where "analogy" is a predicate to verify if the argument list [[c,c'],[d,d'],[a,$X_a$]] is one-to-one or not. Then Agoal is called when the derived goals succeeds and the variable $X_a$ is instantiated to some ground term. For the goal

← reason(fact2(f($X_a$,d'))),reason(fact2(g($X_a$,c'))),

we have the answer substitution with $X_a$ = a', and

analogy([[d,d'],[c,c'],[a,a']])

succeeds. As a result, we have completed to show $r(c,d) \in S_1^+$. We have also showed that reason(fact1(r(c,d))) succeeds.

Generally some transformation of rule R may fail to derive some facts. In such a case, reason must try to set up another pairing without changing the rule R or to transform another rule R'. However, using Prolog's backtracking, we can perform this act of searching alternative transformations. In fact, Prolog goes back and attempts to re-satisfy

        prematch(Goal,Tgoal,Tgoals),

        transform(Goal,Tgoal,Tgoals,Fgoals,Agoal).

Re-satisfying prematch, we have another rule to be transformed. Similarly, re-satisfying transform, we have another pairing for the same rule tried to transform before.

## 5. Concluding remarks

Based on the formalism of analogy, we have succeeded to treat analogical reasoning formally. As a result, we obtain a method to realize the analogical reasoning in a logic programming system. The implementation of the method has been developed for DCL U-station, and is written by CProlog.

The analogy treated in the present paper is a "syntactic" one. Extending the notion of analogy, we are preparing the theory of analogy which takes semantic consideration into account.

## Acknowledgement

The author is grateful to Prof. Setsuo Arikawa for valuable discussions.

## References

[1] Haraguchi, M. (1985): Towards a Mathematical Theory of Analogy, Bull. of Inform. Cybernetics, 21, 29-56.

[2] Plotkin, G.D. (1970): A Note on Inductive Generalization, Machine Intelligence 5, 153-216.

[3] Polya, G. (1954): Induction and Analogy in Mathematics, Princeton University Press.

[4] Winston, P.H. (1980): Learning and Reasoning by Analogy, Comm. ACM, 23, 689-703.

[5] Winston, P.H. (1983): Learning New Principles from Precedents and Exercises, Artificial Intelligence, 19, 321-350.

**SYNCHRONIZATION AND COMMUNICATION IN THE 'SUBJECT'**

T. Hisano and M. Suwa

Electrotechnical Laboratory
1-1-4 Umezono, Tsukuba Science City 305, Japan

ABSTRACT

A new type of communication between concurrent processes called 'subjects' and a synchronization mechanism are presented. Since the communication is carried out only based on reading the internal states of a subject, it is available at any time even in the case of a failure of some subjects.

1. INTRODUCTION

A 'subject' is a conceptual entity which models the knowledge of a problem solver. Since problem solvers in a real problem domain should be designed to deal with concurrent phenomena, a formalism suitable for specifying them is needed. The phrase 'problem solving based upon subjects' is used for denoting such a formalism. The basic component in the formalism is a subject which can be thought of as an atomic problem solver. The objective of introducing the formalism is to represent a solution by means of subjects (Hisano 1984).

Each subject in this formalism consists of two sets of procedures and a data structure representing its internal states. One procedure set includes any procedures to define and accomplish the goals of the subject and is concealed from other subjects. Whereas, the other includes only those procedures to access the data structure to read the internal states of the subject and is revealed to other subjects.

This paper describes a new type of communication between subjects and a synchronization mechanism which can ensure correct communication. The communication is carried out only based on reading the internal states of a target subject, and therefore, is highly available even in the case of a failure of some subjects. Such a communication type is called 'reference'. Subjects communicate with others by using this type of communication.

In Chapter 2 communications are divided into three types: rendezvous, interference, and reference. A general description of subjects is presented in Chapter 3. Synchronization and time sequence of events are then presented in Chapter 4 and 5. Examples of application are illustrated in Chapter 6 and comparisons of the formalism proposed by authors with others are discussed in Chapter 7.

2. COMMUNICATION TYPES

Communications among concurrent processes are divided into three types: rendezvous, interference, and reference. Let $A$ be a process

producing information, let $B$ be a process consuming the information, and let $f$ denote the information flow. Definitions of three types of communications are as follows:
(1) Rendezvous is a communication type in which both $A$ and $B$ directly control $f$.
(2) Interference is a communication type in which only $A$ controls $f$.
(3) Reference is a communication type in which only $B$ controls $f$.

Figure 1 illustrates these three types. The characteristics of the respective types are described in the following sections.

## 2.1 Rendezvous Type Communication

In rendezvous type communication both process $A$ at the information producing side and process $B$ at the information consuming side perform synchronization and communication under their respective control. The advantage of this type of communication is, therefore, that both processes are aware of the occurrence of the communication. In other words, each communication is under the control of the processes concerned. The disadvantage is, on the other hand, that dead locks may occur in the case where an input request does not correspond to any output request for some reason.

## 2.2 Interference Type Communication

Generally, interference in a process is the phenomena that the process is affected by others without previous notice. Interference type communication begins with an output request issued by process $A$. The information is then transferred to process $B$, irrespective of its status. An example of this type of communication is the message passing in the object-oriented programming formalism (Yonezawa 1984), which is a method for transmitting messages and for dealing with an

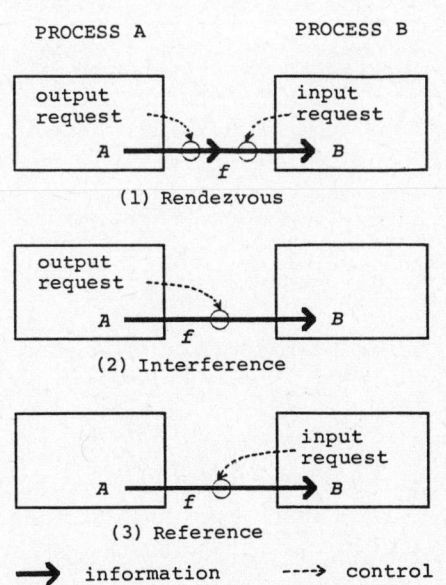

Fig. 1. Three types of communications. The solid lines show information flows, and the dotted lines show control over the flows.

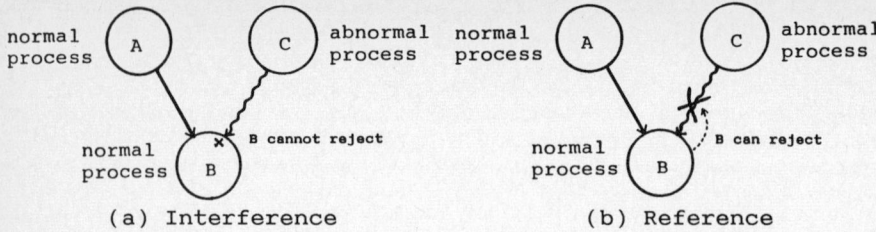

Fig. 2. Communication under conditions that some processes might be abnormal. Process A and B are operating normally and process C is malfunctioning. (a) In the interference type communication, B cannot reject the communication with C. (b) In the reference type communication, if B knows the abnormality of C it can reject the communication with C and secure the communication only with A.

information flow and control in a uniform way. An object in the formalism, equivalent to a process, becomes active when it receives a message. After executing the operation requested by the message, an object becomes inactive until it receives the next message. During the execution, the object may send messages to other objects. The sending object usually performs message passing by specifying the receiving object, but the receiving object cannot specify the sending object. Consequently, the receiving object can neither select the sending object nor reject the message passing itself.

The advantage of the interference type communication is that processes can be used as libraries by making use of the unsymmetry of communication. If a process is defined to perform according to the contents of the received messages, the process can be considered as the instance of an abstract data type.

This unsymmetry of communication, however, may cause disadvantages. For example, since it is difficult to verify a large-scale concurrent system, it should include some steps to recover from erroneous operations. In the interference type communication, one process cannot keep on communicating with a specific process under the condition that some processes might be abnormal as shown in Fig. 2(a). In other words, if there is a malfunctioning process which continues to send messages to another process, the process cannot reject them, causing interference to its communication with normal processes. This means that the interference type communication is likely to be affected by the malfunction of a process.

## 2.3 Reference Type Communication

Reference type communication is performed under the control of a process which needs to get information. Information producing process A, or *referred-to* process, cannot anticipate the communication. Information consuming process B, or *referring* process, refers to the internal state of A without any interference. The referring process makes reference by using a reference procedure defined in the referred-to process. On that occasion, the control is not switched to the referred-to process. Subjects can communicate with others by using this type of communication.

The advantages of the reference type communication are
(1) the communication is under the control of the referring process,

(2) the internal states of a process are guaranteed against any interference of other processes.

As shown in Fig. 2(b), let us suppose that referring process A and referred-to process B are operating normally and process C is malfunctioning[1]. Since C cannot modify the internal states of B, B is protected against the destruction of the internal state. In addition, if B knows the abnormality of C, it can reject the communication with C and secure the communication only with A. Thus, this type of communication can prevent error propagation from C to B and exclude C from the system by ignoring the whole information flow from C.

However, it is possible that the referring process may be kept waiting for a long time when the referred-to process modifies the internal state frequently. The reason is that the reference is repeated if it obtains an incorrect result.

## 3. GENERAL DESCRIPTION OF THE SUBJECT

### 3.1 What Is the Subject ?

Each subject in this formalism consists of two sets of procedures and a data structure representing its internal states. One procedure set includes any procedures to define and accomplish the goals of the subject and is concealed from other subjects. It is called 'concealed set of procedures.' At least one procedure is always activated to accomplish the goals. Whereas, the other includes only those procedures to access the data structure to read the internal states of the subject and is revealed to other subjects. It is called 'revealed set of procedures.'

### 3.2 The Behavior and Characteristics of the Subject

A subject is a process. As to the communication mechanism, in order for the subject to get information provided by other subjects, it uses the reading procedures in their revealed set of procedures and reads their internal states. When the subject gets the information of its own, it also uses the reading procedures in its revealed set of procedures.

The characteristics of the subject are as follows:
(1) The internal states cannot be modified from outside.
(2) The subjects organize a hierarchical structure with an inheritance mechanism.
(3) Each subject performs concurrently and can be independent of the others.

**The Encapsulation of the Internal State:** The internal states of a subject is represented as abstract data. That is, they can be read only by means of the read procedures.

**Hierarchy:** The subjects are classified into two categories: set-subjects and instances. The subjects organize a hierarchical

---

[1] Note that the malfunction of a process means the occurrence of an incorrect state resulting from an incorrect algorithm in a program which has not been verified, but not the occurrence of hardware failures. We assume that the verified program and procedure are assured of the correct operation.

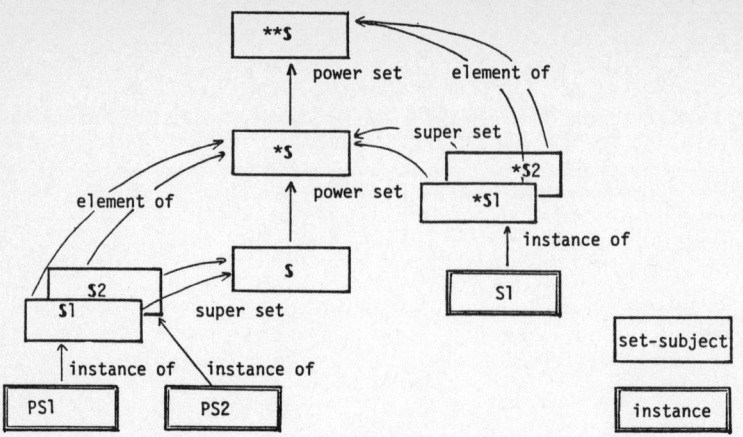

Fig. 3. The hierarchical structure of subjects. The subjects can organized a hierarchical structure with an inheritance mechanism.

structure based on the categories as shown in Fig. 3.

**Inheritance:** The behavior of an instance is specified both by procedures described in itself and by ones in the set-subjects which are the 'super sets' of the instance or their 'super sets.' Procedures which are common among instances can be located in their set-subject. This hierarchical structure makes it possible to introduce the inheritance mechanism to prevent duplicate description.

**Concurrency:** Subjects are always activated. Each subject performs concurrently.

**Independence:** The information flow among subjects is restricted to one way from inside to outside and the control does not pass over the boundary of each subject. Therefore, a subject cannot directly control other subjects. This means that each subject is perfectly independent of others with respect to the information and control flow.

### 3.3 An Implementation

An example of the implementation of subjects is described in this section. It is implemented in URANUS (Nakashima 1985) and utilizes its multiple world mechanism. In this implementation, therefore, procedures are realized as predicates.

**Declaration of the Two Types of Subjects:** A set-subject *subject* is declared using a predicate[2], SUBJECT, as follows:

```
(SUBJECT subject
        (ELEMENT-OF power-set)
        (SUPER super-set)
        definition-of-predicate ...)
```

---

[2] The prototype system of a problem solving system based on subjects is implemented in URANUS (an extended Prolog). We use 'predicate' as a synonym of 'procedure'.

where ELEMENT-OF designates *power-set* as the power-set-subject of *subject*, and SUPER designates *super-set* as the super-set-subject of *subject*.

An instance *subject* is also declared as follows:

(SUBJECT *subject*
    (INSTANCE-OF *set*)
    *definition-of-predicate* ...)

where INSTANCE-OF designates *set* as the set-subject of *subject*.

**Definition of Predicates:** For realizing the two different types of predicate sets, the concealed and the revealed, the multiple world mechanism of URANUS is employed. The data structure representing the internal states and the set of reading predicates are stored in the revealed world (or P region.) All the other predicates are in the concealed world (or Q region.)

Predicates for P region and Q region are defined using predicates ASSERTP and ASSERTQ respectively as shown in the following examples:

(ASSERTP *(predicate-name . args) predicate-call* ...)
(ASSERTQ *(predicate-name . args) predicate-call* ...)

*Predicate-calls* in an ASSERTP must contain no side-effects. If a predicate with side-effects is called, the calling fails. On the other hand, *predicate-calls* in an ASSERTQ are not restricted in type.

Goals of subjects are predicates whose head of ASSERTQ (i.e. *(predicate-name . args)*) is nil. Nondeterminism is achieved by defining two or more goals. At least one goal must exist in each instance, including the inheritance from the set-subject. As soon as an instance is declared, an arbitrary goal in the instance is activated.

## 4. SYNCHRONIZATION IN THE REFERENCE TYPE COMMUNICATION

In the reference type communication, those subjects, of which internal states are under modification, must be excluded from the references. A solution to the synchronization problem of the reference type communication is presented in this chapter.

### 4.1 Synchronization Problem

A subject modifies its internal states with no relation to the others. In addition, any other subjects should be able to refer to the internal states of the subject at any time. As a result, the referring subject must make reference in cooperative operation with the modification of the referred-to subject in order to read the internal states correctly. Meeting that request is equivalent to solving the readers/writers problem in the case of a single writer. Lamport (1977) has already provided an interesting solution to the problem. The solution does not assume mutual exclusion of access to shared data. The synchronization problem for subjects in the reference type communication is solved on the basis of Lamport's solution.

## 4.2 Operations at the Referred-to Side

In an environment where each operation can potentially modify any objects it accesses, Eswaran et al. (1976) have proved that all operations must be 'well-formed' and of 'two-phase' in order to guarantee consistency. An operation is well-formed if the operation
(1) locks an object before accessing it,
(2) does not lock an object which is already locked, and
(3) before it ends, unlocks each object it locked.

An operation is of two-phase if no object is unlocked before all objects are locked by the operation.

The data structure representing the internal states of a subject is thought to be a sharable object to which all subjects can refer, and which only the subject itself occupies during modification. Any operation modifying the internal state is well-formed and of two-phase, since the internal state is locked before any other modification and it is unlocked before the completion of the operation.

The procedures to achieve the goals of a subject are executed in a temporary area where the internal states are inherited. The reason is that in case of failure of procedures with side-effects, the side-effects must be canceled. If one of the procedures is successfully executed, then the internal states are locked, updated according to the result of the execution, and unlocked. The internal states should not be locked during the execution of procedures. The reason is that locking time should be as short as possible in order to increase the probability of successful reference.

Locking and unlocking internal states are implicitly carried out using so called the Lamport variables, which are written in one order and read in the reverse order. A subject has the Lamport variables $v1$ and $v2$ as a part of the internal states. The Lamport variable $v1$ increases in advance of all internal state transitions, and the Lamport variable $v2$ reaches $v1$ after the completion of all other internal state transitions. When $v1 \neq v2$, the internal states are locked and, when $v1 = v2$, they are unlocked.

## 4.3 Operations at the Referring Side

A subject can communicate with another subject by using the referring predicate REFER*, as follows:

(REFER* *subject predicate-call*)

The predicate REFER* calls a predicate *predicate-call*, defined by the referred-to *subject*. Predicate REFER* can be used anywhere in the goals.

Predicate REFER* will be successfully executed under the following conditions:
(1) The internal states of the referred-to subject are not locked. In other words, $v1$ is equal to $v2$ in the subject.
(2) The predicate-call is successful.
(3) The referred-to subject has not modified its internal states during reference. In other words, the current value of $v1$ in the referred-to subject is equal to the previous $v1$ and $v2$.

When the predicate REFER* fails for the reason that the conditions 1 and 3 do not hold, it is said to be suspended. If a goal contains a suspended predicate, the goal immediately fails. If condition 2 does not hold, the predicate fails, causing the goal to backtrack.

## 5. TIME SEQUENCE

It is assumed that a transition from a consistent internal state to a new one is an event. It will be seen that a single process is defined to be a set of events with a total ordering. Here is introduced the concept of the precedent relation as the time sequence of events.

*Definition.* The precedent relation "->" on a set of events is the smallest relation satisfying the following conditions:
(1) If a1 and a2 are events in a same subject, and a1 occurs before a2, then a1 -> a2.
(2) If a1 is an event of any subject A and b1 is an event of another subject B referring to A in which a1 has already occurred, then a1 -> b1.
(3) If a -> b and b -> c, then a -> c.

The events a and b are said to be concurrent if ~(a -> b) and ~(b -> a). A space-time diagram as shown in Fig. 4 facilitates understanding the precedent relation among events. The precedent relation, a -> b, indicates that it is possible for a to causally affect b.

### 5.1 Logical Clocks

Next a logical clock is introduced into the subjects by the same way as Lamport (1978). The logical clock is a way of assigning a number to an event. The assigned number is thought of as the time at which the event occurred. More precisely, the clock Ci for each subject Si is a function which assigns a number Ci(e) to every event e in the subject Si. Since the precedent relation denotes the time sequence of events, the following clock conditions must hold between the precedent relation and the logical clock.

Clock condition 1:
    For given events a and b in Si, if a -> b, then Ci(a) < Ci(b).

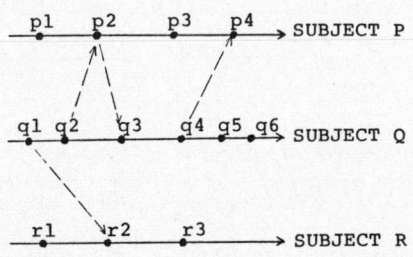

----> information flow by reference

Fig. 4. Space-time diagram. The horizontal direction denotes time and the vertical direction, space. The solid lines in the horizontal direction denote subjects, the points events, and the broken lines the reference type communication. The precedent relation, a -> b, means that there is a path from a to b along the subject line (solid) and the communication line (broken). For example, p1 -> p2, q1 -> r2 and q1 -> p4.

Clock condition 2:
  For given events a in Si and b in Sj, if a -> b, then $C_i(a) < C_j(b)$.

The following rules manage the clock so that all clocks in subjects can satisfy the above clock conditions.

Rule 1:
  Each subject Si increments its clock Ci between two successive events.
Rule 2:
  If the event b of any subject Sj results from the referring to any subject Si in which the event a has occurred, Sj sets Cj greater than or equal to its present value and greater than Ci.

Evidently, the rules 1 and 2 insure that the clock conditions 1 and 2 are satisfied respectively. Hence, if each subject manages its clock according to the rules 1 and 2, its clock defines the time sequence of events as a logical clock.

All kinds of communications among subjects use Lamport variables to solve the synchronization problem. The logical clock in each subject also uses Lamport variables. The logical clock Ci of subject Si is defined with the Lamport variables **v1i** and **v2i** as follows:

$$C_i = \begin{cases} v1i & \text{if } v1i = v2i \\ \text{unknown} & \text{if } v1i \neq v2i \end{cases}$$

The increment of **v1i** and **v2i** can be determined so that Ci conforms to the rules 1 and 2. In other words, subject Si lets the increment **dv** of **v1i** and **v2i** be **dv** = 1 against the rule 1, and **dv** = $\max(C_r - C_i) + 1$ against the rule 2 where $r$ is a set of subjects that the Si has referred to.

## 5.2 Referring According to the Logical Clock

The reference predicate REFER* causes an event to occur regardless of the logical clock of the referred-to subject. The reference predicate REFER is introduced to ensure the reference according to the logical clock. The successful execution of REFER is conditioned on the precedent relation among events. In making reference to a subject by REFER, the event occurs synchronously with an event in the referred-to subject.

Predicate REFER will be successfully executed under the following conditions:
(1) The internal states of the referred-to subject are not locked. In other words, the **v1** is equal to the **v2** in the subject.
(2) The predicate-call is successful.
(3) The referred-to subject has not modified its internal states during referring.
(4) For any event a in the referring subject, an event b which satisfies ~(b -> a) exists in the referred-to subject. In other words, the logical clock Cj in the referring subject Sj is not in advance of the logical clock Ci in the referred-to subject Si.

Conditions 1, 2 and 3 are the same as for predicate REFER*. When the execution of predicate REFER fails for the reason that the conditions 1, 3 and 4 do not hold, it is said to be suspended. If the goal contains a suspended predicate, the goal immediately fails. If the condition 2 does not hold, the predicate fails, causing the goal to backtrack.

The referring subject precedes the referred-to subject, if all the conditions are satisfied. However, REFER in the same subject does not consecutively succeed, since condition 4 is unsatisfied any longer after an event has occurred.

## 6. APPLICATION EXAMPLES

Any subject can use predicate REFER* which refers to the internal state of the referred-to subject, and predicate REFER which causes an event in time sequential order to communicate with another subject. In this section, the communication among subjects using these predicates is illustrated.

### 6.1 The Monitoring of Program Execution

Suppose that one program B should judge whether another program A is normal or not from the results of the execution. The program A operates independently of the program B. The program B must monitor the program A, not influencing the execution of the program A. In addition, the program B needs to choose monitoring items optionally without modifying the program A. As stated in Chapter 2, no program can monitor the execution of another program without interference in any communication type except the reference type.

An execution-monitoring program with subjects is illustrated below.

```
(SUBJECT A
        (INSTANCE-OF program)
        (ASSERTQ NIL program-of-A))
(SUBJECT B
        (INSTANCE-OF program)
        (ASSERTQ NIL (REFER* A *internal-state-of-A)
                    (CHECK *internal-state-of-A)))
```

[Program Explanation]: The program-of-A is the program of the subject A. When the subject A is declared, the program-of-A begins its operation. The subject B can refer to the execution results of the subject A by using (REFER* A *internal-state-of-A) and judge the execution status of the subject A by using (CHECK *internal-state-of-A).

### 6.2 Concurrent Production System

Next the concurrent production system CPS is considered. Suppose that the subject STM is the short-term memory of CPS, the subjects Ri (i = 1 ... n) are the production rules, and the subject CR is for conflict resolution. Each Ri refers to STM and if its IF part matches then Ri immediately executes its THEN part. Ri, however, writes the results in its internal state. CR refers to all rules and selects the optimum production rule R. After that, STM writes the results of R in its internal state. A program for CPS is illustrated as follows:

```
(SUBJECT STM
        (INSTANCE-OF stm)
        (ASSERTQ NIL (AND (CHECKED T)
                          (CANDIDATE *R)))
                    (REFER *R (RESULT *RESULT))
                    (WRITE *RESULT)))
```

```
(SUBJECT CR
        (INSTANCE-OF cr)
        (ASSERTP (CHECKED NIL))
        (ASSERTP (CANDIDATE NIL))
        (ASSERTQ NIL (REFER* R1 (AND (RULE *IF *THEN)
                                      (RESULT *RESULT)))
                    (CHECK *IF *THEN *RESULT))
        (ASSERTQ NIL (REFER* R2 (AND (RULE *IF *THEN)
                                      (RESULT *RESULT)))
                    (CHECK *IF *THEN *RESULT))
        ... )

(SUBJECT R1
        (INSTANCE-OF rule)
        (ASSERTP (RULE (REFER STM if) then))
        (ASSERTP (RESULT NIL))
        (ASSERTQ NIL apply-rule-and-set-result))

(SUBJECT R2
        (INSTANCE-OF rule)
        (ASSERTP (RULE (REFER STM if) then))
        (ASSERTP (RESULT NIL))
        (ASSERTQ NIL apply-rule-and-set-result))
     ....
```

[Program Explanation]: Each statement apply-rule-and-set-result of a production rule Ri sets the results of applying (RULE (REFER STM if) then) in predicate RESULT. The subject CR selects the optimum rule R by using (CHECK ...) and places it in predicate CANDIDATE. The subject STM refers to CR and writes the results in the short-term memory by using (WRITE *RESULT).

## 7. COMPARISON WITH OTHER APPROACHES

The formalism 'problem solving based on subjects' is compared with other approaches and remarks are made on the difference between them.

**Distributed Process (Hansen 1978):** The Distributed Process performs two kinds of operations, the initial statement and the external requests. These operations are executed one at a time by interleaving. A process begins by executing its initial statement. If it terminates or waits for a condition to become true, another operation is started as the result of an external request. When this operation in turn terminates or waits, the process will either begin yet another operation (requested by another process) or it will resume an earlier operation. However, the Distributed Process has no mechanism to limit the access rights of individual processes. Once a process has waited, it cannot be ensured when it will resume or which operations in external requests will be started next. It will therefore be seen that the communication of the Distributed Process using an external request is the interference type.

**Concurrent Prolog (Shapiro and Takeuchi 1983):** Concurrent Prolog employs the behavioral reading of definite clauses. A unit goal is analogous to a process, a conjunctive goal is analogous to a system of processes, and variables shared between goals function similarly to communication channels. To support process synchronization, Concurrent Prolog introduces a new syntactic construct, called read-only variables. A process suspends if it requires the instantiation of its read-only variables. In the communication using read-only variables, the receiving process cannot specify the sending process.

**Smalltalk-80 (Goldberg and Robson 1983):** Smalltalk-80 is an object-oriented programming language. Objects and messages are used to implement the entire programming environment. The communication between objects is represented by message passing. Namely, the communication is the interference type.

**URANUS (Nakashima 1985):** URANUS is an extended Prolog. URANUS features a variety of control structures and a multiple world mechanism. A subject employs several worlds of URANUS. The extended functions of URANUS have facilitated the implementation of a problem solving system based on subjects. Each subject has the capability equal to URANUS itself except for a part of the multiple world mechanism.

## 8. CONCLUSION

The subject is a basic unit for concurrent programming. The internal state of a subject is independent of the other subjects and is prevented from any interference. In an environment where some abnormal processes may exist, this property is very important. It is necessary to solve a synchronization problem instead, so that the subject can ensure the correct referring operation. The subject is provided predicates REFER* and REFER for reference using Lamport's theorem. Predicate REFER not only guarantees the correct referring but also has the function of referring in order of event occurrences.

## ACKNOWLEDGMENTS

The authors are grateful to Dr. H. Kashiwagi, Director of Computer Systems Division, the Electrotechnical Laboratory, for his supports and encouragements. Helpful discussions with H. Nakashima, M. Ishikawa, Y. Tamura and K. Niki, the colleagues of Man-Machine Systems Section, are also acknowledged.

## REFERENCES

Eswaran KP, et al. (1976) The Notions of Consistency and Predicate Locks in a Database System. CACM 19:624-633
Goldberg A, Robson D (1983) Smalltalk-80: the language and its implementation. Addison-Wesley
Hansen PB (1978) Distributed Processes: A Concurrent Programming Concept. CACM 21:934-941
Hisano H, Suwa M (1984) Knowledge Representation for Building Cooperative Problem Solver Based on SUBJECTS. 84-AI-36, IPSJ (in Japanese)
Lamport L (1977) Concurrent Reading and Writing. CACM 20:806-811
Lamport L (1978) Time, Clocks, and the Ordering of Events in a Distributed System. CACM 21:558-565
Nakashima H (1985) URANUS Reference Manual. ETL-RM-85-1
Shapiro E and Takeuchi A (1983) Object Oriented Programming in Concurrent Prolog. New Generation Computing 1:25-48
Yonezawa A (1984) On Object-oriented Programming. Computer Software 1:29-41 (in Japanese)

ZERO : Frame + Prolog

H.Ito*    H.Ueno**

* Japan Information Processing Development Center (JIPDEC), 3-5-8, Shibakoen, Minato-ku, Tokyo 105, Japan
** Department of Systems Engineering, Tokyo Denki University, Hatoyama, Saitama 350-03, Japan

ABSTRACT

In this paper we describe a language specification and its implementation of ZERO, a frame-based language, in terms of embedding Prolog into it. ZERO is a general purpose frame-based knowledge representation language and is an extension of FMS which was developed by us. The extension is a feature to handle Prolog programs as attached procedures in the form of a set of clauses which is activated by a message sent from another frame. By combination of Prolog statements (Horn clauses) and Lisp-based procedures, highly flexible intelligent systems could be achieved. The ZERO system has three major features which are developed to embed Prolog into the system; a Prolog-based message passing, an extension of unification mechanisms and a function for non-deterministic behavior by backtracking for a frame system.

1. Introduction

From the viewpoint of knowledge-based systems (Harmon) design (Hays-Roth), representation of domain specific knowledge is a key. In the past, various knowledge representation languages have been developed to represent knowledge and to utilize it. In this paper we describe the system which embeds Prolog statements based on a logic programming language into a frame structure. The ZERO system has been implemented as frame-based system, which contains Prolog system as a part. The purpose of this work is to develop a powerful and flexible knowledge programming language useful to build a knowledge base and an inference control mechanism. Such language must be transparent for the users and easy to write a program.

Already, we have developed a frame-based knowledge representation language, FMS [Frame Manipulation System] (Ito). In a frame-based language, the users must write inference mechanisms by means of procedures attached to slots of frames (called attached procedures) themselves, because a frame-based knowledge representation system does not have such mechanisms. It is one of the reasons why this kind of language is flexible.

General features of a frame-based model include:

(1) A knowledge base is represented as a frame system in a hierarchical data structure.

(2) Each frame represents a certain conceptual object.

(3) Frames are composed of a collection of values (facts) and attached procedures to handle them.

Due to above features, the frame systems can manage a large amount of knowledge, and the user can implement flexible and appropriate inference mechanisms. The existing general purpose frame systems (such as

---

This report describes a research done at Tokyo Denki University.

FMS, Units (Stefik)) have functions for defining and utilizing a variety of knowledge. They do not provide, however, general inference mechanisms other than inheritance control mechanisms used in the generalization hierarchy and calling procedures like demons. Therefore, the users have to design and implement sophisticated inference mechanisms, an inference engine, presently, by means of attached procedures. For this reason, the users are required to do heavy work, and the transparency of a knowledge base becomes bad, because most frame-based languages are implemented in Lisp and the attached procedures must be written in Lisp-like style.

While, there is another knowledge representation system which is based on mathematical logics. This type of languages provides a clearly defined semantics, and we have well understood those properties. Prolog (Clocksin) is one of such systems, which is known as a logic programming language (Lloyd). In a predicate logic-based system, users can represent procedural knowledge declaratively. From this point, decrease of the user's burden and systematical usage of a knowledge base can be available. Because the Prolog system has the inference control mechanism, the users need to write only declarative knowledge in a form of Horn clauses using the inference mechanism. It has the following features.

(1) Powerful pattern matching mechanism (called unification).

(2) Non-deterministic behavior by backtracking.

(3) The information retrieval function by non-distinctions between input and output.     etc.

A collection of Prolog statements has a flat structure. The flatness seems to be weak for building and handling a large knowledge base. For this reason, Prolog may not be an appropriate representation tool for problems which have a structure. In this case, it is hard to understand the contents of a knowledge written in a flat structure. Therefore, knowledge information is needed to be organized and used systematically. It is difficult to describe large and complex problems in Prolog. In these cases problems should be divided into small subproblem. Each subproblem is easy to represent and to handle in Prolog. Then, Prolog statements make a list of the facts and rules about the subproblem.

Our long-term purpose is not only just to combine FMS and Prolog but also to integrate frame and logic. If it is possible that a knowledge base is handled formally, then we can get the systematical strategies for computing about the knowledge defined in the frame system, and we can give a formal semantics to the frame model. Furthermore, in order to think the frame system as a kind of conceptual model (Davis), it is necessary to specify both structures and behavior of the conceptual objects in a problem which should be specified by systematical notions. Hence, it is possible to consider that the frame-based language and the logic-based language are appropriate to specify structures and functions, respectively. For this reason, we have combined a frame-based knowledge representation language and Prolog as a first step. We supposed that all of the knowledge can not be easily to be represented in the form of clauses. The ZERO knowledge representation provides for clauses as one facility to represent knowledge. A piece of knowledge is partially represented in the form of a clause. The idea of the design is that advantages of both a frame and a logic should be combined in representing knowledge. The above two tools, i.e., a frame and a logic, would work complementary. The Prolog system implemented in ZERO is an extension of usual one, which is designed to handle a message passing, to manipulate frames and slots defined in the form of clauses and to deal with non-deterministic behavior by backtracking to manage the side effects, e.g., setting of a slot value (see 3.1), to the frame system.

In general, the language which are introduced to manipulate symbolic data needs the symbolic manipulation facilities like Lisp. From this point of view, in general Prolog can be thought as a list processing language. In the ZERO system, since Prolog plays a role of a program description language to write an inference procedure, the facilities for the list processing are required. That is, attached procedures are written in Prolog. We call them attached clauses in a sense of attached procedures which are a set of clauses attached to a slot of a frame. Attached clauses are defined in a slot as a slot value. In short, the ZERO system includes Prolog using a framework of FMS. By combining frame and logic, the ZERO system might become a powerful knowledge representation language in sense that users could easily understand the represented knowledge. And, the ZERO users can use programs which are written in Lisp and/or Prolog. From the point of view of transparency, writting attached procedures in Prolog seem to be much better because of its declarativeness. This should be true for some applications. While Lisp should be better for other cases. The users can choose languages to write attached procedures/clauses. Therefore, the users can choose better one from the two procedural knowledge representation tools, i.e., Lisp or Prolog, according to the properties of a problem given to the user. In this sense, the transparency of the knowledge base would be increased.

In the past few years, ideas on combining logic and other representation have been reported. As other approaches, there are some knowledge representation models, such as Krypton (Brachman) and Programmer's Apprentice (Rich). In those models, two sorts of knowledge representation models are defined in parallel. On the other hand, there is one system which is called HSRL (Allen), it has similar design notions to ZERO. HSRL emphasized retrieval features in a logical system. In ZERO, we considered the relation among setting of a slot value and unification, the role of a set of clauses defined in a frame and the treatment of non-deterministic behavior. In Krypton and Programmer's Apprentice, a logic and another representation model are combined weakly in sense that the two representation models exist in parallel. While in ZERO and HSRL, two types of knowledge representation model are combined harder such that a logic feature is included within another language. In HSRL, the formula defined in the schema function to get a slot value. In ZERO, a collection of clauses as attached clauses is thought that it forms a world in sense of a set of formulas (Horn clauses).

In this paper we describe the conceptual structure of the knowledge base, the major functions and the implementation. The ZERO system is written in UTILISP (Chikayama) and is working on FACOM M series computers.

## 2. An Overview of ZERO

### 2.1. The Purpose and Design Policy

Designing objects of ZERO are as follows:

(1) The ZERO system provides a useful knowledge representation language and the system as the environment for users who want to study knowledge engineering and Artificial Intelligence.

(2) The ZERO system is an implementation tool for development of INTELLITUTOR (Ueno 1984) which is an intelligent tutoring system

for programming.

(3) ZERO is designed as a case study of combining and integrating the predicate calculus and the frame model.

Furthermore, as a fundamental issue, we are considering that a frame model should be well treated by means of combining a framework of logic into it.

The Design policy of the ZERO system is that we should keep characteristics and advantages of both different representation models as much as possible. The kernel representation model is a frame model. In this model, the inference control mechanism is not fixed for specific problems. This mechanism must be implemented by the users themselves by means of attached clauses in Prolog and procedures in Lisp. At present, we do not consider the mathematical side of logic, but are considering how to represent knowledge declaratively, in a form of clauses under the framework of the frame model.

## 2.2. Structure of The ZERO System

ZERO provides Prolog features as a part. In the ZERO system, the ZERO interpreter interprets and evaluates the elements of the knowledge base and the inference programs. It should be emphasized that the side effects, i.e., updates and creations of slots and frames as intermediate results, which be occurred on the knowledge base during the processing of reasoning can not be avoided and must be managed by this interpreter. The ZERO interpreter deals with the management of the message passings among the frames and with the interpretation of frames and slots which are expressed in predicates as in Prolog. Here, the ZERO interpreter contains features of a Prolog interpreter as a part.

Fig. 1 shows the conceptual structure of the ZERO knowledge base. The ZERO knowledge base consists of a database which is a collection of Prolog statements and a frame system which is created by the FMS module. The database stores user-defined predicates and built-in predicates as in Prolog statements.

## 2.3. Knowledge Representation

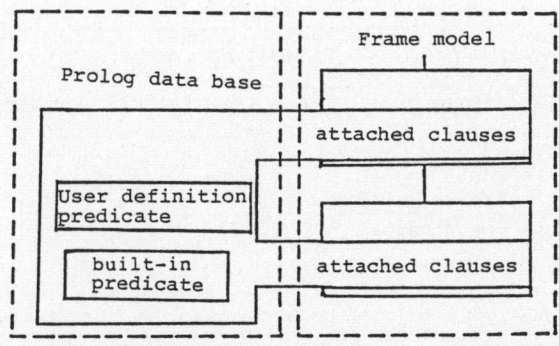

Fig. 1 The conceptual structure of ZERO knowledge base.

## 2.3.1. Data Structure of Frame

Fig. 2 shows a data structure for a frame and a slot. A frame system as a knowledge base consists of a set of frames. Each frame has a unique name through the whole frame system. And a frame consists of a set of slots. There are several types of slots which play specific roles in the frame system. For example, the frame-type slot indicates the node type in a generalization hierarchy. The ZERO knowledge representation provides two node types of frames; instances and classes. A frame whose node type is an instance is called an instance node frame and a frame whose node type is a class is called a class node frame. Each slot consists of ten fields; slot name, inheritance-role, from, datatype, value, default, option, if-needed, if-added and if-removed. The slot name is an identifier in the frame. The inheritance-role indicates a value restriction over the hierarchical structure from an ancestor frame to its potential progenies, i.e. modes of inheritance. The option field provides a flexibility of usage. The users can use this field for various objects. If-needed, if-added and if-removed fields are assinged for demons.

In order to handle a set of clauses as a slot value in ZERO, a new datatype "clauses" has been appended to the datatypes provided in FMS. A datatype "clauses" indicates that the value field of the slot must be filled with a set of clauses as attached clauses. This is described detailly in (Ito).

| Frame-name | Frame-type |
|---|---|
| A-Kind-Of slot | |
| D.Descendants slot | |
| Description-information slot | |
| CreatedBy slot | |
| ModifiedBy slot | |
| Slot 1 | |
| Slot 2 | |
| : | |
| Slot n | |

Frame-type: instance
              class

| Slot name | Inheritance-role | From | Data-type | Value | Default | Option | if-needed |
|---|---|---|---|---|---|---|---|
| | | | | | | | if-added |
| | | | | | | | if-removed |

Inheritance-role: S Same value   Data-type: ATOM TEXT TABLE BOOL
                  U Unique value            LISP FRAME FLIST EXPR
                  R Restriction value       CLAUSES etc.
                  M Member value
                  O Option value
                  I Independent value
                  A Anomaly value

Fig. 2 The data structures for frame and slot.

## 2.3.2. Horn Clauses

The form of a Horn clause in ZERO is shown in Fig. 3. In Fig. 3, (1), (2) and (3) represent a rule, a fact and a goal respectively. Here, A,B1,B2,...,Bn are predicates represented in S-expression. Each variable has one prefix symbol '*'. We use a S-expression to represent a clause, because we can use the features of UTILISP (e.g., structure editor, pretty printer) and FMS (e.g., the storage of a knowledge base, printout functions of a frame and a slot) without modifications.

In designing the Prolog interpreter, we referred to some documents in (Nilsson, Nakashima, etc.).

## 3. Fundamental Mechanisms

### 3.1. Frame Model and Predicate

In general, it is important that usage of appropriate predicate may allow us to represent a problem simply and suitably and permit us to solve it easy(Chan). In terms of ZERO we understand that this point means - what kinds of information in a frame system should be permitted to users to use as predicates -. Because, if the representation of a predicate in the system is unfamiliar for the user. The semantics of formulas may be hard to understand for him.

In FMS, each frame is defined as a clearly distinct frame type, such as an instance and a class. However, from the point of view of predicate logic there exists such a case as a frame behaves like an instance. For example, frames "bird" and "penguin" are defined where "penguin" is defined as an instance frame, one of the progeny frames of class node frame "bird". There two frames contain slot "can-fly" whose value field is filled with the information representing whether a bird and a penguin can fly or not. In this case, the bird can fly, but the penguin can not fly. The reason is as follows. The values of the slots in two frames, "bird" and "penguin", are "true" and "false" respectively. Therefore, each slot defined in the two frames works independently on a node type. As another example, let's define slot "weight-range" in above two frames. The values of the "weight-range" indicate the range of the weight for the two conceptual objects. This kind of slots should be useful to manage data. Also, in this example, the values of the slots in the two frames function corresponding to the role of the slots. The former case should be related to an inference using default value, the latter could be thought that a frame defined in the frame system has an inherent information. In such cases, the frame does not work a class nor a type in logic. Therefore, it should be thought that these frames are combined with each other as a simple frame hierarchy. Moreover, not all properties defined in the slots of an ancestor frame inherited to potential progeny frames (Ito). A class frame is manipulated as like a one-place predicate. The ZERO system deals with a frame name as a predicate symbol or as an argument in an atomic formula representing a part of a frame hierarchy. Instance frame names, however, can not be used as predicates.

The relation between a slot and a predicate is as follows. A slot of a frame represents properties of a conceptual object. Therefore, a slot

```
(1)    (A B1 ····Bn )
(2)    ( A )
(3)    (? B1 ···· Bn )
```

Fig. 3  The representation of Horn clause in ZERO.

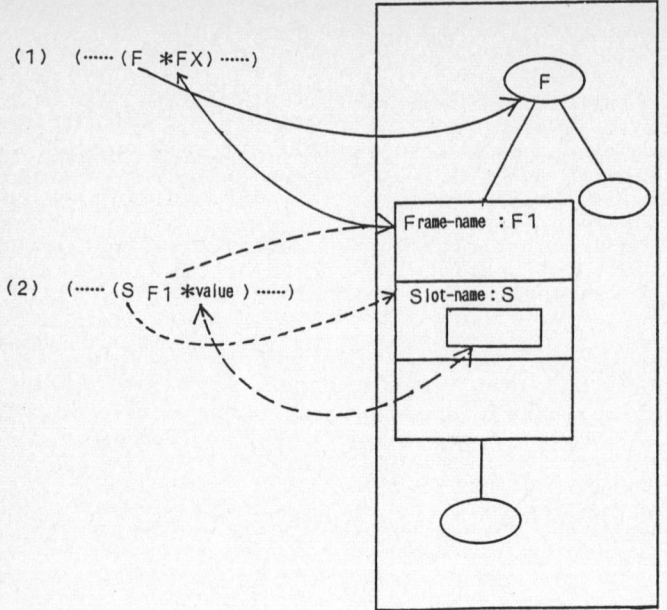

Fig. 4  The relation of frame and slot for predicates.

is corresponding to a two-place predicate. Although a slot consists of several fields, the ZERO system treats the slot as a two-place predicate. The first argument is a frame name and the second one is a slot value (Fig. 4). This representation makes procedural knowledge easy to represent and to understand. In the FMS system, a slot value is systematically managed by mechanisms for datatypes, inheritance-roles, and frame types. On the other hand, the form of two-place predicate is usable for information retrieval. Also, the unification mechanism can be applied to the generalization hierarchy. We describe the reason why the representation of a slot is simplified. The representation of a slot using two-place predicate is understandable for both user and system. It is possible to consider that description using many parameters to get something (i.e., frame name, value) become a burdensome for the user, and although there is a loose of information (e.g., inheritance-role, datatype, etc.) such information should not be used to retrieve data defined in a frame system as key parameters. When the user want to get such information, the user can use FMS facilities. A general form to represent a slot is "((S F VALUE))". Where, S, F and VALUE are a slot name, a frame name and a slot value respectively. This expression is read as "S of F is VALUE." or "There is a relation S between F and VALUE." (see Fig. 4).

## 3.2. Non-decidability

In the ZERO system, refuting a given goal clause is getting a situation on a frame system required. It can be thought that in a frame model side effects are occurred by non-deterministic behavior during proving a goal statement as described before. The ZERO system must manage the side effects.

The causes of non-deterministic behavior are as follows:

(1) Non-deterministic behavior included in Prolog features. The definition of a predicate may be defined by some different bodies.

(2) Non-deterministic behavior of the frame system of ZERO itself. A frame in the frame system behaves as individual.

The case (1) is usual Prolog facility. We describe about the case (2). As we described in section 3.1, the names of a frame and a slot are used for predicate symbols in formulas. Variables will occur in a formula. Those variables represent frames/slot values and are bound to the frame name or to the value of slot using a unification mechanism of the frame system. If the unification is succeeded, the value of the variable is preserved as an environment which is a collection of bindings of variables and values. If the proof procedure fails, the situation of the frame system and the environments must go back to the former situation by backtracking.

In the current implementation, the recoveries in a frame system by backtracking are achieved only by setting and removing a slot value. Setting and removing a slot value are side effects to the frame system. In a non-deterministic programming system in the frame system, the system must recover the side effects. However, conventional Prolog systems does not provide a facility of recovery from side effects. Because such features are not suitable to the concept of a logic programming language. In the ZERO system, if the system does not provide a feature of recovery from side effects, the side effects will affect to the inference process which may cause non-appropriate reasoning.

## 3.3. Attached Clauses

There are two sides of interpretations for attached clauses; they are (1) a program to achieve a certain function, (2) representation of a piece of knowledge in the form of clauses. In the first case, attached clauses consist a procedural program which achieves a certain function. In this case, a message sent from another frame used the predicate Messagep which is one of the built-in predicates in the ZERO system.

The second case is considered as follows. In general, a many-place predicate (includes a one-place predicate) can be rewritten in a form of a two-place predicate (Deliyanni). This is one of problems in designing a suitable knowledge representation. Since a many-place predicate must be translated into a set of two-place predicates. Perhaps, it will happen that a piece of the representation in the form of two-place predicate may not fit with our intuition. This means that if a user does not analyze a problem himself, he can not represent it in the form of two-place predicate. In cases that a description becomes obscure and that it is hard to translate the form of a many-place predicate into a form of a two-place predicate, the system should deal with the forms of many-place predicates instead. Hence, a slot for attached clauses is thought that the slot stores a set of facts and rules. Therefore, the storage which stores facts and rules as slot values may enable him to apply a variety of queries. However, if he use attached clauses only to store facts and rules, the working storage will become garbages of facts and rules, because information in the form of the clauses are not examined by mechanisms of the datatype and the inheritance-role, etc.

## 4. Implementation

### 4.1. Getting of Slot Value and Inheritance

The mechanism of the inheritance-role 'A' is most typical and popular inheritance of properties. The widely used inheritance-role is 'A'

```
┌─────────────────────────────────────────┐
│ Mammal          class                   │
│ A-kind-of       value : root            │
│ Be-found-in     IR : A                  │
│                 value : land            │
│ Clauses         : ----                  │
│                 -- (be-found-in         │
│                          Focus-Frame    │
│                              *x )       │
└─────────────────────────────────────────┘

┌─────────────────────────────────────────┐
│ Whale           class                   │
│ A-kind-of       value : Mammal          │
│ Be-found-in     IR : A                  │
│                 value : sea             │
│ Clauses         :----                   │
│                 -- (be-found-in         │
│                          Focus-Frame    │
│                              *x ) ---   │
└─────────────────────────────────────────┘
```

Fig. 5  The description of mammal and whale.

(anomaly) in ZERO. For example, let suppose that there is the frame named mammal and the frame named whale which is defined as one of the progeny frames of "mammal" frame. Furthermore, the slot "be-found-in" is defined in both frames, which has the inheritance-role 'A'. The value of the slot "be-found-in" both in frame "mammal" and "whale" are "land" and "sea" respectively as in Fig. 5. In this example, the atomic formula "(be-found-in focus-frame *x)" appears in attached clauses in both frames. Here, "focus-frame" is a special purpose declarative constant. The value of "focus-frame" is rewritten by the procedure for the processing of a message passing provided in the ZERO system. Focus-frame stores a current frame name which indicates the frame which is focused by the ZERO interpreter. Therefore, in both frames "mammal" and "whale", the atomic formula is interpreted as follows.

Mammal:(be-found-in mammal land)
Whale :(be-found-in whale sea)

The values for the variable *x are defined in each frame. If the value in the frame "whale" is inherited from its parent frame by means of the mechanism of inheritance-role 'A', then *x is bound to the value "land". Since first-order logic provides monotonic reasoning, it can not be applied directly to these processing. However, in Prolog, such reasoning can be realized using operator demo (Bowen). From points of view of the understandability for human and the representability of knowledge, we think that a frame model is more appropriate than Prolog.

### 4.2. Setting of Slot Value and Unification

Setting a slot value is filling a value field of the slot with something, and a unification is finding a substitution, which is called most general unifier. There are no fundamental differences between setting of slot value and a unification. The design policy in ZERO is that the system manipulates knowledge in the form of clause same as knowledge in the form of a frame and a slot. The issue is to consider about information generated during evaluation process of Prolog program, and about what such information affect on the existing frame system FMS. It can be supposed that the value of a slot is found during the Prolog program evaluation process. For example, we consider the next program.

[Example]
((check *x)(slot frame *x)(perm *x *y) (pred ...) ...)
((perm a al))
((perm b bl))
((perm c cl))

When the goal clause (? (check *x)) is given, the system generates the subgoal ((slot frame *x)(perm *x *y)(pred ...) ...). If the slot value indicated by frame "frame" and slot "slot" are not determined, the predicate "perm" is called. At this time, the value of *x is determined. This process is same as setting the slot value by 'a' in slot "slot" of frame "frame". In this program, predicate "perm" is defined as several facts. The first argument for predicate "perm" is given the constant a, b and c, in each fact respectively. Then if predicate "pred" fails, the value of *x is instantiated as b and c, in that order. Setting of the slot value is not evidently indicated, but above process includes the side effect to the slot "slot". Hence, if predicate "check" succeeds then it shows that the value of slot "slot" is assigned by the value of *x. The ZERO system has several checking mechanisms in terms of setting a slot value (Ito). Those examinations must be needed to apply the value which is dynamically generated during the Prolog program evaluation process. In present implementation, when a slot value has been set and the rest of all of atomic formulas in a goal clause have been succeeded, the set value is checked. For example, if the predicate "perm" succeeds the checking mechanism is applied to the slot value. Here, if information as a slot value is not appropriate for slot "slot" and frame "frame", then predicate "check" will be false and a goal clause will not succeed.

4.3. <u>Message passing</u>   -- <u>Predicate MESSAGEP</u> --

ZERO includes predicate Messagep for the mechanism of a message passing. However, ZERO does not have the conventional mechanisms for message passings and the message passing mechanism in ZERO is restricted. In short, the procedure of the message passing is the evaluation of the attached clauses and attached procedures. In case of attached clauses, the goal clause is defined by only one atomic formula, and the function of the message passing is the decision on goal clause whether its goal can be proved or not. There are two kinds of forms to send a message. The difference comes from difference from the types of procedures which receives a message. The procedure types are attached clauses in Prolog or procedures in Lisp. The forms of the messages are as follows:

(1)  For attached clauses.
     messagep (slot-name frame-name arg-list)

(2)  For attached procedures.
     messagep (slot-name frame-name arg-list value)

In both cases, the value field which is specified by a frame name and a slot name is filled with clauses, attached clauses, or a function name, an attached procedure. A clause which includes predicate Messagep becomes false when the number of arguments is not appropriate.

The evaluation procedure of attached clauses is as in the following. The goal clause is isolated from activated attached clauses, at first.

Next, the unification is applied between an arg-list (arguments list) and the arguments in the goal clause. If this unification fails the formula which sends a message becomes failure. Otherwise, the evaluation of attached clauses starts with goal statement defined in attached clauses as conventional initial goal statement in the Prolog interpreter does. Here, the arguments in the goal statement are converted into new arguments through the unification which is applied between the arguments of goal and the elements of arg-list. The proof procedure for the attached clauses is same as the conventional Prolog system, but the form of a goal statement is restricted. The goal clause must consist of only one atomic formula. This constraint easily enable the ZERO system to unify between elements of the arg-list and the arguments in the goal statement.

In case of attached procedures, the procedure which is a receiver of a message is written in Lisp. The number of arguments is four in the case (1). The forth argument is used to receive the result of the evaluation of Lisp function. Another difference between (1) and (2) is that the value of arguments of the elements of arg-list in (2) is instantiated before a Lisp function is evaluated.

By means of the function of predicate Messagep, it is tried to combine an attached procedure and attached clauses. However, in present implementation, the ZERO system does not take care of the side effects which may happen during the evaluation of Lisp programs. Therefore, the users must pay special care to the side effects.

## 5. Conclusion

ZERO is designed as general purpose frame-based knowledge representation language, and to cover the weakness of both frame and Prolog have. The method applied to combine frame model and Prolog is embedding the Prolog features into the frame model. The understandability of representation and the utilization of knowledge seems to be improved by this way.

On the other hand, the modularity of program is introduced into pure Prolog as attached clauses. By introducing the ideas of modularity and structurization into Prolog, an integration of the knowledge bases can be achieved. In pure Prolog, conflicts of predicate names may happen by program misses. Therefore, the Prolog system is not appropriate to use for knowledge integration. If Prolog programs is embedded into a frame system, it is possible to consider that the frame system may work as a module management system.

In terms of combining frame and Prolog, the behavior of demons becomes one of questions. Because, the behavior of Prolog is non-deterministic, while the behavior of demons is deterministic. When a side effect occurs in a frame system which includes Prolog, corresponding demons are activated. On the other hand, the Prolog interpreter executes pattern-matching to get a slot value. If demons are activated when such a pattern matching is applied on the frame system, the efficacy of a reasoning process becomes meaningless. And, the inference control programs have confusion. Therefore, it is necessary to implement a control mechanism to maintain the consistency between the demons and the pattern matching procedures. This mechanism will be implemented in the near future.

From the point of view of usability for practical applications, the current ZERO system seems not to be powerful enough to solve large problems applied in actual domains because of limitations of capacity and efficiency. We are expanding the ZERO system to meet large problems.

Acknowledgements

The authors would like to thank Dr. M. Takizawa and K. Moriya of members at JIPDEC for their helpful comments on this paper. We would like to thank the reviewer at LPC'85 for helpful advices and comments. We would also like to thank M. Ando and Y. Oomori at Tokyo Denki University for their cooperation to implementations of this system. We would like to acknowledge all members at JIPDEC who gave us the chance to write this report.

References

Allen B, Write J (1983) Integrating Logic and Schemata. Proc. IJCAI 83, 340-342
Bowen K, Kowalski R (1982) Amalgamating Language and Metalanguage in Logic Programming. In: Clark K, Tarnland S (ed) Logic Programming, Academic Press, New York, 153-172
Brachman R, Fikes E, Levesque H (1983) Krypton: A Functional Approach to Knowledge Representation. Computer, Vol. 16, No. 10, 67-73
Chang C, Lee R (1973) Symbolic Logic and Mechanical Theorem Proving. Academic Press, New York
Chikayama T (1981) UTILISP Manual. University of Tokyo
Clocksin W, Mellish C (1984) Programming in Prolog. Second edition, Springer-Verlag, Berlin
Davis R (1984) Reasoning from First Principles in Electronic Troubleshooting. In: Coombs M (ed) Developments in Expert Systems. Academic Press, London, 1-21
Deliyanni A, Kowalski R (1979) Logic and Semantic Networks. CACM, Vol. 22, No. 3. 184-192
Harmon P, King D (1985) Expert Systems : Artificial Intelligence in Business. John Wiley and Sons, New York
Hayes-Roth F, Waterman D, Lenat D (1983) Building Expert Systems. Addison-Wesley, Massachusetts
Ito H, Ueno H (1983) Implementation of a Frame-Based Knowledge Representation Language, FMS. Knowledge Engineering and Artificial Intelligence 30-4, Japan Information Society (in Japanese)
Lloyd J W(1984) Foundations of Logic Programming, Springer-Verlag, Berlin
Minsky M (1975) A Framework for Representing Knowledge. In: Winston P (ed) Psychology of Computer Vision, McGraw-Hill, New York, 211-277
Nakashima H (1983) Prolog. Sangyo-Tosho, Tokyo (in Japanese)
Nilsson M (1984) The World's Shortest Prolog Interpreter? In: Capbell (ed) Implementations of Prolog. John Willy and Sons, New York, 87-92
Rich C (1982) Knowledge Representation Languages and Predicate Calculus : How to have Your Cake and Eat it Too. Proc. AAAI-82
Smith R G, Friedland P (1980) Unit Package User's Guide. Stanford Heuristic Programming Project Memo HPP-80-28
Stefik M (1979) An Examination of a Frame Structured Representation System. Proc. IJCAI 79, 845-852
Ueno H (1983) An End-User Oriented Language to Develop Knowledge-Base Expert Systems. Compcon 83 Fall, 523-529
Ueno H (1984) An Intelligent Programming Assistant System INTELLITUTOR - Background and Philosophy -. Knowledge Engineering and Artificial Intelligence 37-5, Japan Information Processing Society (in Japanese)

PRESET   —   A Debugging Environment for Prolog

Hidehisa Takahashi and Etsuya Shibayama

Department of Information Science
Tokyo Institute of Technology
Ookayama Meguro-ku, Tokyo 152

ABSTRACT

   This paper describes PRESET, a debugging environment for the programming language Prolog. PRESET is implemented in C-Prolog and has two major components: Predicate Diagnoser and Why/Whynot Explanation System. Predicate Diagnoser detects bugs which can be found in prior to execution, such as misspellings and illegal calls.  Why/Whynot Explanation System is based on the top-down procedure diagnosis method. It can explain not only where bugs exist but also "why" they are wrong, which most of the existing debugging tools for Prolog do not indicate.

1. Introduction

E. Y. Shapiro [1] proposed some algorithms which through the interaction with the user detect an incorrect clause with quite short steps. In order to use these algorithms, however, the user must entirely grasp the specification of every predicate. Thus, it may possibly be difficult to apply them to a program which another programmer made or which involves very complicated procedures. Furthermore, these algorithms only point out a clause which contains a bug, and they do not tell the user why it works erroneously.

We implemented PRESET as an initial step to the ideal debugging environment of Prolog. PRESET contains two debugging tools: Predicate Diagnoser and Why/Whynot Explanation system. Predicate Diagnoser detects errors which can be found before execution such as misspellings. Most misspellings are corrected automatically using this. Why/Whynot Explanation System is based on the top-down procedure diagnosis method. This system supports the user to find not only where a bug exists but also why the bug is erroneous. Namely, it tells not only "where" but also "why" the program works incorrectly.

We will first discuss features of existing debugging tools for Prolog in the chapter  2. Next, we will introduce PRESET in the chapter 3. Lastly, conclusion and future research will be presented in the chapter 4.

## 2. Debugging Tools for Prolog

Both DECsystem-10 Prolog[2] and C-Prolog[3] have the built-in debugging tool called Tracer. However, it is considered that Tracer is not suitable for efficient debugging in Prolog, and thus more effective strategy is required for debugging Prolog programs.

Divide-and-query proposed by E. Y. Shapiro[1] is a program diagnosis algorithm for Prolog and detects an erroneous clause in quite short steps. This algorithm computes the middle node of a computation tree, and then queries the user whether the execution result of the goal corresponding to the node is satisfiable or not. According to the user's answer, it localizes a bug and finally detects an erroneous clause. However, supposing that we are to debug an erroneous program which contains assert/retract such as the following push/pop program (stack([X|Xs]) should be retracted in the body of pop):

> push(X) :- retract(stack(Xs)), assert(stack([X|Xs])).
> pop(X) :- stack([X|Xs]), assert(stack(Xs)).

Using divide-and-query, a query which we cannot answer such as

> Query: pop(a)?

may be given. This suggests that such a program cannot be debugged by divide-and-query.

It is also the case that divide-and-query may not work correctly if a given program contains a cut symbol and causes backtracking. Suppose that we want a procedure which returns X/2 if X is even and X otherwise, and that we write the following program:

> f1(X,Y) :- even(X), !, Y is X/2.
> f1(X,X).
> even(X) :- 0 is X mod 3.

Since the body of the procedure even is erroneous (it must be "0 is X mod 2"), this program does not work correctly. For example, if we call the goal f1(4,X), the answer "X=4" will be given instead of "X=2". However, divide-and-query cannot detect the bug and displays the second clause of f1 to be incorrect. This problem is caused by the cut symbol. The procedure f1 is equivalent to the following procedure f2:

> f2(X,Y) :- even(X), Y is X/2.
> f2(X,X) :- \+even(X).

Namely, the cut symbol which appears in f1 implicitly means that the second clause is chosen if and only if X is not even. If '\+even(X)' is specified explicitly in the second clause like f2, divide-and-query can localize the bug on this goal. On the other hand, if the second clause has no body like f1, it cannot localize the bug any further.

Our system is an improved version of Shapiro's algorithms so that the execution process can be shown in the top-down order. The problems of the divide-and-query we described above has been settled in our system.

More recently, several programming environments for Prolog are developed. Several researchers extend the box model[4] in various ways, and propose debugging facilities based on these extended box models[5,6], whereas we improved Shapiro's work. Numao[5] proposed a screen oriented Prolog programming environment called PROEDIT, where the box model is extended so that the flow of control between subgoals can be displayed. It can show the execution process in the top-down order like our system. A new model of computation proposed by Francez et. al.[6] is also based on the ideas of the box model. They also proposed a Prolog oriented editor. On the contrary, Komorowski and Omori proposed a generic software engineering shell for logic programming[7]. They formalize some aspects of programming methodology and provide heuristics for avoiding errors. The open-world assumption is also employed in their system.

## 3. The PRESET System

In this chapter we introduce PRESET, which has been implemented as an initial step to the ideal debugging environment for Prolog. PRESET can be divided broadly into two subsystems: Predicate Diagnoser and Why/Whynot Explanation System. The former detects bugs in prior to execution, whereas the latter explains the execution process of a program in the top-down order.

### 3.1. Predicate Diagnoser

As long as we use such a programming language as Lisp or Pascal, a misspelling scarcely leads to a serious problem. (Most of misspellings are detected as errors during compilation and/or execution.) On the contrary, when using Prolog, we often consume a very long time to get rid of misspellings. However, most of misspellings of a Prolog program can be detected before execution. Namely, the head of a clause which is never called and a goal which always fails probably contain such bugs. Predicate Diagnoser is implemented for the sake of removing such bugs.

### 3.1.1. Classification of Statically Detectable Errors

There are three cases in which a statically detectable error in a clause-body falsifies the execution: (1) undefined predicate, (2) improper arity and (3) irreducible goal. Also in clause-heads, some bugs are statically detectable. For example, consider the incorrect quicksort given in Program 1. A typical error of (1) is in the clause <4>: we should have spelled "partition" instead of "partetion". In the body of <3> a procedure partition occurs which has only three arguments although its arity should be four. This is an example of (2). The goal "quicksort(x2,Y2)" in <1> does not match any clause-head of the predicate quicksort since the first argument is "x2", which should be "X2". That case falls under the heading of errors of (3). The head of the clause <2> is "qicksort([],[])" instead of "quicksort([],[])", which is an example of the statically detectable errors in a clause-head.

## 3.1.2. Detecting Errors

Predicate Diagnoser examines each goal in every clause-body whether a bug exists or not. If a goal does not match any head of a clause, the system infers that the goal contains a bug, since the execution of the goal is expected to fail always. On the contrary, if it matches one or more, one of them may possibly be selected in execution. Therefore the system does not infer that the goal contains a bug. (In order to deal with higher order predicates, the system also examines their arguments as if they were goals.) Each goal infered by the system that it contains a bug is indicated with a warning message according to the type of the bug we classified in 3.1.1 and the system fixes it by the user's recommendation. The user can choose system's action in the following: E)dit this procedure, K)eep this procedure as it is, L)ist this procedure, A)bort, and B)reak. If the user inputs 'e', for example, he can modify the procedure using the editor specified in advance.

We now show an example session of debugging Program 1 with Predicate Diagnoser:

```
            <Warning>
            quicksort([A|X],Y) :-
                partition(X,A,X1,X2),
                quicksort(X1,Y1),
                quicksort(x2,Y2),
```
---
```
        <1> quicksort([A|X],Y) :-
                partition(X,A,X1,X2),
                quicksort(X1,Y1),
                quicksort(x2,Y2),
                append(Y1,[A|Y2],Y).
        <2> qicksort([],[]).

        <3> partition([X|Xs],A,[X|X1],X2) :-
                X < A, partition(Xs,A,X1).
        <4> partition([X|Xs],A,X1,[X|X2]) :-
                X>= A, partetion(Xs,A,X1,X2).
        <5> partition([],_,[],[]).

        <6> append([A|X],Y,[A|Z]) :- append(X,Y,Z).
        <7> append([],Y,Y).

            Program 1: An Incorrect Quicksort
```

```
            append(Y1,[A|Y2],Y).

        Irreducible goal : quicksort(x2,_67).
        Action? e

        *** modify quicksort with the editor ***

        <Warning>
        partition([X|Xs],A,[X|X1],X2) :-
            X < A, partition(Xs,A,X1).

        Improper arity : partition/3.
        Action? e

        *** modify partition with the editor ***

        <Warning>
        partition([X|Xs],A,X1,[X|X2]) :-
            X>= A, partetion(Xs,A,X1,X2).

        Undefined Predicate : partetion.
        partetion --> partition
        Correct? y
        Corrected.

        qicksort/2 will never be called.

        Completed.

        yes
        | ?-
```

The strategy employed in Predicate Diagnoser, however, judges that a goal which is dynamically asserted during execution and a procedure which is invoked to start the program are erroneous. In order to distinguish them from actually erroneous ones, two kinds of commands for PRESET are available. If we write "%!defined_by_assert(p1)." in a program file, the system regards p1 as dynamically defined predicate and does not display any message even if the goal whose predicate is p1 matches none. By putting the command "%!top_level_predicate(p1)." in a file, we can declare that the procedure p1 is directly called by the user. Note that C-Prolog regards each line followed by '%' as a comment line. Further, with such commands, the program will become easier to be read as well as to be debugged.

### 3.2. Why/Whynot Explanation System

If we use Predicate Diagnoser together with divide-and-query, we will be able to debug more effectively. However, problems of divide-and-query shown in the chapter 2 still remain unsettled. We implemented Why/Whynot

Explanation System as an answer to the problems. It is based on the top-down procedure diagnosis method and is designed to show the process of execution plainly as well as where and why the program is wrong.

### 3.2.1. The Strategy of Why/Whynot Explanation System

Why/Whynot Explanation System is composed of two modules: Why-module and Whynot-module.

Why-module explains the execution process of a goal which returns a wrong result in the following manner:

1. examine whether the given goal successes (if it fails, call Whynot-module);
2. display the successful clause which matches the given goal;
3. if some clauses are tried before the successful clause is selected:
   3.1. display the message "backtracking caused";
   3.2. query the user whether he needs the information of backtracking;
   3.3. if the answer is "yes", call Whynot-module on each clause-body which had been tried before the successful clause was selected;
4. for each subgoal:
   4.1. compute the subgoal and display the result;
   4.2. query the user whether he wants an explanation of the result;
   4.3. if the answer is "yes", call Why-module recursively on the subgoal.

Whynot-module explains the execution process of a failure goal as follows:

1. examine whether the given goal fails (if it successes, call Why-module);
2. for each clause whose head matches the goal:
   2.1. display the clause;
   2.2. for each subgoal of the clause:
      2.2.1. if the execution of the subgoal successes:
         2.2.1.1. display the result;
         2.2.1.2. query the user whether he wants an explanation of the result;
         2.2.1.3. if the answer is "yes", call Why-module on the subgoal;
      2.2.2. if the execution fails:
         2.2.2.1. inform the user that the subgoal fails;
         2.2.2.2. query the user whether he wants an explanation of the result;
         2.2.2.3. if the answer is "yes", call Whynot-module recursively on the subgoal;

2.2.2.4. backtrack, i.e. search another solution of the youngest subgoal among those which still have alternatives; if there exists such a subgoal, apply 2.2 from the subgoal.

### 3.2.2. Explanation of Backtracking

In the chapter 2, we described that divide-and-query may not work correctly on some programs which contain cut symbols and cause backtracking. On the contrary, since Whynot-module explains for each failure clause why its execution fails as the explanation of backtracking, we can debug such a program using Why/Whynot Explanation System.

The following is the same program as shown in the chapter 2.

```
f1(X,Y) :- even(X), !, Y is X/2.
f1(X,X).
even(X) :- 0 is X mod 3.
```

We described that divide-and-query indicates the second clause of f1 as a wrong one. With Why/Whynot Explanation System, we can find the actual bug, "0 is X mod 3", as follows:

```
why f1(4,X).
Matched:
f1(X,X).
Backtracking caused. Explain(y/n)? y

1st matched:
f1(X,Y) :- even(X), !, Y is X/2.

even(4) fails.
Explain(y/n)? y

Matched:
even(X) :- 0 is X mod 3.

0 is 4 mod 3 fails.
(is: System Predicate)
ok?
```

### 3.2.3. Explanation of Programs Which Contain Assert/Retract

We also pointed out that divide-and-query cannot be applied to the following program, which contains assert/retract:

```
push(X) :- retract(stack(Xs)), assert(stack([X|Xs])).
pop(X) :- stack([X|Xs]), assert(stack(Xs)).
```

On the other hand, Why/Whynot Explanation System can debug even if a program contains assert/retract.

When the user answers the system's query in the affirmative, the system re-computes the current goal in order to explain the process of its execution. If assert (or retract) is executed during its re-computation, some predicates are defined (removed) over again and the program may be modified unexpectedly. This problem is solved by remembering the modifications of the program and undoing the modifications before re-computation.

Suppose we define the following procedure f for the sake of testing the push/pop program:

```
f(X,Y,Z) :-
    assert(stack(X)), pop(Y), pop(Z).
```

Now we test it on f([1,2,3],X,Y). Consequently we get a wrong answers: "X=1" and "Y=1". The bug can be found by Why/Whynot Explanation System as follows:

```
why f([1,2,3],X,Y).
Matched:
f1(X,Y,Z) :-
    assert(stack(X)), pop(Y), pop(Z).

assert(stack([1,2,3]))
==> assert(stack([1,2,3])).
(assert: System Predicate)
Ok?

pop(_6)
==> pop(1).
Explain(y/n)? n

pop(_7)
==> pop(1).
Explain(y/n)? y

Matched:
pop(X) :-
    stack([X|Xs]), assert(stack(Xs)).

stack([_7|_1505])
==> stack([1,2,3]).             ------ (a)
Explain(y/n)?
```

(a) means that the argument of the predicate 'stack' is not updated although the 'pop' operation has been done. Therefore we see why the program is wrong: the 'pop' operation did not update the predicate 'stack'.

## 4. Conclusions and Future Research

We have implemented PRESET, which is designed as an initial step to the ideal debugging environment for Prolog. We consider that such a facility as Predicate Diagnoser of PRESET should have been supported by Prolog systems themselves. The algorithm employed in Why/Whynot Explanation System can show the user "why" the program is wrong, and consequently some problems of divide-and-query have been settled. We hope that this algorithm contributes to a coming debugging system for Prolog.

However, the PRESET system, especially Why/Whynot Explanation System still has many problems. For example, the algorithm of Why/Whynot Explanation System requires the re-computation frequently, and thus it works quite slowly. Furthermore, we cannot apply Why/Whynot Explanation System to a program which does not terminate. Shapiro designed an algorithm which diagnoses such a program[1]. However, the algorithm comes into effect only when the same goal appears while execution. Recently, researches on eliminating infinite loops in Prolog are intensively made by Covington[8,9], Nute[10], Poole and Goebel[11], and so on. It is quite difficult to deal with an infinitely looping program, and we consider that one of our problem will be there.

## Acknowledgements

We would especially like to thank Prof. A. Yonezawa of Tokyo Institute of Technology for his kind advice and encouragement. We would also like to thank all the members of Yonezawa Lab. for their useful comments on our research.

## References

[1] Shapiro, E. Y., Algorithmic Program Debugging, MIT Press, 1982.

[2] Bowen, D. L., Byrd, L., Pereira, F. C. N, Pereira, L. M. and Warren, D. H. D, DECsystem-10 Prolog User's Manual, Dept. of Artificial Intelligence, University of Edinburgh, 1982.

[3] Pereira, F., C-Prolog User's Manual, Dept. of Artificial Intelligence, University of Edinburgh, 1983.

[4] Clocksin, W. F. and Mellish, C. S., Programming in Prolog, Springer-Verlag, 1981.

[5] Numao, M., PROEDIT - A Screen Oriented Prolog Programming Environment, Proc. of the Logic Programming Conference '85, 1985 (In Japanese).

[6] Francez, N., Goldenberg, S., Pinter, R. Y., Tiomkin, M. and Tsur, S., An Environment for Logic Programming, Proc. of the ACM SIGPLAN 85 Symposium on Language Issues in Programming Environments, ACM SIGPLAN Notices, Vol. 20, No. 7., 1985.

[7] Komorowski, H. J. and Omori, S., A Model and an Implementation of a Logic Programming Environment, Proc. of the ACM SIGPLAN 85 Symposium on Language Issues in Programming Environments, ACM SIGPLAN Notices, Vol. 20, No. 7, 1985.

[8] Covington, M. A., Eliminating Unwanted Loops in Prolog, ACM SIGPLAN Notices, Vol. 20, No. 1, 1985.

[9] Covington, M. A., A Further Note on Looping in Prolog, ACM SIGPLAN Notices, Vol. 20, No. 8, 1985.

[10] Nute, D., A Programming Solution to Certain Problems with Loops in Prolog, ACM SIGPLAN Notices, Vol. 20, No. 8, 1985.

[11] Poole, D. and Goebel, R., On Eliminating Loops in Prolog, ACM SIGPLAN Notices, Vol. 20, No. 8, 1985.

[12] Takahashi, H. and Shibayama, E., PRESET - A Debugging Environment for Prolog, Proc. of the Logic Programming Conference '85, 1985 (In Japanese).

PROEDIT - A Screen Oriented Prolog Programming Environment

M. Numao and H. Maruyama

Science Institute, IBM Japan Ltd.
5-19 Sanbancho, Chiyoda-ku, Tokyo 102, Japan

ABSTRACT

A screen oriented programming environment for Prolog was designed and implemented. To visualize the control flow of the execution of a Prolog program, A new execution model is proposed, which is based on the box model, but has been extended so that control flow between subgoals is displayed over time. It is written for VM/Prolog which runs under the VM/CMS operating system. The system is actually being used by researchers in IBM laboratories.

1. INTRODUCTION

In recent years, the Prolog language (Clocksin 1981) has been gaining in popularity among AI researchers. Prolog is suitable for the research and development of applications in AI because it has a built-in pattern matching function and search mechanism which allows easier coding of symbolic manipulation algorithms. However, there are still far more programs written in Lisp than there are in Prolog. One reason for this is that Prolog does not yet have a programming environment that is as good as Lisp's (Alberga 1981; Mikelsons 1982). Since AI programming is based on trial and error, a poor environment is a great disadvantage for a language. In addition, debugging a Prolog program seems more difficult than debugging a program in a language such as Lisp or Pascal, because Prolog has a very complex execution model. Specifically, the non-deterministic nature of the language makes it difficult to apply ideas from debuggers written for other languages, where execution moves sequentially through the text of a program.

Currently, there seem to be two different approaches to debugging Prolog programs. One is to trace the execution of the program so that the user can find his errors, another is to use diagnostic programs. Diagnostic programs search through the computation tree of the program, and ask the user to verify each predicate. From this information, the source of the problem can be determined. Important works in this area include Algorithmic Program Debugging by Shapiro (1983), and Rational Debugging by Pereira (1984). We have chosen to explore the area of program tracing because we believe that a good execution model best allows the user to understand his program's behavior and find his bugs. In addition, it circumvents some of the problems of the diagnostic approach. For example, the main problem of the diagnostic approach is that it is not suitable for use on large programs since the debugging process is controlled by the system. A large program generates a large number of queries, which quickly becomes frustrating to the programmer.

The remainder of this paper is divided into four sections. The first is an architectural overview of the system. In the second section we first introduce the two current execution models, and discuss their limitations. Then we propose our Execution Flow model (Numao 1985). The third shows its visual representation on a terminal screen. The fourth section concludes our work.

## 2. THE SYSTEM OVERVIEW

The PROEDIT system is a programming environment which allows the user to edit, execute, and debug Prolog programs through a screen oriented user interface. It is written for VM/Prolog, running under the VM/CMS operating system. The system was implemented using VM/Prolog, the VM/CMS command language REXX, and the XEDIT screen editor. There are three major parts of PROEDIT: the session manager, the source file editor, and the execution monitor.

### Session Manager

The session manager allows the user to execute Prolog goals entered at the keyboard. When a goal produces unexpected results, the user can immediately enter the execution monitor to analyze the goal's behavior and call the source file editor to edit the predicate definition. In addition, the history of the session is contained in a file that is displayed in the session manager screen. This file contains both the user inputs and PROEDIT's responses. Since it is just a file, it can be changed using editor commands, and any command in the history can be moved to the command line for re-execution. Figure 1. shows a typical session manager screen.

```
************************* PROEDIT/SM ***************************
 1 /** PROEDIT Logging start at 16:34:58 on 6 Jun 1985 **/
 2 <-addax( human( turing )).
 3 <-addax( human( socrates )).
 4 <-human( X ).
 5 human( turing ) .
 6 ;
 7 human( socrates ) .
 8 ;
 9 fail .
10 <- read( X ) & write( X ).
11 >> hello.
12 hello.
13 read( hello ) & write( hello ).
14 <-reconsult( sample ).
15 reconsult( sample ).

1=? 2=Add 3=File 4=Help 5=Top 6=Bot 7=Bwd 8=Fwd 9='='
====> step config( X ).

Fig. 1.    The Session Manager Screen.
```

### Source File Editor

When a predicate name is given by the user, the Source File Editor searches the file which contains the predicate definition and puts the definition lines into the buffer in an editable form. Because all predicates defined have their original file name associated with them when loading the file into the Prolog workspace, the source file editor can retrieve the file and definition line. After editing the definition, it automatically updates both the file and the Prolog workspace.

**Execution Monitor**

The Execution Monitor keeps track of the Prolog execution search tree and provides a perspective view of succeeded subgoals and failed subgoals for a focused goal in a two dimensional representation. Since the view distinguishes success or failure of the subgoals by symbols and distinguishes the alternative clauses and backtracked subgoals by vertical positions, the user can easily find out which subgoals contribute to success and which to failure for the top goal. Cursor operations allow the inspection of the bindings of in/out variables for each subgoal and the shifting of the focus to an arbitrary position in the search tree. Also it allows the user to perform top-down debugging. This graphic representation is based on the execution flow model which will be described in the next section.

## 3. EXECUTION FLOW MODEL

**Current Execution Models**

For a user to be able to debug his program, it is important to have an execution model by which he can easily trace and understand the program's execution. That is, if the user can understand what his program is doing, he can find the portion of the program that causes the error and correct his mistake. The two models that are currently in use are the tree model and the box model. The tree model is based on the fact that execution of a Prolog program creates a computation tree that shows the resolution process of a given goal. Therefore, a tree representation such as a proof tree or computation tree gives a good perspective view of the goal resolution process. Because each node in a tree represents a subgoal, it is clear how a given goal was divided into subgoals, which were then further divided into subgoals, and so on. But this tree representation has problems: it cannot show the backtracking and unification mechanisms that are a main feature of the Prolog language. Backtracking reverses the direction of the flow of control, and unification causes variable bindings to be set remotely when a variable in the corresponding node is bound. Furthermore, if backtracking occurs the variable bindings are cleared and set to new values. It is difficult to show the trace of the control flow and the history of variable bindings with the tree representation.

The box model, on the other hand, gives a good representation of how control flows through a given subgoal. For this reason, the box model is considered to be the best model, and many existing Prolog systems support debuggers/tracers based on it. In the box model, each goal or subgoal is represented by a box. The flow of control in and out of the boxes is represented by arrows which are named call, exit, redo, and fail. The call arrow shows the initial invocation of the procedure, with control passing into the box. The exit arrow shows that the goal was satisfied, and that control moves out of the box. The redo arrow indicates that the system is backtracking in an attempt to find alternatives, so there is another invocation of the procedure. The fail arrow shows that the goal was not satisfied, and that the system must backtrack.

In later sections, we will use the sample program shown in Fig. 2. The program produces configurations for the IBM 5550 (Japanese PC). The top level predicate "config" finds the configuration by a generate and test sequence. The "generate" predicate generates all possible combinations of system unit type and memory size on backtracking. The "test" predicate checks whether a generated combination satisfies the user's request (Japanese word processor, color display and 24-dot font size in this case).

```
config(X) <- generate(X) & test(X).

generate(SU + Mem) <- sys_unit(SU) & memory(Mem).

sys_unit(5551e).      memory(384).
sys_unit(5551g).      memory(512).
sys_unit(5551h).      memory(640).

test(X) <- jwp(X) & color(X) & dot24(X).

jwp(* + 512).    color(5551e + *).    dot24(5551g + *).
jwp(* + 640).    color(5551h + *).    dot24(5551h + *).


Fig. 2.    Sample program.
```

The box model representation of part of this program is shown in Fig. 3.

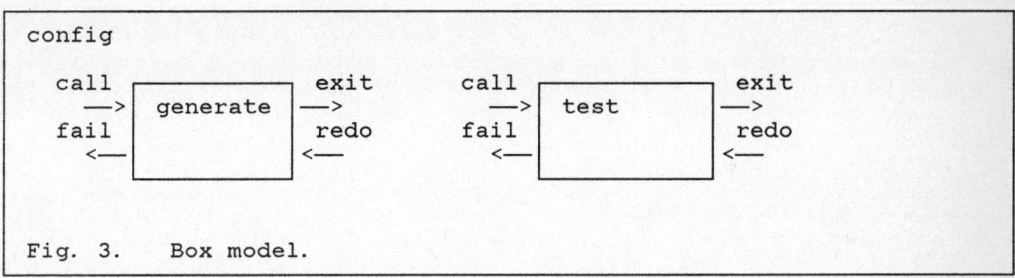

Fig. 3.    Box model.

In this figure, it is clear how the predicates are called or recalled, and how control flows if they succeed or fail. The results of the execution are readily apparent, because control moves to the right if it succeeds and to the left if it fails. What is not apparent, however, is the effect of changes over time. Since each call of a predicate results in a change of variable bindings, having only one box per predicate does not adequately represent the execution of the program. In order to do so, it is necessary to generate a separate box for each call.

## Execution Flow Model

To solve the problems of the box model, we have created the execution flow model (modified box model). In our model the unit of interest is a clause; this is natural to the programmer and helpful in debugging because a clause is a sentence of Prolog code. This model shows the flow of control between subgoals by using a two dimensional representation. It is very similar to the box model in that there are four

possible ways for control to flow: call, exit, redo, and fail.  The main
difference is that the initial calls are represented by the top row of
boxes, and then each subsequent call to a procedure is represented by
a new box, placed under the box that represents the previous invocation
of that procedure.  Therefore, each box represents a change in variable
bindings, and execution moves from left to right, and from top to bottom.  This method allows the user to see the actual flow of control,
as opposed to the box model, which shows all the possibilities without
specifying which path was actually followed.  The execution flow model
of the sample program is shown in Fig. 4.

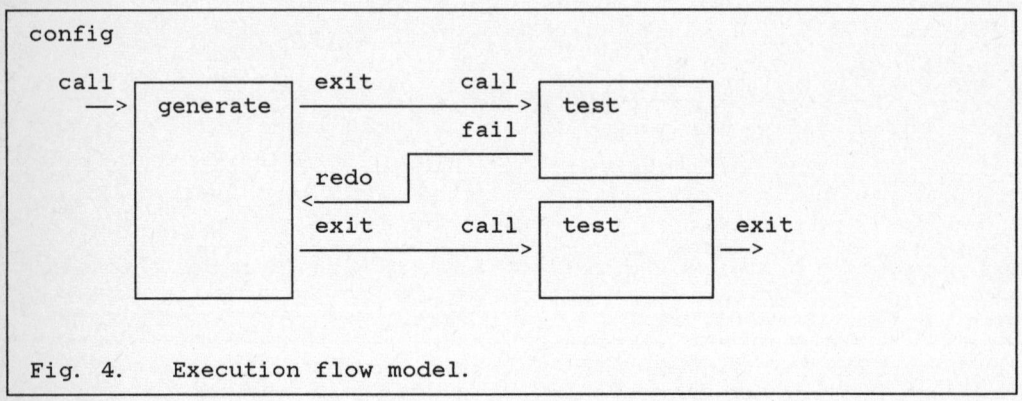

Fig. 4.   Execution flow model.

This figure shows that the goal "<-config(X)" succeeded with the second
alternative solution generated by the "generate" predicate.  In this
model, the variable bindings for a particular call could be shown next
to the exit arrow, and the clearing of variables could be shown next
to the redo arrow.  Due to space limitations we have not indicated the
variable bindings in this representation, but this problem is resolved
in the next section.


## 4. EXECUTION VISUALIZATION

A graphic representation which is suitable for displaying on a terminal
screen was developed using the execution flow model.  Rather than
drawing boxes and arrows separately, we have combined them to form five
kinds of flow of control within a predicate, each with its own representation.  The types and their representations are as follows:

    call and exit:  predicate name (e.g. generate)
    call but fail:  predicate name with underline (e.g. test)
    redo and exit:  right arrow (->)
    redo but fail:  left arrow with underline (<-)
    outside fail :  double left arrow with underline (<<=)

The first four are analogous to the boxes used in the box model, but
the fifth is different.  It represents a request for an alternative
solution that comes from outside the parent goal.  This means that the
goal being recalled was the closest alternative solution to the goal
that failed, even though the goal that failed was not within the parent
goal.  An example of the execution flow model's representation is shown
in Fig. 5.

```
    config     generate     test
                  ->        test
```

Fig. 5.   Graphic representation of the execution flow model

The actual screen representation of the Execution Flow Model used in our execution monitor is shown in Fig. 6.

```
************************  PROEDIT/EM  ****************************
goal : config(V1) : exit
rule : config(V1) <- generate(V1) & test(V1)

config    generate    test
             ->       test
             ->       test
             ->       test
             ->       test
             ->       test
             ->       test
             ->       test




call : test(5551e+512)
fail : test(5551e+512)

1=? 2=Up 3=Clear 4=Left 5=Down 6=Right 7=In 8=Out 9=Top
===>
```

Fig. 6.   The sample program's execution

Note that the program was called to solve the goal "<-config(X)". This figure shows the top level of the program execution. The goal line at the top of the screen shows the parent goal that the program is trying to resolve. The rule line shows the applied rule to resolve the parent goal. The center section contains the trace of the execution of the parent goal. The trace shows that the parent goal "config(X)" was unified with the rule head "config". Next the body of "config" is executed: "generate" is called and it succeeds, but "test" fails; control backs to "generate" which succeeds with another substitution, but "test" fails again, and so on until finally, on the last line, "test" succeeds and the whole parent goal succeeds. The "test" in bold-face indicates the current subgoal. The flow of control in and out of the current subgoal is shown by the "call:" and "fail:" lines directly underneath the trace. The variable bindings set by the current subgoal are also shown here. For the current goal, they indicate that it was called but failed. The numbers at the bottom stand for the function keys on the terminal, and tell the user how to make a subgoal the current, and how to move into or out of a goal. Fig. 7 shows the results of a move into the current subgoal, which makes the current subgoal of Fig. 6 become the parent goal of Fig. 7.

The goal line shows the parent goal has changed to "test(5551e+512)". The trace shows that the reason of failure of "test" was due to the failure of the subgoal "dot24".

```
************************   PROEDIT/EM   ***************************
goal : test(5551e + 512) : fail
rule : test(V1) <- jwp(V1) & color(V1) & dot24(V1)

   test     jwp         color      dot24
                         <-
             <-








unify: test(5551e + 512)



1=?  2=Up  3=Clear  4=Left  5=Down  6=Right  7=In  8=Out  9=Top
===>

Fig. 7.   Screen after moving inside the current goal
```

The ability to step inside a predicate in this fashion makes top-down debugging simple and effective. When a programmer sees a predicate that looks wrong, he can step inside it until he finds the source of the problem. This approach is much more user friendly than that of a box model tracer such as the one shown in Fig. 8 which has in excess of 100 lines of output, both because it is easier to read and because it allows the user to focus on a particular area without seeing parts of the program with which he is not concerned.

```
 1 : call ==> config(V1) .
  2 : call ==> generate(V1) .
   3 : call ==> sys_unit(V1) .
   3 : exit ==> sys_unit(5551e) .
   3 : call ==> memory(V1) .
   3 : exit ==> memory(384) .
  2 : exit ==> generate(5551e + 384) .
  2 : call ==> test(5551e + 384) .
   3 : call ==> jwp(5551e + 384) .
   3 : fail ==> jwp(5551e + 384) .
  2 : fail ==> test(5551e + 384) .
  2 : redo ==> generate(5551e + 384) .
   3 : redo ==> memory(384) .
   3 : exit ==> memory(512) .
  2 : exit ==> generate(5551e + 512) .
  2 : call ==> test(5551e + 512) .
   3 : call ==> jwp(5551e + 512) .
   3 : exit ==> jwp(5551e + 512) .
   3 : call ==> color(5551e + 512) .
   3 : exit ==> color(5551e + 512) .
   3 : call ==> dot24(5551e + 512) .
   3 : fail ==> dot24(5551e + 512) .
             . . .
 1 : exit ==> config(5551h + 512) .

Fig. 8.   Trace of the sample program.
```

## 5. CONCLUSION

We have designed and implemented a screen oriented Prolog programming environment named PROEDIT. It offers an integrated programming environment for the logic programming language; the user can create, run, and debug his programs within the PROEDIT environment. There are three major parts of PROEDIT: the session manager, the source file editor, and the execution monitor. The session manager allows the user to execute Prolog goals entered at the keyboard; the editor allows the user to edit files from within PROEDIT; and the execution monitor shows the user a graphic representation of the execution of a program.

An execution model for the execution monitor was also proposed. It is based on the ideas of the box model, but the model has been extended so that it can show the flow of control between subgoals over time. This model, and its graphic representation based on the model, help the Prolog programmer to understand his program's execution, and allow him to do top-down debugging. The information the system gives a user includes the flow of control of the execution of the program, the history of variable bindings, the rules that apply to a particular subgoal, and the results of the subgoals inside a rule. This system has the same power to find bugs as the algorithmic debugger, and is much more user friendly. Some diagnostic programs can be very frustrating, because the user doesn't know what is happening inside the system. Our debugger allows the user to see what he wants to see, but doesn't burden him down with extraneous information.

The version in use runs on color terminals, so that color coding is used rather than underlining to distinguish between types of flow of control. The system is installed in more than 15 IBM laboratories, and is currently used by many researchers. In our institute, the system is being actively used to write programs such as a natural language parser, a text critiquing system, and an expert system. All of our colleagues who are Prolog programmers prefer our approach to the line-by-line box model tracer provided by the Prolog interpreter. This shows, we believe, that our visualization technique is one of the most natural ways for programmers to understand Prolog execution.

## REFERENCES

Alberga C, et al. (1981) A Program Development Tool. 8th Annual ACM Symposium on Principles of Programming Languages
Clocksin WI, Mellish CS (1981) Programming in Prolog. Springer-Verlag
Mikelsons M (1982) Interactive Program Execution in LISPEDIT. ACM SIGPLAN/SIGSOFT, Symposium on High Level Debugging
Numao M, Fujisaki T (1985) Visual Debugger for Prolog, The Second Conference on Artificial Intelligence Applications. IEEE
Pereira LM (1984) Rational Debugging of Logic Programs. Department de Infomatica, Universiade Nova de Lisboa
Shapiro EY (1983) Algorithmic Program Debugging. MIT press

Software Prototyping with MENDEL

Shinichi Honiden, Naoshi Uchihira, and Toshiaki Kasuya

Systems and Software Engineering Division, Toshiba Corporation,
1-1-1, Shibaura, Minato-ku, Tokyo 105, JAPAN

Abstract
Software prototyping with MENDEL, which is Prolog based concurrent object oriented language, is described. MENDEL can deal with following characteristics such as: 1) meta inference, 2) object concurrency, 3) linkage to C language, 4) propositional temporal logic, 5) Prolog predicates for performance prediction simulator. The object generation in MENDEL, that is a program tranformation of concurrency and temporal dependence requirement specifications, is also described.

1. INTRODUCTION

Prototyping method is currently attracting software engineers as a software specification method, though prototyping method has not been used in software engineering field so much as in other engineering fields. The reasons for attracting them can be summarised as follows:
1) Growing criticism to the waterfall type life cycle model. For example, this criticism comes from the difficulty to predict the realization of the defined requirements at the requirement definition stage.
2) An increasing need for operability confirmation. A need from the software end user is to confirm the operability and handling ease of a completed system at the requirement definition stage.
3) The need of correctness verification. With the conventional method, it is difficult to verify whether the system meets the intention of the user.
4) The integrated environment for software development. The integrated environment makes it possible to easily create a prototype.
5) An increasing attention on software reusability. The software reusability has been recognized as the most important feature in software engineering.

Various prototyping methods have been proposed, such as using the existing programming language (Duncan 1982), a program generator wherein the application field is limited (Barstow 1982), software reusability (Jones 1984), and using executable requirement specification language (Balzer 1982). At present, no prototyping definition has been established, nor has a standard method been established. Though several prototyping methods (Davis 1982 and Duncan 1982) for a real time system have been proposed, many problems still remain to be solved.

Under these circumstances, the authors have planned a prototyping tool for real time systems, satisfying such requirements as:
1) Object-based software development,
2) Concurrent execution of the object,

3) Time concerned model,
4) Software reusability,
5) Logic programming language based specification,
and developed a Prolog based concurrent object oriented language, MENDEL.

Section 2 describes software prototyping for the real time system. Section 3 outlines the MENDEL. Section 4 explains its application to software prototyping.

## 2. PROTOTYPING IN REAL TIME SYSTEM

The objective application is a process control system, which is a computer system for controlling a process system. Process systems are, for example, large-capacity atomic or thermal power generation system, a steel roll mill process, and a distribution supply system for electricity. Function and performance verifications are important for these process control systems.

Major items for function verification in the real time system are the dynamic relationships between functions or between realization units, for example, correctness of data delivery, detection of deadlock, access to common data, and synchronization. These items cannot be adequately verified with the conventional verification methods such as SADT, PSL/PSA, and RSL/REVS. In SADT, nothing is done beyond indication of a format error or an arrow missing in a figure. In PSL/PSA, only the consistency verification is accomplished. In RSL/REVS, only the inspection of configuration correctness and data flow is performed. Therefore, in order to perform function verification for the items, some prototype system (called the function prototype in this paper), that actually behaves like the completed system, is necessary.

The maximum response time in the real time system is strictly stated as one of the performance requiremernts. If the response time exceeds the allowable response time, then the system would generate defective products. Accordingly, it is important to estimate the response time of the system at the system design stage as precisely as possible. Simulation methods have been used for the response time estimation, but have not been utilized sufficiently. Since a great deal of manpower and time are required for creating a simulation model, simulation methods are isolated far from the main path of the software production process. Therefore, when simulator modeling is incorporated in the prototyping process and a simulation model is created, a prototype for performance verification (called the performance prototype in this paper) is realized.

## 3. MENDEL

When various kinds of systems in this world are concerned with the modeling, it is quite natural to develop models which modify the internal states in response to external messages and issue messages. In this respect, the internal and external objects of MENDEL can only transmit information through pipe caps. An attribute name is assigned to each pipe cap and is used by the internal object to refer to the input-output messages. This attribute name not only identifies the pipe cap, but also regulates the input-output message attributes (specifications). The relation between the objects is created according to the transmission pipe binding pipe caps, as shown in Fig. 1. The transmission pipe is a one-to-one asynchronous one-way path.

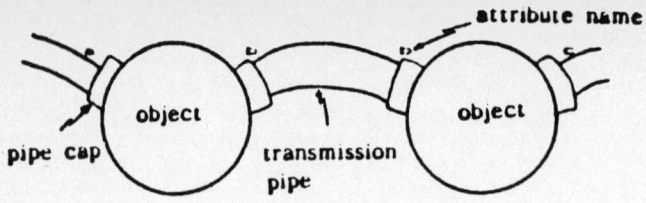

Fig. 1 Object and communication pipe

A. META-INFERENCE

The transmission pipe between pipe caps is automatically created in MENDEL. If a certain goal (input-output specification) is given for a group of objects, the binding agent selects the necessary objects by inference, in order to accomplish that goal, and binds the transmission pipes. (Fig. 2) This inference is called a meta-inference, which infers a strategy to derive a solution. The meta-inference is performed according to the knowledge concerning the object interface specifications (meta-knowledge), and the inference rules of the binding agent. To accomplish a given goal, the necessary object is found by trial and error. The meta-inference in MENDEL can be considered as a method-search with a broadcast function. If there exist multiple paths to accomplish a given goal, the meta-inference selects the most suitable object method by broadcasting from the input-output attributes declared by each object. Since it is necessary to establish some kind of evaluation standards, the meta-inference has many strategies. If every method is appended at processing time, the path with the shortest processing method is selected. When the processing time is not fixed, the method, in which the least number of pipes are required, is used.

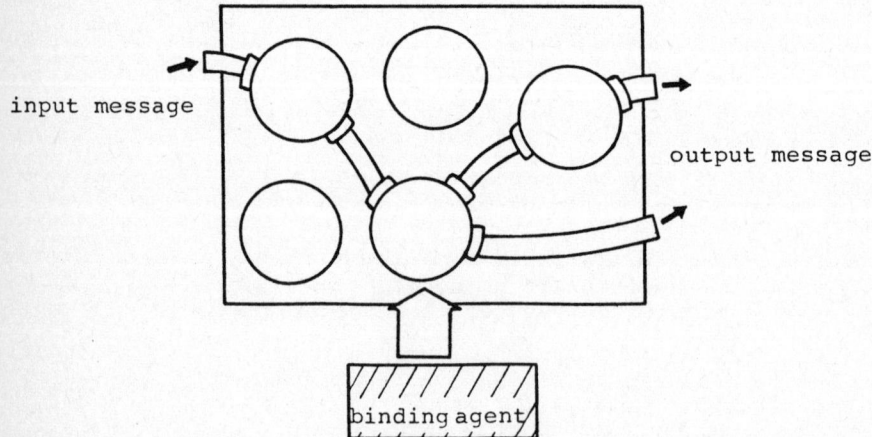

Fig. 2 Binding agent and meta-inference

## B. MENDEL SYNTAX SUMMARY

The object consists of the meta-knowledge and the object-level knowledge.

Meta-knowledge is the knowledge concerning the concept "which way can be used?, and which way must be used?". For object-level knowledge, the processing contents are described from the externally input messages. The external independence of the object-level knowledge can be increased by dividing the meta-knowledge and the object-level knowledge. In the MENDEL objects, there are classes and instances. Initially, there exists only the class of sets in the system. The binding agent selects and binds the necessary classes. When the binding is completed, the object is called an instance. It is possible to create multiple instances from an identical class.

Object-level knowledge consists of some methods. The input values (attribute values) are obtained from each pipe. The attribute names of pipe cap are called the port table. The object starts the appropriate method, if messages are received in this port table. The method is declared as follows.
```
      Method (attribute ? logical variable name) ...
            (attribute ! logical variable name ...)
            -- Prolog clause body
         Prolog clause (characteristic knowledge in the method)
```

When the logical variable after an attribute"?" is accepted from the port table, the method is started. When the method is completed, and the logical variable after an attribute"!" is unified, the unified value is sent to the transmission pipe through the port table. The MENDEL description is shown in Fig. 3.

```
EmployeeAccess
(
 spec:(
       supers( Employees ).
       method( name? sex? idnumber! ).
       method( name? age? idnumber! ).
       method( sex? age? idnumber! ).
      )
 body:(
       method( name?X sex?Y idnumber!Z
              <-database( Z, X, Y, _ ).
             )
       method( name?X age?Y idnumber!Z
              <-database( Z, X, _, Y ).
             )
       method( sex?X age?Y idnumber!Z
              <-database( Z, _, X, Y ).
             )
      )
)
```

Fig. 3 Example of MENDEL

Meta-knowledge includes the following three items.
1) Input-output description of the method.
2) Super class definition.
3) Definition of internal state variables.

The input-output specifications for object methods are expressed using the system predicate "method".
    method (attribute ? ... destination ID :attribute ! ...)
The destination ID, that includes these categories, specifies the destination of messages
    object name - specifies the object name directly
    METAPHOR - decided by meta-inference
    BROADCAST - is broadcasting (transmission (!) only)
The default value is METAPHOR. The binding agent performs the binding using this meta-knowledge. The basic binding rule is to connect pipe caps, which have the same attribute name.
The definition of a super class uses the system predicate "supers" (statement).
    supers (upper position object name ...)
When this is specified from the upper level object, its object inherits the undefined predicate.
This is the definition of internal state variables.
    variables (variable name! initial value)

The system predicate "communicate" is called the expanded module call. If the given attribute and the desired attribute are specified, the appropriate object is selected and the binding between appropriate pipe caps is completed. The desired attribute value is obtained by operating each object concurrently. Since the object selection and binding are left to meta-inference, the program description is unnecessary. For a meta-inference, the following is expressed.
Communicate METAPHOR (attribute! logical variable name ... attribute? logical variable name ...)
This communicate sentence is not only written for a Prolog clause of a object body part, but also used for the goal call to enter a MENDEL program.

The description of concurrency and hierarchy is also possible by using the communicate statement. The portions surrounded by the communicate statement become the AND-parallel description. In the communicate statement, the Prolog predicate can be considered to be the object. On one hand, concerning the hierarchy, if the goal clause in the communicate statement is given, an inference configuration, which is bound by the meta-inference is formed. If a communicate statement appears in the instance body part, the lower level configuration is formed by the meta-inference.

For the processing units (tasks) of real-time systems to be executed concurrently, the synchronization problems must be taken into consideration. In MENDEL, message passing from concurrent object is not the procedure call format adapted in Smalltalk-80 (Goldberg 1983). When messages are transmitted in Smalltalk-80, the program control is transferred to the object receiving the messages, and the method, which corresponds to those messages, is executed. Then, the return value is then sent to the transmission side object. Since each concurrent object execution is difficult using rules like this, the concurrent object-oriented language requests the no-return message passing for transmission only. For the concurrent object, the messages are sent asynchronously from the concurrently operating

object, and the method is selected according to the combination of those messages. In the example
    method (a?, b?, c?, d!)
when a?, b?, c? are transmitted from different objects, this method is not selected until a?, b?, c? are all completed. Consequently, when multiple messages are transmitted from different objects, the initial method is selected, when the messages are totally completed. In MENDEL, the synchronous structure for this purpose exists internally. The selection method for MENDEL is considered to be attached to a Dijkstra's guarded command (Dijkstra 1975). For the declared message, when a certain compound "and" condition becomes true (i.e., when all messages are completed and the conditions of all message contents are satisfied), the guard is permitted. When the object method is selected, and another message is sent to the object during execution, the most recent message will be processed.

The following system predicate is provided in MENDEL for simulation description use.
    $decresource (resource name) : resource declaration
    $seize (resource name) : resource secured
    $release (resource name) : resource release
    $dectime (time) : simulation time unit declaration
    $hold (time) : period of time of hold

C language is called from MENDEL by using the system predicate, and is performed by the $usercall command. The first argument of the $ usercall command is the C language filename. The second and succeeding parameters are the arguments of the object function. Symbols ? and ! are attached before each argument, to distinguish input and output parameters.

For process control systems, which use external production control devices, it is difficult to express the system adequately by only using the usual predicate calculus. Therefore, to apply the expert system in the real time process control system, it is necessary to overcome this problem. MENDEL adapts temporal logic to solve the problem. Deadlock may occur, especially when the execution order of the concurrently operating object is not regulated. Definitions of the sequential relationship between the objects are necessary. In MENDEL, it is possible to regulate a message exchange without producing deadlock by meta-inference.

## 4. SOFTWARE PROTOTYPING WITH MENDEL

The objective for prototyping support systems for real time systems is to create a MENDEL object by program transformation from concurrency, and temporal dependence requirement specifications. Program transformation is realized by either algorithms or expert systems.

The meta-knowledge of MENDEL are first generated from the requirement specifications by program transformation. In MENDEL, the requirement specification consists of the system transitional logic and the required proposition. The system transitional logic is expressed by the Petri net. The "fact" in each transition unit is described below. The description format is defined as:
    transition (transition name, input place name, output place name)
The required proposition is described by temporal logic of relationship between each transition, and also determines the system

operations described by system transitional logic. The exchange of
messages between objects to avoid deadlock is realized by these two
descriptions. This means that the MENDEL meta-knowledge is
generated. The generation is performed by the method expanded from
the tableau method in the temporal logic. (Manna and Wolper 1982)
The procedure is as follows:
1) A tableau graph is generated by the tableau method.
2) The system is checked to make sure that no deadlock condition
   exists.
3) The meta-knowledge concerning message exchange is created.

A simple example is shown in Fig. 4. Processes P1 and P2 are
exchanging S, which is the critical section at this time. In these
relationships, P1 is sending the begin-1 and end-1 message to S, and
P2 is sending the begin-2 and end-2 message to S. The corresponding
system transitional logic for these relationships is shown in Fig. 5,
and the required proposition is shown in Fig. 6. The MENDEL meta-
knowledge is created from these definitions as shown in Fig. 7. In
this case, P1, P2, S and the object N which shows the tableau
position are created.

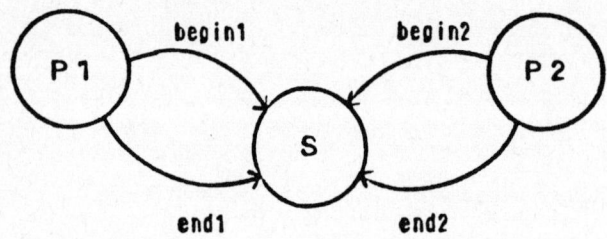

Fig. 4 Example of mutual exclusion

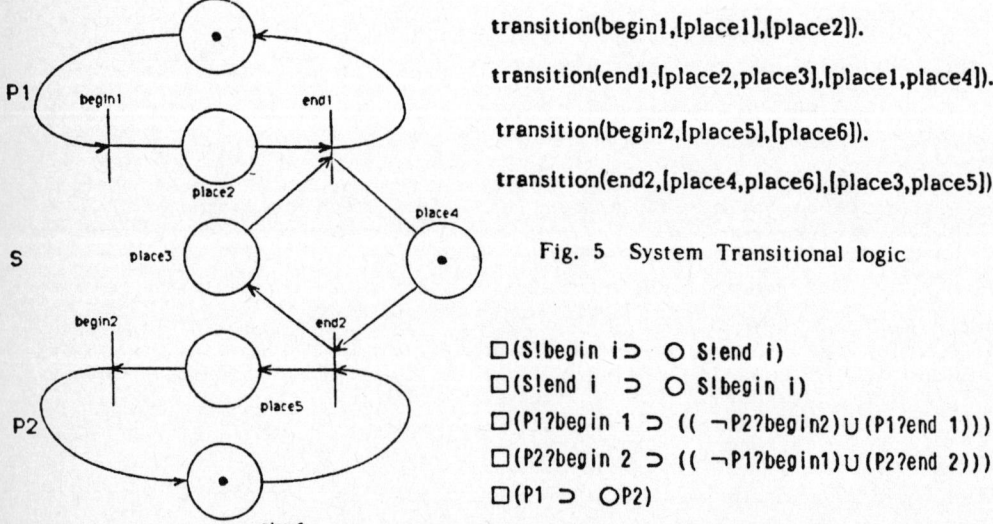

transition(begin1,[place1],[place2]).

transition(end1,[place2,place3],[place1,place4]).

transition(begin2,[place5],[place6]).

transition(end2,[place4,place6],[place3,place5]).

Fig. 5 System Transitional logic

$\Box$(S!begin i $\supset$ $\bigcirc$ S!end i)
$\Box$(S!end i $\supset$ $\bigcirc$ S!begin i)
$\Box$(P1?begin 1 $\supset$ (( $\neg$P2?begin2) U (P1?end 1)))
$\Box$(P2?begin 2 $\supset$ (( $\neg$P1?begin1) U (P2?end 2)))
$\Box$(P1 $\supset$ $\bigcirc$P2)

Fig. 6 Required proposition

```
S
(spec(
    method(begin1?,N-out?´1´,N-in!´2´)
    method(begin2?,N-out?´1´,N-in!´3´)
    method(end1?,N-out?´2´,N-in!´1´)
    method(end2?,N-out?´3´,N-in!´1´)
    )
)
P1
(spec(
    method(N-out?´1´,begin1!)
    method(N-out?´2´,end1!)
    )
)

P2
(spec(
    method(N-out?´1´,begin2!)
    method(N-out?´3´,end2!)
    )
)
N
(spec(
    method(N-in?,N-out!)
    )
)
```

Fig. 7 Part of meta-knowledge


MENDEL is considered as a software prototyping tool. If the objects (components) exist, a program is created from reusable components. Unless the objects (components) exist, a program is created from specification description.

When components exist, a component combination, which satisfy the requirement, is selected and combined by meta-inference. Thus, it is possible to configure a prototype rapidly. Component detection is also possible using the specification level, since information concerning object-level knowledge can be described by meta-knowledge.

When no component exists, the prototyping is accomplished in the following manner.

1) The input-output attributes which are generated by the tableau method, are described in the object meta-knowledge. The message flow can be checked by tracing the meta-knowledge for each object, depending on the meta-inference at this level.
2) The pseudo-execution accompanying the exchange of messages relating to the value is also possible by defining the top level clause for the body part of each method.
3) The body part is described by Prolog clauses.
4) Since the system operating under UNIX is mostly written by C language, the predicates defined by Prolog are realized successively in C language.

The steps above show the progressive stages for the prototypes.

The performance prototype is also important for real time systems. MENDEL provides two level prototyping, that is, the design level and the programming level. In the design level, only meta-knowledge is defined. In the programming level, meta-knowledge and object-level knowledge are described. In the former case, system predicates SEIZE and RELEASE for performance evaluation are added to meta-knowledge, and meta-inference selects the path with the shortest processing method and predicts roughly performance items. In the latter case, more detailed simulation becomes possible by adding object-level knowledge.

The simulator, in which a computer system is modeled as a queuing network, reports a performance evaluation result including items, such as the response time for each object, the resource use efficiency, and the queue distribution. The problem with regard to correct correspondence between the design model and the simulation model is eliminated, since data on function and performance are written on the same object.

5. CONCLUSION

A summary of MENDEL and its use as a prototyping tool has been briefly described. The intelligent programming environment, the MENDELS, is under development. MENDELS is configured from the MENDEL interpreter and the object manager, which includes DWIM (Do What I Mean), intelligent debugger, and intelligent editor etc.

ACKNOWLEDGEMENTS

The authors would like to thank Akira Ito, Masahiko Arai, and Shinsuke Tamura of Systems and Software Engineering Division in Toshiba Corporation for providing essential support.

REFERENCES

Jones T.G. (1984) Reusability in Programming:A Survey of the State of the Art. IEEE Trans. Software Eng. 10 5:488-493
Dijkstra E.W. (1975) Guarded Commands,Nondeterminacy and Formal Derivation of Programs. CACM 18 8:453-457
Goldberg A. etal (1983) Smalltalk-80 Language and its implementation. Addison-Weslay
Manna Z.,Wolper P. (1982) Synthesis of Communication Processes from Temporal Logic Specification. Lecture Notes in Computer Science 131,Springer-Verlag,p 253
Balzer R.M. etal (1982) Operational Specification as Basis for Rapid Prototyping. ACM Sigsoft Software Eng. Notes 7 5:3-16
Davis A.M. etal (1982) Rapid Prototyping using Executable Requirements Specification. ACM Sigsoft Software Eng. Notes 7 5:39-44
Duncan A.G. (1982) Prototyping in ADA:Case Syudy. ACM Sigsoft Software Eng. Notes 7 5:54-60
Barstow D. (1982) Automatic Programming System to Support Experimental Science. Proc. 6th ICSE,p 360
Zave P. (1981) Executable Requirements for Embedded System. Proc. 5th ICSE,p 295
Gomma H. etal (1981) Prototyping as a Tool in the Specification of User Requirements. Proc 5th ICSE,p 333
May D. (1983) occam. SIGPLAN Notices 18 4:69-79

# RETRIEVAL OF SOFTWARE MODULE FUNCTIONS USING FIRST-ORDER PREDICATE LOGICAL FORMULAE

H. Yoshida, H. Kato, and M. Sugimoto

FUJITSU LIMITED
1015 Kamikodanaka Nakahara-ku, Kawasaki, Japan

## ABSTRACT

This paper introduces a method to retrieve software modules from a module library in order to reuse them for new software. It is effective for a programming environment in which specifications of software modules are formalized using first-order predicate logical formulae. This method uses resolution and heuristics to determine reusability of current modules in the library. A prototype system has been developed using C-Prolog on a VAX11/780.

## 1. PREFACE

In logic programming, a programming language has its logical basis in Horn clauses which are subsets of first-order predicate logical formulae. A language for specifications of logic programs will be somewhat close to logical expressions. For this reason, first-order predicate logical formulae can be taken as one of the candidates for the specification description language. However, first-order predicate logical formulae are both difficult to write and read, and thus require a user interface. The TELL system (Enomoto et al. 1984) currently being researched by the Tokyo Institute of Technology is an attempt to integrate a natural-language interface into formal specification descriptions written in first-order predicate logical formulae. In other words, the specification description language TELL/NSL, which is the core of the TELL system, is a natural language (English) with limited syntax, and software specifications written in this language can be translated unambiguously into first-order predicate logical formulae through syntactic analyses.

Well-written software specifications not only facilitate maintenance, but also make it easier to reuse old software. If useful software is stored in a library and can be retrieved easily, it can be reused, which improves productivity significantly. Although automatic retrieval is desirable, simply matching characters is not a practical method of retrieval. A retrieval method based on software functions is required. It is important to grasp the "semantics of specifications" as intended by the designer for semantical matching. This paper discusses a method for retrieving software module functions in a programming environment, such as the TELL system, that can formalize semantics of specifications using first-order predicate logical formulae. This method uses resolution and heuristics to match first-order predicate logical formulae. This paper briefly introduces specification description language TELL/NSL in Section 2. It presents an overview, and the algorithm of the method in Sections 3 and 4, and reports on a prototype system developed using C-Prolog on a VAX11/780 in Section 5.

## 2. SPECIFICATION DESCRIPTION LANGUAGE TELL/NSL

The four types of modules that can be described using TELL/NSL are as follows:

(1) functional definition (equivalent to a predicate or function),

(2) class definition (equivalent to an abstract data type),

(3) action definition (equivalent to a parallel process), and

(4) dynamic class definition (equivalent to shared data of processes).

This retrieval method currently applies only to functional definitions.

Figure 1 is an example of a top level module definition for solving the eight queens puzzle described in TELL/NSL. This specification can be translated into Formula (1) below.

Arrangement X is an <u>eight queens solution</u>

  means that

    1) Eight queens are placed in X.

    2) No queen is checking any other queen in X.

end eight queens solution.

Fig. 1  A sample specification (by TELL/NSL)

$$\forall c \; [eight\_queens\_solution(c) \equiv \\ \exists S \; [|S|=8 \wedge \forall q [_\wedge q \varepsilon S \equiv placed(q,c)]] \\ \wedge \sim \exists q1 \exists q2 \; [q1 \neq q2 \; checking(q1,q2,c)]] \quad (1)$$

TELL/NSL is a pseudo-natural language which can be translated into first-order predicate logical formulae. It is characterized by natural stepwise refinement through lexical decomposition. That is, one word corresponds to each module, and the specification description of each module explains the meaning of the word in natural language. The words in the explanatory statement provide further explanations as auxiliary modules which are subcontractors of the original module. Thus, the module structure and the inter-module interface of the entire software are determined naturally based on the explanatory statement in natural language. The specifications of each module define the logical association with the auxiliary modules and are translated into relatively simple logical formulae. Therefore, a sufficient response speed can be expected even if the resolution principle is used for those logical formulae. Since there is a tendency to generate many small modules, reusing modules by functional retrieval would be highly effective.

## 3. FUNCTIONAL RETRIEVAL

A functional retrieval system using this method is used, for example, in the following sequence:

(1) The specifications of individual modules using TELL/NSL, their translated logical formulae, and programs that have been verified to satisfy the logical formulae are stored in a library.

(2) Anyone can then use TELL/NSL to develop a new module by describing the specification of the module.

(3) A syntactic analysis is then performed on the specification of the new module, which is then translated into a first-order predicate logical formula and input into the functional retrieval system.

(4) The functional retrieval system compares the input logical formula with the formulae of the modules in the library to determine whether they are reusable.

(5) The developer modifies the program of a module determined to be reusable and obtains a program of the new module.

Since this method uses the resolution principle to determine the equivalence of logical formulae, a specifications is determined to be reusable if it is logically equivalent to the input specification, regardless of differences in characters or expressions. For example, module eight_queens_puzzle with a specification that can be translated as shown in Formula (2) below is reusable as module eight_queens_solution shown in Figure 1.

$$\forall c \; [\text{eight\_queens\_puzzle}(c) \equiv \\ \forall q1 \forall q2 \; [\text{checking}(q1,q2,c) \Rightarrow q1=q2] \\ {}^\wedge \exists S \; [|S|=8 {}^\wedge \forall q \; [q \varepsilon S \equiv \text{placed}(q,c)]]] \quad (2)$$

In reality, however, modules with equivalent functions are seldom stored in the library. To use the functional retrieval system effectively, modules that are "similar" to some extent must also be retrievable. The problem is under what condition the two specifications should be considered similar. Because the main purpose of the functional retrieval system is to promote reuse of programs, it must be able to obtain the desired program easily, merely by modifying the programs of the retrieved modules. Therefore, the functional retrieval system must not only to answer "similar," but also provide guidelines as to what part of the program text should be modified and how. The method tentatively checks whether each of the following three cases and any of their combinations apply, to determine whether two specifications are "similar":

(a) Difference in the order of parameters

Two specifications are equivalent except for the order of formal parameters. For example, modules successor and predecessor having specifications that are translated as shown in Formulae (3) and (4), respectively, are logically equivalent if the two formal parameters are exchanged.

$$\forall x \forall y \; [\text{successor}(x,y) \equiv x=\text{increment}(y)] \quad (3)$$

$$\forall z \forall w \ [predecessor(z,w) \equiv increment(z)=w] \quad (4)$$

Therefore, if Formula (3) is input, the functional retrieval system will return Formula (5), provided that predecessor is stored in the library.

$$\forall x \forall y \ [successor(x,y) \equiv predecessor(y,x)] \quad (5)$$

By taking the program text of module predecessor out of the library and by replacing all occurrences of the first parameter z with y and all of the second parameter w with x, the user can obtain the program of the new module successor.

(b)  Turning a parameter into a constant

Two specifications will be equivalent if some constant is given as an actual parameter. For example, module n_queens_solution having the specifications that can be translated as shown in Formula (6) will be reusable as module eight_queens_solution shown in Figure 1 if constant 8 is given as the first parameter.

$$\forall n \forall c \ [n\_queens\_solution(n,c) \equiv \\ \exists S \ [|S|=n \wedge \forall q \ [q \varepsilon S \equiv placed(q,c)]] \\ \wedge \sim \exists q1 \exists q2 \ [q1 \neq q2 \wedge checking(q1,q2,c)]] \quad (6)$$

Therefore, if Formula (1) is input, the functional retrieval system will return Formula (7).

$$\forall c \ [eight\_queens\_solution(c) \equiv n\_queens\_solution(8,c)] \quad (7)$$

By taking the program text of module n_queens_solution out of the library and by replacing all occurrences of the first parameter n with 8, the user obtains the program of the new module eight_queens_solution.

(c)  Difference in auxiliary modules

Two specifications will be equivalent if the subcontracting auxiliary modules are replaced with similar ones. For example, in module sort and module generate_test having the specifications that can be translated as shown in Formula (8) and Formula (9), respectively, the original modules are equivalent assuming that auxiliary modules parmutation and generated, and sorted and tested are logically equivalent.

$$\forall x \forall y \ [sort(x,y) \equiv permutation(x,y) \wedge sorted(y)] \quad (8)$$

$$\forall z \forall w \ [generate\_test(z,w) \equiv generated(z,w) \wedge tested(w)] \quad (9)$$

Therefore, if Formula (8) is input, the functional retrieval system will return Formula (10), and Formulae (11) and (12) which are assumed equivalences of auxiliary modules.

$$\forall x \forall y \ [sort(x,y) \equiv generate\_test(x,y)] \quad (10)$$

$$\forall x \forall y \ [permutation(x,y) \equiv generated(x,y)] \quad (11)$$

$$\forall x \ [sorted(x) \equiv tested(x)] \quad (12)$$

By taking the program text of module generate_test out of the
library and by replacing all occurrences of the auxiliary module
names generated and tested with permutation and sorted,
respectively, the user obtains the program of the new module sort.
It should be noted that this method does not verify the assumptions
in Formulae (11) and (12). Therefore, modules having completely
different functions may be retrieved by this method. However, as
shown above, the program of module generate_test can easily be
reused regardless of whether Formulae (11) and (12) are satisfied.
Auxiliary modules parmutation and sorted of the new module sort can
be used as is if they already exist as modules. If they are new
modules, specifications are defined for them and reusable modules
are functionally retrieved from the library as for sort, in which
case the retrieved modules need not be generated or tested.

## 4. PRINCIPLES OF RETRIEVAL

Parameters of each module are represented by universally quantified
logical variables in a logical formula which is a translation of
specifications. Therefore, the similarities shown in Sections (a)
and (b) of the preceding section can be determined, because their
logical variables or their logical variables and constants are
unified during the verification process that uses the resolution
principle. The determination of the similarity shown in Section
(c), on the other hand, is a high order unification, and is realized
by heuristics.

The procedures and heuristics used are explained below.

(a) Terminology and notation

Predicate names are represented by lower case alphabetics, such as
p, f, and g, while the ordinary logical formulae are represented by
upper case alphabetics, such as F and G. The set of parameters X1,
X2, ..., Xn of predicate p is represented by "$\underline{X}$" as a tuple.
Therefore, call of p is represented by "$p(\underline{X})$". The operation for
properly rearranging the order of tuple elements is called
permutation. Tuple $\underline{X}$ rearranged by parmutation $\pi$ is represented by
"$\underline{X}\pi$". Tuple <X1, X2, ..., Xi, Y1, Y2, ..., Yj> for the two tuples
$\underline{X}$=<X1, X2, ..., Xi> and $\underline{Y}$=<Y1, Y2, ..., Yj> is called concatenation
of $\underline{X}$ and $\underline{Y}$, and is represented by "$\underline{X} + \underline{Y}$".

Call of a predicate and its negation is called a literal. In
particular, call $p(\underline{X})$ of predicate p and its negation $\sim p(\underline{X})$ are
called positive literal of p and negative literal of p, respectively.

A clause is a set of literals. A clause consisting of only one
literal is called a unit clause; in particular, a clause consisting
of only one literal of predicate p is called the unit clause of p.

(b) Procedures

Hereafter, the new module to be retrieved will be named f, and the
module with which its equivalence is to be verified will be named
g. Modules f and g are defined in Formulae (13) and (14).

$\forall \underline{X} [ f(\underline{X}) \equiv F(\underline{X}) ]$     (13)

$\forall \underline{Y} [ g(\underline{Y}) \equiv G(\underline{Y}) ]$     (14)

In the first phase, it is determined whether functions of module g satisfy those of module f. Functions are verified if a parameter tuple $\underline{Z}$ of module g that satisfies Formula (15) can be found for a parameter tuple $\underline{X}$ of module f.

$$\forall \underline{X} [g(\underline{Z}) \Rightarrow f(\underline{X})] \quad (15)$$

In this case, since Formula (15) to be verified is unknown, the normal resolution principle cannot be applied as is. In this retrieval method, therefore, parameter tuple $\underline{X}$ of module f is fixed to obtain Formula (18) as the unit clause of module g, using Formulae (16) and (17) as axioms.

$$\sim F(\underline{X}) \quad (16)$$

$$\forall \underline{Y} [G(\underline{Y}) \Rightarrow g(\underline{Y})] \quad (17)$$

$$\sim g(\underline{Z}) \quad (18)$$

If Formula (18) can be resolved, formula (19) is considered to be satisfied, and Formula (15) is considered to have been verified by Formulae (19) and (13).

$$\sim F(\underline{X}) \Rightarrow \sim g(\underline{Z}) \quad (19)$$

At this time, tuple $\underline{Z}$ is normally a permutation of tuple $\underline{X}$ (or a concatenation of tuple $\underline{X}$ with a tuple consisting of several constants).

With Formula (15) alone, module g may be a partial solution of module f. Therefore, Formula (20) which is the opposite of Formula (15) is also verified in the second phase.

$$\forall \underline{X} [f(\underline{X}) \Rightarrow g(\underline{Z})] \quad (20)$$

Formula (21) can be resolved from Formulae (15) and (20). Thus, module g which is reusable as f is discovered.

$$\forall \underline{X} [f(\underline{X}) \equiv g(\underline{Z})] \quad (21)$$

(c) Heuristics

(1) Forced factoring of literals

This is a unique heuristic in the first phase of this method, which is used to improve the efficiency of the resolution principle. That is, if the resolved clause contains multiple negative literals of g and if they can be factored, an attempt is made to forcibly factor them so that the resolved clause contains only one negative literal of g. If the literals cannot be factored, the resolved clause is deleted, because the clause to be finally resolved in the first phase must not be an empty clause. That is, it must be a unit clause of g, such as Formula (18).

(2) Assumption of similarity of auxiliary modules

This is a heuristic used to find a pair of modules, h and k, where h is an auxiliary module of f, k is that of g, and the verification process would advance on the assumption that h and k are equivalent. In the first phase, the two clauses C1 and C2 that satisfy the following conditions are searched for among the resolved clauses:

- C1 contains positive literal h($\underline{V}$) of h and C2 contains negative literal ~k($\underline{W}$) of k. Or, C1 contains negative literal ~h($\underline{V}$) of h and C2 contains positive literal k($\underline{W}$) of k.

- There is a permutation π of the tuple, the class of the corresponding elements of $\underline{V}$π and $\underline{W}$ is equal, and each of $\underline{V}$π and $\underline{W}$ has a most general unifier σ.

- If C1 contains negative literal ~g($\underline{Y}$) of g, and C2 contains ~g($\underline{Z}$) of g, $\underline{Y}$σ and $\underline{Z}$σ are unifiable.

If the above conditions are satisfied, and if h and k (when parameters are rearranged by permutation π) can be equivalent, a new clause can be resolved from C1 and C2. Even if multiple negative literals of g appear in the clause, the new clause will not be excluded, by the heuristics of (1) above. Verification continues with Formula (22) added to the axiom.

$$\forall \underline{V} \ [h(\underline{V}) \equiv k(\underline{V}\pi)] \quad (22)$$

Formula (22) is also used as one of the axioms in the second phase.

(3) Handling of recursive definitions

Strictly speaking, to determine whether two recursively defined modules are equivalent, the mathematical induction on the data structure of the two must be used. However, it is difficult to do so automatically with a computer. And one can often decide that the two modules appear to be equivalent without using such a precise method. What must be noted here is how the recursive calls appears in the body of the modules. The decision based on the style of calling the subcontractors is the same as that of heuristic (2) above. So the method similar to that of (2) can be used to determine the equivalence of recursive modules.

In the first phase, the two clauses C1 and C2 that satisfy the following conditions are searched for among the resolved clauses:

- C1 consists of only negative literal ~f($\underline{V}$) of f and negative literal ~g($\underline{Z}$) of g.

- C2 consists of only positive literal g($\underline{W}$) of g and negative literal ~g($\underline{Z}$) of g.

- Both tuple $\underline{A}$ consisting of only constants (including a tuple whose length is 0) and permutation π exist, ($\underline{V} + \underline{A}$)π and $\underline{W}$ have the most general unifier σ, and ($\underline{X} + \underline{A}$) and $\underline{Z}$σ are equal.

When the above conditions are satisfied, the first phase terminates with Formula (23) considered to be satisfied.

$$\forall \underline{X} \ [g(\underline{Z}\sigma) \Rightarrow f(\underline{X})] \quad (23)$$

Recursive calls are processed in the same way in the second phase.

It will be shown that this heuristic is correct for a module recursively defined for the list structure. For simplicity, it is assumed that both f and g have two parameters. The first parameter is used for input and the second parameter is used for output, and they are defined by Formulae (24) and (25).

$$\forall x \forall y \, [f(x,y) \equiv F(x,y)] \quad (24)$$

$$\forall x \forall y \, [g(x,y) \equiv G(x,y)] \quad (25)$$

In the first phase, parameters x and y of module f are fixed to resolve the unit clause of module g using Formulae (26) and (27) as axioms, and heuristic (3) checks that a clause as shown in Formulae (28) and (29) is resolved.

$$\sim F(x,y) \quad (26)$$

$$\forall v \forall w \, [G(v,w) \Rightarrow g(v,w)] \quad (27)$$

$$\sim f(cdr(x),y) \lor \sim g(x,y) \quad (28)$$

$$g(cdr(x),y) \lor \sim g(x,y) \quad (29)$$

If the clauses of Formulae (28) and (29) are resolved, then Formulae (30) and (31) can be resolved from Formulae (24), (25), (26) and (27).

$$\forall x \forall y \, [g(x,y) \wedge f(cdr(x),y) \Rightarrow f(x,y)] \quad (30)$$

$$\forall x \forall y \, [g(x,y) \Rightarrow g(cdr(x),y) \lor f(x,y)] \quad (31)$$

Now, it will be verified that Formula (32) is satisfied by using the mathematical induction on a list structure.

$$\forall x \forall y \, [g(x,y) \Rightarrow f(x,y)] \quad (32)$$

(1) When x is nil

Since literal g(cdr(x),y) means "$\exists z [cdr(x,z) \wedge g(z,y)]$", it is false in this case, and Formula (33) can be resolved from Formula (31).

$$\forall y \, [g(nil,y) \Rightarrow f(nil,y)] \quad (33)$$

(2) When x is cdr(a)

Assuming Formula (34), Formula (35) can be resolved from Formulae (30) and (31).

$$\forall y \, [g(cdr(a),y) \Rightarrow f(cdr(a),y)] \quad (34)$$

$$\forall y \, [g(a,y) \Rightarrow f(a,y)] \quad (35)$$

## 5. PROTOTYPE SYSTEM AND EXAMPLE OF REUSE

A prototype of the functional retrieval system using this method has been realized using C-Prolog on a VAX11/780. The program consists of approximately 2000 lines, and whether logical formulae are equivalent is determined using ordered linear resolution (Chang et al. 1973). Of the heuristics discussed in Section 4, heuristics (1) and (3) are used as required, if they are applicable. Heuristic (2) is considered only when the resolution principle comes to a deadlock.

This prototype operates as one of the modules composing the program development environment (Sugimoto et al. 1984), whose specification description language is TELL/NSL. The prototype is also used as a subcontractor of another module called the semi-automatic synthesis system. The semi-automatic synthesis system is used interactively by the software designer. This system functions include specification description by TELL/NSL, translation of logical formulae by parser, retrieval of reusable modules by the functional retrieval system, reference and modification of the retrieved modules, and storing of the modified modules into the library.

Figure 2 is an example of synthesis of program on_the_same_column, which reuses the module on_the_same_row.

(a) New Specification (by TELL/NSL)

    **Queen q1 and queen q2 are
               on the same column of arrangement x**
  means that
   1) The x_coordinate of the position of q1 in x is
      the x_coordinate of the position of q2 in x.
  end

(b) Translated Logical Formula of (a)

$$\forall q1,q2,x\ [\text{on\_the\_same\_column}\,[q1,q2,x] \equiv$$
$$\text{x\_coordinate}\,[\text{position}\,[q1,x]]$$
$$= \text{x\_coordinate}\,[\text{position}\,[q2,x]]]$$

(c) Retrieved Module Name

    on_the_same_row

(d) Translated Logical Formula of (c)

$$\forall q1,q2,x\ [\text{on\_the\_same\_row}\,[q1,q2,x] \equiv$$
$$\text{y\_coordinate}\,[\text{position}\,[q1,x]]$$
$$= \text{y\_coordinate}\,[\text{position}\,[q2,x]]]$$

(e) Assumption of the Equivalence

$$\forall x\ [\text{x\_coordinate}\,[x] \equiv \text{y\_coordinate}\,[x]]$$

(f) Program of (c) (by Prolog)

```
on_the_same_row(Q1,Q2,X):-
    position(Q1,X,P1),
    y_coordinate(P1,Z),
    position(Q2,X,P2),
    y_coordinate(P2,Z).
```

(g) Modified Program of (a)

```
on_the_same_column(Q1,Q2,X):-
    positon(Q1,X,P1),
    x_coordinate(P1,Z),
    position(Q2,X,P2),
    x_coordinate(P2,Z).
```

Fig. 2   An example of program synthesis

(1) The user inputs specification (a) of the program to be obtained.

(2) The semi-automatic synthesis system converts specification (a) into logical formula (b) using the parser.

(3) Then, the semi-automatic synthesis system calls the functional retrieval system and retrieves similar modules.

(4) The functional retrieval system returns the name of the similar module (c), its logical formula (d), the logical formula of conditions under which the two agree (e), and the program (f).

(5) Viewing (f), the user determines it to be usable, modifies the program (f) based on (e), and obtains the program (g).

(6) The semi-automatic synthesis system stores the generated module into the library.

The user then repeats this cycle, if necessary, for further refinement (generating auxiliary modules).

6. CONCLUSION

This paper presents a method for retrieving reusable software modules by verifying the equivalence of first-order predicate logical formulae given as specifications. As long as the specifications are for programming environments that can be stipulated by first-order predicate logical formulae, this method can be applied, regardless of the implementation language.

This method is not, however, sufficient to retrieve all modules having specifications logically equivalent to those input by the user. It is also true that the specifications of the retrieved modules are not always equal to new specifications. This is mainly because the auxiliary modules and the specifications of the data structure to be operated by them are not referenced when determining whether two modules are equivalent. For software development, however, it is desirable to determine the usable modules at the earliest possible stage to promote the reuse of modules, as well as to enable retrieval without complete detailed descriptions of the specifications. Therefore, the objective of this method is not to verify the logical equivalence including specifications of the modules (auxiliary predicates and data classes) being referenced, but to find similarities in their "reference formats." The method is based on the theory that if the reference formats in specifications are similar, the interfaces based on the programs that implement them are also similar and, therefore, can be easily used. In this method, the equivalence of specifications of auxiliary predicates is determined solely by how they are called and how parameters are given. The recursive equivalence is determined solely by the format of recursive call without using mathematical induction on the data structure. Using this method, a software designer can use any part of the reusable modules at each step of the stepwise refinement. The designer can also further refine unusable parts.

ACKNOWLEDGMENTS

This study has been carried out as a part of the fifth generation computer project. We would like to thank Institute for New Generation Computer Technology for giving us the opportunity to conduct this study.

We would also like to thank Prof. Enomoto (current Director of International Institute for Advanced Study of Social Information Science, Fujitsu), Assistant Prof. Yonezaki, and Dr. Saeki of Tokyo Institute of Technology for their valuable guidance on TELL.

REFERENCES

Chang C, et al. Symbolic logic and mechanical theorem proving, Academic Press, U.S.A. 1973.

Enomoto H, et al. NATURAL LANGUAGE BASED SOFTWARE DEVELOPMENT SYSTEM TELL, ICOT TR-067, Tokyo, 1984.

Sugimoto M, et al. Design concept for software development consulation system, ICOT TR-071, Tokyo, 1984.

# TEMPORAL LOGIC PROGRAMMING LANGUAGE Tokio
## Programming in Tokio

T. Aoyagi, M. Fujita*, T. Moto-oka

Department of Electronic Engineering, University of Tokyo
(* Currently assigned to Fujitsu Laboratories.)

## ABSTRACT

We introduce Tokio, a sophisticated extension of Prolog. Tokio is based on interval temporal logic (ITL) (Moszkowski 1983), and includes many useful ITL operators. We will discuss how those temporal operators work. Some simple execution examples of Tokio are also included. Finally, we compare and contrast Tokio with other logic programming languages. Tokio is especially well suited for hardware description. We are now developing a total logic design assistance system based on Tokio.

## 1. WHY Tokio?

Prolog, a logic programming language, is based on first-order predicate logic and, therefore, has the following characteristics which differentiate it from other programming languages such as Pascal:

1) Each program is easily understood and program validity can easily be verified.

2) Program descriptions naturally include parallelism ie. concurrent processing does not change the meaning of the program.

3) Structured data that includes ambiguities can be processed by using logical variables.

However certain operations that are easily described in conventional programming languages are not so easily described using Prolog. A typical example is the description of a changing states. For example, to increment the value of a variable by one, that is :

$X:=X+1$

Prolog requires an extra argument to receive the resultant value, as follows.

    add1(X, Y) :- Y is X+1.

This is because logical variables in Prolog can be bound only once.

In X:=X+1, the X on the left and that on the right are evaluated at different times. This is an illustration of how conventional programming languages employ the "time" concept. If a language could incorporate both Prolog capabilities and the "time" concept, it could perform various types of operations that are not easily described in Prolog, while retaining the desirable Prolog characteristics listed above. Tokio was developed for this purpose.

The following sections provide details on Tokio. Specifically, Section 2 introduces the background required for programming in Tokio, Section 3 contains simple examples, Section 4 describes the position of Tokio, and Section 5 discuss the future of Tokio.

## 2. WHAT IS Tokio?

### 2.1. Tokio time

Tokio is based on Local Interval Temporal Logic (ITL) (Moszkowski 1983). In this chapter, some of the temporal operators found in ITL are introduced. Time in Tokio has discrete attributes. Time is represented by an integer (see Fig. 2.1). The integer is called 'time value'.

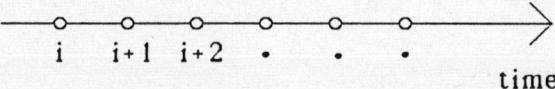

Fig. 2.1 Tokio time

The period between two time values is called an interval. An interval is determined by a pair of integers (I.beg, I.fin). The condition:

    I.beg <= I.fin

must always be true (see Fig. 2.2).

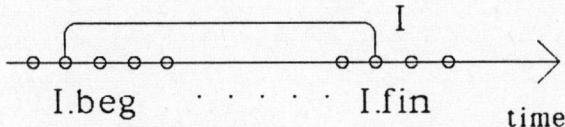

Fig. 2.2 Interval

### 2.2. Time-Related Execution Control

Implementation of the time concept in Prolog requires temporal operators that will determine when a Prolog goal is executed in the

Tokio time. An interval is used to specify "when in the Tokio time." For example, "execute the goal in interval I" may be specified. A Tokio program that includes no temporal operators is executed at the beginning of the interval. For example, if the following clause is given:

    P :- Q,R.

Here, goals Q and R are executed at the beginning (I.beg) of the same interval (I) as shown in Figure 2.3.

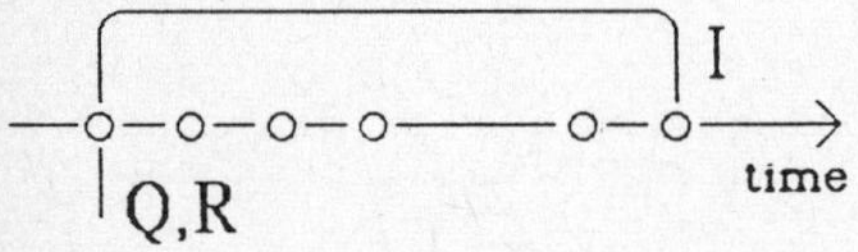

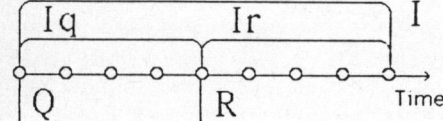

Fig. 2.3 When no temporal operators are used

## &&

We introduce here the so-called chop operator which specifies the sequence of execution of two goals. The chop operator is indicated by the symbol "&&"*.

    P :- Q && R.

The chop operator divides interval Ip, in which P is executed, into two shorter intervals: Iq, in which Q is executed, and Ir, in which R is executed (see Fig. 2.4).

Fig. 2.4 Chop operator

## @

The symbol "@" represents the "next" operator which specifies execution in the next interval. The next interval is Inext (I.beg+1, I.fin) that immediately follows the current interval I (I.beg, I.fin). This symbol is used in the following format:

    P :- @Q.

---

* ";" is usually used to indicate chop (Moszkowski 1983), but to avoid confusion with Prolog's "or" operators, here we use "&&" instead of ";".

Since goal Q does not have temporal operators, goal Q is executed at the next time (the beginning of Inext) immediately following the time of P execution (see Fig. 2.5).

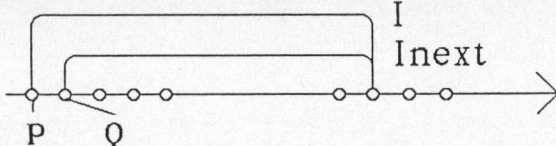

Fig. 2.5 Next operator

#

The symbol "#" represents the "always" operator which indicates that the specified goal is to be executed at all time values in the given interval. For example:

    P :- #Q.

This executes goal Q at all time values in the interval in which P is executed (see Fig. 2.6).

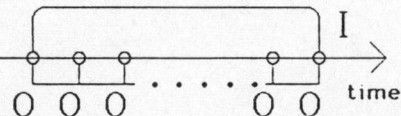

Fig. 2.6 "Always: operator

<>

The symbol "<>" represents the "sometime" operator which indicates that the specified goal is to be executed at least one time value in the given interval. For example:

    P :- <>Q.

This executes goal Q at some time value in the interval in which P is executed (see Fig. 2.7).

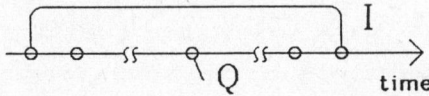

Fig. 2.7 "sometime" operator

keep

The "keep" operator indicates that the specified goal is to be executed at all time values except the final in the given interval. For example:

    P :- keep(Q).

The goal Q does not execute at Ip.fin (see Fig. 2.8).

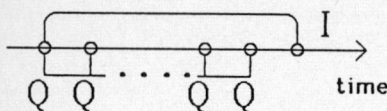

Fig. 2.8 "keep" operator

### fin

The "fin" operator indicates that the specified goal is to be executed at the final time value in the given interval. For example:

    P :- fin(Q).

The goal Q is executed at the final time value (Ip.fin) of interval Ip in which P is executed (see Fig. 2.9).

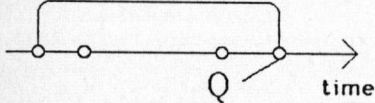

Fig. 2.9 "fin" operator

### 2.3. Variable Evaluation

A Tokio variable may have a different value for each time. In other words, a Tokio variable is a sequence of logical variables along the time axis. Usually, a unification of two Tokio variables means that the all values in the sequence are unified.

However we need another kind of unification which makes it possible to process the values of a Tokio variable at specific times. We introduce some predicates for that purpose.

### =

Symbol "=" is used to unify the current values of two Tokio variables. For example:

X = Y.

This fetches the current values from Tokio variables X and Y, and unifies two current values (see Fig. 2.10).

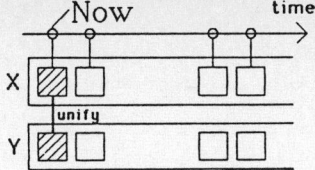

Fig. 2.10 Unification at "now"

<-

The symbol "<-" is used to unify the current value (the value at the first time value (I.beg) of the current interval I) with the value at the final time value (I.fin) of the interval (see Fig. 2.11).

X <- Y.

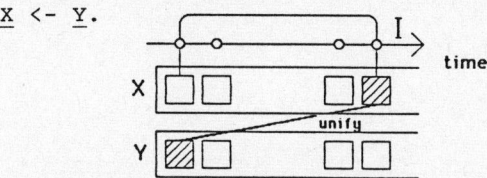

Fig. 2.11 Temporal assignment (<-)

@

Symbol "@", representing the "next" function*, can be prefixed to a Tokio variable to generate a sequence of logical variables, starting with the variable's value at the next time value. In a Tokio program, the "next" function is not allowed in a argument of predicate. This function is allowed only in the "=" predicate. This restriction precludes circularly structured temporal variables. The use of "@" with "=" enables the unification of current time and next time (see Fig. 2.12).

@X = Y.

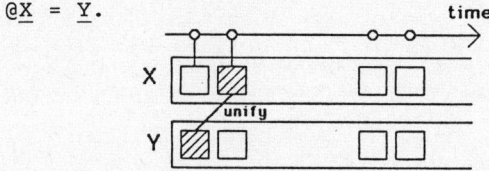

Fig. 2.12 Unification of "now" and "next"

---

* This next function should be distinguished from the next operator, even though we use the same symbol. The next operator is prefixed to a predicate, while the next function is prefixed to a variable.

## 2.4. Interval Determination

Interval I begins with integer I.beg and ends with I.fin. The I.fin value is obtained non-determinately during execution. Tokio executes the given goal by assuming that I.beg is the current time. To specify the interval, there are several operators in Tokio.

### length

Predicate "length" defines the length of the interval. Length(N) causes the I.fin value to be I.beg + N.

### empty

Predicate "empty" is equivalent to length(0).

### notEmpty

This means interval is not empty, i.e. there must be a next time value.

If there are none of these predicates, the end of interval (I.fin) can be indicated as I.beg + N, where N is 0 or a positive integer, and is found non-determinately. In other words, the value of N depends on the results of the backtrack operation.

In Prolog, Non-determinate operation is defined to find solutions in a manner dependent on the order in which clauses appear. This ordering has no declarative meaning, although it significantly affects program execution. This also applies to the length determination made by Tokio. That is, the length can be logically determined in any order but, in terms of Tokio program execution, the order is very significant.

An interpreter is used according to the following algorithm:

1) If "length" is provided, the length is determined by that.

2) If "length" is not provided, the length is determined in the order of 0, 1, 2, 3, ...N. The value of N here is limited by "length" of the parent interval. The interval of P && Q is called the parent interval relation to the interval of P or Q alone.

3) For practical reason, we don't allow length 0 in two cases. The one case is the whole interval. The other is the former interval of chop. If there are no such restrictions, many predicates are evaluated in an empty interval.

## 3. SIMPLE EXAMPLE

Figure 3.1 is an example of simple programs written in Tokio. The operation of the programs should be clear from the explanation given in Chapter 2. The Prolog operator "t" is a Tokio interpreter.

```
% cprolog
C-Prolog version 1.5
| ?- t length(2),
    (write(0) && write(1)).
t0:0
t1:1
t2:
yes
| ?- t length(2),
    (write(0) && write(1))
    && fail.
t0:0
t1:1
t2:
t1:
t2:1
no
| ?- t length(2), @write(0)
    && length(2), #write(1).
t0:
t1:0
t2:1
t3:1
t4:1
yes
| ?- t length(2), <>write(0).
t0:
t1:0
t2:
yes
| ?- t length(2), <>write(0)
    && fail.
t0:
t1:0
t2:
t1:
t2:0
no
| ?- t length(2),keep(write(0
))
    && length(3),#write(1).
t0:0
t1:0
t2:1
t3:1
t4:1
t5:1
yes
| ?- t length(2),fin(write(0)
).
t0:
t1:
t2:0
yes

| ?- t length(3),X=1,@X=X+1,
    #write(X).
t0:1
t1:2
t2:_447
t3:_540
X = $t(1,$t(2,
        $t(_447,$t(_540,_536)
)))
yes
| ?- t length(3),
    X=1,X<-X+1,#write(X).
t0:1
t1:_500
t2:_686
t3:2
X = $t(1,$t(_500,
    $t(_686,$t(2,_875))))
yes
| ?- [user].
| add1(X):-X<-X+1.
| user consulted 92 bytes
yes
| ?- t length(2),X=1,
    add1(X),#write(X).
t0:1
t1:_520
t2:2
X = $t(1,$t(_520,$t(2,_709)))

yes
| ?- [user].
| counter(X) :- #(@X=X+1).
| user consulted 108 bytes
yes
| ?- t length(5),X=1,
counter(X),#write(X).
t0:1
t1:2
t2:3
t3:4
t4:5
t5:6
X = $t(1,$t(2,$t(3,
    $t(4,$t(5,$t(6,
    $t(7,_1580)))))))

yes
| ?-
[ Prolog execution halted ]
%
script done
```

Fig. 3.1 Simple program example

The interpreter used here is a reduced version. The full set of Tokio functions includes if-then-else structure, static variables, more functions and debugging facilities. "t0", "t1" and so on are current time information output by the debugger used in Tokio.

## 4. WHERE IS Tokio?

### 4.1. Comparison with Prolog

In Prolog, a sophisticated program can be written by using recursive calls instead of repeat-fail loops, but this method would require another variable for each call. For examples:

```
p(X) :- q(X, X1), p(X1).
```

Variable X1 is generated each time a recursive call is made. In Tokio, their type of operation can be stated simply by advancing the timer as follows.

```
p(X) :- q(X) && p(X).
```

Thus, Tokio does not require any extra variable when looping.

This characteristic of Tokio, in which recursive calls require no extra variables, makes it possible to use abstract statments like "while" as shown below.

```
while P do Q :- if P then ( Q && while P do Q) else empty.
```

In Prolog, this kind of abstract description is prohibited because recursive calls are meaningless if the variable included in head P is identical to that in body P.

### 4.2. Comparison with concurrent Prolog

In a strongly synchronized stream parallel mode, Tokio descriptions are superior to other concurrent Prolog descriptions. Suppose that the following program is written in concurrent Prolog: (Shapiro 1983)

```
?- producer(A),consumer(A?).
consumer([A|A1]) :- work(A) | consumer(A1?).
```

In Tokio, this operation can be written as follows:

```
?- #producer(A), #work(A).
```

where "work" use the current value of A.

Tokio and concurrent Prolog are identical in that they both use shared variables for inter-process communication. Tokio, however, does not require read-only symbols or list structures for stream expression.

Concurrent Prolog also uses variables for inter-process synchronization. that is:

    p(A), q(A?)

This Prolog description can be indicated in Tokio as follows:

    p(A) && q(A)

Conversely, if the following Tokio description is to be written Prolog:

    p && q

then an extra variable will be required for synchronization.

## 5.  THE FUTURE OF Tokio

We are developing a high-speed Tokio processor. It will facilitate an integrated design support system (Fujita 1984) in which the hardware description in Tokio will be verified and compiled up to the actual hardware.

In addition, by utilizing the capabilities acquired through the transition of time, logical expressions representing possible world semantics will be directly executed in Tokio.

REFERENCES

[1]  M. Fujita "Specifying Hardware in Temporal Logic & Efficient Synthesis of State Diagram Using Prolog", Int. Conf. of Fifth Generation Computer System 1984, Tokyo, November 1984.

[2]  B. Moszkowski, "A Temporal Logic for Multi Level Reasoning about Hardware", IEEE Computer Magazine, February 1985.

[3]  B. Moszkowski, "Executing Temporal Logic Programs", Technical Report No. 55 University of Cambridge, Computer Laboratory 1984.

[4]  E. Shapiro, "A subset of Concurrent Prolog and its Interpreter", TR-003, ICOT 1983.

IMPLEMENTATION OF TEMPORAL LOGIC PROGRAMMING
LANGUAGE Tokio

S. Kono, T. Aoyagi, M. Fujita*, H.Tanaka

Department of Electronic Engineering, University of Tokyo
* Currently assigned to Fujitsu laboratories

ABSTRACT

The temporal logic programming language, "Tokio" can be executed by a resolution of Interval Temporal Logic. The resolution consists of three parts, which are: the unification of the temporal variable, reduction including temporal operator, and interval control. The implementation of Tokio includes automatic interval length determination and stream-like temporal variable representation. At the end of this report, an abbreviated version of a Tokio interpreter written in Prolog will be shown.

## 1. TEMPORAL LOGIC PROGRAMMING LANGUAGE Tokio

Tokio is a concurrent logic programming language designed for hardware description, based on first order linear time temporal logic (LTTL) (Wolper 1981) and first order local interval time temporal logic (ITL) (Moszkowski 1983). Since ITL fully embraces first-order predicate logic, Tokio includes the capabilities of Prolog.

When compared to Prolog's unification and reduction processing, Tokio processing consists of the following three elements:

-- Unification of temporal logic variables that possess different values at different times.

-- Ordinary reduction and future reduction

-- Division of time intervals

The following chapters summarizes ITL used as an extension of LTTL, and discuss the methods of implementing the above three elements.

## 2. LOGIC OF Tokio

Tokio executes Local ITL on the basis of LTTL. This chapter describes ITL and Tokio logic. In non local ITL, the value of a variable can be determined for time intervals. On the other hand in the Local ITL the value of a variable can be determined for time axis.

Local indicates that the value of variables is only determined at the beginning of an interval, and does not depend on the final time of the interval. In this sense, LTTL and local ITL are equivalent. But ordering descriptions is easier in ITL than in LTTL because times are treated as intervals. The use of LTTL is also convenient, if it includes an automatic synthesis system and a verification system for logical circuits (Fujita 1983). The language to be proposed, therefore, must permit ITL descriptions by expanding LTTL's capabilities.

In Tokio, the LTTL operator @ (next) is a basic temporal operator. @p means that p is true at the next time, that is LTTL has a discrete time concept, as does Tokio. In ITL's view, @p creates a new interval and p is true in this interval. The other important operator is "&&" chop of ITL. p && q means that p is true in some interval and q is true in the succeeding interval.

To execute chop by a next operator, Tokio uses two variables. One is for the fin time of time interval, and the other for the indicator of interval terminating. Tokio propositions are generally determined for time axis, and variable values are associated with the interval. For an atomic predicate, except for the few temporal operators, the truth value of the predicate is dependent only on the time. Previous "@" operator sets the later variable to "not empty". That is, there must be a next time. The "next" operator of this type is called a "strong next". There is a "weak next" (wnext), which does not set the variable of interval terminating. In the weak next, if there is no next time that is the end of the interval, the whole formulae is true.

The Tokio program is a kind of Horn clause. The primitive temporal operators such as next or chop are not allowed in head of the Horn clause. This is a useful subset of first order theory. Using these Horn clauses, the other LTTL operators are defined easily. For example, using weak next the operator "#", "always" is defined as follows. This operator corresponds to the square of LTTL.

    #P :- P,wnext(#P).

The syntax of the Horn clause is that of C-Prolog (Pereira 1984) In the following sections we discuss the unification and reduction of Horn clauses of ITL.

## 3. UNIFICATIONS FOR TEMPORAL VARIABLES

For a first-order predicate, the truth value is always determined from the meaning of its argument for all times. Accordingly, unification in Tokio is executed at all times. Operator "=" is only used to fetch the current value of a variable. The "@" (next) function is used to fetch a future variable value*. To avoid a circularly structured

---
* This next function should be distinguished from the next operator, even though we use the same symbol. The next operator is prefixed to a predicate, while the next function is prefixed to a variable.

temporal variable, the "@" function is only allowed in the expression "=". In the leading discussion, there are two kinds of unification in Tokio. One is unification in the head of a Horn clause, which we call a full time unification. The other is a unification in a "=" predicate, and we call this a one time unification.

In principle, a temporal logical variable has values for all time (may be infinite). Specific finite values are only referenced, however. In Tokio, the value of a variable is generated incrementally according to time advance. When the value of some time is generated, that variables is called differentiate. In a full time unification, the unification for non differentiated variable is a simple assignment for it. The differentiated variable is represented by the following list.

```
$t—$t—$t—$t—$t—5
 |   |   |   |   |
 0   1   2   3   4
```

Fig 3.1 temporal variable structure

The leaves of 0-4 means the value at times 0-4. The leaf of 5 represents non differentiated parts. $t is a tag or functor for differentiated variables.

examples
    eq(X,X).
    ?-@A = 1,@ @B = 2, @ @ @(eq(A,B)).

This results in the temporal logic variable structures shown below. Underscored number represents uninstanciated variable.

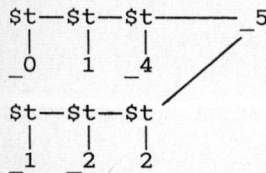

Fig 3.2 temporal variable structure

In the Prolog interpreter of Tokio, a variable is expressed by the $t(Now,Next) structures by using Prolog functors. unfiyAll specifies unification at all times. unifyNow is the predicate used for obtaining the current portion of the variable. Similarly, unifyNext obtains the future portion. Both unifyNow and unifyNext generate a new structure if the specified structure is unified with a differentiated variable. Specifically, repetition by functor and arg generates copies of the structure. During the actual, more detailed implementation stage, such copy generation is achieved by structure sharing. This method, however, does not improve storage efficiency, because of its multiple environments. Unification at the current time only, represented by "=", is enabled by unifyNow.

Note how unification is done for structures that are static in terms of time, and variables vary according to time. By using this method, the execution speed is maximized when variables are not differentiated. The other characteristic of this method is that Tokio can be implemented in a form similar to Prolog. But treatment of the constants on an interval is not so efficient in this implementation. This method is effective because structures do not usually exist at the clause head in actual Tokio programming in our experience.

## 4. FUTURE REDUCTION

In Tokio, reduction is done in two directions: future and current axis. Reduction in the current direction is identical to reduction in Prolog. Reduction in the future direction occurs when a new interval is generated by "@" (next) or "&&" (chop). Tokio executes these two types of reductions in the order of time values. In other words, a reduction generated by "next" is performed after all current reductions are completed. This necessitates the preparation of a queue, called "next quee", which consists of the literals to be reduced. In the simplest implementation, the "next queue" is organized as a FIFO queue.

The next queue contains literals with assigned variable for future times, that have been created by unifyNext. The next queue will be closed with backtracking in the current axis direction. A backtrack may be performed beyond the current time, which is called "backtrack to the past". "Cut" may be considered when backtracking in Tokio. For a backtrack in the current axis direction, the cutting feature can be supplied in the same way as in Prolog. Implication and negation without temporal operators are executed by cutting, although another mechanism is required for negation related to time intervals. The five primary negation operations related to intervals are listed below.

```
        empty       :- wnext(false).
        notEmpty    :- not(empty).
        halt(P)     :- #(if P then empty else notEmpty).
        fin(P)      :- #(if empty then p).
        keep(P)     :- #(if notEmpty then p).
```

These operations are all related to interval determination. The definitions of empty and notEmpty using the weak next definition are somewhat technical, and are not suited for implementation. The end of an interval is directly used to determine whether to execute "fin" or "keep". In other words, the execution of "fin" or "keep" cannot start until completion of the interval has been verified. Therefore, both a fin queue and a keep queue are required.

The end of an interval is signified by the execution of either an "empty" or a "notEmpty". Execution of theses predicates is done by setting a flag that indicates interval completion. The formula fails, of course, if a conflict is caused by the flag. The flag must be reset by a backtrack. If neither "empty" nor "notEmpty" is executed, "empty" flag is set currently. In this case, the interval completes in this time. If backtrack is reached at this point, the flag is reset and the length of the interval is extended. In this way, the length of an interval is adjusted to gradually increase, starting from 1.

In the Tokio interpreter, <u>t reduce</u> generates <u>i reduce</u> for each time. The time precedes until only true remains or exceeds the end of the interval. At <u>i reduce</u>, <u>reduce</u> operation is done in the same way as in Prolog, which reduces the literals with the exception of the temporal operators. Then, <u>force finite</u> is used to cut unlimited intervals. Depending on the result of the cutting operation, either "fin" or "keep" is executed by <u>exec fin keep</u>. The queue structure represented by Q is always retained by <u>reduce</u>. Q contains queues for "fin", "keep", and "next", and a flag indicating "empty". It also retains the current time and "fin" time.

## 5. DIVIDING INTERVALS

The chop operator is used to divide an interval. Specifically, it divides interval p&&q into two shorter intervals during which p and q will be executed respectively. These shorter intervals are executed independently of each other by i reduce. "fin" and "keep" are executed during each interval. Each interval is identified by its interval variables, i.e., the flag indicating the end of interval and fin_time indicating the end time. This means that each interval can be expressed using the following structures:

$i(p,q,fin_time)

where p is executed during that interval and q will be executed during the following interval. q is executed at "fin" of p, which differs from fin(q).

## 6. THE INTERPRETER

The Tokio interpreter written in Prolog shown here can execute basic Tokio programs. The execution speed is approximately 40 times slower than that of the original Prolog. The compiler of Tokio to Prolog has also been written, which operates 5 times faster than the interpreter. At present, an interpreter and a compiler written in the C language, are being developed. The interpreter will be the almost as fast as C-Prolog, and the compiler will be 5-10 times faster.

## 7. DIFFERENCE FROM TEMPURA

Tempura is a Lisp-like language based on ITL, and is written in Lisp. When compared to Tokio, the method of executing Tempura is simpler. However Tokio can handle a wider range of ITL executions than Tempura. The following restrictions apply to Tempura:

- Tempura programs are written in Lambda format, including temporal operators. It has no unfications.

- Tempura does not support the backtrack feature.

- Two or more consecutive "next" operations, such as @ @ A, are not allowed.

- Cross-references, such as exchange of two variables' values, are not allowed.

Tempura, however, is provided with more intrinsic functions than Tokio. Tempura has better storage efficiency than Tokio written in Prolog, mainly because it does not perform backtracking.

## 8. CONCLUSION

The Tokio language has been designed to execute ITL on the basis of LTTL. It supports both mathematical fundamentals and actual simulations for hardware description. Several students in our university are using Tokio. Programs written in Tokio include the Unify Processor which is a prototype of PIE, Parallel Inference Engine, and systolic array for matrix multiplication and pipeline merge sorter. We are now planning to develop a system based on Tokio to verify and synthesis logical circuits that include functional relationship.

## REFERENCES

[1] M. Fujita, "Temporal Logic Based Hardware Description and Its Verification with Prolog", New Generation Computing, Vol. 1, No. 2, pp. 195-203 1983.

[2] B. Moszkowski, "Reasoning about Digital Circuits", Report No. STAN-CS-83-970, Department of Computer Science, Stanford University, July 1983.

[3] F. Pereira, "C-Prolog Users Manual Version 1.5" EdCAD, Edinburgh Univ. 1984.

[4] E. Shapiro, "A subset of Concurrent Prolog and its Interpreter", TR-003, ICOT 1983.

[5] K. Ueda, "Guarded Horn Clauses", TR-103, ICOT, 1985

[6] D. Warren, "AN ABSTRACT RPOLOG INSTRUCTION SET", Technical Note 309, SRI International, October 1983.

[7] P. Wolper, "Temporal logic Can Be More Expressive", 22nd Annual Symposium on Foundation of Computer Science, October 1981.

```
/* Tokio interpreter Reduced Version */

t(A):-t_reduce(A,0,Fin).      % entry

/* temporal reducer
        t_reduce(Formula,Now,Fin) */

t_reduce(true,Now,Fin):-integer(Fin),Now>Fin,!.
t_reduce(Formula,Now,Fin):-
        nl,write((t)),write(Now),write(':'),
```

```
        i_reduce(Formula,Next,Now,Fin,_),
        NextT is Now+1,
        t_reduce(Next,NextT,Fin).

/* interval reducer
        i_reduce(Formula,Next,Now,Fin,OuterFin)
        reduce now formula and
        execute either
        keepQueue or finQueue */

i_reduce(Formula,Next1,Now,Fin,OuterFin):-
        qcl(Next,EmptyFlag,Q1,Q2),
        reduce(Formula,Q1,Now,Fin),
        force_finite(EmptyFlag,Now,Fin,OuterFin),
        exec_fin_keep(Next,Next1,Q1,Q2,Now,Fin).

/* interval terminate works */

exec_fin_keep(Next,true,Q1,Q2,Now,Fin):-
        Now==Fin,!, get_fin(F,Q1),
        reduce(F,Q2,Fin,Fin).
exec_fin_keep(Next,Next,Q1,Q2,Now,Fin):-
        get_keep(K,Q1),
        reduce(K,Q2,Now,Fin).

/* cut off infinite interval
        force_finite(EmptyFlag,Now,Fin) */

force_finite(free,Now,Fin,OuterFin):-
        var(Fin),Fin is Now+1,
        (nonvar(OuterFin),OuterFin=Fin,! ; true).
force_finite(_,Now,Fin,OuterFin).

/* reducer
        reduce(F,Q,Now,Fin) */

reduce((A,B),Q,Now,Fin):-qap(Qa,Qb,Q),!,
        reduce(A,Qa,Now,Fin),
        reduce(B,Qb,Now,Fin).
reduce(A,Q,Now,Fin):-systemp(A),!,
        exec(A,Q,Now,Fin). % system predicate
reduce(A,Q,Now,Fin):-
        t_clause(A,B),reduce(B,Q,Now,Fin).

t_clause(A,B):-
        functor(A,Head,N),functor(AA,Head,N),
        clause(AA,B),
        unify_all(A,AA).

/* system predicate exec(Formula,Q,Now,Fin) */

exec(true,Q,_,_):- !,nonq(Q).
exec(length(N),Q,Now,Fin):- !,
        nonq(Q),Fin is Now+N.
```

```
exec(empty,Q,Now,Fin) :- nonq(Q),!,Now=Fin.
exec(notEmpty,Q,Now,Fin) :- !,
        enq_nonEmpty(true,Q).
exec(halt(F),Q,Now,Fin):-reduce(F,Q,Now,Fin),
        !,Now=Fin.
exec(halt(F),Q,Now,Fin):- unifyNext(F,Fn),
        enq_nonEmpty(halt(Fn),Q).
exec(#F,Q,Now,Fin):-qap(Q1,Q2,Q),enq_nxt(#Fn,Q1),
        unifyNext(F,Fn),!,
        reduce(F,Q2,Now,Fin).
exec(@F,Q,Now,Fin):-!,              % strong next
        enq_nonEmpty(Fn,Q),
        unifyNext(F,Fn).
exec(wnext(F),Q,Now,Fin):-          % weak next
        enq_nxt(Fn,Q),
        unifyNext(F,Fn),!.
exec(fin(F),Q,Now,Fin):-!,(
        (Now==Fin,!,reduce(F,Q,Now,Fin)) ;
        qap(Q1,Q2,Q),enq_fin(F,Q1),
        unifyNext(F,Fnn),enq_nxt(fin(Fnn),Q2)).
exec(keep(F),Q,Now,Fin):-!,
        qap(Q1,Q2,Q),enq_nfin(F,Q1),
        unifyNext(F,Fnn),enq_nxt(keep(Fnn),Q2).
exec((A && B),Q,Now,Fin):-!,
        sub_exec(A,B,Q,Now,Fin,SubFin).
exec($int(A,B,SubFin),Q,Now,Fin):-!,
        sub_exec(A,B,Q,Now,Fin,SubFin).
exec(A=B,Q,Now,Fin):- qap(Q1,Q2,Q),!,
        eval(A,Va,Q1,Now,Fin),
        eval(B,Vb,Q2,Now,Fin),
        unifyNow(Va,V),
        unifyNow(Vb,V).
exec(A<--B,Q,Now,Fin):-!,eval(B,Vb,Q,Now,Fin),
        unifyNow(Vb,A1),unify_all(A,A1).
exec(S,Q,Now,Fin):-unifyNow(S,SN),!,
        SN,nonq(Q).

/*      subinterval execute
        sub_exec(Former,Later,Q,Now,Fin,SubFin) */

sub_exec(F,L,Q,Now,Fin,SubFin):-
        i_reduce(F,Fnext,Now,SubFin,Fin),
        sub_exec_later(L,Fnext,Q,Now,Fin,SubFin).

sub_exec_later(L,Next,Q,Now,Fin,SubFin):-
        Now==SubFin,!,
        reduce(L,Q,Now,Fin).
sub_exec_later(L,Next,Q,Now,Fin,SubFin):-
        unifyNext(L,Ln),
        enq_finNext(L,$int(Next,Ln,SubFin),Q).


/*      function evaluate
        eval(Formula,Value,Queue,Now,Fin) */
```

```
eval(Atom,Atom,Q,Now,Fin):- (atomic(Atom) ; var(Atom)
        ; functor(Atom,$t,2)),
        nonq(Q),!.
eval(@Var,Next,Q,Now,Fin):-!,
        eval(Var,NowValue,Q,Now,Fin),
        unifyNext(NowValue,Next).
eval(A+B,V,Q,Now,Fin):-!, qap(Q1,Q2,Q),
        eval(A,Va,Q1,Now,Fin),
        eval(B,Vb,Q2,Now,Fin),
        unifyNow(Va,Vna),unifyNow(Vb,Vnb),
        V is Vna+Vnb.
eval(S,S,Q,_,_) :- nonq(Q).

/* queue structures
            1         2         3         4
q(Next-Next,Fin-Fin,Keep-Keep,EmptyFlag)
*/

qcl(Next,EmptyFlag,
    q(Next-Next1,Fin0-true,Keep0-true,EmptyFlag),
    q(Next1-true,Fin1-true,Keep1-true,EmptyFlag)).

qap(q(Next2-Next1,Fin2-Fin1,Keep2-Keep1,EmptyFlag),
    q(Next1-Next ,Fin1-Fin ,Keep1-Keep ,EmptyFlag),
    q(Next2-Next ,Fin2-Fin ,Keep2-Keep ,EmptyFlag)).

nonq(q(Next-Next,Fin-Fin,Keep-Keep,EmptyFlag)).

enq_nxt(N,                          % weak next
    q((N,Next)-Next,Fin-Fin,Keep-Keep,EmptyFlag)).
enq_nonEmpty(N,                     % strong next
    q((N,Next)-Next,Fin-Fin,Keep-Keep,nonEmpty)).
enq_fin(F,
    q(Next-Next,(F,Fin)-Fin,Keep-Keep,EmptyFlag)).
enq_nfin(K,
    q(Next-Next,Fin-Fin,(K,Keep)-Keep,EmptyFlag)).
enq_finNext(F,N,
    q((N,Next)-Next,(F,Fin)-Fin,Keep-Keep,nonEmpty)).

get_fin(F,Q):-arg(2,Q,F-_).
get_keep(K,Q):-arg(3,Q,K-_).
get_nonEmpty(EmptyFlag,Q):-arg(4,Q,EmptyFlag).

nonEmpty(Q,Now,Fin):-Now==Fin,!, fail.
nonEmpty(Q,Now,Fin):-get_nonEmpty(nonEmpty,Q).

/* unifiers */

unify_all(G,D):-
        (var(G) ; var(D)),!,G=D.
unify_all(F1,D):-
        functor(F1,$t,2),!,
        unify_flt(F1,D).
unify_all(D,F1):-functor(F1,$t,2),!,
```

```
        unify_flt(Fl,D).
unify_all(Sa,Sb):-
        functor(Sa,H,N),functor(Sb,H,N),
        unify_arg(N,N,Sa,Sb).

unify_arg(0,N,_,_):-!.
unify_arg(M,N,Sa,Sb):-
        arg(M,Sa,Aa),arg(M,Sb,Ab),
        unify_all(Aa,Ab),M1 is M-1,!,
        unify_arg(M1,N,Sa,Sb).

unify_flt($t(Now,Nxt),$t(Now,Nxt1)) :-!,
        unify_all(Nxt,Nxt1).
unify_flt($t(Now,Nxt),S) :-
        unifyNow(S,Now),
        unifyNext(S,Nxt1),
        unify_all(Nxt,Nxt1).

unifyNow(X,X1):-atomic(X),!,X=X1.
unifyNow($t(Now,_),Now1):-!,Now=Now1.
unifyNow(S,Sn):-
        functor(S,H,N),functor(Sn,H,N),
        unifyNowArg(N,N,S,Sn).

unifyNowArg(0,_,_,_).
unifyNowArg(M,N,Sa,Sb):-
        arg(M,Sa,Aa),arg(M,Sb,Ab),
        unifyNow(Aa,Ab),M1 is M-1,!,
        unifyNowArg(M1,N,Sa,Sb).

unifyNext(X,X):-atomic(X),!.
unifyNext($t(_,Next),Next1):-!,Next=Next1.
unifyNext(S,Sn):-
        functor(S,H,N),functor(Sn,H,N),
        unifyNextArg(N,N,S,Sn).

unifyNextArg(0,_,_,_).
unifyNextArg(M,N,Sa,Sb):-
        arg(M,Sa,Aa),arg(M,Sb,Ab),
        unifyNext(Aa,Ab),M1 is M-1,!,
        unifyNextArg(M1,N,Sa,Sb).

/* predefined utilities */

<>(F)           :- true && F.
A gets B        :- keep(B = @A).
% stable(A)     :- A gets A.
stable(A)       :- keep(A = @A).
% B <- A        :- stable(C),A=C,fin(B=C).
B <- A          :- C<--A,fin(B=C).
skip            :- length(1).
```

# Heuristic Prolog: Logic Program Execution by Heuristic Search

K. Nakamura

School of Science and Engineering, Tokyo Denki University,
Hatoyama-machi, Saitama-ken, 350-03 Japan.

**ABSTRACT** This paper presents a language and its system called Heuristic Prolog. The language is an extension of the Edinburgh version Prolog for execution of logic programs by heuristic (best-first) search in addition to depth-first search. The user can specify both the nodes in the search tree to be executed concurrently and priority of the nodes by means of a special built-in predicate. Some example programs in Heuristic Prolog are included to show the capability of the language.

## 1. INTRODUCTION

Most Prolog systems employ depth-first search to execute the programs. This search strategy is comparatively simple to implement, and the users of the system can directly specify the control of program execution by the use of the cut operator and by the order of clauses and sub-goals in the program. It is generally accepted, however, that employment of more flexible search strategy than depth-first is essential to realize "true" logic programming more deeply.

The search strategy have been investigated in the field of artificial intelligence (Nilsson 1971). Heuristic search, also known as best-first search, is generally employed in problem solving to utilize knowledge of the problem for efficient search.

We extended H-Prolog system we have been developing (Nakamura 1984a) to execute programs by heuristic (best-first) search in addition to depth-first search for the purpose of investigating its application and implementation. The system and its language are called Heuristic Prolog. The user can specify the nodes in the search tree to be executed concurrently and give the nodes their priority in terms of a special built-in predicate in the program.

## 2. SPECIFICATION OF HEURISTIC SEARCH IN THE PROGRAMS

We assume that a logic program and a query are executed by SLD-resolution. The execution is represented by a search tree, in which each node corresponds to a goal list (or a sequence of goals), and the root of the tree to an query (an initial goal list). By concurrent execution we mean a serial computation for more than one goal list in turn.

Syntactically, a program in Heuristic Prolog is not different from those in Edinburgh version of Prolog (Clocksin and Mellish 1981), except that it may contains goals of the form hold(E,K).

The predicate hold is realized as a special built-in predicate. The goal hold(E,K) means that the goal list following this goal is executed concurrently.

The arguments E and K are expressions which have integer values. The value E represents the estimation of the goal list: the lower value of E represents higher priority. The value K is a bound of the number of goal lists which are executed concurrently. We intend that the value of K is used to restrict the number of concurrent goal lists in the case each of the goal lists corresponds to a method to solve the problem. If K is uninstantiated variable, the number of goal lists is unbound.

The Heuristic Prolog system has a queue of goal lists to be executed concurrently. The system computes a query and a program as follows.

(1) The query and the program are executed by depth-first search as in conventional Prolog system until a hold goal is encountered.

(2) Whenever a goal of the form hold(E,K) is encountered in the execution, the system interrupts its computation, places the goal list following this goal in the queue, and causes backtracking. If the number of the goal lists in the queue exceeds K, the goal list with the lowest priority is abandoned.

(3) After all the derived goal lists are either proved to be true or false or included in the queue, the system resumes execution of the goal list with the highest priority. If the queue is empty, the system displays that there is no (more) solution.

Fig. 1 illustrates a search tree, in which the nodes a, b, c, and d are specified to be executed concurrently. The queue contains the goal lists corresponding to nodes a, b, and c after the first cycle of the depth-first execution. Suppose that the goal list b has the

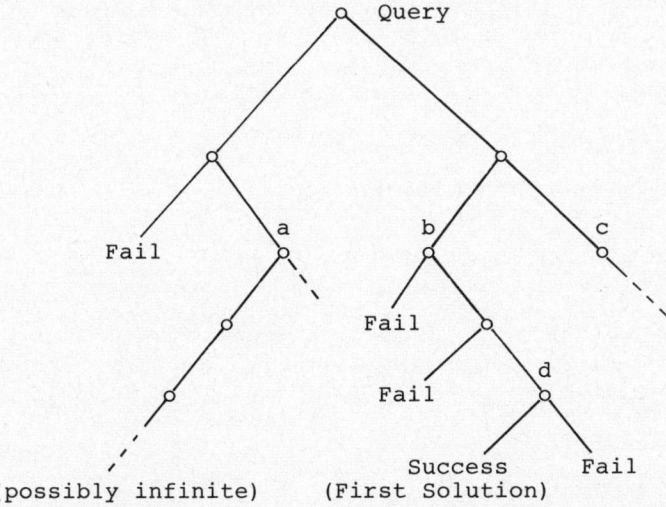

**Fig. 1**   An illustration of Concurrent Execution

lowest estimated value. Then it is executed next, and the goal list d is added to the queue. If this goal list has also the highest priority, the first solution is derived from it.

Another possible method to specify the concurrent execution in the programs is to use some meta-rules.

## 3. THE SYSTEM

In this section, we describe how the built-in predicate hold and the top level of the interpreter work.

The goal lists in the queue are sorted according to the priority of the goal lists. When a goal of the form hold(E,K) is executed, the goal lists following this goal is inserted into the queue. The predicate hold is equivalent to that defined by

        hold(E,K) :- goallist(L),
                    EV is E, KV is K,
                    qassert(EV,KV,L), !, fail.

Where goallist and qassert are supposed to be the built-in predicates such that
(1) goallist(L) returns the goal lists following this goal to L, and
(2) qassert(E,K,L) inserts the goal list L into the queue.

The place of the insertion in the queue is determined by the value of E, and the number of the goal lists in the queue is restricted to the value of K.

The top level of the Heuristic Prolog system works as if it is defined by the clauses

        interpret(Q) :- Q.
        interpret(_) :- qretract(L),interpret(L).

It is assumed that the goal list Q is executed by depth-first search, and the goal qretract(L) retracts the top goal list from the queue and returns it to L.

## 4. ESTIMATION OF GOAL LISTS BY THEIR LENGTH AND DEPTH

A generally applicable estimation of a goal list is obtained from its length and depth, i.e. the number of resolutions to derive it, because:

(1) a shorter goal list can be considered to be nearer to the solution; and
(2) the estimation by the depth can be used to prevent an infinite loop in the execution.

The depth can be counted by adding an additional variable D to every clauses and an additional argument to each predicate term as

$$p(\ldots,D) :- D1 \text{ is } D + 1, q_1(\ldots,D1),\ldots,q_n(\ldots,D1).$$

The length of the goal lists is obtained by the goals

            ...,goallist(GL),length(GL,L),...,

where length(GL,L) returns the length of the list GL to L. The concurrent execution is specified by the goal

hold(D + L,K).

This method can be generally applied to avoid infinite loop in the computation of Prolog programs.

## 5. EXAMPLE PROGRAMS IN HEURISTIC PROLOG

### 5.1 A Tree Search Problem

Problem: Given a tree in which each terminal node is attached a number, find the route from the root to the terminal node with the least number.

For example, the tree in Fig. 2 is represented by the unit clauses:

```
branch(root,a).
branch(root,b).
branch(root,c).
branch(a,d).
branch(a,e).
branch(b,f).
branch(b,g).
branch(f,h).

terminal(c,4).
terminal(d,2).
terminal(e,3).
terminal(g,-3).
terminal(h,0).
```

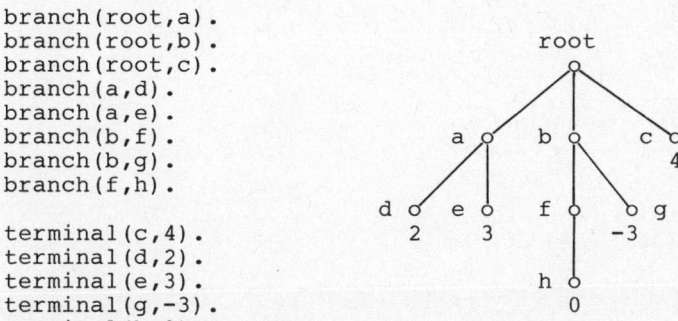

Fig. 2  The Tree Represented by the Clauses

Program:
```
search(N,[N|L]) :- branch(N,M),search(M,L).
search(N,[N]) :- terminal(N,E),!,hold(E,1).
```

For the following query, the path represented by a list of nodes is returned to the variable L.

?-search(root,L).

L = [root,b,g]

### 5.2 Search for the Shortest Route in a Road Map

Problem: Given a database representing a road map, find the shortest route between two points. The database is a set of unit clauses of the form

road(p,q,d),

which means that there is a road between two points p and q with the distance d.

A logic program and the query to find a route between p and q and the distance are:

```
route(X,Y,[X,Y],D,DX) :- road1(X,Y,D1),
        DX is D + D1.
```

```
route(X,Z,[X,R],D,DX) :- road1(X,Y,D1),
                         D2 is D + D1,
                         route(Y,Z,R,D2,DX).

road1(X,Y,D) :- road(X,Y,D).
road1(X,Y,D) :- road(Y,X,D).

?- route(p,q,R,0,DX).
```

The predicate term route(X,Y,R,D,DX) means that there is a route R (a sequence of points) between points X and Y with the distance DX. The variable D is instantiated to the distance from the starting point p to the point X.

The execution of this program and query may fall into an infinite loop in the ordinary depth-first Prolog system. In order to correct this program to find the shortest route, we add some goals and unit clauses for the heuristic search.

The following program in Heuristic Prolog uses an estimated distance between the starting point and the goal point before each time it choose a new point. The estimated value for a point Y is calculated by the predicate eval as in Fig. 3. We represent a coordinate (x,y) of a point p by the unit clauses pos(p,x,y).

Estimated Distance from Y
to the goal point: (x + y)

**Fig. 3** The Estimation of the Distance Used
in the Shortest Route Problem

Unit clauses representing a road map:

```
road(a,b,1).
road(b,c,5).
road(a,e,5).
road(a,g,4).
road(c,e,4).
road(e,f,4).
road(c,d,4).
road(f,d,5).

pos(a,0,0).
pos(b,0,-1).
pos(c,3,1).
pos(d,4,4).
pos(e,1,3).
pos(f,2,6).
pos(g,-1,2).
```

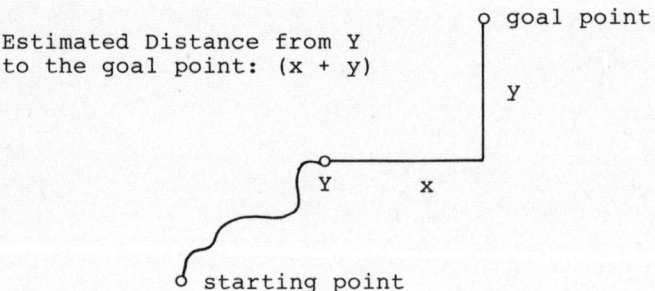

**Fig. 4** An Example Road Map

Program:
```
        route(X,Y,[X,Y],D,DX) :- road1(X,Y,D1),
            DX is D + D1.
        route(X,Z,[X|R],D,DX) :- road1(X,Y,D1),
            D2 is D + D1,
            eval(Y,Z,D2,E),hold(E,10), /* heuristic control */
            route(Y,Z,R,D2,DX).

        road1(X,Y,D) :- road(X,Y,D).
        road1(X,Y,D) :- road(Y,X,D).

        eval(Y,Z,TD,E) :-
            pos(Y,A,B),pos(Z,C,D),
            E is TD + abs(A - C) + abs(B - D).
                /* abs(x) returns the absolute value of x */
```

An example execution:
```
        ?-route(a,f,X,0,D).

        X = [a,e,f]
        D = 9
        MORE (y/<ret>) ? y

        X = [a,b,a,e,f]
        D = 11
```

## 5.3 Word Transformation by Permutation

Problem: For two words A and B, find the shortest sequence of replacement of successive two characters that transforms A into B.

Fig. 5 shows a graph representing a search for a word transformation problem. Here is the program in Heuristic Prolog.

```
        trans(X,X,[X],0).
        trans(X,Y,[X|P],D1) :- perm(X,Z),
            diff(Z,Y,1,M),hold(M,_),
            trans(Z,Y,P,D),
            D1 is D + 2.

        perm([X,X1|X2],[X1,X|X2]).
        perm([X|X1],[X|Y1]) :- perm(X1,Y1).

        diff([],_,_,0) :- !.
        diff([Z|Z1],Y,I,M) :- thpos(Z,Y,D),
            A is abs(I - D),
            I1 is I + 1,
            diff(Z1,Y,I1,A2),
            M is A2 + A.

        thpos(Z,[Z|_],1) :- !.
        thpos(Z,[_|K],X) :- thpos(Z,K,X1),X is X1 + 1.
```

The predicate term perm(X,Y) means that Y is a word obtained from X by replacement of two successive characters. The goal diff(Z,Y,1,M) returns the estimated difference between the words Z and Y to M, using the predicates <u>thpos</u> and <u>diff</u>. We can obtain the following results by this program.

```
?-trans([i,p,l,s],[l,i,s,p],X,D).

X = [[i,p,l,s],[i,l,p,s],[l,i,p,s],[l,i,s,p]]
D = 6
MORE (y/<ret>) ? y

X = [[i,p,l,s],[i,l,p,s],[i,l,s,p],[l,i,p,s]]
D = 6
```

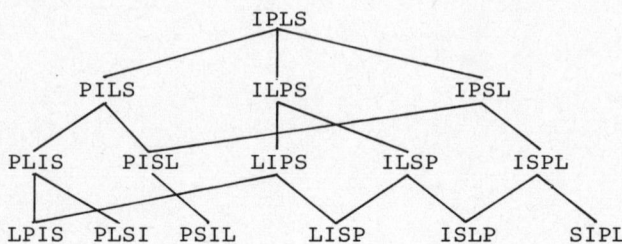

**Fig. 5** A Graph for a Word Transformation Problem
(This figure is from Shimura (1983))


## 6. IMPLEMENTATION

In order to employ the search strategy other than strict depth-first, the system requires to process multiple goal lists and/or to have multiple variable environments. There are the following two methods to represent the goal lists in the queue of Heuristic Prolog system.

(1) Copying: The queue contains the complete copies of goal lists.
(2) Structure sharing: Each goal list in the queue is represented by a set of source goal lists and their variable environments. This method is based on Boyer and Moore (1972).

We implemented the first versions of Heuristic Prolog in H-Prolog, and then we add the built-in predicate hold to the H-Prolog system written in the C language. The copying method is employed in both implementation. A little change is necessary in the top level of the interpreter of the H-Prolog system to realize Heuristic Prolog. The queue is realized by a bi-directional linear list.

An advantage of the copying method is that we can reduce the necessity of garbage collection and last call (end recursion) optimization, because the system needs to contain only the copied goal lists in the queue at the beginning of each execution cycle. On the other hand, the copying method is not efficient when the goal lists in the queue become very long.

We also built an experimental system employing structure sharing which requires no copying. In this system, a variable may have multiple values one of which is "valid" at a time. The multiple environment used in this system is discussed in (Nakamura 1984b).

## 7. CONCLUDING REMARKS

We have presented a language and its implementation for execution of logic programs by heuristic search in addition to depth-first search. It would not be difficult for most implementers of Prolog to add the built-in predicate hold to their systems and to implement this language without affecting efficiency of the systems.

The example programs are computed efficiently by the extended H-Prolog system. In general, the programs in Heuristic Prolog are simpler than the equivalent programs in conventional Prolog. It is shown that Heuristic Prolog is compact language suitable to find optimal or sub-optimal solutions by heuristic search.

**ACKNOWLEDGEMENT** The author acknowledges Isamu Shioya and Satoshi Matsuura for their assistance in the implementation of Heuristic Prolog.

## REFERENCES

Boyer RS and Moore JS (1972) The sharing of structure in theorem proving. In: Melzer B, Michie D (eds) Machine Intelligence 7, Edinburgh University Press.

Clocksin WF and Mellish CS (1981) Programming in Prolog, Springer-Verlag, p279

Nakamura K (1984a) Associative evaluation of Prolog programs. In: Campbell CA (ed) Implementations of PROLOG, Ellis Horwood.

Nakamura K (1984b) Associative concurrent evaluation of logic programs, J Logic Programming 2: 285-295

Nilson NJ (1971) Problem-Solving Methods in Artificial Intelligence, McGraw-Hill, New York, p255

Shimura M (1983) Kikai Chinow Ron (Theory of Machine Intelligence), (in Japanese) Shoukoudou Inc, Tokyo, p310

# AND-OR QUEUING IN EXTENDED CONCURRENT PROLOG[1]

Jiro Tanaka*[2], Takashi Yokomori**, Makoto Kishishita***[3]

* International Institute for Advanced Study of Social Information Science (IIAS-SIS) Fujitsu Limited, 1-17-25, Shinkamata, Ohta-ku, Tokyo 144, Japan
** IIAS-SIS, Fujitsu Limited 140 Miyamoto, Numazu-shi, Shizuoka 410-03, Japan
*** Fujitsu Social Science Laboratory, 7-5-9, Nishigotanda Shinagawa-ku, Tokyo 141, Japan

## ABSTRACT

We have modified Concurrent Prolog (CP) Interpreter (Shapiro 1983) and implemented Extended Concurrent Prolog (ECP) Interpreter (Fujitsu 1985), which has OR-parallel, set-abstraction and meta-inference facilities. In Shapiro's CP interpreter only the AND-related goals are enqueued to the scheduling queue. None of OR-related clauses is dealt with. However, our ECP interpreter has only one scheduling queue to which all the AND-related goals and all the OR-related clauses are enqueued. This scheduling method is designated "AND-OR queuing." AND-OR queuing makes it possible to handle all kinds of AND-relations and OR-relations in a uniform manner.

## 1 INTRODUCTION.

Concurrent Prolog (CP) (Shapiro 1983) is a parallel logic language which includes a commit operator and read-only annotation as language constructs. We have extended Shapiro's Concurrent Prolog (CP) Interpreter and implemented Extended Concurrent Prolog (ECP) Interpreter (Fujitsu 1985), which has OR-parallel, set-abstraction and meta-inference facilities. A "scheduling queue" is often used in implementing a parallel logic language on a sequential machine. Processes reduced in parallel are enqueued to the scheduling queue. They are dequeued from the queue and reduced one by one. In this paper, focusing on the role of the "scheduling queue," we outline the implementation method for realizing extended features, and show how one can nicely handle those features in a uniform manner.

## 2 EXTENDED CONCURRENT PROLOG.

As mentioned above, ECP is an extension of CP with OR-parallel, set-abstraction and meta-inference features. Each feature is based on the conceptual specification of Kernel Language Version 1 (KL1) (Furukawa 1984). We briefly explain these features in the following sections.

### 2.1 AND-parallelism and OR-parallelism

AND-parallelism and OR-parallelism are the basic parallel inference mechanisms of ECP. AND-parallelism is the mechanism which evaluates AND-related goals in parallel. This

---
[1] This research has been carried out as a part of Fifth Generation Computer Project.
[2] Current address: ICOT Research Center, Institute for New Generation Computer Technology Mita-kokusai-building 21F, 1-4-28, Mita, Minato-ku, Tokyo 108, Japan
[3] Current address: IIAS-SIS, Fujitsu Limited, 1-17-25, Shinkamata, Ohta-ku, Tokyo 144, Japan

function can be realized by enqueuing goals to the tail of the scheduling queue, dequeuing a goal from the head of the queue, and enqueuing the newly created goals to the tail of the queue. This AND-parallelism has already been implemented in Shapiro's Interpreter. On the other hand, OR-parallelism is the mechanism which realizes the parallel evaluation of guards, when there exists more than one potentially unifiable clause with the given goal. This OR-parallelism was not implemented in Shapiro's Interpreter. The following program is an example of exploiting OR-parallelism.

```
solve(P,Mes):- call(P) | ... .
solve(P,Mes):- find_stop(Mes) | ... .
```

When "solve" is called, the above two clauses are executed in parallel by OR-parallelism. The first clause executes "P." However, as soon as "stop" is found in "Mes" in the second clause, the second clause is committed and the first clause is aborted. This realizes the "solve" with abort.

## 2.2 Set-abstraction

Set-abstraction is a mechanism for realizing the all-solution-search feature in a parallel environment. The following two predicates have been proposed (Fujitsu 1984).

```
eager_enumerate({X|Goals}, L)
lazy_enumerate({X|Goals}, L)
```

In the above description, "Goals" is the sequence of the goals defined in a Pure Prolog world. We assume that the Pure Prolog world is defined as follows:

```
pp(( <head> <- <body> )).
```

That is, the Pure Prolog world is asserted as the set of "facts" which have a functor name "pp."

These two "enumerate" predicates solve the Goals in the Pure Prolog world and put the set of all solutions in L in stream form. The following is an example of "eager_enumerate."

```
eager_enumerate({X | grand_child(jiro,X)}, L)
```

We assume that the Pure Prolog world is defined as follows:

```
pp((grand_child(X,Z) <- child(X,Y),child(Y,Z))).
pp((child(jiro,keiko) <- true)).
pp((child(yoko,takashi) <- true)).
pp((child(jiro,yoko) <- true)).
pp((child(keiko,makoto) <- true)).
```

In this case, L is instantiated as [takashi,makoto].

The difference between "eager_enumerate" and "lazy_enumerate" is the way it instantiates the second argument. "eager_enumerate" instantiates it actively. "lazy_enumerate" instantiates it passively in accordance with the request from the stream consumer. In the following example, a solution list "L" is created in accordance with the request from "display."

```
:- lazy_enumerate({X | prime(X)}, L?),
    display(L, Mes?), keyboard(Mes).
```

## 2.3 Meta-inference

Meta-inference means to solve a given goal using knowledge defined in a user-defined world (Furukawa 1984). We set up the predicate "simulate" with the following form.

```
simulate(World, Goals, Result, Control)
```

Here, "World" is the name of a world, "Goals" is the goal sequence to be solved, "Result" is the computation result, and "Control" is the stream through which we can stop and resume the computation. We assume that knowledge of the world is given as a set of facts whose principal functors are the name of the world. That is, knowledge of the world has the following format.

```
world_name((<Head> <- <Guard> | <Body>)).
```

As an example of meta-inference, we give the "shell" example (Clark 1984) which can run the foreground and background jobs. In this example, the foreground job always checks its control information while running. The background job runs steadily without looking up its control information.

```
shell([], _).
shell([fg(G)|N],C) :-
    simulate(f_world,G,R,C)&
    remove(C, NewC)&
    shell(N?,NewC).
shell([bg(G)|N],C) :-
    simulate(b_world,G,R,_),
    shell(N?,C).

:- shell([bg(primes),fg(primes)],C), control(C).
```

In this example, the "primes" programs to compute the infinite sequence of prime numbers runs both foreground and background jobs. Execution of the foreground job can be controlled by "C."

## 3 THE IMPLEMENTATION OF ECP

We have explained the extended features of ECP in the previous section. However, Shapiro's interpreter is not enough to realize these features. We need to implement AND-relations and OR-relations well using a scheduling queue.

In Shapiro's interpreter, a scheduling queue only contains AND-related goals. It is created for each OR-relation. Therefore, many local scheduling queues are created at program execution time. After extensive consideration, we have decided to make scheduling queues global. In our approach, only one global scheduling queue is created. All AND-related and OR-related goals are contained in one scheduling queue. We can imagine that the AND-OR tree created at program execution time is encapsulated in this scheduling queue.

We have named this scheduling method "AND-OR Queuing." Using this method, it becomes possible to handle all kinds of AND-relations and OR-relations in a consistent way. In this section, we describe the queuing method for each feature.

## 3.1 AND-parallelism and OR-parallelism

As we mentioned before, AND-parallelism has already been satisfied by enqueuing AND-related goals in the scheduling queue. To deal with OR-parallelism, we have decided to enqueue OR-relations sandwiched in between two kinds of markers.

For example, assume that the head of the scheduling queue is a goal "P" and the potentially unifiable clauses for "P" are as follows:

```
P1 :- G11, G12 | B1.
P2 :- G21, G22 | B2.
```

In this case, we put goals at the tail of the scheduling queue as follows:

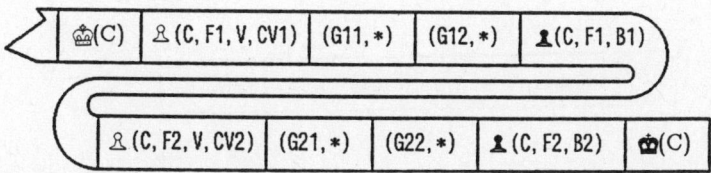

Here, OR-clauses are sandwiched in between the markers ♛ and ♚. The guard part of each clauses is placed between the markers ♝ and ♟. Notice that markers ♛ and ♚ express the OR-relation and that markers ♝ and ♟ express the AND-relation. The symbol "*," the second argument of each goal, shows that the goal should be solved by using the global database world. The argument C, common to all markers, contains the information whether one of the OR-clauses is committed or not. The argument $F_i$ of the marker ♝ shows whether the i-th OR-clause has failed or not. Note that this argument only needs to show that the i-th OR-clause has failed. Since the i-th OR-clause is committed as soon as the i-th OR-clause succeeds, it does not need to show that the i-th argument succeeded. The argument V is a list of variables which contains all variables in the original goals. The argument $CV_i$ is the copied list of V. The argument $B_i$ of the marker ♟ is the body part of each clause.

Goals between markers are processed in exactly the same manner as the ordinary goals when goals are picked up from the scheduling queue. However, when markers are picked up, they are processed as follows:

(1) When marker ♛(C) or ♚(C) is picked up, the marker is aborted if "committed" is set in argument "C." Otherwise, the marker is put on the tail of the scheduling queue.

(2) When marker ♛ is picked up and the top of the queue is marker ♚, i.e., the markers ♛ and ♚ are neighbors, this shows that all guards failed for a given goal. Since the "failure" of all guards means the "failure" of the given goal, "failure" is transmitted to the AND-relations to which they belong.[1]

---

[1] If the goal is at the top level, it means the total failure of the computation. For more detailed description, see the last paragraph of 3.3.

(3) When marker ♞(C,Fi,V,CVi) is picked up, it checks whether "committed" is set in argument "C" or "failed" is set in argument "Fi." In these cases, all goals from ♞ to ♟ are removed from the scheduling queue.

(4) When marker ♞(C,Fi,V,CVi) is picked up and the top of the queue is marker ♟(C,Fi,Bi), i.e., the markers ♞(C,Fi,V,CVi) and ♟(C,Fi,Bi) are neighbors, it means that all goals of a guard succeed. In this case, we set "committed" to the argument C, unify V and CVi, and schedule Bi.

(5) When marker ♟(C,Fi,Bi) is picked up, the marker is simply put on the tail of the scheduling queue.

## 3.2 Set Abstraction

We consider the case where the following goal is taken from the scheduling queue.

```
eager_enumerate({X| P(X),Q(X)}, L)
```

In our implementation, the goal is appended to the tail of the scheduling queue in the following way.

⟨ ♚ | ♞ ♟(M,{X | P(X),Q(X)},pp) | ♛(M,L) ⟩

Two pairs of markers appear again. The meanings of these markers are slightly different from the previous ones. However it is still true that the markers ♚ and ♛ express OR-relation, and the markers ♞ and ♟ express AND-relation. The markers ♚ and ♛ surround the OR-relation and work as a solution collector. The solutions are collected in "M" in stream form. The markers ♞ and ♟ compute one solution. The computed value is substituted into the argument "M."

When markers are taken from the scheduling queue, they are processed as follows:

(1) When marker ♚ is picked up and the top of the queue is marker ♛, i.e., the markers ♚ and ♛ are neighbors, this means that all solutions for the given goal have already been computed. We put [] onto the tail of the argument "L" in this case.

(2) When marker ♞ ♟(M,{X | ...}, pp) is picked up, we find definition clauses for the leftmost goal of this set. If more than two clauses are found, it is broken up into several goals. The argument "M" is also reproduced by fission.

(3) When marker ♛(M,L) is picked up, the argument "M" is checked. If it is instantiated, its value is sent to the stream "L" and the marker is appended to the tail of the scheduling queue.

The following is an example of fission. Assume that the marker is picked up, and P is defined in the Pure Prolog world as follows:

```
pp((P(X) <- B1,B2)).
pp((P(X) <- B3)).
pp((P(X) <- true)).
```

There are three clauses. The marker ♞ ♟ breaks up into three goals and they are appended to the scheduling queue in the following form:

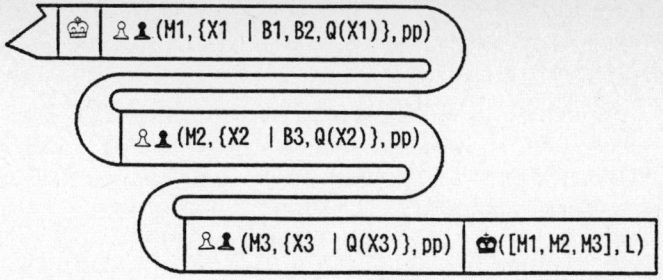

We can get all solutions for the given goal by invoking fission. Notice that the solutions are computed by the depth-first search based on OR-parallelism. We have explained all-solution computing in the case of "eager_enumeration." The basic mechanism for "lazy_enumeration" is exactly the same as that for "eager_enumeration."

## 3.3 Meta-inference

We assume that the goal "simulate" is taken from the scheduling queue. In our implementation, the goal is put on the tail of the scheduling queue in the following form.

Markers ♞ and ♟ appears again. The arguments "R," "C" and "W" express the Result, Control, and World name, respectively.

The following summarize the actions when markers are taken from the scheduling queue.

(1) When marker ♞(R,C) is picked up and "failure" is already set in argument "R," all goals from ♞ to ♟ are removed from the scheduling queue.

(2) When marker ♞(R,C) is picked up and the top of the queue is marker ♟, i.e., it is empty between marker ♞ and marker ♟, we set "success" to the argument "R."

(3) When marker ♞(R,C) is picked up and "C" is instantiated as [ ..., abort | variable], all goals from ♞ to ♟ are removed from the scheduling queue and "abortion" is set to the variable "R."

(4) When marker ♞(R,C) is picked up and "C" is instantiated as [ ..., stop | variable], all goals from ♞ to ♟ are enqueued onto the tail of the scheduling queue without reducing these goals.

(5) When marker ♞(R,C) is picked up, it checks whether "C" is a variable or instantiated as [ ..., cont | variable]. In this case, the marker is just appended to the tail of the scheduling queue.

(6) When marker ♟ is picked up, the marker is appended to the tail of the scheduling queue.

Just as before, the markers ♞ and ♟ express AND-relation. If a goal between ♞ and ♟ fails, "failure" is set to "R." Goals between ♞ and ♟ are processed as exactly same as the ordinary goals, except that goals are reduced in a specified world. No special problems are created if OR-parallelism, set abstraction and meta-inference are nested within each other.

## 4 ECP INTERPRETER

In previous sections we explained the various features of ECP and the realization of these features in the scheduling queue. We have extended Shapiro's CP Interpreter (Shapiro 1983) and created the ECP Interpreter. In this section, we will explain the details of this ECP interpreter.

### 4.1 Shapiro's CP Interpreter

As mentioned above, our ECP interpreter is based on Shapiro's CP interpreter. Shapiro's interpreter is written in Prolog. The following program is a simplified version of his interpreter. The actual implementation is more complicated since it includes deadlock detection, system predicates and debug/trace features.

```
(1) cp(A):-
        schedule(A, X-X, Head-Tail),
        solve(Head-Tail).
(2) solve([]-[]):-!.
    solve([A|Head]-Tail):-
        system(A), !, A,
        solve(Head-Tail).
    solve([A|Head]-Tail):-
        reduce(A, B),
        schedule(B, Head-Tail, NewHead-NewTail), !,
            solve(NewHead-NewTail).
(3) reduce(A,B):-
        guarded_clause(A, (G|B)),
        cp(G), !.
    reduce(A,A).
(4) guarded_clause(A,B):-
        copy_functor(A, A1),
        clause(A1, B),
        unify(A, A1).
(5) schedule(true, Head-Tail, Head-Tail) :- !.
    schedule((A,B), Head-Tail, Head2-Tail2) :- !,
        schedule(A, Head-Tail, Head1-Tail1),
        schedule(B, Head1-Tail1, Head2-Tail2).
    schedule(A, Head-[A|Tail], Head-Tail):- !.
```

The meaning of this program is as follows:

(1) To solve a CP goal, the goal must be scheduled into the scheduling queue first. The "solve" predicate actually solves the goal.

(2) The "solve" predicate solves goals in the scheduling queue expressed as a D-list. If the scheduling queue is empty, the process terminates. Otherwise, a goal is taken

from the queue. If the goal is a system predicate, it is executed and the rest of goals are solved. If the goal is not a system predicate, the goal "A" is reduced to the new goals "B," and "B" is scheduled to the scheduling queue.

(3) The "reduce" predicate solves user-defined goals. The "guarded_clause" predicate looks for a potential unifiable guarded clause for a given goal "A." We solve the guard part of the unifiable clause. If it succeeds, "B" is the body part of that clause. If it fails, it backtracks and "guarded_clause" looks for another candidate clause. When all candidate clauses have failed, the "reduce" predicate does nothing and the second argument is equated to the first argument.

(4) The "guarded_clause" looks for a potential unifiable clause "B" for a given goal "A." The "copy_functor" makes the copied goal "A1" by copying the top level functor from the given goal "A." The "clause" finds a potentially unifiable clause "B" from "A1." If this succeeds, the "unify" predicate unifies A and A1.

(5) The "schedule" predicate contains the given goals to a scheduling queue. As mentioned before, the scheduling queue is expressed as a D-list. The "schedule" predicate enqueues nothing if the given goal is "true." If the given goal is "(A,B)," "A" is scheduled first and "B" is scheduled next. If the given goal is "A," it is simply appended to the tail of the scheduling queue.

## 4.2 Our ECP Interpreter

We have extended Shapiro's CP Interpreter (Shapiro 1983) and created the ECP Interpreter. The differences between our ECP interpreter and Shapiro's interpreter are as follows:

- Shapiro's interpreter processes OR-relations by backtracking as shown in (3) in the previous subsection. Since the "reduce" predicate in (3) calls the top-level predicate "cp" for each OR-relation, one scheduling queue is created for each OR-relation as mentioned in section 3. We have implemented OR-relations by appending them to the global scheduling queue with markers.

- Shapiro's interpreter does not distinguish "fail" and "suspend" on processing goals. However, we distinguish them so that the failure of a guard can be handled in OR-parallelism.

- Shapiro's interpreter does not directly realize OR-parallel, set-abstraction and meta-inference features. We directly implemented these using one global scheduling queue.

Our ECP interpreter is written in DEC-10 Prolog on the DEC2060 and in C-Prolog on the VAX11/780. The interpreter consists of the scheduling part, the marker processing part, and the Pure Prolog processing part. In terms of program size, these are approximately 150 lines, 170 lines, 50 lines respectively. The processing speed is two or three times slower than Shapiro's system since our system realizes OR-parallelism. The slow speed is caused by the fact that so many markers and goals are contained in the scheduling queue when we have a nested guard.

Our system was created to meet ICOT's research objectives. Therefore, our system has still several problems, such as the consumption of memory, exhaustion of stack space and others.

## 5 ECP PROGRAM EXAMPLE

We examine the "shell" program in this section. This is a more realistic version of the shell program discussed in 2.3 (Clark 1984). The shell program in 2.3 can run only one foreground job and multiple background jobs. We can control the execution only for the foreground job. However, in our "realistic" version, there is no distinction between foreground and background jobs, so we can run and control multiple jobs at the same time. In this "shell" program, every job has a process-ID and the execution of jobs can be controlled by commands which include process-IDs. A job may be aborted, suspended and resumed. The realistic "shell" program is shown below:

(1) shell :- shell(I?, []), in(I).

(2) shell([proc(ID,Goals)|Input], IDlist) :-
     true | print_result(IDlist,IDlist1),
         print_process(ID,Goals),
         simulate(*, Goals, R, C),
         shell(Input?, [(ID,R,C)|IDlist1]).

   shell([wproc(ID,W,Goals)|Input], IDlist) :-
     true | print_result(IDlist,IDlist1),
         print_wproc(ID,W,Goals),
         simulate(W, Goals, R, C),
         shell(Input?, [(ID,R,C)|IDlist1]).

   shell([Com | Input], IDlist) :-
     otherwise | print_result(IDlist,IDlist1),
         print_com(Com),
         send(IDlist1, Com, NewIDlist),
         shell(Input?,NewIDlist).

(3) send([],_,[]).
   send([(ID,R,C)|IDList],Com,
         [(ID,R,NewC)|IDList]) :-
             Com =.. [M,ID] | C = [M|NewC].
   send([(ID,R,C)|IDList],Com,
         [(ID,R,C)|NewIDlist]) :- otherwise |
             send(IDlist,Com,NewIDlist).

The meaning of this "shell" program is as follows:

(1) "shell" is the top level predicate. It calls the two-argument-"shell" and "in."

(2) Two-argument-"shell" is the main part of this program. The first argument of "shell" is a stream which receives commands from the goal "in." The second argument is the list of processes controlled by "shell." This list of processes is called "IDlist." A process is expressed as (ID,R,C), where ID is an identifier of a process, R is a variable which sends a message to the outside, and C is a variable which controls its execution.

This "shell" behaves as follows:

- When it receives the message "proc(ID, Goals)" at its first argument, it calls "simulate," executes "Goals" in the global database world, and adds this process "(ID,R,C)" to the "IDlist."

- When it receives the message "wproc(ID, W, Goals)" as its first argument, it calls "simulate," executes "Goals" in world "W," and adds this process "(ID,R,C) to the "IDlist."

• When it receives other commands, such as "stop(ID)," "cont(ID)" or "abort(ID)," as its first argument, it sends that command to the control variable of the specified process.

The predicates "print_process," "print_wproc" and "print_com" are used just for printing out the message which "shell" received. The predicate "print_result" is used to print out the result when a process is aborted or ends successfully. In such cases, it prints out the process termination information and removes that process from the given "IDlist."

(3) "send" transmits a message such as "stop(ID)," "cont(ID)" or "abort(ID)" to the process with a process identifier "ID." It looks for the "IDlist." If it finds the process, it sends the message to the control variable of that process.

The following is an execution example of this "shell" program.

```
?- solve(shell, R).
> proc(p01,primes)
> wproc(p02,s,prime(10))
2
3
        2 (s)
        3 (s)
5
> stop(p01)
        5 (s)
        7 (s)
> cont(p01)
> result([p02,success])
7
11
> abort(p01)
> result([p01,abortion])
```

Here, we invoked two processes. One is the process "p01" which generates the infinite sequence of prime numbers. The second is the process "p02" which computes prime numbers up to 10 following the definition of prime in the world "s." In this example, we stopped "p01" after it printed out 2, 3 and 5, and resumed after "p02" printed out 2, 3, 5 and 7. The process "p02" is terminated after it prints out all primes up to 10. We also terminated process "p01" by sending the abort message to "p01."

## 6  RELATED WORKS

Here, we would like to survey various research on extended features of Concurrent Prolog.

(1) For OR-parallelism, Levy (1984) proposed the implementation method using a global queue. His method is based on the lazy copying scheme, but it has been pointed out that this method still has bugs. ICOT also tried OR-parallelism using several implementation schemes (Miyazaki 1984; Sato 1984; Tanaka 1984). For these methods, implementations were written in Pascal or Lisp. On the other hand, our implementation was done in a logical way using Prolog.

(2) The research in set abstraction is preceded by POPS (Hirakawa 1984). POPS is a Pure Prolog interpreter written in Concurrent Prolog. It enumerates all solutions for the given goals in stream form. In our approach, the enumeration of all solutions is directly realized by the scheduling queue.

(3) The key issue in meta-inference is how to implement the interpreter of the target language. In this field, research has been done by writing meta-interpreters (Shapiro 1984, Clark 1984). We have implemented meta-inference predicates directly onto the scheduling queue. Compared with the traditional approach, our approach is more direct.

## 7  CONCLUSION

In this paper, we described the rough outline for realizing extended features of ECP. Related work in this field was also surveyed. Although we have omitted here, there are various problems which occur in the actual implementation. One is the problem of copying variables involved in the realization of OR-parallelism.

We proposed the "AND-OR queuing" method. It is surprising that the various features of ECP, such as OR-parallel, set-abstraction and meta-inference, can be implemented in a consistent manner. From the architectural point of view, it is more realistic to assume one global queue than assuming many local scheduling queues created dynamically. And it leads to the more consistent scheduling. That is,

(1) It realizes OR-parallelism.

(2) In set abstraction, we can reduce other goals while generating solutions.

(3) In meta-inference, we can compute several "simulate" predicates at the same time.

By the way, the scope of this "AND-OR queuing" method is not limited to Concurrent Prolog. This method is also applicable to GHC (Ueda 1985). In this case, implementation is simpler because it does not generate multiple environments in implementing OR-parallelism.

## ACKNOWLEDGMENTS

This research was carried out as a part of the Fifth Generation Computer Project. T.Yokomori and J.Tanaka chiefly designed the ECP interpreter. M.Kishishita actually coded the ECP interpreter.

We would like to thank Akikazu Takeuchi, Kazunori Ueda, and other members of the KL1 implementation group at ICOT for their useful comments and suggestions. We would also like to thank Dr. Furukawa, the chief of the First Research Laboratory, ICOT, Dr. Kitagawa, the president of IIAS-SIS, Fujitsu, Dr. Enomoto, the director of IIAS-SIS, Fujitsu, and Mr. Yoshii, Fujitsu Social Science Laboratory, for giving us the opportunity to pursue this research and helping us with it.

# REFERENCES

Clark K, Gregory S (1984) Notes on Systems Programming in Parlog. Proceedings of the International Conference on Fifth Generation Computer Systems 299-306

Fujitsu (1984) The Verifying Software of Kernel Language Version 1 – Detailed Specification–, PART II. In: The 1983 Report on Committed Development on Computer Basic Technology, in Japanese

Fujitsu (1985) The Verifying Software of Kernel Language Version 1 – the Revised Detailed Specification and the Evaluation Result–, PART I. In: The 1984 Report on Committed Development on Computer Basic Technology, in Japanese

Furukawa K et al. (1984) The Conceptual Specification of the Kernel Language Version 1. Technical Report TR-054. ICOT

Hirakawa H et al. (1984) Eager and Lazy Enumeration in Concurrent Prolog. Proceedings of the Second International Logic Programming Conference 89-100

Levy J (1984) A Unification Algorithm for Concurrent Prolog. Proceedings of the Second International Logic Programming Conference 333-341

Miyazaki T et al. (1985) A Sequential Implementation of Concurrent Prolog Based on Shallow Binding Scheme. Proceedings of 1985 Symposium on Logic Programming 110-118

Sato H et al. (1984) A Sequential Implementation of Concurrent Prolog - based on the Deep Binding Scheme. Proceedings of the First National Conference of Japan Society for Software Science and Technology 299-302, in Japanese

Shapiro E (1983) A Subset of Concurrent Prolog and its Interpreter. Technical Report TR-003. ICOT

Shapiro E (1984) Systems Programming in Concurrent Prolog. Conference Record of the 11th Annual ACM Symposium on Principles of Programming Language 93-105

Tanaka J et al. (1984) A Sequential Implementation of Concurrent Prolog – based on the Lazy Copying Scheme. Proceedings of the First National Conference of Japan Society for Software Science and Technology 303-306, in Japanese

Ueda K (1985) Guarded Horn Clauses. Technical Report TR-103. ICOT

# GUARDED HORN CLAUSES

Kazunori Ueda

C&C Systems Research Laboratories, NEC Corporation[1]
Kawasaki, Japan

ABSTRACT

A set of Horn clauses, augmented with a *'guard'* mechanism, is shown to be a simple and yet powerful parallel logic programming language.

## 1. INTRODUCTION

A set of Horn clauses allows procedural interpretation (Kowalski 1974). It was given a semantics as a sequential programming language by Prolog (Roussel 1975), and Prolog has proved to be a simple, powerful, and efficient sequential programming language (Warren, Pereira, Pereira 1979).

As Kowalski (1974) points out, a Horn clause program allows parallel or concurrent execution as well as sequential execution. However, although a set of Horn clauses may be useful for uncontrolled search as it is, it is inadequate for a parallel programming language which is capable of describing important concepts such as communication and synchronization. We need some additional mechanism to express these concepts. This paper shows that only one construct, *guard*, is adequate for our purposes.

In the following chapters, we introduce guarded Horn clauses. The name Guarded Horn Clauses (abbreviated to GHC) will be used also as the name of our language. Comparison of GHC with other logic/parallel programming languages is included. The language GHC is intended to be the machine-independent core of the Kernel Language for ICOT's Parallel Inference Machine.

## 2. DESIGN GOALS AND OVERVIEW

Our goal is to obtain a logic programming language that allows parallel execution. It is expected to fulfill the following requirements:

(1) It must be a parallel programming language 'by nature'. It must not be a sequential language augmented with primitives for parallelism. That is, the language must assume as little sequentiality among primitive operations as possible, in order to preserve parallelism inherent in a Horn clause program. This would lead to a clearer formal semantics, as well as to an efficient implementation on a novel architecture in the future.

(2) It must be an expressive, general-purpose parallel programming language. In particular, it must be able to express important concepts in parallel programming—processes, communication, and synchronization.

(3) It must be a simple parallel programming language. We do not have much experience with either theoretical or pragmatic aspects of parallel programming. Therefore, we must first establish a foundation of parallel programming on a simple language.

(4) It must be an efficient parallel programming language. We have a lot of simple, typical problems to

---

[1] Author's current address: Institute for New Generation Computer Technology, 1-4-28, Mita, Minato-ku, Tokyo, 108 Japan

be described in the language as well as complex ones. It is very important that such programs run as efficiently as the comparable ones written in existing parallel programming languages.

Concurrent Prolog (Shapiro 1983) and PARLOG (Clark and Gregory 1984a) seem to lie near the solution. Both realize processes by goals and communication by streams implemented as lists. Synchronization is realized by read-only variables in Concurrent Prolog and by one-way unification in PARLOG.

GHC inherits the *guard* construct and the programming paradigm founded by these languages. What is the most characteristic with GHC is that the guard is the only syntactic construct added to Horn clauses. In GHC, synchronization is realized by the semantic rules of a guard.

GHC is expected to fulfill all the above requirements. We have succeeded in rewriting most of our Concurrent Prolog programs. Miyazaki and Ueda have independently written GHC-to-Prolog compilers in Prolog by modifying different versions of Concurrent Prolog compilers on top of Prolog (Ueda, Chikayama 1985).

## 3. SYNTAX AND SEMANTICS

### 3.1. Syntax

A GHC program is a finite set of guarded Horn clauses of the following form:

$$H :\!- G_1, \ldots, G_m \mid B_1, \ldots, B_n. \quad (m \geq 0, n \geq 0).$$

where $H$, $G_i$'s, and $B_i$'s are atomic formulas that are defined as usual. $H$ is called a clause head, $G_i$'s are called guard goals, and $B_i$'s are called body goals. The operator '|' is called a commitment operator. The part of a clause before '|' is called a guard, and the part after '|' is called a body. Note that *a clause head is included in a guard*. A set of all clauses whose heads have the same predicate symbol with the same arity is called a procedure. Declaratively, the above guarded Horn clause is read as "$H$ is implied by $G_1, \ldots,$ and $G_m$ and $B_1, \ldots,$ and $B_n$".

A goal clause has the following form:

$$:\!- B_1, \ldots, B_n. \quad (n \geq 0).$$

This can be regarded as a guarded Horn clause with an empty guard. A goal clause is called an empty clause when $n$ is equal to 0.

In this paper, we use symbols beginning with uppercase letters for variables and ones beginning with lowercase letters for function and predicate symbols, following DECsystem-10 Prolog (Bowen et al. 1983). The nullary predicate 'true' is used for denoting an empty set of guard or body goals.

### 3.2. Semantics

The semantics of GHC is quite simple. Informally, to execute a program is to reduce a given goal clause to the empty clause by means of input resolution using the clauses constituting the program. This can be done in a fully parallel manner under the following rules of suspension:

- *Rules of Suspension*
  (a) Any piece of unification invoked directly or indirectly in the guard of a clause cannot bind a variable appearing in the caller of that clause with
    (i) a non-variable term or
    (ii) another variable appearing in the caller.
  (b) Any piece of unification invoked directly or indirectly in the body of a clause cannot bind a variable appearing in the guard of that clause with
    (i) a non-variable term or

(ii) another variable appearing in the guard

until that clause is selected for commitment (see below).

A piece of unification which can succeed only by making such bindings is suspended until it can succeed without making such bindings *(end of the rules of suspension)*.

Note that a set of variables whose instantiation is inhibited by the above rules can vary as computation proceeds. When a variable X in the set $S$ is bound to a non-variable term T (in a way not disallowed above), we include all the variables in T in $S$ and remove X itself from $S$.

Another rule we have to add is the *commitment* rule. When some clause succeeds in solving (see below) its guard for a given goal, that clause tries to be selected exclusively for subsequent execution of the goal. To be selected, it must first confirm that no other clauses belonging to the same procedure have been selected for the same goal. If confirmed, that clause is selected indivisibly; we say that the goal is committed to that clause and also that that clause is selected for commitment.

We say that a set of goals *succeeds* (or is *solved*) if it is reduced to the empty set of goals by using a selected clause for each initial or intermediate goal: We are interested in a reduction path in which only selected clauses are involved. We do not introduce the notion of failure here, but it will be discussed in Section 6.1.

It must be stressed that under the rules stated above, anything can be done in parallel: Conjunctive goals can be executed in parallel; candidate clauses for a goal can be tested in parallel; head unification involved in resolution can be done in parallel; head unification and the execution of guard goals can be done in parallel. However, it would have to be even more stressed that we can also execute a set of tasks in a predetermined order as long as it does not change the meaning of the program.

The rules of suspension could be more informally restated as follows:

(a) The guard of a clause cannot export any bindings to (or, make any bindings which is observable from) the caller of that clause, and

(b) the body of a clause cannot export any bindings to (or, make any bindings which is observable from) the guard of that clause before commitment.

Rule (a) is used for synchronization, so it could be called the rule of synchronization. Rule (b) is rather tricky; it states that we can solve the body of a clause not yet selected for commitment. However, the above restrictions guarantee that this never affects the selection of candidate clauses nor the other goals running in parallel with the caller of the clause. So Rule (b) is effectively the rule of sequencing.

In Concurrent Prolog, the result of unification which is performed in a guard (including a head) and which would export bindings is recorded locally. In GHC, such unification simply suspends. Suspension of unification due to some guard may be released when some goal running in parallel with the goal for which the guard is being executed has instantiated the variable that caused suspension.

An example may be helpful in understanding the rules of suspension. Let us consider the following program:

```
Goal:            :- p(X), q(X).                (i)
Clauses:  p(ok)  :- true | ... .               (ii)
          q(Z)   :- true | Z=ok.               (iii)
```

The predicate '=' is a predefined predicate which unifies its two arguments. This predicate must be considered as predefined, because it cannot be defined in the language.

Clause (ii) cannot instantiate the argument X of its caller to the constant 'ok', since this unification is executed in the guard. This clause has to wait until X is instantiated to 'ok' by some other goal. On the other hand, Clause (iii) can instantiate X to 'ok' after it is selected for commitment, and this clause can be selected almost immediately. Therefore, no matter which of the two goals of Clause (i) starts first, the head unification of Clause (ii) can succeed only after the 'Z=ok' goal in Clause (iii) is executed.

The semantics of the following program should be more carefully understood:

```
Goal:              :- p(X), q(X).                (i)
Clauses:  p(Y) :- q(Y) | ... .                   (ii')
          q(Z) :- true | Z=ok.                   (iii)
```

To solve the guard of Clause (ii'), we have to do two things in parallel: unifying X and Y (i.e., parameter passing), and solving q(Y). Let us first assume that parameter passing occurs first. Then the goal q(Y) tries to unify Y (which is now identical to X) with 'ok'. However, this unification cannot instantiate X because it is indirectly invoked by the guard of Clause (ii'). Let us then consider the other case where the goal q(Y) is executed prior to parameter passing. The variable Y is bound to 'ok' because this itself does not export bindings to the caller of Clause (ii'), namely p(X). However, this binding causes the subsequent parameter passing to suspend because it would export binding. Hence, no matter which case actually happens, Clause (ii') behaves equivalently to Clause (ii) as for bindings given to the variable X.

Some important consequences of the above rules follow:

(1) Any unification which is intended to 'export' bindings to the caller of a clause through its head arguments must be specified in the body. Such unification must be specified by using the predefined predicate '=' which unifies its two arguments. As stated before, the predicate '=' cannot be defined in the language and should be considered as a predefined predicate.

(2) The unification of the head arguments of a clause may, but need not, be executed in parallel. It can be executed sequentially in any predetermined order.

(3) The unification of head arguments and the execution of guard goals can be executed in parallel. That is, the execution of guard goals can start before the unification of head arguments has completed. However, the usual way of execution that solves guard goals only after head unification is also allowed; it does not change the meaning of a program.

(4) The execution of the body of a clause may, but need not, start before that clause is selected. The bindings made by the body is unobservable from the guard before commitment, so the meaning of the program is independent of whether the body starts before or only after commitment.

(5) We need not implement a multiple environment mechanism, a mechanism for binding a variable with more than one value. This mechanism is in general necessary when more than one candidate clause for a goal is tried in parallel. In GHC, however, at most one clause, a selected clause, can export bindings, thus eliminating the need of a multiple environment mechanism.

Unfortunately, the properties (2) and (3) do not hold if we introduce the concept of failure. For example, the following goal

```
Goal:                    :- and(X, false).
Clause:  and(true, true) :- true | true.
```

fails if the arguments are unified in parallel, but suspends if they are unified from left to right (Gregory 1985).

## 4. PROGRAM EXAMPLES

### 4.1. Binary Merge

```
merge([A|Xs], Ys,     Zs) :- true | Zs=[A|Zs1], merge(Xs, Ys, Zs1).
merge(Xs,     [A|Ys], Zs) :- true | Zs=[A|Zs1], merge(Xs, Ys, Zs1).
merge([],     Ys,     Zs) :- true | Zs=Ys.
merge(Xs,     [],     Zs) :- true | Zs=Xs.
```

The goal 'merge(Xs, Ys, Zs)' merges two streams Xs and Ys (implemented as lists) into one stream Zs. This is an example of nondeterministic programs. The language rules of GHC do not state that the selection of clauses should be fair. In a good implementation, however, the elements of Xs and Ys is expected to appear on Zs almost in the order of arrival.

Note that no binding can be exported from the guard; the binding to Z must be done in the body. This programming style, however, serves to clarify causality. In most cases, the bi- (or multi-) directionality of a logic program is only an illusion; it seems far better to specify the data flow which we have in mind and to enable us to read it from a given program.

Note that the declarative reading of the above program gives the usual, logical specification of the non-deterministic merge—arbitrary interleaving of the two input streams makes the output stream.

### 4.2. Generating Primes

```
primes(Max, Ps) :- true | gen(2, Max, Ns), sift(Ns, Ps).
gen(N, Max, Ns) :- N <= Max | Ns=[N|Ns1], N1 := N+1, gen(N1, Max, Ns1).
gen(N, Max, Ns) :- N >  Max | Ns=[].
sift([P|Xs], Zs) :- true | Zs=[P|Zs1], filter(P, Xs, Ys), sift(Ys, Zs1).
sift([],     Zs) :- true | Zs=[].
filter(P, [X|Xs], Ys) :- X mod P=:=0 |                  filter(P, Xs, Ys).
filter(P, [X|Xs], Ys) :- X mod P=\=0 | Ys=[X|Ys1], filter(P, Xs, Ys1).
filter(P, [],     Ys) :- true        | Ys=[].
```

The call 'primes(Max, Ps)' returns through Ps a stream of primes up to Max. The stream of primes is generated from the stream of integers by filtering out the multiples of primes. For each prime P, a filter goal 'filter(P, Xs, Ys)' is generated which filters out the multiples of P from the stream Xs, yielding Ys.

The binary predicate ':=' evaluates its right-hand side operand as an integer expression and unifies the result with the left-hand side operand. The binary predicate '=:=' evaluates its two operands as integer expressions and succeeds iff the results are the same. These predicates cannot be replaced by the '=' predicate because '=' never evaluates its arguments. The predicate '=\=' is the negation of '=:='.

The readers may wish to improve the above program by eliminating unnecessary filtering.

### 4.3. Bounded Buffer Stream Communication

```
test(N) :- true | buffer(N, Hs, Ts), ints(0, 100, Hs), consume(Hs, Ts).
buffer(N, Hs, Ts) :- N > 0 | Hs=[_|Hs1], N1:=N-1, buffer(N1, Hs1, Ts).
buffer(N, Hs, Ts) :- N=:=0 | Ts=Hs.
ints(M, Max, [H|Hs]) :- M <  Max | H=M, M1:=M+1, ints(M1, Max, Hs).
ints(M, Max, [H|_ ]) :- M >= Max | H='EOS'.
consume([H|Hs], Ts) :- H\='EOS' | Ts=[_|Ts1], consume(Hs, Ts1).
consume([H|Hs], Ts) :- H ='EOS' | Ts=[].
```

This program illustrates the general statement that demand-driven computation can be implemented by means of data-driven computation. It uses the bounded-buffer concept first shown by Takeuchi and Furukawa (1983) in a logic programming framework. The predicate 'ints' returns a stream of integers through the third argument in a lazy manner. It never generates a new box by itself; it only fills a given box created elsewhere with a new value. In the above program, the goal 'consume' creates a new box by the goal 'Ts=[_|Ts1]' every time it has confirmed the top element H of the stream. The top and the tail of the stream are initially related by the goal 'buffer(N, Hs, Ts)'.

The binary predicate '\=' is a negation of the predicate '='. It succeeds when its two arguments are proved to be ununifiable; it suspends until then.

### 4.4. Meta-Interpreter of GHC

```
call(true ) :- true | true.
call((A, B)) :- true | call(A), call(B).
call(A = B ) :- true | A = B.
call(A      ) :- A \= true, A \= (_, _), A \= (_ = _) |
    clauses(A, Clauses), resolve(A, Clauses, Body), call(Body).
resolve(A, [C|Cs], B) :- melt_new(C, (A :- G|B2)), call(G) | B = B2.
resolve(A, [C|Cs], B) :- resolve(A, Cs, B2) | B = B2.
```

This program is basically a GHC version of the Concurrent Prolog meta-interpreter by Shapiro (1984). The predicate 'clauses' is a system predicate which returns in a *frozen* form (Nakashima, Ueda, Tomura 1984) a list of all clauses whose heads are potentially unifiable with the given goal. Each frozen clause is a ground term in which original variables are indicated by special constant symbols, and it is *melted* in the guard of the first clause of 'resolve' by 'melt_new'. The goal 'melt_new(C, (A :- G|B2))' creates a new term (say T) from a frozen term C by giving a new variable for each frozen variable in C, and tries to unify T with '(A :- G|B2)'.

The predicate 'resolve' tests the candidate clauses and returns the body of arbitrary one of the clauses whose guards have been successfully solved. This many-to-one arbitration is realized by the nest of binary clause selection performed in the predicate 'resolve'.

It is essential that each candidate clause is melted after it has been brought into the guard of the first clause of 'resolve'. If it were melted before passed into the guard, all variables in it would be protected against instantiation from the guard.

## 5. IMPORTANT FEATURES OF GHC

### 5.1. Simplicity

GHC has only a small number of primitive operations all of which are considered small:

(1) calling a predicate leaving all its arguments unspecified, i.e., after making sure only that they are new distinct variables,

(2) unifying a variable with another variable or with a non-variable term whose arguments are all new distinct variables, and

(3) commitment.

Operation (1) is effectively resolution without unification. From a viewpoint of parallel execution, resolution in the original sense (Robinson 1965) need not be considered as an indivisible operation. Resolution can be decomposed into goal rewriting and unification, and the latter can be executed in parallel with the newly created goals, as stated in Section 3.2.

Operation (2) shows that the unification of a variable and a non-variable term is not necessarily a primitive operation. For example, the unification 'X=f(a)' can be decomposed into the two operations 'X=f(Y)' and 'Y=a', where Y is a new variable. This is suggested also by Hagiya (1983).

Furthermore, the semantics of guard and commitment is powerful enough to express the following notions:

(1) conditional branching,
(2) nondeterministic choice, and
(3) synchronization.

This feature is much like CSP (Hoare 1978), but CSP provides additional constructs '?' (input command) and '!' (output command) for synchronization. The Relational Language (Clark, Gregory 1981) was the first to introduce the guard concept to logic programming for the purpose similar to ours[2]. However, GHC has removed the restrictions on the guard of the Relational Language together with mode declarations and annotations.

### 5.2. Descriptive Power

We have succeeded in rewriting most of the Concurrent Prolog programs we have. In particular, we have written a GHC program which performs bounded buffer communication, and a meta-interpreter of GHC itself (see Section 4.4).

### 5.3. Efficiency

It cannot be immediately concluded that GHC can be efficiently implemented on parallel computers. The efficiency of GHC owes very much to the future research on the language itself and its implementation. However, GHC is more favorable than Concurrent Prolog for implementation: It needs no mechanism for multiple environments; it provides more information on synchronization statically. We made a compiler of GHC subset which compiles a GHC program into Prolog (Ueda, Chikayama 1985), and an 'append' program ran at more than 13kLIPS on DEC2065. The current restriction is that user-defined goals are not allowed in guards. Another GHC-to-Prolog compiler was made by Miyazaki. Although less efficient than ours, his compiler is capable of handling nested guards.

For applications in which efficiency is the primary issue but little flexibility is needed, we could design a restricted version of GHC which allows only the subclass of GHC and/or introduces declarations which help optimization. Such a variant should have the properties that additional constructs such as declarations are used only for efficiency purposes and that a program in that variant is readable as a GHC program once the additional constructs are removed from the source text.

## 6. POSSIBLE EXTENSIONS

This chapter suggests some possible extensions. The extensions shown below are currently not part of GHC. Their necessity, implementability, compatibility with other language features, and so on are yet to be examined before they are actually introduced.

### 6.1. Finite Failure and the Predicate 'otherwise'

The semantics of GHC as described in Section 3.2 does not introduce the concept of failure. However, failure of unification can be readily introduced into the language. We can say that a set of goals fails if it contains or derives some unification goal and its two arguments are instantiated to different principal functors. Then a suspended unification may turn out to fail as well as to succeed afterwards.

Another kind of failure is caused by a goal for which there prove to be no selectable clauses. Calling a non-existent predicate also falls under this category. This kind of failure must be detected as failure only under the *closed world assumption*; otherwise, that goal would have to suspend until somebody add a selectable clause into the program.

The predicate 'otherwise' proposed by Shapiro and Takeuchi (1983) can be introduced to express 'negation as failure'. The predicate 'otherwise' can appear only as a guard goal. A goal 'otherwise' succeeds when the guard of all the other candidate clauses for the given goal have failed; until then it suspends. This predicate could be conveniently used for describing a *default* clause.

### 6.2. Metacall Facilities

We sometimes want to see whether a given goal succeeds or fails without making the test itself fail. Consider,

---
[2] IC-Prolog (Clark, McCabe 1980) was the first to introduce the guard concept to logic programming, but the purpose was rather different.

for example, a monitor program. A monitor program may create several processes, some of which are user programs and others are service programs. In this case, the user programs must be executed in a fail-safe manner because if one of them should fail, so does the whole system. Furthermore, a monitor program must have some means to abort its subordinate user programs.

Let us consider a program tracer next. A program tracer must execute a given program, generating trace information every moment. Even if the program fails, the tracer should generate appropriate diagnostic information without failing. The tracer may even have to trace the execution of guards, which is really an impure feature since information should be extracted from the place from where no bindings must otherwise be exported.

A partial evaluator is another example. A partial evaluator rewrites a program clause by executing the goals in the clause. For example, the first clause in the program

```
p(Y) :- q(Y) | ... .
q(Z) :- true | Z=ok.
```

in Section 3.2 can be partially evaluated to the following clause:

```
p(ok) :- true | ... .
```

To do such rewriting, it must be possible to execute a given goal to obtain a finite set of substitutions and, in the case of suspension, a finite set of remaining (suspended) goals. In this case, the initial goal and the result must be represented in a frozen form. For if ordinary variables were used, the solver of the initial goal could not know when that goal had been fully instantiated, nor could we know when all bindings had been made. The delay of binding is not guaranteed to be bounded.

We are considering language facilities which support all such applications as described above. However, we have not reached a satisfactory solution yet. The metacall facilities proposed by Clark and Gregory (1984b) was a candidate solution, but it proved to have some semantical problems. Their two-argument metacall 'call(Goal, Result)' tries to solve Goal possibly generating output bindings, and it unifies Result with 'succeeded' upon success and with 'failed' upon failure. However, consider the following example (Sato, Sakurai 1984):

```
:- call(X=0, _), X=1.
```

If the first goal is executed first, X becomes 0. Then the unification X=1 fails and so does the whole clause. If the second goal is executed first, X becomes 1. But since the first goal never fails, the whole clause succeeds. This is a new kind of nondeterminism resulting from the order of unification; without this facility, all nondeterminism would result from the arbitrary choice of selectable clauses.

Let us consider another example:

```
:- call(X=0, _), call(X=1, _).
```

The semantics of a GHC variable is intended to allow the above goal to be rewritten as follows (Ueda 1985),

```
:- call(X=0, _), X = Y, call(Y=1, _).
```

because they are logically equivalent. However, this rewriting shows that the failure of unification cannot be confined in either 'call'. The failure can creep out and topple the whole goal. This means that the metacall facilities as proposed by Clark and Gregory cannot protect a system program from unpredictable behavior of a user program. Further investigation is necessary to have a better solution.

## 7. IMPLEMENTATION OUTLINE

The purpose of this chapter is to demonstrate that the suspension mechanism of GHC can be implemented.

We will first show an easy-to-understand but possibly inefficient method: pointer coloring. Here we do not consider the suspension of bodies. The body of a clause is assumed to start after the clause has been selected.

When a term in a goal and a variable in the guard of a clause are unified, we color the pointer which indicates the binding. A term dereferenced using one or more colored pointers cannot be instantiated. When the clause is selected, colored pointers created in its guard are uncolored. For this purpose, the guard of a clause must record all pointers colored for that guard. Uncoloring can be done in parallel with the other operations in the body.

Care must be taken when the term in a goal to be unified with the variable in the guard is itself dereferenced using colored pointers. Consider the following example:

```
       :- p(f(A)).              (i)
p(X) :- q(X) | ... .            (ii)
q(Y) :- true | Y=f(b).          (iii)
```

If the variable Y should directly point to the term f(A) by a colored pointer and uncolor it upon selection of Clause (iii), the variable A would be erroneously instantiated to the constant 'b'. There are a couple of possible remedies:

(1) Disallow pointers which go directly out of nested guards and use a chain of pointers instead.

(2) Let each pointer know how many levels of guards it goes through.

(3) (Miyazaki 1985) Allow pointers to go directly through nested guards. However, let each colored pointer know for what guard it is colored. When directly pointing a term dereferenced using colored pointers, that new pointer must be recorded in the guard which records the last colored pointer in the dereferencing chain.

The pointer-coloring method explained above is general. In many cases, however, we can analyze suspension statically. The simplest case is the following clause:

```
p(true) :- ... | ... .
```

The head argument claims that the corresponding goal argument must have been instantiated to 'true' for this clause to be selected. We can statically generate the code for this check, and need not use colored pointers in this case.

In general, if a guard calls only system predicates for simple checking (e.g., integer comparison), compile-time analysis is easy because no consideration is needed on other clauses. On the other hand, if it calls a user-defined predicate, global analysis is necessary to determine which unification may suspend and which unification cannot. There will be no general method for static analysis, but in many useful cases, static analysis like PARLOG's compile-time mode analysis (Clark and Gregory 1984c) will be effective.

## 8. COMPARISON WITH OTHER LANGUAGES

### 8.1. Comparison with Concurrent Prolog and PARLOG

GHC is like Concurrent Prolog and PARLOG in that it is a parallel logic programming language which supports committed-choice nondeterminism and stream communication. However, GHC is simpler than both Concurrent Prolog and PARLOG.

Firstly, unlike Concurrent Prolog, GHC has no read-only annotations. In GHC, the semantics of guards enables process synchronization.

Secondly, Concurrent Prolog needs a multiple environment mechanism while GHC and PARLOG do not. In Concurrent Prolog, bindings generated in each guard are recorded locally until commitment and are exported into the global environment upon commitment. However, this mechanism contains semantical problems whose solution would require an additional set of language rules, as Ueda (1985) pointed out. More importantly, we have not obtained any evidence that we need multiple environments in stream-AND-parallel programming.

Thirdly, unlike PARLOG, we require no mode declaration for each predicate. PARLOG's mode declaration is nothing but a guide for translating PARLOG program into Kernel PARLOG (Clark and Gregory 1984c), so we can do without modes. In fact, GHC is more similar to Kernel PARLOG than to PARLOG. However, unlike Kernel PARLOG, we have only one kind of unification. Although each unification operation occurring in a GHC program might be compiled into one of several specialized unification procedures, GHC itself needs (and has) only one.

Another difference from (Kernel) PARLOG is that a (Kernel) PARLOG program requires compile-time analysis in order to guarantee that it is legal, i.e., it contains no unsafe guard which may bind variables in the caller of the guard (Clark, Gregory 1984c). On the other hand, a GHC program is legal if and only if it is syntactically legal; it can be executed without any semantic analysis.

## 8.2. Comparison with Qute

Qute (Sato, Sakurai 1984) is a functional language based on unification. Qute allows parallel evaluation which corresponds to AND-parallelism in logic programming languages, but the result of evaluation is guaranteed to be the same irrespective of the particular order of evaluation. That is, there is no observable nondeterminism.

Although Qute and GHC are independently developed and look differently at a glance, their suspension mechanisms are essentially the same. The Qute counterpart of GHC's guard is the condition part of the *if-then-else* construct, from where no bindings can be exported.

The major difference between Qute and GHC is that Qute has no committed-choice nondeterminism while GHC has one. Qute does not have committed-choice nondeterminism (though Sato and Sakurai (1984) suggests it could) because it pursues the Church-Rosser property of the evaluation algorithm. GHC has one because our applications include a system which interfaces with the real world (e.g., peripheral devices).

Another difference is that Qute has sequential AND while GHC does not. We deliberately excluded sequential AND, because our programming experience with Concurrent Prolog has never called for this construct. One may think that sequential AND could be used for the specification of scheduling and for synchronization. However, the primitives for scheduling should be introduced at a different level from that of GHC, and sequential AND as a synchronization primitive is of no use in the intended computation model of GHC which allows delay for communication by shared variables.

## 8.3. Comparison with CSP

GHC is similar to CSP (Communicating Sequential Processes)(Hoare 1978) in the following points:

(1) Both encourage programming based on the concept of communicating processes.
(2) The guard mechanism plays an important role for conditional branching, nondeterminism and synchronization.
(3) Both pursue simplicity.

The major difference is that CSP tries to rule out any dynamic constructs—dynamic process creation, dynamic memory allocation, recursive call, etc.—while GHC does not. Another major difference is that CSP has a concept of sequential processes while GHC does not. To put them differently, CSP is at the level nearer to the current computer architecture. GHC is more abstract and has a smaller set of primitives: it uses unification instead of input, output, and assignment commands, and it uses recursive call instead of a repetitive command.

## 8.4. Comparison with (sequential) Prolog

Comparison with sequential Prolog must be made from the viewpoint of logic programming languages, not of parallel programming languages.

First of all, GHC has no concepts of the order of clauses or the order of goals in a clause. GHC is undoubtedly nearer to the Horn clause logic in this point. The semantics of Prolog must explain its sequentiality; without it, we cannot discuss some properties of a program such as termination.

GHC deviates from first-order logic in that it introduces the guard construct. It will be hard to give a semantics to the guard within the framework of first-order logic. However, Prolog also suffers from the same situation because of the notorious but useful cut operator. The commitment operator of GHC is the parallel of the cut operator. However, since the commitment operator has been introduced in a more controlled way, it should be easier to give a formal semantics to it.

One problem with Prolog is that the use of 'read' and 'write' predicates prevents the declarative reading of a program. In GHC, we no longer need imperative predicates because the concept of streams can well be adapted to input and output. Large data structures such as mutable arrays and databases can also be logically and efficiently handled by using transaction streams as interface (Ueda, Chikayama 1984).

## 8.5. Comparison with Delta Prolog

Delta-Prolog (Pereira, Nasr 1984) is an extension of Prolog which allows multiple processes. Communication and synchronization are realized using the notion of *event*. The underlying logic which explains the meaning of events is called Distributed Logic.

One of the differences between Delta-Prolog and GHC is that Delta-Prolog retains the sequentiality concept and the cut operator of Prolog. Both of them seemed to be a peculiarity of Prolog, so GHC did not stick to them. A parallel program in Delta-Prolog may look quite different from the comparable sequential programs in Delta-Prolog itself and in Prolog. On the other hand, a class of GHC programs which have only unidirectional information flow (like pipelining) is easily rewritable to Prolog by replacing commitment operators by cuts, and a class of Prolog programs which use no deep backtracking and each of whose predicates has only one intended input/output mode is also easily rewritable to GHC.

## 9. CONCLUSIONS

We have proposed a parallel logic programming language Guarded Horn Clauses. Its syntax, informal semantics, programming examples, important features, possible extensions, implementation technique of synchronization mechanism, and comparison with other languages have been described.

We hope the simplicity of GHC will make it suitable for a parallel computation model as well as a programming language. The flexibility of GHC makes its efficient implementation difficult compared with a CSP-like language. However, a flexible language could be appropriately restricted in order to make simple programs run efficiently. On the other hand, it would be very difficult to extend a fast but inflexible language naturally.

### ACKNOWLEDGMENTS

The author would like to thank Akikazu Takeuchi, Toshihiko Miyazaki, Jiro Tanaka, Koichi Furukawa, Rikio Onai and other ICOT members, as well as the members of ICOT Working Groups, for useful discussions on GHC and its implementation. Thanks are also due to Ehud Shapiro, Steve Gregory, Anthony Kusalik and Vijay Saraswat for their comments on the earlier versions of this paper. Katsuya Hakozaki, Masahiro Yamamoto, and Kazuhiro Fuchi provided very stimulating research environments.

This research was done as part of the R&D activities of the Fifth Generation Computer Systems Project of Japan.

# REFERENCES

Bowen DL (ed), Byrd L, Pereira FCN, Pereira LM, Warren DHD (1983) *DECsystem-10 Prolog User's Manual*. Dept of Artificial Intelligence, Univ. of Edinburgh

Clark KL, Gregory S (1981) *A Relational Language for Parallel Programming*. In: Proc ACM Conf on Functional Programming Languages and Computer Architecture. ACM

Clark KL, Gregory S (1984a) *PARLOG: Parallel Programming in Logic*. Research Report DOC 84/4. Dept of Computing, Imperial College, London

Clark KL, Gregory S (1984b) *Notes on Systems Programming in PARLOG*. In: Proc Int Conf on Fifth Generation Computer Systems 1984. Institute for New Generation Computer Technology, Tokyo, 299-306

Clark KL Gregory S (1984c) *Notes on the Implementation of PARLOG*. Research Report DOC 84/16. Dept of Computing, Imperial College, London

Clark KL McCabe F (1980) *IC-PROLOG—Language Features*. In: Tärnlund, S-Å (ed) Proc Logic Programming Workshop. Debrecen, Hungary

Gregory S (1985) *private communication*

Hagiya M (1983) *On Lazy Unification and Infinite Trees*. In: Proc Logic Programming Conference '83. Institute for New Generation Computer Technology, Tokyo (in Japanese)

Hoare CAR (1978) *Communicating Sequential Processes*. Comm ACM 21: 666-677

Kowalski R (1974) *Predicate Logic as Programming Language*. In: Proc IFIP 74. North-Holland, Amsterdam New York Oxford, 569-574

Miyazaki T (1985) *unpublished manuscript*. Institute for New Generation Computer Technology, Tokyo

Nakashima H, Ueda K, Tomura S (1984) *What Is a Variable in Prolog?* In: Proc Int Conf on Fifth Generation Computer Systems 1984. Institute for New Generation Computer Technology, Tokyo, 327-332

Pereira LM, Nasr R (1984) *Delta-Prolog: A Distributed Logic Programming Language*. In: Proc Int Conf on Fifth Generation Computer Systems 1984. Institute for New Generation Computer Technology, Tokyo, 283-291

Robinson JA (1965) *A Machine-Oriented Logic Based on Resolution Principle*. J ACM 12: 23-41

Roussel P (1975) *Prolog: Manual de Reference et d'Utilisation*. Groupe d'Intelligence Artificielle, Marseille-Luminy

Sato M, Sakurai T (1984) *Qute: A Functional Language Based on Unification*. In: Proc Int Conf on Fifth Generation Computer Systems 1984. Institute for New Generation Computer Technology, Tokyo, 157-165

Shapiro EY (1983) *A Subset of Concurrent Prolog and Its Interpreter*. ICOT Technical Report TR-003. Institute for New Generation Computer Technology, Tokyo

Shapiro EY (1984) *Systems Programming in Concurrent Prolog*. In: Conf Record of the 11th Annual ACM Symp on Principles of Programming Languages, ACM, 93-105

Shapiro EY, Takeuchi A (1983) *Object Oriented Programming in Concurrent Prolog*, New Generation Computing, 1: 25-48

Takeuchi A, Furukawa K (1983) *Interprocess Communication in Concurrent Prolog*. In: Proc Logic Programming Workshop '83. Universidade Nova de Lisboa, Portugal

Ueda K, Chikayama T (1984) *Efficient Stream/Array Processing in Logic Programming Languages*. In: Proc Int Conf on Fifth Generation Computer Systems 1984. Institute for New Generation Computer Technology, Tokyo, 317-326

Ueda K, Chikayama T (1985) *Concurrent Prolog Compiler on Top of Prolog*. In: Proc 1985 Symposium on Logic Programming. IEEE Computer Society Press, 119-126

Ueda K (1985) *Concurrent Prolog Re-Examined*. ICOT Tech Report TR-102. Institute for New Generation Computer Technology, Tokyo

Warren DHD, Pereira LM, Pereira F (1977) *PROLOG—The Language and Its Implementation Compared with Lisp*. Sigplan Notices, 12: 109-115

TDProlog : An extended Prolog with Term Description

Satoru Tomura

Language Processing Section, Computer Science Division
ElectroTechnical Laboratory
Ibaraki, Japan

**ABSTRACT**

TDProlog is an extended Prolog with a term description feature. A term description is a pair of a term and a description that the term must satisfy. Declarative and procedural semantics are given. Completeness and soundness of term description is discussed.

In TDProlog, terms are classified into three groups: term descriptions, functional terms and constructive terms. Functional term is defined as a specialized term description. TDProlog provides a way to define a functional term in term rewriting rules. The relation between term description and term rewriting system on functional terms is discussed.

The interpreter of TDProlog is given in Prolog. And TDProlog compiler written in Prolog is also explained. The compiler translates TDProlog programs into Prolog programs. The compiler can deal with mode declarations that help the compiler to execute some unifications at the compilation time.

Bench mark programs show that TDProlog programs run 2 to 5 times slower than Prolog programs and run 9 to 15 times faster than Uranus programs.

## 1. INTRODUCTION

TDProlog(Term Description Prolog) is an extended Prolog and provides a term description feature in addition to Prolog's features. Term description was proposed by Nakashima(1984,1985a). It is an extension of executable pattern in Prolog/KR (Nakashima 1982), and also has been implemented partially in Uranus(Nakashima 1985b).

We implemented TDProlog on DEC10-Prolog(Bowen 1983). Our intentions are:

(A) Term description feature implemented in Uranus dose not have completeness. Uranus sometimes fails to find a solution even when there exists one. This is because unification in Uranus is restricted to behave deterministic. We intend to make a complete Prolog system with term description. TDProlog has completeness and unification in TDProlog is nondeterministic.

(B) Uranus is implemented on Lisp. Term description feature in Uranus is also directly implemented on Lisp. Its implementation is complicated and hard to understand. We intend to implement this feature on Prolog. This enables us to study well about this feature.

(C) Unification used in TDProlog is a nondeterministic unification. In general nondeterministic algorithm is more powerful but more inefficient than deterministic one. Thus we intend to develop an efficient implementation and measure the cost of it.

In this paper we first introduce term description feature of TDProlog and discuss some properties of it. Next the interpreter of TDProlog in Prolog is shown. Last the compiler system is explained and the result of bench mark test is reported.

## 2. TDPROLOG

TDProlog is an extend Prolog. Its extended feature is term description feature.

### 2.1 Term Description

A term description is an extended term. It is a pair of a term and a predicate form. It means that the term must satisfy the predicate form.

A term description is written as "TERM:PRED" where "TERM" is a term and "PRED" is a predicate form. ":" is an infix operator that constructs a term description from a term and a predicate form. For example, a term description

    N:(N > 0)

means that a logical variable "N" must be a positive number.

We give declarative and procedural semantics of term description below.

The declarative semantics of term description is given by equivalent Horn clauses which have the same declarative semantics. This equivalent Horn clauses are made by moving all predicate forms of term description into the negative part of Horn clauses. For example, the declarative semantics of the assertion

    p(X:s(X)) :- r(Y:t(Y)).

is that of the corresponding Horn clause

    p(X) :- s(X),r(Y),t(Y).

Note that the order of negative literals of Horn clause ( in the above example, s(X), r(Y), t(Y) are negative literals ) is not significant. The declarative semantics of the query

    ?- p(U:q(U)).

is that of the following Horn clause

    ?- p(U), q(U).

As concerns the declarative semantics, term description provides convenient notation to write Horn clauses.

Procedural semantics of term description is given by the way of executing term description. The execution of term description means the execution of the predicate part of term description. Term description is executed only when the term description is unified with a nonvariable term. That is,

(1) When a variable is unified with a term description, the variable becomes to be equal to the term description and the term description is not executed.

(2) When a nonvariable term is unified with a term description, the term part of the term description is unified with the nonvariable term and the predicate part of the term description is executed.

## 2.2 Functional Term and Constructive Term

In TDProlog terms are grouped into three classes: term descriptions, functional terms and constructive terms. Functional term is provided as a special case of term description. Syntax of functional term is the same as a term with a prefix operator "!". Terms other than term descriptions and functional terms are constructive terms. For example, "!g(a,b)" is a functional term and its arity is 2. "g(a,b)" is a constructive term. Semantics of functional term is given by an equivalent term description. A functional term

    !f(t1,...,tn)

is equal to the term description

    V:f(t1,...,tn,V)

where "V" is a new logical variable that dose not appear elsewhere in that clause.

## 2.3 Term Rewriting Rules for Functional Terms

Usually, a definition of a functional term is given by the assertion of a predicate which has the same name and whose arity is the arity of the functional term plus 1. For example, the definition of a functional term "!g(X,Y)" is given by the assertion of the predicate "g" whose arity is 3. TDProlog provides another convenient way to give a definition of a functional term. The definition can be given in the form of term rewriting rules by using the assertion of rewriting predicate "==>". The following two styles of rewriting rules are available:

  (A) Unconditional rewriting rule:
      !f(t1,...,tn) ==> s.

  (B) Conditional rewriting rule:
      !f(t1,...,tn) ==> s :- cond.

where "t1",... "tn" and "s" are terms, and "cond" is a predicate form. These are equivalent to the following assertions of predicates respectively.

  (A)    f(t1,...tn,s).
  (B)    f(t1,...tn,s):- cond.

The way to define a functional term in the form of rewriting rules
provides the convenient notation to use functional terms.

## 2.4 Example of Term Descriptions

Several ways to define a predicate "fact" that computes factorial
number are shown below:

(1) Without term description:

```
fact(0,1).
fact(N,F) :- N>0, N1 is N-1, fact(N1,F1), F is N*F1.
```

(2) With term description:

```
sub1(X,Y) :- Y is X-1.
times(X,Y,Z) :- Z is X*Y.
fact(0,1).
fact(N:N>0, F:times(N, F1:fact(N1:sub1(N,N1), F1), F)).
```

(3) With functional terms:

```
!sub1(X) ==> Y :- Y is X-1.
!times(X,Y) ==> Z :- Z is X*Y.
!fact(0) ==> 1.
!fact(N:N>0) ==> !times(N,!fact(!sub1(N))).
```

## 3. INTERPRETER OF TDPROLOG

The interpreter of TDProlog written in Prolog is shown below.  It
consists of two predicates: "solve" and "=TD=".

Predicate "solve" executes its argument as a predicate on TDProlog.

```
solve( true ) :- !.
solve( fail ) :- !, fail.
solve( (P,Q) ) :- solve(P), solve(Q).
solve( (P;Q) ) :- solve(P); solve(Q).
solve( P ) :- !, functor(P,F,N), functor(H,F,N),
    clause(H,Body,_), headUnify(P,H,N), solve(Body).

headUnify(P,H,N) :- mapArgs(P,H,N,=TD=).
```

where predicate "mapArgs" is defined by

```
mapArgs(X,Y,0,P) :- !.
mapArgs(X,Y,N,P) :- !, M is N-1, mapArgs(X,Y,M,P),
    arg(N,X,Xn), arg(N,Y,Yn), C =.. [P, Xn, Yn], call(C).
```

and "mapArgs(X,Y,N,PRED)" means that

(1) X has the same principal functor of Y and

(2) both of the arity of X and Y is N

(3) For each corresponding argument of X and Y, predicate PRED is
applied.

TD-unification is a unification algorithm used in TDProlog.

Predicate "=TD=" implements TD-unification on Prolog.  The definition
of "=TD=" is given below.

```
X   =TD= Y     :- (var(X); var(Y)), !, X = Y.
X:P =TD= Y     :- !, X =TD= Y, solve(P).
X   =TD= Y:Q   :- !, X =TD= Y, solve(Q).
X   =TD= Y     :- !, functor(X,F,N), functor(Y,F,N),
                 mapArgs(X,Y,N,=TD=).
```

## 4. PROPERTIES ON TDPROLOG

### 4.1 Completeness and Soundness of TDProlog

Declarative and procedural semantics of term description are
described above.  Let's discuss the completeness and soundness of
TDProlog.  First we give the meanings of completeness and soundness.

   Completeness: If a program of TDProlog holds in a declarative
      semantics, then the execution of it always terminates and
      succeeds.

   Soundness: If the execution of a program terminates and succeeds,
      then it always holds in a declarative semantics.

The definition of completeness is too strong.  The base language of
TDProlog, that is Prolog, itself is not complete.  So we introduce
weak completeness.  Prolog has weak completeness.

   Weak completeness : If the execution of a program terminates and
      fails, then it never holds in a declarative semantics.


### A. Completeness

Term description has been implemented in Prolog/KR and its successor
Uranus partially.  However term description in them does not have
weak completeness.  This is because unification in Uranus is
restricted to behave deterministic.  Unification in Uranus finds at
most one solution.  During unification of the head unification does
backtrack to find a solution. But after unification of the head finds
one solution once, it does not backtrack anymore.  For instance,
let's consider the following program.

```
        mem(A,[A! _]).
        mem(A,[_!X]) :- mem(A,X).
        p(Y:mem(Y,[a,b,c]).
        ?- p(X:mem(X,[a,c]),p(X:mem(X,[b,c]).
```

If TDProlog executes this program, it finds the solution X=c
correctly.  But Uranus fails because "X:mem(X,[a,c])" has two
solutions (X=a, X=c) but Uranus finds only one of them(X=a). We show
the related part of interpreter of Uranus in Prolog below.

```
        headUnify(P,H,N) :- mapArgs(P,H,N,=TD=),!.
```

The last cut operator("!") in the clause of "headUnify" suppress the
backtracking after "headUnify" succeeds once.  The difference between
Uranus and TDProlog is this last cut operator.  Since TDProlog does
not cut the search in "headUnify", TDProlog have weak completeness.

## B. Soundness

Term description is executed only when unification demands it. Thus if unification does not need the execution of a term description, the term description is never executed. Therefore sometimes the execution of a program terminates with some term descriptions which are not executed. In such case if the predicates of the term description which are not executed does not have any solution, it happen that the program succeed but the program has no solution. That is TDProlog is not sound. For instance, let's consider the following query.

```
?- X=1:(X=2).
```

In the declarative semantics, it is interpreted as

```
?- X=1,X=2.
```

Of course it has no solution. But in TDProlog the program above are terminated successfully. It is because it terminates without the execution of predicate part "(X = 2)".

Current TDProlog has no soundness. However if the procedural semantics of term description is changed as the following, TDProlog has soundness.

(1) When a program have no side effects, after the top level query succeeds, all the term description which are not executed are executed.

(2) When a program contains predicates that have side effects such as input output predicates and meta predicates that manipulate the knowledge database, before a predicate with side effect is invoked, all the delayed predicates are executed.

## 4.2 Term Rewriting System vs. Term Description

Functional terms and its rewriting rules in TDProlog compose conditional term rewriting system on the logic programming language. We defined functional terms by means of term description. On the other hand, term description can be defined by means of functional terms and its rewriting rules, i.e. restricted term rewriting system. Translation rule from term description into conditional term rewriting system is as follows:

An occurrence of term description

```
TERM:PRED
```

is replaced by newly created functional term

```
!FTERM
```

The functor of "FTERM" is a unique symbol which does not appear elsewhere. Each argument of "FTERM" is a variable which occurs in "TERM:PRED". And the rewriting rule on the functional term "!FTERM" is defined as:

```
!FTERM  ==> TERM :- PRED.
```

For example, a program with term descriptions

    p(f(X,g(X)):q(X,Y), X:r(X,Z))

is equal to a program with term rewriting system

    p(!g001(X,Y), !g002(X,Z))

and the rewriting rules

    !g001(X,Y) ==> f(X,g(X)) :- q(X,Y).
    !g002(X,Z) ==> X :- r(X,Z).

Therefore term description is equivalent to conditional term rewriting system.


## 5. TDPROLOG SYSTEM

It is relatively easy to implement TDProlog interpreter on Dec10-Prolog. This is because TDProlog is similar to Prolog. However the interpreter system has some problems.

 (1) It has poor efficiency in speed.
 (2) There in no easy way to implement cut operator.

On the other hand, to make a compiler that translates TDProlog programs into Dec10-Prolog programs has merits described below.

(1) We can gain execution speed in two stages: By unfolding the interpreter and by compiling translated Dec10-Prolog programs into machine codes (by Dec10-Prolog compiler).

(2) The compiler from TDProlog into Prolog can be implemented easier than the compiler from TDProlog into machine codes.

(3) Cut operators in TDProlog are directly translated into DEC10-Prolog's cut operators.

Thus we adopted the compiler system for TDProlog system instead of interpreter system.

### 5.1 Internal representation of Term Description

TDProlog system translates external representation of term description

        TERM : PRED

into internal structure

        '$TD'(TERM,PRED,FLAG,MODE)

Here "FLAG" indicates whether the predicate "PRED" has been already executed and its success has been confirmed. When the predicate "PRED" is not executed, "FLAG" is a variable. When the predicate is executed and succeeds, "FLAG" is instantiated to the symbol "true". If the term description is shared by several predicates, this mechanism eliminates the re-execution of the same predicate. "MODE"

indicates that this term description is in term description form
(MODE = td) or is in functional term form (MODE = fn). This
information is used when an internal representation is displayed as
its external representation which the user typed in. So in TDProlog
the user need not know its internal representation at all.

## 5.2 Compiler

The compiler of TDProlog unfolds the interpreter of TDProlog and if
there are some predicates such that they can be executed at
compilation time, the compiler executes them at compilation time.
For example, let predicate "p" in TDProlog be defined as

```
p(a1) :- q(b1).
p(a2) :- r(b2).
```

Then the execution of "p(t1)" in TDProlog is equivalent to the
execution of "solve( p(t1) )" on Prolog. This form can be
transformed by unfolding predicate "solve":

```
solve( p(t1) ) <-->
        functor(p(t1),F,N), functor(H,F,N),
        clause(H,Body,_),
        mapArgs(p(t1),H,N,=TD=),
        solve(Body).
```

Two predicate invocations of "functor" can be executed at compilation
time. The execution of them instantiates the following variables as:

{ F <-- p, N <-- 1, H <-- p(X1)}

where X1 is a new variable.

Thus the following equation holds.

```
solve( p(t1) ) <-->
        clause(p(X1),Body,_), mapArgs(p(t1),p(X1),1,=TD=),
        solve(Body).
```

By using the definition of "p", "clause(p(X1),Body,_)" can be
executed at compilation time. The following hold.

```
clause( p(X1),Body,_) <-->
        Body=q(b1), X1=a1;
        Body=r(b2), X1=a2
solve( p(t1) ) <-->
        mapArgs(p(t1),p(a1),1,=TD=), solve(q(b1));
        mapArgs(p(t1),p(a2),1,=TD=), solve(r(b2))
```

By expanding the "mapArgs", we get the following.

```
solve( p(t1) ) <-->
        t1 =TD= a1, solve( q(b1) );
        t1 =TD= a2, solve( r(b2) )
```

This means that a specialized "solve" for predicate "p" can be
defined as:

```
solve( p(t1) ) :- t1 =TD= a1, solve( q(b1) ).
solve( p(t1) ) :- t1 =TD= a2, solve( r(b2) ).
```

Then the new definitions are introduced:

```
p_(X) :- solve( p(X) ).
q_(X) :- solve( q(X) ).
r_(X) :- solve( r(X) ).
```

and by folding those predicates we get:

```
p_(A1) :- A1 =TD= a1, q_(b1).
p_(A1) :- A1 =TD= a2, r_(b2).
```

This is a compiled Prolog code which TDProlog compiler produces.

## 5.3 Mode Declaration

We can generate more efficient code when the mode of arguments of predicates are specified. For instance, if an argument of a predicate is guaranteed to be variable when the predicate is invoked, unification with the argument can be executed at compilation time. For that purpose, TDProlog provides mode declaration facility similar to that of DEC10-Prolog compiler.

Syntax of mode declaration is as follows,

```
:-mode p(m1,...,mn).
```

where "m1",..., "mn" are one of "+","-","?". These mean:

- **+ (Input mode)** : When the predicate is invoked, the argument is always a nonvariable term.

- **- (Output mode)** : When the predicate is invoked, the argument is always a variable.

- **? (Undefined mode)** : When the predicate is invoked, the state of that argument is not defined.

Modes can be declared to rewriting rules of functional terms.

```
:-mode !f(m1,...,mn) ==> mk.
```

This gives us the same result when we declare as follows.

```
:-mode f(m1,...,mn,mk).
```

If the mode declaration is omitted, all arguments are interpreted as undefined mode.

We now show how the efficient code can be generated with mode declaration. We use the predicate "app" which concatenates lists as an example.

A program in TDProlog:

```
app([],X,X).
app([A!X],Y,[A!Z]) :- app(X,Y,Z).
```

is compiled into a program in Prolog:

```
        app(A1,A2,A3) :- unifyNil(A1),unify(A2,A3).
        app(A1,A2,A3) :- unifyList(A1,P1,P2),
                unifyList(A3,L1,P3),unify(P1,L1),
                app(P2,A2,P3).
```

where "unifyNil" and "unifyList" are specialized unification predicates defined as:

```
        :- mode unifyNil(?).
        unifyNil([]) :- !.
        unifyNil('$TD'(T,D,Flag,Mode)) :- var(Flag),!,
              unifyNil(T), solve(D), Flag = true.
        unifyNil('$TD'(T,D,true,Mode)) :- !, unifyNil(T).

        :- mode unifyList(+,-,-).
        unifyList([A!B],A,B):- !.
        unifyList('$TD'(T,D,Flag,Mode),X,Y) :- var(Flag),!,
              unifyList(T,X,Y), solve(D), Flag = true.
        unifyList('$TD'(T,D,true,Mode),X,Y) :- !,
              unifyList(T,X,Y).
```

When the mode declaration is specified as,

```
        :- mode app(+,+,-).
```

the compiled code generated by TDProlog compiler is

```
        app(A1,A2,A2) :- unifyNil(A1).
        app(A1,A2,[P1!P3]) :- unifyList(A1,P1,P2),
                app(P2,A2,P3).
```

In the first clause, the third argument "A3" is output mode. Thus "unify(A2,A3)" can be executed at compilation time and we conclude that "A2 = A3" holds. We get the code.

In the second clause, the third argument "A3" is output mode. Thus "unifyList(A3,L1,P3)" can be executed and it is proved that "A3 = [L1!P3]" holds. Moreover we can see that "L1" and "P3" are also output mode from the mode declaration of "unifyList", thus we can execute "unify(P1,L1)" at compilation time also. Then we get "P1 = L1".

Next we show the effect of mode declaration on term description. We use "fact" which calculates the factorial of number "N".

```
        !fact(0) ==> 1.
        !fact(N:N>0) ==> !times(N,!fact(!sub1(N))).
```

The compiled code is:

```
        fact(A1,A2) :- unifyConst(0,A1),unifyConst(1,A2).
        fact(A1,A2) :- unify(A1,'$TD'(N,N>0,_,td)),
                times(A1,!fact(!sub1(A1)),A2).
```

where "unifyConst(C, T)" unify the second argument "T" with the first argument "C" which is grand term and dose not contain term description.

On the other hand, if we supply the next mode declaration,

```
:- mode !fact(+) ==> ?.
```

TDProlog compiler generates more efficient code.

In the second clause, we can see that the variable "A1" is always instantiated to nonvariable term when it is invoked. So "unify(A1,'$TD'(N,N>0,_,td))" can be executed at compilation time. By expanding the restriction "N>0" into body, we get

```
unify(A1,'$TD'(N,N>0,_,td))
<--> unify(A1,N), solve(N>0), _ = true.
```

At this moment, "N" is output mode. So we can also execute "unify(A1,N)" at compilation time. We now get optimized compiled code

```
fact(A1,A2):-
        A1>0,times(A1,!fact(!sub1(A1)),A2).
```

In this case the mode declaration eliminates the internal representation for term description ( '$TD'(N, N>0, _, td) ) from the compiled code.


## 5.4 Results of Benchmark Test

The execution speed of TDProlog, Prolog, Prolog/KR are shown on some examples. The value within parentheses is the value with mode declarations. The computer on which examples runs is DEC2060. Prolog is Prolog-20 Version 1.0 and Prolog/KR is Version S-17.5 on Maclisp. "ms" stands for milliseconds and "LIPS" stands for logical inferences per second.

(1) Concatenate a list with 500 elements and a null list.

```
:- mode(+,+,-).
app([A! X],Y,[A! Z]) :- app(X,Y,Z).
app([],X,X).

?- app([1,2, ... ,500],[],X).
```

| | | | |
|---|---|---|---|
| TDProlog | : | 127(86)ms | 3937( 5826)LIPS |
| Prolog | : | 20(15)ms | 25050(33400)LIPS |
| Prolog/KR | : | 1182(--)ms | 424(-----)LIPS |

(2) Reverse of lists that takes time in the order of the fourth power of the length of the list.

```
:- mode rev4(+,-).
rev4([], []).
rev4([X! Y], Z) :- rev4(Y,W), app4(W,[X],Z).

:- mode app4(+,+,-).
app4([],X,X).
app4([X,Y,Z) :- rev4(X,[Rx! _]), rev4(X,[_! Ry]),
    rev4(Ry,Rz), app4(Rz,[Rx! Y],Z).

?- rev4([1,2,3,4,5,6],X).
```

| | | | |
|---|---|---|---|
| TDProlog | : | 555(376)ms | 11774(17380)LIPS |
| Prolog | : | 261(239)ms | 25038(27343)LIPS |

Prolog/KR :     8627(---)ms         785(-----)LIPS

(3) Prime sieve

!integers(N) ==> [N¦ !integers(!add1(N))].

!sift([P¦R]) ==> [P¦ !sift(!sieve(P,R))].

sieve(P,[X¦Y],Z) :- sieve_if(P,X,Y,Z).
sieve(_,[],[]).

sieve_if(P,X,Y,Z) :- remainder(X,P,0),!,
     Z=(!sieve(P,Y)).
sieve_if(P,X,Y,Z) :- Z=[X ¦ !sieve(P,Y)].

primes(N) :- printn(!sift(!integers(2))),N).

printn(_,0).
printn([X¦Y],N) :- write(X), write(=), printn(Y, !sub1(N)).
?- primes(10).

```
TDProlog    :     144ms
Prolog      :     ---ms
Prolog/KR   :     1561ms
```

Sample programs show that TDProlog programs run 2 to 5 times slower than Prolog programs and run 9 to 15 times faster than Uranus programs. And sample programs also show that appropriate mode declarations make the programs 30% faster.

## ACKNOWLEDGMENTS

The author gives many thanks to Hideyuki Nakashima and Kokichi Futatsugi and Ichirou Ogata at ETL.

## REFERENCE

Bowen DL(ed.), Byrd L, Pereira LM, Warren DHD (1983) DECsystem-10 PROLOG User's Manual, Dept. of Artificial Intelligence, Univ. of Edinburgh

Nakashima H (1982) Prolog/KR - Language Features, Proc. of the First International Logic Programming Conf., pp. 65-70

Nakashima H (1984) Term Description, Proc. of the Logic Programming Conference'84 (in Japanese)

Nakashima H (1985a) Uranus Reference Manual, Research Memorandum 85-1, Information Processing Group, Electrotechnical Laboratory

Nakashima H (1985b) Term Description : A Simple Powerful Extension to Prolog Data Structures, Proc. of IJCAI-IX

# DESIGN AND EVALUATION OF A PROLOG COMPILER

M. Kishimoto, T. Shinogi, Y. Kimura, and A. Hattori

FUJITSU LIMITED
1015 Kamikodanaka Nakahara-ku, Kawasaki 211, Japan

## ABSTRACT

This paper discusses a Prolog compiler for the FACOM α, a symbolic data processing machine. The compiler includes several optimization algorithms, such as separated predicate frames, extended mode declaration, and fast goal invocation. Compiled programs run at 30 to 40 KLIPS.

## 1. INTRODUCTION

A Prolog compiler has been created that runs on the FACOM α, a dedicated machine for symbolic data processing (Akimoto 1985). This paper discusses the design philosophy of the compiler, optimization methods, execution results, and evaluates them.

This Prolog language processor is based on DEC-10 Prolog. The language is identical to DEC-10 Prolog except for part of the syntax and the built-in predicates (Warren 1977).

The Prolog language processor is intertwined with the LISP language processor. The interpreter is started by executing the LISP function PROLOG.

The Prolog interpreter and garbage collector (GC) are implemented by microprograms. The garbage collector is shared by both the LISP and Prolog language processors, using data tags to differentiate the object code. Most of the Prolog I/O routines and built-in predicates are coded in LISP, but some are written in Prolog. The compiler discussed in this paper is also written in LISP.

When executed by the interpreter, programs run at about 12 thousand logical inferences per second (KLIPS), several times slower than required for practical use. A compiler speeds up execution of predicates to 30 to 40 KLIPS.

Section 2 of this paper outlines the compiler and the machine instructions. Section 3 explains the extended mode declarations, which greatly improve execution speed, and methods of fast goal invocation. Section 4 presents some measured results of the execution characteristics of compiled predicates and evaluates the performance.

## 2. COMPILER DESIGN

### 2.1 Data Structures

Compiled predicates have basically the same data structures as when they are interpreted, as shown below.

(1) Structure sharing is used. The data length is 4 bytes, consisting of a 3-byte pointer and a 1-byte data tag. Molecules consist of 8 bytes, including a skeleton and environment.

(2) A compound term is a tuple (LISP vector type) or a CONS cell. For compound terms that do not include variables, there are two special types: constant list, and constant tuple.

(3) Logical inferences are performed using three stacks. The local stack is implemented in hardware. The global stack and trail stack are in main storage, where they can be compacted by the garbage collector.

## 2.2 Separation of Control Frames

In the interface to the compiled predicates, the actual arguments are placed on the local stack before the predicate is called. Since the FACOM α is a stack machine, it does not have any registers manipulated by machine instructions. The method of calling the predicate after its actual arguments have been prepared is the same as the Warren's structure copying method, except for the following differences (Warren 1983, Tick 1984):

(1) Actual arguments are passed on the local stack instead of registers. The compiler is therefore spared the complex task of register allocation. Tail recursion can be performed by changing pointers on the local stack, because it is not necessary to globalize the unsafe variables. Unsafe variables, however, must be considered in in-predicate loop as described below (Warren 1980).

(2) Actual arguments are dereferenced before being passed to predicates. The compiler can determine whether dereferencing is necessary, so it generates code without needless dereference processing. Therefore logical inference can be performed with less dereferencing than when dereferencing is postponed until it becomes necessary.

The FACOM α accesses the local stack by the frame pointer. In Prolog, however, it is determined at run time whether recent choice pointer (RCP) frames are allocated. Since the frame length cannot be calculated at compilation time, stack access by the frame pointer cannot be used. This problem is solved by separating the predicate frame into two parts (Figure 1).

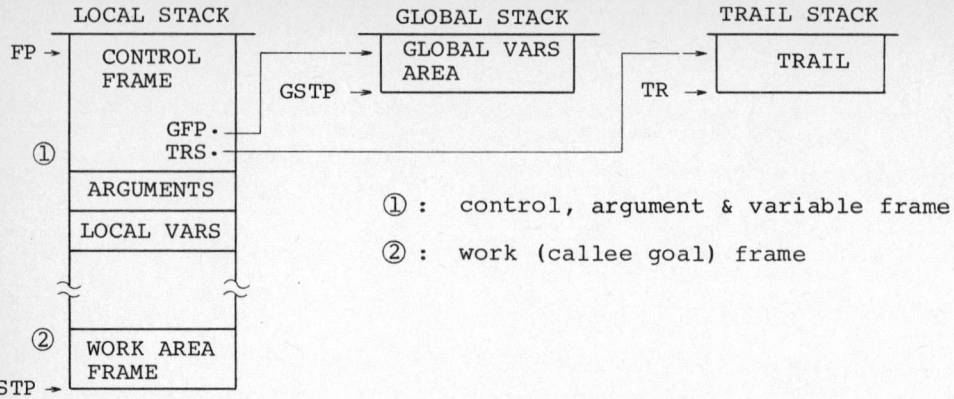

Fig. 1  Layout of the stacks for the Prolog processor

① Control, argument, and variable frame

The compiler can calculate the size of this frame, which is accessed by means of the frame pointer.

② Predicate call (work) frames

This frame is work area used for goal invocation in the clause body. Since there may be an RCP frame between this type of frame and a frame of type ①, access is relative to the stack top pointer rather than the frame pointer.

The contents of the control frame are nearly the same as ones for the interpreter. Three entries are used for different purpose to have compiled predicates run faster.

2.3  Unification

When a compiled predicate is executed, machine instructions corresponding to a body of a clause set actual arguments and invoke a goal. While other machine instructions corresponding to the head of the clause perform unification with actual arguments. If there is a mode declaration, unification is performed in the order of (1) input actual arguments, (2) normal actual arguments, (3) output actual arguments. If each argument is a compound term, all levels of objects are compiled to unify in the depth first manner. Unification is performed at high speed on the hardware stack, without using registers, since there are no registers available to the machine instructions.

In Warren's implementation (Warren 1980), the GET-LIST instruction simply checks whether an argument is a list, then sets a pointer to the compound term. In contrast, the FACOM α GET-LIST instruction checks whether an argument is a list, then decomposes it, and pushes first the cdr part then the car part onto the local stack. (See Figure 2.) The decomposed elements are dereferenced at this time, but no molecules are generated, and the environment pointer (ENV) is explicitly carried about. Molecules are generated (by the

MAKE-MOLECULE instruction) only ahead of a unification for variables (by GET-LOCAL-VARIABLE and other instructions). Suppressing generation of molecules speeds up unification of complex compound terms.


(a)   sample predicate and query

q([X|Y]).        % predicate
?- q([a,b,c]).   % query


(b)   codes for list unification

(LS A1)   % push first argument
(LS ENV)  % push environment
(GL)      % unify list


(c)   Before (GL)     (d)   After (GL)

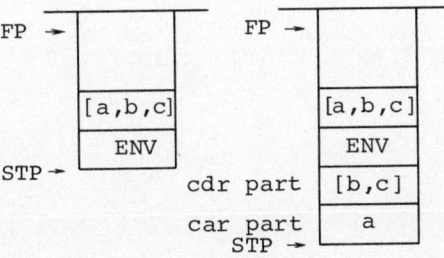

Fig. 2    List unification


2.4   Design of Machine Instructions

The FACOM α has 156 dedicated instructions for LISP. From the standpoints of both function and speed, these instructions are inadequate for Prolog processing, so 65 new machine instructions were added. All machine instructions are implemented by microprogram. A high execution speed achieved by using a 6-byte instruction prefetch buffer, a machine instruction dispatch memory, and other hardware features. The following points were considered in the design of the machine instructions.

(1)   More run-time decisions are made in Prolog than in conventional languages. The semantics of the machine instructions are therefore set at a high level, and decisions are performed on the microprogram level at run time. The number of branch instructions is held down to improve the hit ratio on the instruction buffer.

(2)   Dereferencing, molecule-making, and other common functions are performed by dedicated instructions to eliminate redundant processing at compilation time.

The instructions newly created for Prolog can be classified as follows:   (1) GET instructions to perform unification; (2) PUT instructions to set actual arguments; (3) PROCEDURAL instructions to handle inter-predicate control; (4) INDEXING instructions to select candidate clauses; (5) miscellaneous instructions.

## 3. OPTIMIZATION METHODS

This section discusses extended mode declaration and fast goal invocation, two special methods of optimization used in this compiler.

### 3.1 Speed-up by Mode Declaration

This compiler completely compiles compound terms appearing at the head of a clause. The DEC-10 Prolog like mode declarations (+, -) are therefore extended to allow a deeper mode declaration (++). It declares that all the variables even in compound terms are instantiated. (See Figure 5.) This declaration is satisfied by the first and the third items in Figure 5. In the second item, it is against the mode declaration that the actual argument of variable L1 is uninstantiated. Use of the (++) mode declaration enables an efficient object code to be generated for objects in a compound term.

(a) Declaration

```
append([X|L1],L2,[X|L3]):-
:-mode append(++,++,-).
```

(b) Usage

```
?-append([a,b,c ]   [d ],ANS).
    X=a    L1= [b,c ]   -- OK
?-append([a|Y ]   [d ] ,ANS).
    X=a    L1= UNDEF   -- NO
?-Y= [b|Z ],
  append ( [a|Y ]   [d ], ANS).
    X=a    L1= [b| UNDEF] --  OK
```

Fig. 5   Deeper mode declaration

In an interface in which actual arguments are passed after dereferencing, variables in argument positions with the (+) mode declaration and variables appearing in compound terms in argument positions with the (++) mode declaration are always instantiated (never references). A variable that appears at least once in such a position is called an instantiated variable.

For instantiated variables, dereferencing is unnecessary, so unification can be replaced by the store instructions, and setting of arguments by the load instructions.

A similar situation in which dereferencing can be eliminated is called a real reference. Since an actual argument is set after dereferencing, an argument with the (-) mode declaration is a reference, and the referenced location is always an uninstantiated variable value cell. In general, a reference indicates a constant

or a value cell of a different variable, so it is unsafe to write
without dereferencing. The dereferencing can be omitted, however,
in a real reference. A (-) mode actual argument is always a real
reference during the interval from invocation of the predicate to
the first unification.

Another new mode declaration used in this compiler is a half
instantiated mode declaration (?#, -#). Half instantiated means
that dereferencing would produce a value other than a reference.
The (?#) mode declaration signifies the normal (?) mode declaration
when a goal is called. It also declares that the argument is half
instantiated after the goal termination. Similarly, the (-#) mode
declaration is the input mode declaration (-) when a goal is
called. It also declares that the argument is instantiated after
exit. The half instantiated mode declarations (?#, -#) can be used
to enable the compiler to detect not unsafe variables. The compiler
determines that neither variables declared as input nor half
instantiated in the goal invocation are unsafe.

Ordinarily, mode declarations can be used only in relation to their
own predicates. In this system, mode declarations can also be used
in relation to invoked goals. As an example, the predicate
NOT_TAKE1 in Figure 6 is a part of 8-QUEEN. From the mode
declaration for the NOT_TAKE1 predicate, it cannot be determined
that variables N1 and M1 are safe. But, both variables are proved
not to be unsafe, and recursion can be changed to in-predicate
loop. Since ":- mode is (?#, ++)" is declared for the built-in
predicate. The compiler is equipped with ready-made mode
declarations for the built-in predicates as shown in Figure 7.

```
not_take1( [],N,M).

not_take1( [X|L] , N,M)
   :- X =\= N,
      X =\= M,
      N1 is N+1,
      M1 is M+1,
      not_take1(L,N1,M1).

:- mode not_take1(++,+,+).
```

Fig. 6    Predicate NOT_TEKE1

```
% ARITHMETIC
  :- mode is(?#,++),
          '>'(++,++),
          '=:='(++,++),
          ...
          .

% CONVENIENCE
  :- mode length(+,?#).

% DATA BASE
  :- mode recorded(+,?,?#),
          recoreda(+,?,?#),
          recoredz(+,?,?#),
          erase(+),
          ...
          .
```

Fig. 7   Mode declaration of built-in predicates


3.3   High-Speed Invocation

Goal invocation is speeded up by the following means.  Except for (1), these means are compiler options, because balanced against the high speed are trade-offs such as that non-compiled predicates cannot be invoked, and modifications in predicates are not reflected afterwards.

(1)   Continuation call

Continuation calls are used to speed up termination.  Continuation calls use the same amount of stack as ordinary calls, though they are applicable even to indeterminate clauses.

(2)   Linked call (direct call)

Linked calls are used to speed up calls among compiled predicates. In an ordinary call, a predicate definition is searched from the predicate name and arity, but in a linked call a direct branch is made to the address of the predicate difinition.

(3)   Tail recursive call (TRO) (Warren 1980)

A tail recursive call can be used only with a determinate clause, but it greatly reduces consumption of the local stack.

(4)   Forming of loops within predicates (in-predicate loop)

When a clause is determinate and the last goal is itself, a recursive call is converted to a loop (iteration).  Since loops within predicates are always formed using relative branch instructions, they execute even faster than the combination of a linked call (2) and a tail recursion (3).


4.   PERFORMANCE MEASUREMENTS

We measured the speed performance and dynamic characteristics of the compiled predicate.  This section presents and discusses the results.

## 4.1 Execution Time

Table 8 shows some of the execution times for the problems in the Prolog contest (Okuno, 1984). Execution time was measured for 12 cases to examine how the optimization methods explained in Section 3 contribute. The results indicated in Table 9. Following conclusions are lead from them.

(1) A comparison of sets of cases with the same invocation method but different mode declarations (for example ①, ⑤ and ⑨) shows that the (+, -) mode declaration provides a boost in speed of 0% to 20%. The (++, -#) mode declaration provides a boost in speed of 35% to 70%.

(2) Goal invocation is speeded up by linked call and tail recursion. In terms of execution time, the linked call is faster than the tail recursive call. When in-predicate loops are used, speed is improved by a maximum of 45% compared with the ordinary call.

Table 8   Result of benchmark

[msec]

| Benchmark program | Interpreted code | Compiled code |
|---|---|---|
| APPEND    (30) | 2.74 | 0.75 |
| NREVERSE  (30) | 39.8 | 15.5 |
| QSORT     (50) | 52.1 | 18.6 |
| DATABASE-1 | 51 | 2 |
| LISP (FIB10) | 1156 | 443 |

Table 9    Result in each case

(a)   Optional case explanation

| CASE | Mode | Goal invocation |
|---|---|---|
| ① | x | Normal invocation |
| ② | x | Linked call |
| ③ | x | Tail recursive optimization |
| ④ | x | Trans iteration |
| ⑤ | o | Normal invocation |
| ⑥ | o | Linked call |
| ⑦ | o | Tail recursive optimization |
| ⑧ | o | Trans iteration |
| ⑨ | ⊙ | Normal invocation |
| ⑩ | ⊙ | Linked call |
| ⑪ | ⊙ | Tail recursive optimization |
| ⑫ | ⊙ | Trans iteration |

x:   Without mode, declaration

o:   With +, - mode declaration

⊙:   With ++, -# mode declaration

(b)   Result

| CASE | NREVERSE | | QSORT | |
|---|---|---|---|---|
|  | msec | KLIPS | msec | KLIPS |
| ① | 33.1 | (15) | 31.9 | (23) |
| ② | 28.9 | (17) | 28.7 | (25) |
| ③ | 27.9 | (18) | 29.8 | (24) |
| ④ | 26.5 | (19) | 26.7 | (27) |
| ⑤ | 29.6 | (18) | 30.1 | (24) |
| ⑥ | 25.3 | (20) | 26.9 | (27) |
| ⑦ | 26.9 | (18) | 28.0 | (26) |
| ⑧ | 26.9 | (18) | 28.0 | (26) |
| ⑨ | 22.3 | (22) | 23.7 | (31) |
| ⑩ | 18.3 | (27) | 20.5 | (35) |
| ⑪ | 19.5 | (25) | 21.6 | (33) |
| ⑫ | 15.5 | (32) | 18.6 | (39) |

4.2   Stack Consumption

Consumption of the three stacks was measured during execution of compiled code and we compare it with consumption during execution of interpreted code. Several programs were run, and stack consumption was measured for eight of the same cases as in Section 4.1. Table 10 gives the results.

Table 10    Stack consumption

[Word = 4 byte]

| Program | CASE | LOCAL | GLOBAL | TRAIL |
|---|---|---|---|---|
| NREVERSE | INT | 472 | 2822 | 435 |
|  | ① | 477 | 2763 | 0 |
|  | ② | ↓ | ↓ | ↓ |
|  | ③ |  |  |  |
|  | ④ | ↓ | ↓ | ↓ |
|  | ⑨ | 496 | 1023 | 0 |
|  | ⑩ | ↓ | ↓ | ↓ |
|  | ⑪ |  |  |  |
|  | ⑫ | ↓ | ↓ | ↓ |
| QSORT | INT | 754 | 1652 | 268 |
|  | ① | 818 | 1654 | 104 |
|  | ② | ↓ | ↓ | ↓ |
|  | ③ | 197 |  |  |
|  | ④ | ↓ | ↓ | ↓ |
|  | ⑨ | 868 | 1023 | 104 |
|  | ⑩ | ↓ | ↓ | ↓ |
|  | ⑪ | 197 |  |  |
|  | ⑫ | ↓ | ↓ | ↓ |

(1) Local stack consumption was greatly reduced by the tail recursive call and the in-predicate loops. For NREVERSE, stack consumption was not reduced, because the compiler cannot recognize the NREVERSE predicate is determinate.

(2) Without mode declaration, global stack consumption was about the same as in execution by the interpreter. With mode declaration, global stack consumption was reduced because variables were reclassified.

(3) Compilation have candidate clauses narrow down. Clauses that previously had alternatives became determinate, and trail stack consumption was reduced.

4.3    CPU Occupied Rate

The CPU occupied rate was measured during Prolog execution. Figure 8 shows the CPU occupied rate for APPEND and 8-QUEEN for compiled and interpreted codes.

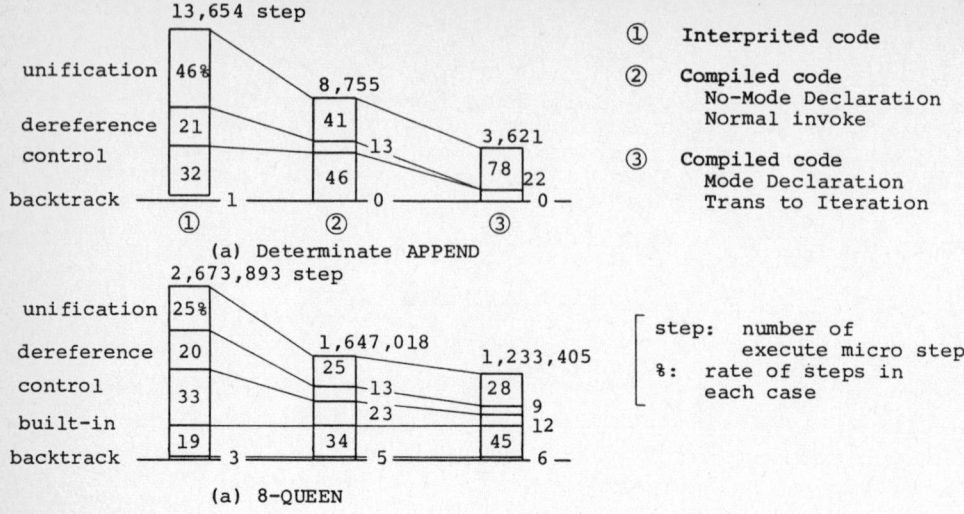

Fig. 8  Dynamic analysis of Prolog execution

(1) More than 80% of the dereferencing done by the interpreter was eliminated by using the mode declarations discussed in Section 3.2. In APPEND, all dereferencing was eliminated.

(2) Special unification, generated by compilation of clause head, cuts the unification operation roughly in half.

(3) It is difficult to speed up the execution of programs like 8-QUEEN which consist of a high proportion of built-in predicates, because the execution time of these predicates is fixed.

## 5.  CONCLUSION

A Prolog compiler for the FACOM α has been created. Compiled predicates run at 30 to 40 KLIPS, about three times faster than when interpreted. Extended mode declarations were added to improve execution speed, giving improvements of 35% to 70% over no declarations, and 25% to 70% over conventional mode declarations. Various invocation methods were evaluated, and a dynamic analysis of compiled predicates was performed to evaluate the FACOM α.

This research was done at the request of the Institute for New Generation Computer Technology (ICOT) as part of the fifth-generation computer project.

ACKNOWLEDGMENTS

The authors wish to acknowledge the guidance received from
Mr. Tanahashi and Mr. Hayashi, and the useful discussions with other
members of the laboratory staff.  They also wish to thank
Mr. Sugino, Mr. Yamazaki, Miss Ino, and Mr. Yamauchi of Fujitsu SSL
for cooperation in developing the compiler and collecting data.


REFERENCES

AKIMOTO H (1985) Evaluation of the dedicated Hardware in FACOM
    ALPHA.  IEEE 1985 COMPCON SPRING

Okuno H (1984) Proposed problems for 3rd LISP contest and 1st
    Prolog contest.  (In Japanese) IPSJ, SYM, 28-4

Tick E, Warren DHD (1984) Towards a pipelined Prolog processor.
    1984 International Symposium on Logic Programming

Warren DHD (1977) Implementing Prolog - compiling predicate
    programs.  DAI Research Report 39-40, Univ. of Edinburgh

Warren DHD (1980) An improved Prolog implementation which
    optimizes tail recursion.  1980 Logic Programming Workshop,
    Debrecen, Hungary

Warren DHD (1983) An abstract Prolog instruction set.  Tech Note
    309, AIC SRI International

The Program Characteristics in Logic Programming Language ESP

Akira Yamamoto, Masaki Mitsui, Hiroyuki Yoshida, Minoru Yokota[*] and Katsuto Nakajima[**]

Systems Laboratory, Oki Electric Co., Ltd., 10-12, Shibaura 4-chome, Minato-ku, Tokyo, Japan

Abstract

This paper describes static and dynamic characteristics of programs written in ESP ( Extended Self-contained Prolog ) running on PSI ( Personal Sequential Inference machine ). All the software modules on PSI are written in ESP. Four actual programs are chosen to measure the number of arguments, alternatives, the ratios of built-in predicate calls to all other calls, and so forth. The results of this measurement are summarized and evaluated.

1. INTRODUCTION

Logic programming languages are attracting attention and many language processors are under development. However, few papers and documents evaluating the programs written in logic programming languages have been presented. This has motivated us to measure and analyze data on both the static and the dynamic characteristics of various programs written in a logic programming language called ESP (Extended Self-contained Prolog).

ESP runs on the personal sequential inference machine (PSI) developed by the Institute for New Generation Computer Technology (ICOT) as a part of Fifth Generation Computer System (FGCS) project.

This paper describes the static and the dynamic characteristics of four ESP application programs. Then, on the basis of the results, characteristics of practical programs are discussed from an architectural standpoint.

2. EVALUATION METHOD

The static and the dynamic characteristics of four ESP programs are analyzed and evaluated.

2.1 ESP Programs

ESP is a system description language based on a logic programming language (Chikayama 1984). ESP has a unification mechanism for parameter passing and a depth-first AND-OR tree search by backtracking

---

[*]Institute for New Generation Computer Technology, Mita-Kokusai Bldg. 21F, 4-28 Mita 1-chome, Minato-ku, Tokyo, Japan
[**]Information Systems and Electronics Development Laboratory, Mitsubishi Electric Corp., 5-1-1 Oofuna, Kamakura City, Kanagawa-Ken, Japan

like DEC-10 Prolog. It also introduces object-oriented and macro description mechanisms. we have been mainly concerned to evaluate those features of ESP related to logic programming languages.

The following four programs are evaluated on PSI.

<u>8 Puzzle:</u> The numbers from one to eight are arranged in a grid of three rows by three columns like the input pattern in Fig. 1. Scrambling the order of these numbers for the initial position in Fig. 1, this program finds the shortest path to reordering them.

Input pattern

| 8 | 7 | 6 |
|---|---|---|
| 1 | * | 5 |
| 2 | 3 | 4 |

Initial position

| 1 | 2 | 3 |
|---|---|---|
| 8 | * | 4 |
| 7 | 6 | 5 |

Fig. 1.   8 Puzzle

<u>BUP translator:</u> This program converts CFG (Context Free Grammar) rules described in DCG (Definite Clause Grammar) format into an ESP program to perform bottom-up parsing. A simple Japanese grammar is chosen as input data for the program.

<u>Window system:</u> This program is one of the modules of PSI operating system. The program generates a window on a bit-mapped display, displays a character in the window and erases the window.

<u>Harmonizer:</u> This system is a sort of the expert system. It generates four-part chorus for a given melody. This program adds the proper accompanied notes to each original melody note to produce chord by chord-generation rules.

2.2  Analyzed Items

2.2.1  Static Characteristics

ESP is based on the Prolog-like high-level machine language called KL0 (Kernel Language version 0). ESP programs are translated by a compiler into KL0 programs, then executed on PSI. All the features of ESP are thus built upon the features of KL0. The static characteristics of the four programs are evaluated by analyzing KL0 program.

A KL0 program is represented by a set of clauses. One clause consists of one head and one body, and one body consists of a group of goals. A goal is either a built-in predicate or a user-defined predicate.

Data is measured to evaluate the static characteristics of the programs on the following items;

1) Execution Control

<u>Clause type:</u> Clauses are divided into four types listed below. The numbers of clauses of each type are counted in each program and the ratio of that clause type (1) is calculated.

- Unit clause     H.
    A clause consisting of a head only.
- Pseudo unit clause    H :-b,...,b.
    A clause with a body consisting of built-in predicates only.
- Transitive clause    H :-B. or H :-b,...,b,B.
    A clause with a body consisting of either a user-defined predicate or a series of built-in predicates followed by a user-defined predicate.
- Regular clause    H :-B,B',...,B'.
    All clauses not belonging to the above three types.

NOTE: In the above description, "H", "B", "b" and "B'" represent a head goal, user-defined predicate, built-in predicate and user-defined or built-in predicate, respectively.

$$\frac{\Sigma \text{ Clauses of a particular type}}{\Sigma \text{ Clauses}} \quad (1)$$

NOTE: The symbol " " sums up the specified clauses or predicates or arguments for the program of interest.

<u>OR relation:</u> An OR relation represents the relationship between two clauses whose head has a predicate of the same name and the same number of arguments. The average number of OR relations is defined as follows (2).

$$\frac{\Sigma \text{ Clauses}}{\Sigma \text{ Predicates}} \quad (2)$$

<u>Built-in predicate:</u> The number of built-in predicates and their ratios (3) are obtained.

$$\frac{\Sigma \text{ Built-in predicates}}{\Sigma \text{ Body goals}} \quad (3)$$

2) Unification

<u>Argument:</u> The average number of arguments in a head goal (4) is calculated. The head arguments and body goal arguments are classified to three data type; variable, constant and structure. "Atom", "integer" and "floating" types belong to the constant data type, while "compound term", "vector", and "string" types belong to the structured data type. The number of arguments and their ratios (5),(6) are obtained separately for head goals and body goals.

$$\frac{\Sigma \text{ Head arguments}}{\Sigma \text{ Clauses}} \quad (4)$$

$$\frac{\Sigma \text{ Head arguments of particular data type}}{\Sigma \text{ Head arguments}} \quad (5)$$

$$\frac{\Sigma \text{ Body arguments of particular data type}}{\Sigma \text{ Body arguments}} \quad (6)$$

## 2.2.2 Dynamic characteristics

After ESP programs are compiled into KL0 programs, they are executed on the PSI under control of SIMPOS (SIM Program and Operating System). The dynamic characteristics of the ESP programs are obtained by analyzing the behavior of the KL0 programs at execution.

KL0 programs are directly interpreted by PSI micro interpreter and dedicated hardware. Measurement points are set at several points in the micro interpreter, and the necessary data is measured in real time as a program passes these points. This method allows data on the same item to be measured for the dynamic and static characteristics.

The dynamic characteristics of ESP programs are measured on PSI under the SIMPOS operating system. And process switch evokes the SIMPOS process management routine during program execution. Therefore the dynamic characteristics in Window partially include those of the process management, because process switch occurs in Window.

To evaluate dynamic characteristics of the programs, data is measured on the following items;

1) Execution Control

<u>Clause type:</u> The number of called clauses including those recalled by backtracking and their ratios (7) are obtained for four called clause types; unit clauses, pseudo unit clauses, transitive clauses and regular clauses.

$$\frac{\Sigma \text{ Called clauses of a particular type}}{\Sigma \text{ Called clauses}} \qquad (7)$$

<u>Nondeterministic clause:</u> When unification fails, an alternative clause of the last executed clause is executed (backtracking). A clause that has other choices excluded is called a nondeterministic clause. The number of nondeterministic clauses and their ratios (8) are obtained.

$$\frac{\Sigma \text{ Nondeterministic clauses}}{\Sigma \text{ Called clauses (including those recalled by backtracking)}} \qquad (8)$$

<u>Built-in predicate:</u> The number of built-in predicates is measured and their ratios (9) are obtained.

$$\frac{\Sigma \text{ Executed built-in predicates}}{\Sigma \text{ Executed body goals}} \qquad (9)$$

<u>Fail and backtracking:</u> There are two types of backtracking, shallow and deep backtracking. Shallow backtracking is performed when the clause whose unification failed has alternative clauses executed. Deep backtracking is performed when the clause does not have alternative clauses. For fail and backtracking, the following data are obtained. the number of successful or failed unifications on user-defined predicates and their ratios (10); the ratio of successful or failed unifications on built-in predicates (11); and the number of shallow or deep backtrackings and their ratios (12).

NOTE: Unifications include re-executions due to backtracking.

$\dfrac{\Sigma \text{ Successful (or failed) unifications on user-defined predicate}}{\Sigma \text{ Executed user-defined predicates}}$ \hfill (10)

$\dfrac{\Sigma \text{ Successful (or failed) unifications on built-in predicates}}{\Sigma \text{ Executed built-in predicates}}$ \hfill (11)

$\dfrac{\Sigma \text{ Shallow (or deep) backtrackings}}{\Sigma \text{ Backtrackings}}$ \hfill (12)

<u>Clause indexing:</u> The PSI performs clause-indexing to speed up predicate call, using a non-variable argument in a head goal as a key. The compiler statically analyzes a program to generate an indexing code for a group of clauses where the first head argument in the heads consists of more than two kinds of non-variable symbols and include more than four OR relations. The successful indexing ratio (13) is obtained.

$\dfrac{\Sigma \text{ Successful indexings}}{\Sigma \text{ Executed body goals}}$ \hfill (13)

2) Unification

<u>Argument:</u> Unification is executed between a body goal of calling clause and a head goal of called clause. The average number of arguments appearing in body goals of user-defined predicates at execution is also obtained (14). Arguments are divided into three data types; variable, constant and structure. The numbers of data types of arguments and their ratios of total head and body arguments (15), (16) respectively are also obtained.

NOTE: Head arguments include those recalled by backtracking.

$\dfrac{\Sigma \text{ Executed user-defined predicate arguments}}{\Sigma \text{ Executed user-defined predicates in bodies}}$ \hfill (14)

$\dfrac{\Sigma \text{ Called head arguments of a particular type}}{\Sigma \text{ Called head arguments}}$ \hfill (15)

$\dfrac{\Sigma \text{ Executed body arguments of a particular type}}{\Sigma \text{ Executed body arguments}}$ \hfill (16)

## 3. EVALUATION RESULTS

### 3.1 Static Characteristics

Table 1 shows the results of the analysis of static characteristics.

### 3.1.1 Execution Control

The unit clause ratio and the average of OR relations are high in the 8 Puzzle and Harmonizer (Table 1). Both programs show that clauses with a high OR-relation averages (3.9 in 8 Puzzle and 7.5 in Harmonizer) are unit clauses or pseudo unit clauses. This indicates that the database comprises greater part of the programs.

Pseudo unit clauses in a database have the built-in predicate "cut" for execution order as a body goal. After one pseudo unit clause in the database is selected, "cut" prevents another value of the database from being chosen in the subsequent backtracking.

The built-in predicate ratio is higher than that of user-defined predicates over all programs (Table 1). The four programs show higher built-in predicate ratios than the DEC-10 Prolog programs reported in Onai (1984). This is attributed to assortment of built-in predicates incorporated with data manipulations in KL0.

### 3.1.2 Unification

One head goal has 3.4 arguments on average. This is similar to characteristics of programs written in DEC-10 Prolog (Onai 1984). The ratio of the constant data type of head arguments is highest in the 8 Puzzle and Harmonizer (Table 1), because arguments of unit clauses constituting the database are constant data types. The variable data type accounts for most of the body arguments in all clauses (Table 1).

## 3.2 Dynamic Characteristics

Tables 2 and 3 illustrate the results of the analysis of the dynamic characteristics.

### 3.2.1 Execution Control

The ratio for called regular clauses is more than 50 percent in all programs (Table 2). This indicates that execution environments for more than half of the clauses has to be saved for successful return.

PSI uses clause indexing to speed up processing. The indexing reduces the actual execution count of unification. The ratio of unit clauses and pseudo unit clauses in 8 Puzzle and Harmonizer with database is lower than for the static characteristics, because the clause indexing is successful (Table 2).

One remarkable point is that the built-in predicate ratio is more than about 65 percent (Table 2) in all programs; in particular, 8 Puzzle program is as high as 93 percent.

The non-deterministic clause ratio is more than 70 percent except in Window (Table 2); this suggests that execution environments for a large number of clauses have to be kept for backtracking. The non-deterministic clause ratio is low in Window, because Window is a part of operating system with deterministic processes. However, 49 percent of the called clauses is nondeterministic (table 2). This contradicts the initial prediction that operating system programs would be described deterministically.

About 40 percent of unifications of user-defined predicates fail, except in Window (Table 3). Unification is less likely to fail in Window, because the program is executed uni-directionally.

The failed unification ratio on built-in predicates is low for all programs (Table 3), because unification on some built-in predicates like "cut" never fails and unification on other built-in predicates, for example, arithmetic operations, fails only infrequently.

The shallow backtracking ratio is high for all programs (average about 70 percent). The ratio for BUP is as high as 91 percent (Table 3). This suggests that backtracking is frequently used as case branching.

### 3.2.2 Unification

Average number of body goal argument is 4.2 (Table 2). Constant and structured data types appear on average in 75 percent of body goal arguments at execution (Table 2). This means that many body arguments have a ground value at unification. And if body goals have four arguments, three out of four are used to pass data to the called clause and another one to receive data from the called clause.

Structured data type appears frequently in both body and head arguments in BUP, reflecting the features of the program.

## 3.3 Comparison of Static and Dynamic Characteristics

The dynamic characteristics in Window partially include those of the SIMPOS process management, because process switch occurs in Window. Though comparison between static and dynamic characteristics in Window is not appropriate, it is worth while comparing the characteristics of Window as an operating system program.

### 3.3.1 Features of execution control

Regular clauses appear frequently in dynamic characteristics, but not in static characteristics (Tables 1 and 2). This seems to be because the programs are written in a tail recursive manner. Clause indexing also contributes to this phenomenon. Clause indexing decreases the number of access to the database, which consists of unit clauses and pseudo unit clauses.

Window with a low OR-relation average for static characteristics also has low backtracking ratio for dynamic characteristics (Tables 1 and 3). Though the 8 Puzzle and Harmonizer have large databases, the backtracking ratio is held down by clause indexing.

### 3.3.2 Features of unification

For the static characteristics, constant data appears frequently in head arguments of database in the 8 Puzzle and Harmonizer, while variable data appears in other programs. For the dynamic characteristics, variable data appears frequently for all the programs. The constant data appears less frequently in dynamic characteristic in head arguments of the 8 Puzzle and Harmonizer, because the database is less frequently accessed comparing with static analysis.

Structured data appears frequently in head arguments of BUP in static and dynamic characteristics.

Static characteristics differ from dynamic characteristics in body argument data type. For static characteristics, variable data appears frequently, while for dynamic characteristics, constant or structured data appears. This is because variables in the body goal are bound to values at unification.

### 3.3.3 Features of built-in predicates

The built-in predicates ratio is high for both static and dynamic characteristics. Built-in predicates appear frequently on the program lists and frequently tend to appear during execution.

Low correlation is found between the two characteristics. Especially, the database does not significantly affect the dynamic characteristics by clause-indexing.

## 4. ARCHITECTURAL CONSIDERATIONS

Most head goals have less than 10 arguments. It is enough to optimize unification on clauses up to 10 arguments. Built-in predicates appear frequently in goals. Therefore, faster execution for built-in predicates increase overall execution speed.

It is expected that clause-indexing is effective unless the head argument of the called clause is a variable, because the calling clause's body goal argument is likely to have a ground value at unification. However, clause-indexing is not effective in some cases when the called clauses have few choices, because processing speed of clause indexing is not faster than simple unification.

When the called clause has alternatives, the execution environment must be kept for later backtracking. However, when unification fails or the built-in predicate "cut" appears just after a head's unification, saving the environment is not necessary. The sequence of built-in predicates which appear just after the head's unification is called extended head. In dynamic characteristics, shallow backtracking accounts for a high ratio of total backtracking and "cut"'s appear frequently in extended-heads. Therefore, faster processing can be achieved by delaying the saving of the environments for backtracking until completion of unification and the extended-head processing.

Processing speed will be increased by "argument copying" to duplicate the values from the calling clause arguments to the environments of the called clauses before unification (Yokota 1984), because backtrackings are frequently performed. This method permits copied values to be reused at unification after backtracking.

## 5. CONCLUSION

This report discussed static and dynamic characteristics of four ESP programs and analyzed their features for similarities and differences.

The analyses lead to the following conclusions;
. Built-in predicates appear frequently in both the static and the dynamic analyses.
. Shallow backtracking appear more frequently than deep backtracking.

It is difficult to have general conclusions from limited evaluation result. However, several analyses of the program characteristics could be performed. More detailed characteristics will be obtained by measuring data from a wider variety of programs in future. The results of this report will be useful in the design of machines for logic languages.

## 6. ACKNOWLEDGMENTS

The authors would like to thank to Dr. Toshio Yokoi, chief of the Second Research Laboratory and Dr. Shunichi Uchida, chief of the Fourth Research Laboratory in ICOT, for their valuable suggestions and encouragement. They would also like to extend our thanks to all the researchers at ICOT who provided us with programs for evaluation and contributed to the discussions.

## REFERENCES

Onai R, Shimizu H, Masuda K, Aso M (1984) Analysis of Sequential Prolog Programs, Proc. of The logic Programming Conference'84 Japan

Yokota M, Yamamoto A, Taki K, Nishikawa H, Uchida S, Nakajima K, and Mitsui M (1984) A Microprogrammed Interpreter for The Personal Inference Machine, Proc. of The International Conference on Fifth Generation Computer Systems'84, Japan

Chikayama T (1984) Unique Features of ESP, Proc. of The International Conference on Fifth Generation Computer Systems'84, Japan

Table 1. Static characteristics

|  | 8PUZZLE | BUP | WINDOW | HARMONIZER |
|---|---|---|---|---|
| Total predicates | 25 | 58 | 2392 | 62 |
| Total clauses | 97 | 110 | 2895 | 467 |
| CLAUSE TYPE | | | | |
| Unit clause | 72(74%) | 6( 6%) | 154( 5%) | 296(63%) |
| Pseudo unit clause | 12(13%) | 43(39%) | 948(33%) | 135(29%) |
| Transitive clause | 6( 6%) | 22(20%) | 388(13%) | 14( 3%) |
| Regular clause | 7( 7%) | 39(35%) | 1405(49%) | 22( 5%) |
| Ave. of OR relations | 3.9 | 2.0 | 1.2 | 7.5 |
| Built-in predicates | 91(73%) | 315(65%) | 9116(70%) | 269(79%) |
| Ave. of head arguments | 2.3 | 3.9 | 3.2 | 4.2 |
| DATA TYPE OF BODY ARG. | | | | |
| Variable | 265(79%) | 905(85%) | 22243(72%) | 544(80%) |
| Constant | 62(18%) | 76( 7%) | 8469(27%) | 108(16%) |
| Structure | 10( 3%) | 88( 8%) | 276( 1%) | 25( 4%) |
| DATA TYPE OF HEAD ARG. | | | | |
| Variable | 73(33%) | 284(67%) | 7851(89%) | 409(21%) |
| Constant | 142(64%) | 14( 3%) | 557( 6%) | 1509(77%) |
| Structure | 7( 3%) | 128(30%) | 387( 5%) | 48( 2%) |

Table 2. Dynamic characteristics

|  | 8PUZZLE | BUP | WINDOW | HARMONIZER |
|---|---|---|---|---|
| Total clauses | 78732 | 527 | 2814 | 14635 |
| Unit clause | 30326(39%) | 5( 1%) | 8( 0%) | 2714(19%) |
| Pseudo unit clause | 84( 0%) | 63(12%) | 853(30%) | 2529(17%) |
| Transitive clause | 16( 0%) | 112(21%) | 485(17%) | 311( 2%) |
| Regular clause | 48306(61%) | 347(66%) | 1468(53%) | 9081(62%) |
| Non determ. clause | 59201(75%) | 374(71%) | 1374(49%) | 9944(68%) |
| built-in predicates | 479908(93%) | 503(64%) | 10569(82%) | 15469(70%) |
| Ave. of user goal arg. | 4.0 | 3.2 | 4.7 | 4.3 |
| DATA TYPE OF BODY ARG. | | | | |
| Variable | 35423(25%) | 367(49%) | 1795(17%) | 4561(18%) |
| Constant | 88461(62%) | 127(17%) | 6075(59%) | 15756(62%) |
| Structure | 17681(13%) | 255(34%) | 2463(24%) | 4985(20%) |
| DATA TYPE OF HEAD ARG. | | | | |
| Variable | 88612(45%) | 739(55%) | 11736(88%) | 31979(61%) |
| Constant | 91277(46%) | 148(11%) | 1401(10%) | 15167(29%) |
| Structure | 17697( 9%) | 466(34%) | 261( 2%) | 4967(10%) |
| Clause indexing | 50% | 0% | 12% | 26% |

Table 3. Fail and backtrack

|  | built-in | | user | | backtrack | |
|---|---|---|---|---|---|---|
|  | success | fail | success | fail | shallow | deep |
| 8PUZZLE | 467211 (97%) | 12696 ( 3%) | 48111 (61%) | 30621 (39%) | 26470 (61%) | 16847 (39%) |
| BUP | 372 (75%) | 123 (25%) | 341 (65%) | 186 (35%) | 281 (91%) | 28 ( 9%) |
| WINDOW | 9094 (94%) | 593 ( 6%) | 2417 (86%) | 397 (14%) | 546 (55%) | 444 (45%) |
| HARMONIZER | 12360 (83%) | 2592 (17%) | 8172 (56%) | 6475 (44%) | 7160 (79%) | 1907 (21%) |

Extended Prolog and Its Application to an Integrated Parser
for Text Understanding

Kuniaki Uehara, Takashi Kakiuchi,
Osamu Mikami, and Jun'ichi Toyoda

The Institute of Scientific and Industrial Research,
Osaka University,
8-1 Mihogaoka, Ibaraki, Osaka 567, Japan

Abstract

This paper presents an extended Prolog and its application to an integrated parser for text understanding. The word 'integrated' includes some meanings. First, syntactic, semantic, and contextual analyses occur as an integral part of the parsing process. Second, three distinct metaphors available in the field of computational linguistics, such as procedure oriented, declaration oriented, and actor oriented metaphors are incorporated into a single grammar formalism. Third, two major discourse analyses, expectation-driven and explanation-driven approaches are unified into a single module. The language Prolog discussed here is extended by allowing the inclusion of both 'equality assertions' for defining a new data type and computational entities 'actors' for performing computation via 'message passing'.

## 1 INTRODUCTION

IP is an abbreviation of an Integrated Parser for text understanding. For IP, the word 'integrated' includes some meanings. First, syntactic, semantic, and contextual analyses occur as an integral part of the parsing process. Second, three distinct metaphors available in the field of computational linguistics, such as procedure oriented (i.e., PROGRAMMAR (Winograd 1972) and ATN (Woods 1970)), declaration oriented (i.e., DCG (Pereira 1980) and PAMPS (Uehara 1984)), and actor oriented (i.e., Word Expert Parser (Small 1981) and Object-oriented Parser (Phillips 1983)) metaphors are incorporated into a single grammar formalism. Third, two major discourse analyses, top-down (i.e. scenario-based, expectation-driven) and bottom-up (i.e. coherence-relation-based, explanation-driven) approaches are unified into a single module.

In the previous paper (Uehara 1985), the grammar formalism and control structure of IP were described, the mechanism for text understanding by means of 'prediction' and 'presupposition' was explained, and examples of output from IP were given. This paper is intended to show the implementation details of IP in the framework of logic programming. The language Prolog discussed here is extended by allowing the inclusion of both 'equality assertions' (Kornfeld 1983) for defining a new data type and computational entities 'actors' (Hewitt 1977) for performing computation via 'message passing'.

## 2 IP GRAMMAR

The syntax of an IP grammar is based on a Lexical Functional Grammar

(LFG) proposed by Bresnan et al. (1982), which has grown out of ideas from current transformational linguistics and computational linguistics. In LFG, the parsing of a sentence takes place in three steps. First a constituent structure (c-structure) is generated using a CFG (ignoring schemata). The c-structure is a conventional phrase structure tree. Secondly the schemata associated with non-terminals are instantiated. That is, each meta-variable in the schemata is replaced by the identifier for the node of the c-structure. Finally these instantiated schemata, called a functional description which is a set of equations, are solved to produce a functional structure (f-structure). We claim that the parsing process of a sentence described above can be done more efficiently by doing all the three steps simultaneously (on-line parsing). On-line parsing means that it evaluates the augmentation (schemata) of a rule as soon as the rule is applied.

The following introduction is fairly self-contained, but readers are expected to be familiar with the basic concepts and notations of LFGs.

## 2.1 Data Structure

In IP, the grammatical relation of an input sentence is represented by an f-structure. The f-structure is composed of a set of ordered pairs each of which consists of an attribute and a specification of the attribute's value for the input sentence. An attribute is the name of a grammatical function or a feature. A value is either a symbol, a semantic form, or an f-structure. A symbol is a primitive type of attribute's values. There are two types of semantic forms. One is called an event, which is a logical formula encoding the meaning of the input sentence. The event comprises a predicate name followed by a sequence of one or more arguments. A predicate name is characterized to represent its sense or meaning. An argument will be assigned to an f-structure which specifies the grammatical function of its thematic role. The second type of semantic forms is called an individual. Individuals do not have any arguments. Figure 1 shows the f-structure for the sentence "*John opened the window*".

$$\begin{bmatrix} \text{subject} = \begin{bmatrix} \text{num} = \text{singular} \\ \text{ind} = \text{john} \end{bmatrix} \\ \text{tense} = \text{past} \\ \text{event} = \text{open}( \begin{bmatrix} \text{num} = \text{singular} \\ \text{ind} = \text{john} \end{bmatrix}, \begin{bmatrix} \text{num} = \text{singular} \\ \text{ind} = \text{window} \\ \text{spec} = \text{the} \end{bmatrix}) \\ \text{object} = \begin{bmatrix} \text{num} = \text{singular} \\ \text{ind} = \text{window} \\ \text{spec} = \text{the} \end{bmatrix} \end{bmatrix}$$

Fig. 1 An f-structure.

## 2.2 The Syntax of an IP Grammar

An IP grammar has two kinds of rules: augmented context-free rules (hereafter we will simply say grammar rules) and lexical items, each of which non-terminal is associated with schemata.

A grammar rule is of the form:

<left-hand-side> --> <right-hand-side>.

<left-hand-side> consists of a single non-terminal. <right-hand-side>

is of the form:

<non-terminal₁><schemata₁>, ... ,<non-terminal_k><schemata_k>

A lexical item is of the form:

<terminal> ; <non-terminal><schemata>.

A schema is either a defining schema, which defines the value of some feature, or a constraining schema, which constrains a feature whose value is expected to be defined by a separate specialization. In other words, the defining schema is for constructing an f-structure of a sentence. Whereas the constraining schema is for specifying the grammatical constraint on the sentence. A defining schema is of the form:

<designator> = <designator>          (1)

(1) expresses that the f-structure indicated by the left-hand side is identified with the f-structure indicated by the right-hand side.

A constraining schema is of the form:

<designator> =c <designator>         (2)

(2) is an equational constraint which constrains that the f-structure specified by the right-hand side should be equal to the one of the left-hand side. There are some other types of schemata, such as a membership schema, existential constraining schema, and negative constraining schema. For convenience of our discussion, hereafter we will not refer to them at all.

A designator consists of a meta-variable followed by none or more symbols. A designator is of the form:

<meta-variable> <symbol₀>, ... ,<symbol_n>

Meta-variables are of just two types:

<- , ->                              i)

<= , =>                              ii)

A meta-variable '<-' refers to the f-structure attached to the left-hand side non-terminal of a grammar rule. A meta-variable '->' refers to the f-structure attached to the non-terminal where '->' itself appears. Meta-variables '<=' and '=>' are used to characterize the long-distance dependencies found in relative clauses and questions. Roughly speaking, '<=' and '=>' specify a trace (i.e. 'hole' left by an extraposed constituent) and a marker (i.e. extraposed constituent) respectively. We postpone our discussion of the long-distance dependency to section 4.

The following IP grammar produces the f-structure in Fig. 1.

```
sentence --> np(<-subject = ->),                (1)
             vp(<- = ->).
np --> det(<- = ->),                            (2)
       n(<- = ->).
vp --> v(<- = ->),                              (3)
       np(<-object = ->).
```

```
         the   ;  det(<-spec = the).                                   (4)
         john  ;  n(<-ind = john),                                     (5)
                   (<-num = singular).
         window ; n(<-ind = window),                                   (6)
                   (<-num = singular).
         opened ; v(<-event = open(<-subject,<-object)),               (7)
                   (<-tense = past).
```

## 2.3 The Semantics of an IP Grammar

As was mentioned above, an IP grammar is founded on three readings of grammar rules. Consider, for instance, the grammar rule (1). First of all, we can read this rule declaratively as:

"A 'sentence' is an 'np' followed by a 'vp', where the value of the 'subject' attribute of the 'sentence' is the f-structure of the 'np' and the value of the 'sentence' is the f-structure of the 'vp'."

or procedurally as:

"To construct the f-structure of a 'sentence', first construct the partial f-structure of an 'np' whose attribute is 'subject', then construct the partial f-structure of a 'vp', and finally mix them into a single f-structure of the 'sentence'."

Furthermore, in another point of view, we can understand this control structure as message passing in actor theory proposed by Hewitt: actor oriented reading. The actor oriented paradigm says that the phrase structure tree chosen by a grammar (i.e. c-structure) is taken to be the internal structure of actor computations. Each node of the c-structure, that is, each non-terminal of the grammar rule, is associated with an actor. Each arc can be viewed as the communication path between actors. Meta-variables specify the flow of messages between actors, that is, they provide a mechanism for message sending and receiving. The grammar rule indicates the flow of control between actors, or we can say that the right-hand side of the rule indicates the sequence of behaviors actors should take.

According to actor theory, we can re-interpret meta-variables. A meta-variable '<-' would be read as a form of the verb 'send'. A meta-variable '->' is read as 'receive'. In the actor oriented reading, the above grammar rule is read as:

"Receive an f-structure of an 'np' and send it to a 'sentence' with the attribute 'subject', then receive an f-structure of a 'vp' and send it to the 'sentence'."

The actor oriented paradigm is well suited to applications where the description of entities is simplified by use of uniform protocols. If we are adding the idea of actor theory to our grammar formalism, we can produce a better practical way of writing complex grammars.

## 3 IMPLEMENTATION ISSUES

In actor theory, an actor is organized as a computational entity which has aspects of both procedures and data. Actors are not primarily partitioned into procedures and separate data. All of the action of an actor comes from passing messages between actors. An actor consists of an internal state and script. A script describes what should be done when the actor receives a message. An internal state of an actor can be manipulated when the actor receives a message which specifies the operation to be performed.

An actor is straightforward to implement in the framework of logic programming, especially Prolog. There are two types of actors in IP: one is an actor corresponding to a grammar rule (grammatical actor), the other is an actor corresponding to a lexical item (lexical actor). An actor in IP consists of a set of Prolog statements whose heads have the same predicates. The script of an actor corresponds to a set of bodies of the statements. Each body is called a pattern. The internal state of an actor is represented as a set of equality assertions. An equality assertion is a unit clause with two arguments. It specifies both arguments are equal. Equality assertions are used to define a hierarchical structure, that is, an f-structure. The implementation details will be discussed in the following sections.

3.1 Realization of an Actor

In actor theory, communication between actors is assumed to be done in parallel. However, since achieving parallelism within our implementation would consume more space during parsing and require more difficult implementation technique, IP parses sentences in a traditional top-down serial way with automatic backtracking.

Hewitt's actor model does not make any reference to the sequencing of patterns within the script of an actor. The sequencing information, however, is necessary for IP to parse sentences. It constitutes crucial control information for IP. That is, if an actor has some applicable patterns, it chooses the appropriate pattern depending on the received message, evaluates the pattern, modifies its internal state, and sends a message to the other grammatical actors. All the other patterns are turned out to be inactivated and wait to be executed until the chosen one fails to be sent to another actor. The receiver, an actor to which the message was sent, also evaluates its pattern according to the received message, modifies its internal state, and returns the result of the transmitted message to the sender, an actor which sent the message.

Let us now consider an implementation of actors to illustrate our idea. An actor is represented as a set of Prolog statements. Each head in the Prolog statement specifies the actor name and the body plays the role of the 'pattern' (Kahn 1982). An actor is of the form:

```
head(Message_Type, Message) :- body.
```

The two fields in the head contain the following:

(1) Message_Type is an atom representing the type of a message. It decides whether the body will be an appropriate pattern or not.
(2) Message is instantiated to a term which contains the environment in which the body will be evaluated.

If an actor with the above definition is sent a message which matches Message_Type then the body will be evaluated in the environment resulting from the pattern match. The body specifies the sequence of actions which the actor should take when it receives a message.

For example, the grammar rule (1) depicted above can be translated into the grammatical actor of the form:

```
sentence(parse,F) :-
        f-st(new,F1),
        f-st(define,F.subject=F1),
        np(parse,F1),
        f-st(new,F2),
        f-st(define,F=F2),
        vp(parse,F2).
```

The actor 'sentence' has two arguments. These arguments can be characterized as a template of receiving messages. When the actor receives a 'parse' message with the identifier for the sender F, it constructs the f-structure corresponding to F. The actor 'f-st' should evaluate one of its patterns depending on the type of a received message. When 'f-st' receives a 'new' message, it unifies the second argument with the newly created identifier, where the second argument is used as a communication channel that carries response from the receiver 'f-st' to the sender 'sentence'. When receiving a 'define' message, it evaluates the second argument (defining schema) and constructs an equality assertion which specifies the grammatical relation of an input sentence. The equality assertion will be discussed in section 3.2. In this example, the first two 'f-st' predicates correspond to the schema '<-subject = ->' associated with an 'np' category in the grammar rule (1). The predicate 'np' sends the message to the actor 'np' with the identifier F1.

A lexical item is also translated into the lexical actor. The translated form is similar to the one of a grammar rule. For example, the lexical item (5) is translated into the following form:

```
n(parse,F) :-
        input(get_next_word,john),
        f-st(define,F.ind=john),
        f-st(define,F.num=singular).
```

We assume that the actor 'input' reads and stores an input sentence in its internal state. When receiving a 'get_next_word' message, the actor 'input' will pick up the next word from the input sentence, and return the word as its second argument. In this example, the second argument has already been instantiated to 'john', this actor can be used to check to see if the next input word is 'john' or not.

3.2 The Internal State of an Actor

It was noted that a Prolog statement (i.e., Horn clause) has a form similar to a Context-Free rule. In fact, Pereira et al. proposed an augmented CFG, named Definite Clause Grammar (DCG), in the framework of logic programming. Each non-terminal of a DCG is augmented with arguments representing useful information such as syntactic structures and selectional restrictions.

The DCG, being essentially a set of Prolog statements, has a purely declarative interpretation which is independent of the notions of parsing and generation. Thus, not a few computational linguists claim that it is easy to develop natural language processing programs by use of DCGs.

Prolog, however, is not well suited for defining new data types, or for writing programs that are independent of the physical representation of their data. For example, one may express a segment of the f-structure of Fig. 1 in Prolog list notation such that:

```
            [object, [[num,   singular],
                     [ind,    window],
                     [spec,   the]        ]]
```

The list above represents the f-structure, each of which attribute-value pair is also expressed in list notation. However, we cannot, for example, unify it with the list of the following form:

```
            [object, [[num,   singular],
                     [spec,   the],
                     [ind,    window]     ]]
```

since the order of attribute-value pairs is different from the one depicted above. We must assemble and dissect the list structure, if we want to see some attribute's value. Furthermore, if the structure is highly nested, the operation would become more complicated.

Kornfeld et al. presented an extended version of standard Prolog, called Prolog-with-Equality (Kornfeld 1983). It allows users to include assertions about equality. When a unification of two terms which are syntactically distinct is failed, the two terms may be re-written by using equality assertions so as to prove that both of them are equal. This idea extremely alleviates the above mentioned deficiency.

Following the idea of Prolog-with-Equality, we represent the f-structure as a set of equality assertions. Each assertion corresponds to an attribute-value pair, and is of the form:

$$T1 = T2$$

where both T1 and T2 are terms and '=' is an infix operator. T1 and T2 correspond to an attribute and its value respectively. The assertion is pronounced "T1 is equal to T2".

In addition, we also introduce the unique identifier, which stands for an f-structure. Identifiers (indicated by $f_n$ for any number n) will be substituted for meta-variables in a schema. A designator of the instantiated schema is represented as a term constructed with the functional symbol '.'. The symbol represents a left-associative infix operator which is used in IP for forming compound terms like '$f_1$.subject'. The term can be read as "the f-structure $f_1$'s subject". The instantiated schema is represented as an equality assertion. With this notation, the f-structure shown in Fig. 1 can be expressed as:

$f_1$.subject = $f_2$ (1)
$f_1$.tense = past (2)
$f_1$.event = open($f_2$,$f_3$) (3)
$f_1$.object = $f_3$ (4)
$f_2$.num = singular (5)
$f_2$.ind = john (6)
$f_3$.num = singular (7)
$f_3$.ind = window (8)
$f_3$.spec = the (9)

The equality assertion (1) may be read as "$f_1$'s subject is equal to $f_2$".

In another point of view, the data structure used by IP can be seen a kind of network, consisting of equality assertions. Identifiers of an equality assertion are really pointers to other equality assertions. They could be drawn as links to those other equality assertions if they were shown in a visual way.  Figure 2 shows the network representation of the f-structure in Fig. 1.

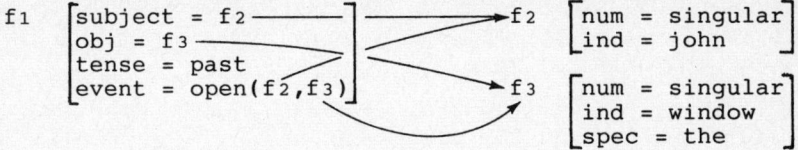

Fig. 2   A Network Representation of the f-structure

Our implementation technique facilitates very rapid creation and discard of f-structures at the sacrifice of somewhat slower access to its components, since reference to the components of an f-structure entails extra work to trace down any chains of equality assertions.

## 3.3 Evaluation of Schemata

Now we will introduce the schema evaluation algorithm. Our algorithm can manipulate f-structures in a simple and uniform way. When the algorithm tries to evaluate the constraining schema 'T1 =c T2', and the two designators T1 and T2 are not syntactically equal, it will look for the equality assertions that make the two designators equal. If this succeeds, the evaluation of the constraining schema also succeeds. When the algorithm attempts to evaluate a defining schema such that 'T1 = T2', it will continue to rewrite both designators using equality assertions until no further application of the assertions is possible. At this point, the algorithm attempts to see that both reduced designators are equal. If this fails, it asserts the new equality assertion by combining these reduced designators with the infix operator '='. Our algorithm is defined as follows:

```
        f-st(constrain,T=cT) :- !.
        f-st(constrain,T1=cT2) :-
                reduce(T1,T3),
                reduce(T2,T4), !,
                eq(T3,T4).              /* system predicate, T3 and T4
                                           are strictly identical */
    reduce(T,T) :- var(T), !.
    reduce(T1,T2) :-
            T1=T3,
            reduce(T3,T2).
    reduce(T1,T2) :-
            T1=..[F|L1],
            reduce_list(L1,L2),
            T3=..[F|L2],
            (not eq(T1,T3), !, reduce(T3,T2);
             fail).
    reduce(T1,T1).

    reduce_list([],[]).
    reduce_list([X|L],[X1|L1]) :-
            reduce(X,X1),
            reduce_list(L,L1).

        f-st(define,T1=T2) :-
                reduce(T1,T3),
                reduce(T2,T4), !,
                merge(T3=T4).
```

```
            merge(T1=T2) :-
                    check_symbol(T1),
                    check_symbol(T2), !,
                    eq(T1,T2).
            merge(T1=T2) :-
                    assert(T1=T2).
```

Where we assume that the predicate 'check_symbol(Term)' checks to see if 'Term' has already been reduced to a symbol or not.

To see how our algorithm works, consider the evaluation of the constraining schema 'f1.subject.num =c singular'. Since the two designators are not equal, 'f1.subject.num' is reduced to 'f2.num' by the application of the assertion (1). Next the assertion (5) is used to get the value of the f2's number attribute, that is, 'singular'. Finally both designators become identical, and the evaluation of the schema succeeds.

## 3.4 Delayed Evaluation of Schemata

One of the important problem inherent in the nature of on-line parsing is that some 'tests' (constraining schemata) may not be evaluated without waiting for the information extracted from the rest of the sentence. In IP, a primitive for delaying evaluation until the value of a designator is determined has been implemented.

Before discussion of the delaying evaluation, we will define a binary functor called 'delay' which represents an uninstantiated designator. The first argument is a variable that is uninstantiated when the term is introduced. The second argument is the delayed constraining schema whose uninstantiated designator is replaced by the variable of the first argument. The 'delay' term could be defined as follows:

            delay(<variable>, <constraining schema>)

Consider, for example, the sentence "*The girl persuaded the baby to go*". The verb phrase "*persuaded the baby to go*" is analyzed by the following rules:

```
            vp  --> v(<- = ->), np(<-obj = ->), vp1(<-vcomp = ->).
            vp1 --> to(<-to = +),(<-inf =c +), v(<- = ->).
```

At the time IP sees the word "*to*", it cannot evaluate the constraining schema '<-inf =c +', since it has not yet seen the rest of the sentence, i.e. "*go*", and cannot decide the infinitive feature of the category 'vp1'. It, thus, creates the equality assertion whose right-hand is the 'delay' term. The uninstantiated designator is placed at the left-hand of the equality assertion:

            fn.inf = delay(X, X=c+)

where we assume that fn represents the f-structure associated with 'vp1'. As soon as the delayed designator 'fn.inf' becomes determined, it is substituted for the first argument of the 'delay' term, and the delayed schema is evaluated.

It is straightforward to incorporate this delaying machinery into the algorithm. To introduce the delaying evaluation, replace the second statement of 'f-st' described above with the following:

```
        f-st(constrain,T1=cT2) :-
               reduce(T1,T3),
               reduce(T2,T4), !,
               constrain(T3=cT4).
```

and add the following statements:

```
        constrain(T1=cT2) :-
               check_symbol(T1),
               check_symbol(T2), !,
               eq(T1,T2).
        constrain(T1=cT2) :-
               delay(T1=cT2).

        delay(F.Attr=cT) :-
               !,assert(F.Attr=delay(X,X=cT)).
        delay(T1=cT2) :-
               delay(T2=cT1).
```

The predicate 'constrain(Schema)' forces to delay the evaluation of 'Schema', if one or both designators are not symbols.

Immediately after the analysis of the word "*go*", IP can find the lexical entry for "*go*" has a '+'-valued infinitive feature. To extend the power of the actor 'f-st' so that it can re-evaluate 'delay' terms, we have the following:

```
        merge(delay(X,Schema)=Y) :-
              check_value(Y),!,force(delay(X,Schema),Y).
        merge(Y=delay(X,Schema)) :-
              check_value(Y),!,force(delay(X,Schema),Y).

        force(delay(X,X=cT),X) :-
              retract(Lhs=delay(X,X=cT)),
              assert(Lhs=X),
              f-st(constrain,X=cT).
```

Note that the predicate 'check_value(Term)' checks to see if 'Term' is a value or not. The predicate 'merge' tests whether the designator Y has been instantiated. If so, the delayed schema 'Schema' is re-evaluated by the actor 'f-st', otherwise the evaluation is suspended.

## 4 LONG-DISTANCE DEPENDENCIES

We now turn to a mechanism for dealing conveniently with the long-distance dependencies such as those that arise in English questions, relative clauses, and other constructions. In the examples so far, equality assertions have been produced from the grammar rules and lexical items by instantiating '<-' and '->' with the identifiers corresponding to the nodes at the top and bottom of a single line in a c-structure. Meta-variables '<=np' and '=>np', however, are instantiated with identifiers that can span over a distance in the c-structure. Each occurrence of '=>np' must be matched with an occurrence of '<=np' that appears within a part of the c-structure called the control domain for '=>np'.

The extraposed constituent is usually known that it is out of place, and that the place where it may be attached to has not yet been encountered in the parsing. It is found first in a left-to-right parse, and captured by a meta-variable '=>np'. In IP, the mechanism for dealing with long-distance dependency is accomplished by use of 'delay' terms in an efficient and uncomplicated way.

The schema '-> = =>np', for instance, would be translated into the goal of the following form:

$$f\text{-}st(define, F=controller(np))$$

where we assume that F has already been instantiated to the identifier for the extraposed constituent.

When the actor 'f-st' receives the message beginning with 'define' followed by the schema 'F=controller(np)', it associates the extraposed constituent with the category 'np', and stores the pair in terms of an equality assertion. The equality assertion produced by 'f-st' is of the form:

$$controllee(np) = delay(X, X=f_n).$$

where we assume that $f_n$ represents the f-structure of the extraposed constituent. The mechanism described so far would be defined as follows:

```
merge(F=controller(Cat)) :-
        f-st(new,F1),
        delay(controllee(Cat)=F1),
        merge(F1=F).

delay(controllee(Cat)=F) :-
        !,asserta(controllee(Cat)=delay(X,X=F)).
```

Subsequently in the parsing of such a sentence, a configuration will be encountered in which the constituent of 'np' is missing. A meta-variable '<=np' at this point will allow the extraposed constituent to be taken from the meta-variable '=>np' and treated just as if it had actually occurred at this position in the sentence.

The schema '<- = <=np', for example, can be translated into the goal of the following form:

$$f\text{-}st(define, F=controllee(np))$$

where F has already been instantiated to the identifier for the missing constituent.

When the actor 'f-st' is sent a message 'define', it searches the equality assertion in which the extraposed constituent is stored. If the extraposed constituent is found, then the predicate 'force' deletes the assertion, and sends 'f-st' a 'define' message. Finally, 'f-st' actor asserts the equality assertion which specifies that the missing constituent is equal to the extraposed constituent. The predicate 'force' is defined as follows:

```
force(delay(X,X=T),X) :-
          retract(Lhs=delay(X,X=T)),
          f-st(define,X=T).
```

The algorithm explained above can simulate the HOLD-VIR mechanism in ATNs. The HOLD action can be achieved in IP with the predicates 'merge' and 'delay'. The role of the HOLD list is analogous to that of equality assertions. The predicate 'force' has the same effect as the VIR arc has.

## 5 CONCLUSIONS

We have explained the implementation issues of IP. Prolog explored here appears quite natural and general. Moreover the added features, an extended datatype and actor-oriented programming paradigm, do not impinge on the efficiency of IP.

We are currently developing the mechanism for text understanding. In IP, processes of explanation-driven and expectation-driven understanding occur as an integral part of the parsing process. The knowledge for expectation, which is an active process called a 'scenario' actor, is associated with a particular lexical actor (i.e. key word). The scenario is a property inheritance net that organizes a hierarchy of events. The event means either an action that people carry out or a simple change of state. When the lexical actor is activated, it sends a message to the corresponding 'scenario' actor. The 'scenario' actor expects what conceptual and contextual structures are likely to occur in the text. The contextual structure extracted from the text is stored in an actor 'context'. The knowledge for explanation, which is also an actor called a 'presupposition' actor can be activated when the expectation fails. The 'presupposition' actor accomplishes the explanation by asking the 'context' actor to search the stored contextual structures. Furthermore, this mechanism can be activated during the parsing of a sentence. The information contained in the text is, thus, available to resolve anaphora and ellipsis. More discussion on text understanding will be treated in the forthcoming paper.

## REFERENCES

Bresnan J (ed) (1982) The Mental Representation of Grammatical Relations, MIT Press, Cambridge, Mass.
Hewitt C (1977) Viewing Control Structures as Patterns of Passing Messages. Artif. Intell. 8: 323-364
Kahn MK (1982) Intermission - Actors in Prolog. In: Clark KL, Tärnlund SA (eds) Logic Programming. Academic Press, New York, 213-228
Kornfeld WA (1983) Equality for Prolog. Proc. of the 8th IJCAI, 514-519
Pereira FCN, Warren DHD (1980) Definite Clause Grammar for Language Analysis - A Survey of the Formalism and a Comparison with Augmented Transition Networks. Artif. Intell. 13: 231-278
Phillips B (1983) An Object-Oriented Parser for Text Understanding. Proc. of the 8th IJCAI, 690-692
Reyle U, Frey W (1983) A Prolog Implementation of Lexical Functional Grammar. Proc. of the 8th IJCAI, 693-695
Small S (1981) Viewing Word Expert Parsing as Linguistic Theory. Proc. of the 7th IJCAI, 70-76
Uehara K, Ochitani R, Kakusho O, Toyoda J (1984) A Bottom-up Parser Based on Predicate Logic - A Survey of the Formalism and Its Implementation Technique. Proc. of the 1984 International Symposium on Logic Programming, 220-227
Uehara K, Ochitani R, Mikami O, Toyoda J (1985) An Integrated Parser for Text Understanding: Viewing Parsing as Passing Messages among Actors. In: Dahl V, Saint-Dizier P (eds) Natural Language Understanding and Logic Programming. North-Holland, New York, 79-95
Winograd T (1972) Understanding Natural Language. Academic Press, New York
Woods WA (1970) Transition Network Grammar for Natural Language Analysis. Comm. of the ACM 13: 591-606

A Travel Consultation System : Towards a Smooth Conversation in Japanese

H. Suzuki, M. Kiyono, S. Kougo, M. Takahashi, S. Motoike, and T. Niki

Tokyo Systems Research Department
Matsushita Electric Industrial Co., Ltd.
17-15, Shinbashi 6-chome, Minato-ku,
Tokyo 105, JAPAN

ABSTRACT

We have developed a travel consultation system which extracts user's requests through natural language (Japanese) conversation and answers destinations that fit the case.

The system has four parts, the parsing subsystem, the user model subsystem, the sentence generator, and the database retriever. All subsystems are written in PROLOG.

The distinctive characters of conversations which our system makes are:
- smoothness and kindness,
- that the system can be a topic introducer, and
- efficiency.

How the system works is as follows:
First, the system parses Japanese sentences that the user inputs. The input sentences are interpreted as user's requests, not as the answer for the previous question. So he can add any requests other than the questioned one. Next, the system guesses the user's type, evaluating user models that the system has. Each user model represents the expected type of users. Then it generates a next question which that type of users would care. This parse-guess-generate sequence are continued till the topics which the user cares are exhausted. At last the system searches the database and shows places that satisfy all requests of the user.

OUR OBJECTIVES AND A SAMPLE DIALOG

Our research objective is to make a 'user friendly' interface. But what 'user friendly' means is a difficult question. Our approach is to create a machine that can communicate by the means that man uses everyday, *i.e.* a natural language conversation.

Most distinguishing characteristics of human conversation by natural language are its *efficiency* and *smoothness*. Grice(1975) argues that there are underlying constraints, and proposes two kind of rules, the cooperative principle and four maxims of conversation. Neustupný(1982) also argues constraints under communication, and proposes nine rules.

| | |
|---|---|
| S：御希望をいれてください。 | Enter your demand please. |
| U：7日間の新婚旅行に行きたいのです。 | We'd like to go 7-day honeymoon. |
| 予算は2人で50万円です。 | We estimate the cost about 500,000yen. |
| 新婚さんの多い所がいいです。 | We'd like to visit where many honeymooners go. |
| S：どのような所に行きたいですか。 | What kind of place do you want to visit? |
| U：ロマンティックな涼しい都会に行きたい。 | We want to visit a cool and romantic city. |
| S：泊まるところは高級ホテルがいいですね。 | You plan to stay at a high class hotel, don't you? |
| U：はい。 | Yes. |
| S：出発はいつごろですか。 | When do you want to depart? |
| U：6月に東京から行くのです。 | We'd like to depart from tokyo in June. |
| S：交通手段は何がいいですか。 | By what do you want to go? |
| U：え。 | Eh? |
| S：飛行機とバスと車と電車と船から選べます。 | Choose one from an airplane, a bus, a train, and a ship. |
| U：飛行機。 | An airplane. |
| S：遠いところがいいですね。 | You want to go far, don't you? |
| U：そうです。 | Yes. |
| S：わかりました。しばらくおまち下さい。 | All right. Wait a minute. |
| S：札幌をお勧めします。 | We recommend SAPPORO. |

Figure 1. An example of dialogs our system made

For to make computer programs keep these rules and constraints, we have to study about six points:
(1) Selection of styles
(2) Generation without ambiguity
(3) Cooperative answering
(4) Reasoning user's answers
(5) Selection of topics
(6) Clarification subdialog

We have implemented some restricted aspects of above six features in our system. Figure 1 shows that our system has the feature (2), (4), (5) and (6). For example, our system does not ask "Where do you want to stay?", but asks "You plan to stay at a high class hotel, don't you?". This is an example of feature (4). Another is an example of clarification subdialog, feature (6). When the user says "Eh?", the system finds out that the user cannot understand the question and clarifies its idea by listing all possible answers.

But what we would like to mention in this article is our new proposal about how to choose next topic at the conversation. So in the next section, our user models are introduced, and the simplified algorithm for selecting topics which employs user models are introduced in the following section.

## USER MODELS CONVEYED TO SELECT TOPICS

We employed user models to select next topics in conversations. We summarize our idea and algorithm here. Detailed descriptions are found in (Suzuki 1985).

We propose to construct user models based on attitudes towards topics. We respected the following five attitudes.
(1) Whether the user cares about such topics. Or he has something to say about a topic or not.
(2) Whether he thinks he needs to say about such a topic or not.
(3) Whether he minds talking about such topics or not.
(4) Whether he can introduce such topics or not.
(5) Whether he remembers a topic or forgets it.

Using these, we classify topics into fourteen groups, and get five classes. Five classes are U, S, SD, R, and X. Class U consists of topics that a user has something to say about, that he thinks he need to say, that he doesn't mind talking about, that he can introduce into the conversation, and that he doesn't forget about. So topics in class U are introduced at the earliest chance by the user. Topics in class S and SD lacks some feature mentioned above, but the user doesn't mind talking about it, anyway. So these topics are to be introduced by consultant, the system. The user expects that the system knows the answer for topics in class SD, *i.e.* he thinks he need not talk about such topics. Topics in class R are topics which the user has nothing to talk about it. Topics in class X are forbidden topics that the user does mind talking about it for various reasons.

So there are two sorts of topics, topics that are to be talked about in the conversation and topics that are not to be mentioned. Topics in U and S are in the former sort, and topics in R and X are in the latter sort. Topics in SD can be considered in two ways. But in this article they are treated in the former sort, *i.e.* they are asked in the tag question form to get the user's confirmation.

A basic user model consists of these topics in the former sort. A user model is a basic user model with restrictions of possible answers for topics in the model.

## SYSTEM CONFIGURATION

Figure 2 shows our system's configuration. Our system consists of four subsystems. We

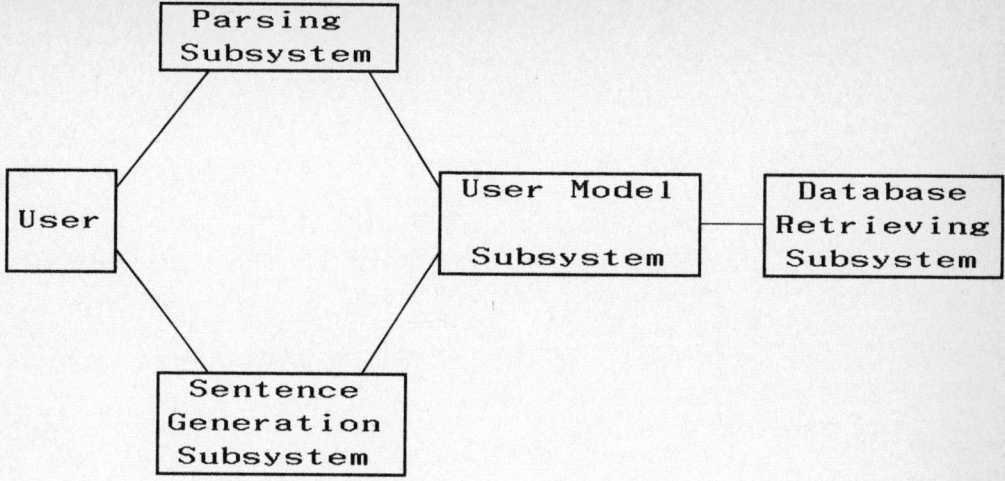

Figure 2. System Configuration

will explain each subsystem in this section.

Parsing Subsystem of Japanese

This parser/analyzer of Japanese sentence has three main job steps.
Step1: Analyzes a given sentence and generates its structural description.
Step2: Based on the structural description above, outputs the meaning representation of the sentence.
Step3: Extracts the attribute-value pairs from the meaning representation.

At step 1, we employed the LFG parser in PROLOG (Yasukawa 1983). But we developed the original grammar. The basic idea of our grammar owes much to Teramura(1982). A rough sketch of our grammar is as follows:
- A sentence has two part, the sentence kernel and the auxiliary part. In the sentence kernel, objective facts are described, and in the auxiliary part, speaker's attitudes towards that facts and tenses and aspects are represented.
- The structure of a sentence kernel is $X^*V$, where X corresponds to a chunk such like a noun phrase with a case particle or adverbial phrase (we call it "hogo") and V corresponds to a chunk such like a verb phrase (we call it "jutsubu").
- A auxiliary part consists of particles that represent tenses, aspects, and speaker's attitudes. The order of them is strictly determined.

Our grammar mainly treats the following four linguistic features of Japanese.
(1) Case government by verbs
(2) Modality
(3) Tense/Aspect particle
(4) Voice and transformation of case government

The analyzing strategy of these features uses the classification of Japanese verbs. To treat the first feature, we described necessary cases in the lexicon of verbs. Here, cases mean surface cases, not deep cases nor gramatical functions. One of the reason why we do not simply apply the LFG theory to Japanese is that in Japanese, any constituent of a sentence can appear at any place before verbs, and even more they can be omitted.

One of the problems about the third feature is that a tense/aspect particle '*teiru*' has two different meaning, progressive tense and stative tense. These problems are treated by the agreement of grammatical feature of verb and adverbs. Voices are solved at lexical level except causative. In Japanese, there are causative particles 'seru' and 'saseru'. But in our grammar, they have their own case government like verbs and make a F-structure.

At step 2, we constructed a meaning representation according to F-structure and its 'sem' feature. Our meaning representation is somewhat situation semantics like, but generating algorithm differs very much from their Aliass described in the book (Barwise 1983). Settings are not used, either. The detailed algorithm is described in our earlier paper (Suzuki 1983).

At step 3, we prepared a list of event-types and roles for each attribute used. If the situation is of that type, then the pair of the attribute and the value that is anchored to the role is generated. Then the subsystem outputs a collection of pairs.

Sentence Generation Subsystem

The sentence generator of Japanese also has three job steps.
Step1: Given an attribute and values, if any, generates its deep case structure description.
Step2: Based on the structure description above, outputs the surface case structure in a grammatical word order.
Step3: Makes morphological adjustment such as verb inflections.

At step 1 and 3, most works are done by lexicons, dictionaries, and tables. No new methods are employed at these steps.

Step 2 is the most significant core of sentence generator. Details are described in our paper (Takahashi 1985). The points of our method are three new data/programs listed below.

(1) A Japanese grammar in a form of transformation rules between subtrees.
(2) A translator which pre-compiles each transformation rule into a Horn clause, with the interpretation of such transformation rules.
(3) An engine which divides a tree into subtrees and reconstructs a tree from the transformed subtrees.

There are basically three kinds of transformation rules in our grammar, addition rules, deletion rules, and movement rules. (Inoue 1976; Shibatani 1978) Our grammar has about 150 rules of such kinds.(Mizutani 1983) In rules, capitalized identifiers, except those starting with the letter 'C', stand for part variables which may unify any structure including a sequence of subtrees. We use '@' and '&' for describing feature checking, and '*' for designating main category of the rule. if '*' is omitted, the top node is considered as the main category. No rules are applied twice to the same main category to avoid infinite loop.

The translator pre-compiles each transformation rule into a Horn clause. The Horn clause, as a PROLOG predicate, means a relation between two trees, an input tree and an output tree. So its body has two parts, one for checking whether an input tree matches the left-side pattern of the rule, and the other for rebuilding the output tree by using the constituents got from the above analysis. A collection of these predicates forms a transformation part of this subsystem. Therefore, at execution, transformations are directly done by PROLOG interpreter/compiler. In this sense, our method is efficient.

The engine part is written in PROLOG. It reduces the input tree to the minimum subtrees and sends them sequentially to the transformation part till no transformation rules are applicable. Then it reconstructs the tree by using the new subtrees.

Figure 3 shows an example of our grammar rules and the result of their translations. This example is an addition rule describing : "if a verb has the feature 'motive', then add the case particle '*ni*' after the noun phrase whose case is locative."


User Model Subsystem


This subsystem has two main jobs, selection of next topics and default reasoning for answers. These are realized by a concurrent algorithm which employs three kind of processes:
- The General Model Process
- User Model Processes
- The Decision Process

The general model process has:
- The set of all topics

```
joshi : [CX1, X11,
         [pred, X21, [doushi@[motive], D], X22],
         X12,
         [case, X23, [*place, X31], X24],
         X13] =>
        [CX1, X11,
         [pred, X21, [doushi, D], X22],
         X12,
         [case, X23, [place, X31, [joshi, ni]], X24],
         X13].

rule(A,B,C,A,B,D,joshi,E,[F↑[joshi([ ],[ ],ni)]]) :-
        divide(C,pred(G,H),I,J,K),
        divide(J,doushi(L,M),N,O,P),
        intersect([motive],M),
        divide(K,case(Q,R),S,T,U),
        divide(T,place(V,W),X,Y,Z),
        not_member(joshi,V),
        !,
        divide(D,pred(G,H),I,A1,B1),
        divide(A1,doushi(L,M),N,O,P),
        divide(B1,case(Q,R),S,C1,U),
        divide(C1,place([joshi|V],W),X,D1,Z),
        divide(D1,joshi([ ],[ ]),Y,F,[ ]).
```

**Figure 3.** An example of transformation rules and their translations

- Default values with applicable conditions

A user model process has data of three kinds:
- A set of topics
- Constraints on values
- Default values with applicable conditions

Figure 4 shows an example of a user model. Our system reads these descriptions and makes PROLOG programs for user model processes automatically.

The decision process are implemented as follows:
Prepare three classes, 'white', 'grey' and 'black'. Put all user models in the white class. If the input are not expected, *i.e.* not in the set of attributes, the model's class goes down one rank. If a model of black class goes down, it vanishes away. The order in a class is determined mainly by evaluating correctness of the default. The top model of the highest class is the current user model, and a topic which is nearest to the current topic is expected as the next topic.

```
        title      honeymoon ::
        attribute meimoku,
                  mood,
                  budget,
                  ......
                  goby ::
        constraint meimoku : [honeymoon],
                  ...... ::
        expect    mood : [romantic],
                  budget > 10 ↦ goby : [airplain] .
```

**Figure 4. An example of a user model description**

As a total, this subsystem works as follows. First, attribute-value pairs are received by the decision process. Then it evaluates the rank of each user model. While evaluating, the candidates for the next topic are also calculated by each user model. Then the decision process adopts the candidate of the highest rank, or the general process if no user models survive.

Database Retrieving Subsystem

The database retrieving subsystem has two parts, the database about destinations and the retrieving system with routing. Entities of the database describe the features of places declaratively like

$$data(temperature, warm, okinawa).$$

So almost all process of retrieving are done by unification facility of PROLOG . But there remains some to be considered. For example, cost of the travel depends not only on the destination but also on starting place and routing, so our retriever has a simple routing process and cost estimating process. Another example is the problem about seasons. One can play golf at Sapporo in summer, but cannot do it in other three seasons. The solution is to translate these constraints into Horn clauses and to check them when retrieving.

CONCLUSIONS AND FUTURE WORKS

Comparison with other systems

Our main concern and interest are to realize a *smooth* conversation. And our system can make a conversation with two features,

(1) Both the system and the user can take the initiative to select new topics.
(2) The system drives the conversation to the end efficiently.

SCHOLAR (Carbonell 1970) also embodies the first feature, that both can take the initiative in conversation. But as for SCHOLAR , the situation is rather different. SCHOLAR is a CAI system of geometry, so usually the system takes the initiative. Only when a user cannot answer questions that SCHOLAR asks, he may take the initiative and can ask a question. The system takes the initiative usually, and a user takes the initiative only in sub-dialogs. So a user cannot take the initiative of the main conversation. But our system has no such limitation. A user can take the initiative at any time during the conversation, by introducing new topics in his answering phase. Then the flow of the topic will change and go for that direction.

GUS (Bobrow 1977) can make a cooperation with the user to drive the conversation to get at the feasible answer. But what GUS does is to use the frame that represents the logical construction of the problem to guide the user. Its course of conversations are fixed and rigid. Our user model represents not only logical constructions but also user's types. Using models, our system can perform more flexible conversation than GUS can perform. Even more, our system's conversation has a property of 'efficiency'. Using models enables the system to anticipate user's answers. We can make yes-no questions rather than just ask him about the topic.

Future Works

We must respect many, at least three, more features about selecting topics.
(1) We considered nothing about heuristic knowledges and rules in the QA field when selecting topics.
(2) If the consultant is human, sometimes, especially at the final stage, he selects the topic which narrows the range of possible answers effectively.
(3) Our algorithm always in the model-selection mode. Humans, however, fix the model so that the conversation become robust to mistakes like slip of the tongue.
The implement method of these features are currently studied.

Other subsystems also have many features not implemented. As for parsing subsystem, analyzing anaphors, including zero anaphors, are very big open problem we have to attack. To generate a natural sentence, mechanisms to respect discourse grammar like word ordering according to the context are needed. These are now in study.

## ACKNOWLEDGMENTS

The Authers are grateful to the members of natural language processing group of ICOT Research Center and the members of AIUEO for their valuable advice. We also thanks to Dr. Noda, Mr. Suzuki, and Mr. Komorida, for their continuous encouragement and various comments.

## REFERENCES

Barwise J, Perry J (1983) Situations and Attitudes. MIT Press, Cambridge, Mass.
Bobrow DG, Kaplan RM, Kay M, Norman DA, Thompson H, Winograd T (1977) GUS, A Frame-Driven Dialog System. Artificial Intelligence 8: 155-173
Carbonell JR (1970) AI in CAI: An Artificial Intelligence Approach to Computer-Assisted Instruction. IEEE transaction on Man-Machine Systems MMS-11: 190-202
Coulthard M (1977) An Introduction to Discourse Analysis. Logman, London Grice HP (1975) Logic and Conversation. In: Morgan JL (ed) Syntax and Semantics III: Speech Acts. Academic Press, New York, p 41
Inoue K (1976) Henkei Bunpou to Nihongo ('Transformational Grammar and Japanese'). Taishukan, Tokyo (in Japanese)
Kaplan RM, Bresnan J (1982) Lexical-Functional Grammar. In: Bresnan J (ed) Mental Representation of Grammatical Relations. MIT Press, Cambridge, Mass., p 173
Mizutani S, Ishiwata T, Ogino T, Kaku N, Kusanagi Y (1983) Bunpou to Imi I ('Grammar and Semantics I'). Asakura, Tokyo (in Japanese)
Neustupný JV (1982) Gaikokujin-tono Communication ('Communication with Foreigners'). Iwanami, Tokyo (in Japanese)
Shibatani M (1978) Nihongo-no Bunseki ('Analysis of Japanese'). Taishukan, Tokyo (in Japanese)
Suzuki H (1984) Nihongobun-no Imi-no Joukyouimirontekina Kijutsu ('Event Types Represent Meanings of Japanese Sentences'). Information Processing Society of Japan, WGNL 42-3 (in Japanese)
Suzuki H, Kiyono M, Kougo S (1985) User-no Kaiwa-no Kata-wo Mochii-ta Shitsumon Outou System ('Selecting Topics in a Dialog according to Users Type'). Information Processing Society of Japan, WGNL 49-3 (in Japanese)
Takahashi M, Suzuki H, Kiyono M (1985) Production System wo Mochii-ta Nihongo Bunseisei ('Generation of Japanese Sentences by Production'), Proceedings of the 30th semiannual meeting of Information Processing Society of Japan: 1675-1676 (in Japanese)
Teramura H (1982) Nihongo-no Syntax to Imi I ('Syntax and Semantics of Japanese I'). Kuroshio, Tokyo (in Japanese)
Yasukawa H (1984) LFG System in Prolog. Proceedings of the 10th International Conference on Computational Linguistics: 358-361

A Prolog-based Korean-English Machine Translation System and Its
Efficient Method of Dictionary Management

J.M. Choi, M.S. Song, K.J. Jeong, H.C. Kwon,
S.Y. Han, and Y.T. Kim

Department of Computer Engineering
Seoul National University
San 56-1, Shinrim-dong, Kwanak-ku
Seoul, Korea


ABSTRACT

This paper describes a Prolog-based Korean-English Machine Translation
System (KEMTS).
KEMTS employs the transfer approach and consists of four separate phases
- morphological analysis, parsing, deep structure generation, and English
generation.
The implementation described here is based on a syntactic analysis of
Hangul(the Korean language) and English, and it applies and extends the
work of Marcus.
KEMTS also makes use of a dictionary management system called DProlog
in order to overcome the inefficiency of the sequential search in Prolog
and to manage the large amount of data conveniently.


INTRODUCTION


Prolog has shown some powerful aspects particularly in natural language
processing because of its pattern matching and unification facilities
(Clocksin and Mellish 1980), so KEMTS adopts it as a main implementation
language.

KEMTS embodies the transfer approach (Tucker 1984), which separates the
process of translation into three general stages : analysis, transfer,
and synthesis.  This approach allows for the separation of source
language analysis from target language synthesis, parsing strategy from
morphological analysis, and so forth.

Although based on the assumption that understanding is necessary for
correct translation of text, the current system does not contain an
understanding component.

KEMTS consists of four phases - morphological analysis, parsing, deep
structure generation, and English generation.  The first three of them
are taking charge of the analysis stage from the general transfer
approach, while the tasks of transfer and synthesis are performed in
the last generation phase.

Deep structure is a language-free representation formalized via Chomsky-
type transformational grammar (Chomsky 1957), and we focus analysis and
synthesis around this medium.

Dictionary elements can be simply represented by predicates in Prolog,
but as the amount of data increases, there occur some negative phenomena
which lower the system performance.  In order to solve this problem,
we propose a dictionary management system named DProlog which supports

an efficient dictionary manipulation by storing dictionary elements in
secondary storage, and by providing a fast search feature using a hashing
mechanism.

DProlog also guarantees the abstraction that each phase of KEMTS can
easily refer to the dictionary information by Prolog syntax, without
the knowledge of the data format stored in secondary storage.

In the following sections, each phase of KEMTS will be explained, and
some results obtained from experiments using this system will be reported
on.

MORPHOLOGICAL ANALYSIS

Most English words are found in the dictionary exactly as written or in
a form that follows from stripping off endings like -s, -ed, -ing.

Compared to English, Hangul morphology is complex because it strings
together simple words to form compounds (Huh 1978; Lee 1970).
For example, the word 'saramdolon' would not occur in the dictionary,
but its components would.  'saram' means a human, 'dol' is a plural
affix, and 'on' is a postposition which has a role of a subjective case
marker.  The case markers like this are very useful in analyzing Hangul
sentences to form the correct parse structure.

In this phase, each Hangul word is classified into grammatically
meaningful morphemes.  This is considered to be unnecessary for English
in which each word itself is one grammatical meaning.

The combination patterns of Hangul words are listed below (here []
indicates the optional case) :

1)  noun
2)  noun [ + plural affix ] + postposition
3)  adnominal (or adverb)
4)  verb (or adjective) stem [ + aux. stem ] + ending

Since matching each word with the dictionary elements is the main task
in this analysis, Prolog's pattern match and backtracking facilities
play an important role.

The outline of the morphological analysis procedure can be informally
defined as follows :

         < the morphological analysis procedure >

    1.  WORD   <---   one input word

    2.  match WORD with noun lexicon ;
        if matched then
            return with 'WORD is an isolated noun' ;

    3.  match WORD with adnominal or adverb lexicon ;
        if matched then
            return with
            'WORD is an isolated adnominal or adverb' ;

    4.  find a postposition P in the end of WORD ;
        if found then
            delete P from WORD ;

```
                    match remaining part of WORD with noun lexicon ;
                    return with
                        'WORD is noun + postposition' ;

    5.  make reverse list of WORD ;
        do next two tasks repeatedly and simultaneously
            until successful match occurs ;

            task1 :  scan WORD forward and match scanned string with
                     verb or adjective lexicon ;
            task2 :  scan WORD backward using reversed list and match
                     scanned string with word endings, or auxiliary
                     stems representing tense or modal ;

        end
        if successfully matched then
            WORD is 'verb (or adjective) [+aux. stem] + ending' ;
            return ;

    6.  error recovery routine
```

The only complicated part in the above procedure is the case of 'verb [+aux. stem] +ending'. We extract the string of each word by forward and backward scanning. In Prolog implementation backward scanning is enabled by the forward scanning of reversed list of input words.


PARSING


The aim of this and the next phase is to produce a parse tree of the sentence, together with sufficient semantic information to enable a complete and correct translation to be generated.

It is well-known that top down backtracking parsers are easy to write in Prolog, and those parsers can be extended to give them the power of ATN's (Pereira and Warren 1980). But this kind of top down parser has all the problems of standard context-free top down parsers ; left recursive rules can cause looping, and backtracking is quite inefficient.

In particular, Hangul has the syntactic constraints that a verb must come last and an embedded clause must come first in a sentence, which forces us to favor the bottom up parsing (Lee 1970; Stabler 1983).

Promising alternatives to context-free rule parsers and ATN parsers are the Wait-and-See Parsers (WASP) (Marcus 1980). WASP uses the deterministic bottom up strategy, and our parser is a Prolog implementation of WASP.

Our WASP consists of three components - a stack, a buffer, and a set of condition action rules. Sentences stream from right to left through the buffer, ending up in a standard looking parse tree.

The condition action rules control the flow of data between the stack and the buffer. The condition part of each rule is allowed to consider the contents of the buffer and the current node. The action part of each rule specifies one of the following actions.
(In these actions, 'OldSt' and 'NewSt' represent for the contents of the stack before and after the actions, respectively, while 'OldBuf' and 'NewBuf' for the contents of the buffer before and after the

actions, respectively) :

1) Create :
   creates a new node(ToBeCreated) and pushes it onto the stack.

   ```
   create(OldSt, ToBeCreated, NewSt) :-
       append(OldSt, ToBeCreated, NewSt).
   ```

2) Attach :
   attaches the first item in the buffer(ToBeAttached) to the top of the stack, and shifts other buffer items left to fill the hole which was previously occupied by the removed item.

   ```
   attach(OldSt,StLast,ToBeAttached,NewSt) :-
       append(StLast,ToBeAttached,St1),
       append(OldSt, [St1],NewSt).
   ```

3) Drop :
   drops the most recently popped node(ToBeDropped) into the first position in the buffer, after shifting existing items to the right.

   ```
   drop(OldSt,NewSt,ToBeDropped,OldBuf,NewBuf) :-
       NewSt = OldSt,
       append(ToBeDropped,OldBuf,NewBuf).
   ```

The condition action rules reside in a partitioned condition action rule memory. Each partition corresponds to a parse-tree node type. Only those rules in the partition associated with the current parse-tree node, the one at the top of the stack, are active.
One of these rules is as follows :

```
cond_act(OldSt,OldBuf,NewSt,NewBuf) :-
    stack_check(OldSt,Rem,LastElm,s),
    OldBuf = [[np|Temp]|NewBuf],
    create(OldSt, [[np|Temp]],NewSt).
```

The parsing procedure is quite simple because all the start, stop, and attach knowledge is locked up in the rules.
Let us look at the parsing procedure.

< parsing procedure >

---

until the sentence is completely parsed or
   no active condition action rule applies do
  1. activate the condition action rules
     associated with the current node
  2. use the first active rule that matches
     the condition of the buffer and the
     current node
end

---

Prolog implementation of this procedure is also simple and as follows :

```
parsing(Tree, [],Tree, []).

parsing(OldSt,OldBuf,NewSt,NewBuf) :-
    cond_act(OldSt,OldBuf,StTemp,BufTemp),
    parsing(StTemp,BufTemp,NewSt,NewBuf).
```

Our Prolog implementation of WASP can be extended to get great coverage of the language without the substantial increase in parsing time that would be expected for a strictly top down parser with some extensions.


GENERATION OF DEEP STRUCTURE


We define the deep structure as a hierarchical structure of clauses included in a sentence. This structure contains information about tense, mood and the meanings of postpositions, endings and auxiliaries (Chomsky 1957; Simmons 1972).

Due to the various features in Hangul, we should consider several problems peculiar to Hangul in this phase (Lee 1970).

First of all, it is necessary to construct the hierarchical structure of clauses in a sentence.
Second, we should analyze the meanings of postpositions, endings, and auxiliaries and add these to the deep structure.
Third, we should add information about tense and mood to the structure.

The information about tense and mood can easily be found in the morphological analysis phase because the auxiliary stems of mood and tense have a unique form corresponding to the meaning.
As a result of this, it is possible to solve the third problem easily by a simple movement mechanism (Chomsky 1957).

A postposition in Hangul is attached to an absolute word such as a noun or a pronoun, and determines the constituent of the absolute word in a sentence.

Generally postpositions are classified into three cases; subjective case, adnominal case, and adverbial case.
Postpositions of subjective case and adnominal case have fixed meanings, but in the adverbial case the meanings change according to sentences. Therefore, we have to decide the meaning of a postposition of adverbial case.

With priority given to a conjugational word such as a verb or an adjective, the meanings of postpositions with which are accompanied by a conjugational word are recorded in the conjugational word dictionary. At the same time, all meanings that each postposition can have are recorded in the postposition dictionary.
And then we compare the meanings of the postposition attached to a conjugational word with the meanings of the postpositions that the related conjugational word can accompany with. In this way we can determine the meanings of a postposition in a sentence.

In order to construct the hierarchical structure of clauses included in a sentence, we should understand the meanings of endings and analyze the relationships between included clauses.
We use the reverse transformations to solve these. The transformations are minutely explained in the literatures of transformational grammar (Chomsky 1957; Pereira and Warren 1980).

In Hangul, there are three kinds of clauses ; noun clauses, adnominal clauses, and adverbial clauses.

It is easy to find the embedded noun clause in a sentence. The nominal ending of noun clause has a unique form corresponding to its meaning, so they can be checked during the morphological analysis phase.

The syntactic structure of a noun phrase modified by an adnominal phrase has the form of 'Adnp(S) + Np(N)', where 'Adnp(S)' is the adnominal phrase which modifies the noun phrase, 'Np(N)'. 'Adnp(S)' is to be transformed into an adnominal clause, the deep structure of 'Adnp(S)', which has all necessary sentential components.

To construct an adnominal clause of 'Adnp(S)', it is required to analyze the relationship between S and Np, and to add the information about the relationship.
We analyze the role of Np playing in S by applying a reverse transformation in Hangul.

In the embedded adverbial clause, each clause accompanies with the adverbial endings.
The method of making the deep structure of an adverbial clause is just to check the adverbial ending, to search the ending dictionary, and to record the meaning of ending in that dictionary.


ENGLISH GENERATION


Hangul differs from English not only in their phonological rules and lexicons, but also in their syntactic rules (Huh 1978; Lee 1970).

Considering this fact, English generation phase includes two processes, namely the substitution of words and the transformation of grammars.

Referencing dictionary elements is the main task in both processes, so we emphasize the clear construction of dictionaries for word and grammar information.

In words substitution, nouns are easily converted by one-to-one mappings of dictionary elements. But the handling of verbs is not the same because verbs of Hangul may be translated into idioms, not a single word of English.

For example, 'samda' of Hangul should be replaced by 'regard A as B', making the corresponding dictionary entry as follows :

       v(sam, [regard,$obj,as,$adv]).

Here '$obj' will eventually be filled with the object constituent, and '$adv' with the adverbial constituent of the sentence.

The grammar transformation converts the word order of Hangul such as S+O+V into that of English such as S+V+O (Boyer and Lapalme 1985). During this transformation, some exceptions can happen in which embedded clauses of Hangul had better be translated into English phrases, usually prepositional phrases.
For example, the English equivalent of a Hangul verb 'wihada' is not a verb of English but a preposition 'for'.


DICTIONARY MANAGEMENT SYSTEM : DPROLOG


KEMTS makes use of the dictionary management system called DProlog in order to overcome the inefficiency of the sequential search in Prolog and to manage the large amount of data conveniently.

DProlog provides facilities which can efficiently use secondary devices and can manipulate the dictionary like an external database. These facilities are very similar to those of the deductive database systems (Chomicki and Grudzinski 1983; Minker and Tran 1981; Naish and Thom 1983).

The main components of DProlog are as follows :

(1)   Unix Prolog interpreter

(2)   The interface between KEMTS and
      the dictionary on secondary device

(3)   The partial match system

Figure 1 shows the architecture of KEMTS using DProlog. The interface of DProlog is implemented in Prolog and the partial match system in C language.

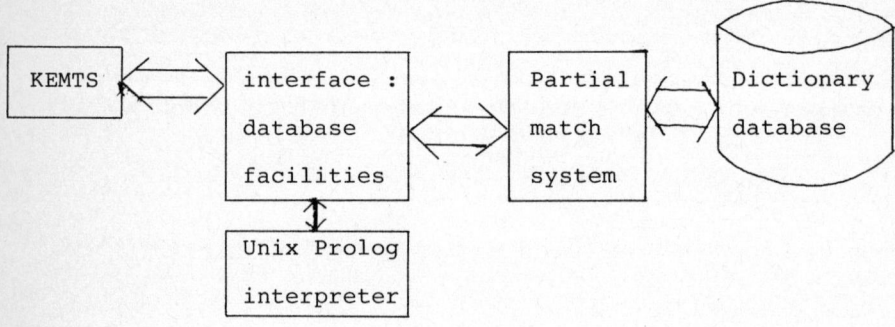

Fig. 1   The architecture of KEMTS


The interface in DProlog is composed of database facilities, each of which can be used like a built-in predicate in KEMTS. A number of relations and a set of procedures make the dictionary of KEMTS constructed by these facilities. Each relation consists of a set of ground unit clauses called dictionary clauses and stored on secondary device. The procedures contain rules about the dictionary.

The interface has the following commands which create, alter and access the dictionary :

(1)   create(file_name(pred_name,pred_spec)).
      It creates the relation named 'pred_name'. All dictionary clauses
      of this relation stored in file named 'file_name' are transformed
      into a hashed file in the dictionary. The information about the
      hash function and the size of relation is specified in 'pred_spec'.

(2)   insert(pred_name(t1,t2,....,tn)).
      It adds the clause 'pred_name(t1,t2,....,tn)' to the dictionary.

(3)   delete(pred_name(t1,t2,....,tn)).

It deletes the clause 'pred_name(t1,t2,....,tn)' from the dictionary.

(4) remove(pred_name).
It removes all relations named 'pred_name' from the dictionary.

(5) listall(pred_name).
It displays all clauses of the relation named 'pred_name'.

(6) ls.
It displays the information about all relations in the dictionary.

The current Prolog interpreter assumes that all ground unit clauses are stored in the main memory. Unfortunately the dictionary clauses which are similar to general ground unit clauses are not in the main memory. Therefore the mechanism which can distinguish the dictionary clauses on secondary device from the other clauses in main memory is required to retrieve the dictionary clauses.

Without any change of the Prolog interpreter, Dprolog distinguishes the dictionary clauses from the others using the communication predicate 'ext'.
The tasks which the communication predicate 'ext' accomplishes are listed below :

(1) 'ext' sends a query to the partial match system and receives the answer set from that system, via Unix pipe.

(2) 'ext' unifies the query and the first clause of the answer set which has not been unified yet.

(3) When a backtracking happens, 'ext' repeats the step 2.

An example is shown in Fig. 2. In this case, it is required only one rule 'srel(X,Y) :- ext(srel(X,Y))' to accomplish the communication in a dictionary procedure.

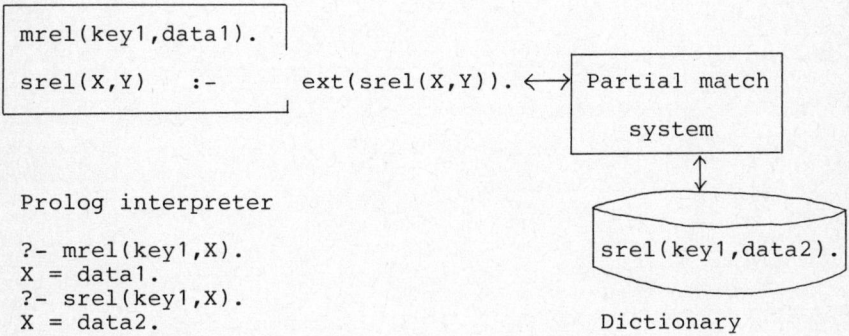

Fig. 2  The communication predicate 'ext'

DProlog stores each relation in a single file and retrieves the
dictionary clauses in that file by partial match retrieval (Ramamohanarao
and Lloyd and Thom 1983; Ullman 1982). Partial match retrieval is a
method for efficient access to the files via multi-key combinations, and
it is appropriate for Prolog.


RESULTS AND CONCLUSION


An experimental Prolog-based Korean-English Machine Translation System
(KEMTS) has been introduced. In order to improve the overall performance
a dictionary management system called DProlog has also been presented.

KEMTS embodies the transfer approach that the translation is carried
out by a syntactic and sentence-by-sentence manner. Another method of
translation named 'the integral method' which uses active dictionary can
be found elsewhere (Tanaka and Isahara 1983).

An example which shows the result of each phase is given in the Appendix.

KEMTS experienced somewhat satisfactory result with performance in the
domain of Korean history, but severe problems may arise in a word
selection when the ambiguity occurs. We have tried to solve this problem
by consulting the remaining parts of the sentence, and this mechanism
will be enhanced by understanding capabilities in the near future
(Carbonell and Cullingford and Gershman 1981; Wilks 1973).


REFERENCES


Boyer M, Lapalme G (1985) Generating sentences from semantic networks.
   In: Dahl V, Saint-Dizier P (eds) Natural language processing and logic
   programming. North-Holland, 181-189
Carbonell J, Cullingford R, Gershman A (1981) Steps toward knowledge-
   based machine translation. IEEE Trans on Pattern Analysis and Machine
   Intelligence 3: 376-392
Chomicki J, Grudzinski W (1983) A database support system for Prolog.
   Proc Logic programming workshop, Algarve Portugal
Chomsky N (1957) Syntactic structures. Mouton, The Hague
Clocksin W, Mellish C (1980) The Unix Prolog system. Software Report 5,
   Univ of Edinburgh
Huh W (1978) Korean phonology, revised edn. Cheung-Eum Sa, Seoul Korea
Lee H (1970) A study of Korean syntax. Pan Korean Book Corporation,
   Seoul Korea
Marcus M (1980) A theory of syntactic recognition for natural language.
   MIT Press, Cambridge MA
Minker J, Tran D (1981) Interfacing predicate logic languages and
   relational databases. TR 1019, Univ of Maryland
Naish L, Thom J (1983) The MU-Prolog deductive database. TR 83/10,
   Univ of Melbourne
Pereira F, Warren D (1980) Definite clause grammars for language analysis
   - a survey of the formalism and a comparison with augmented transition
   networks. Artificial Intelligence 13: 231-278
Ramamohanarao K, Lloyd J, Thom J (1983) Partial match retrieval using
   hashing descriptors. ACM Trans on Database Systems 8: 552-576
Simmons R (1972) Semantic networks : their computation and use for
   understanding English sentences. Tech Report NL-6, Univ of Texas at
   Austin
Stabler E (1983) Deterministic and bottom-up parsing in Prolog.
   Proc Nat Conf on AI, Amer Assoc for AI, 383-386

Tanaka H, Isahara H (1983) An English-Japanese machine translation system using the active dictionary. New Generation Computing 1: 179-185
Tucker A (1984) A perspective on machine translation : theory and practice. Comm ACM 27: 322-329
Ullman J (1982) Principles of database systems, 2nd edn. Computer Science Press, Rockville Maryland
Wilks Y (1973) An artificial intelligence approach to machine translation. In: Schank R, Colby K (eds) Computer models of thought and language. W.H. Freeman and Company, San Francisco


APPENDIX

An example which shows the result of each phase is given below.

Input sentence in Hangul ===>

조선은 국초부터 농본 민생의 기본 정책을 내세워 농업을 천하의 대본으로 삼았다.

The output of morphological analysis ===>

[nn(조선,0), jo(은,1), nn(국초,0), jo(부터,3), nn(농본,0), nn(민생,0), jo(의,2), nn(기본,0), nn(정책,0), jo(을,4), v(내세우,0), ee(어,31), nn(농업,0), jo(을,4), nn(천하,0), jo(의,2), nn(대본,0), jo(으로,3), v(삼,0), vi(았,2), ee(다,11)].

The output of parsing ===>

[[s, [advp, [s, [sjp, [np, [n,조선]],0], [predp, [advp, [np, [n,국초]], [post,부터]], [objp, [np, [adnp, [np, [cn, [n,농본], [n,민생]]]], [np, [cn, [n,기본], [n,정책]]]], [pred, [v,내세우], [tns, 1]]], [dcl,1]], [aux,ㅓ]], [predp, [objp, [np, [n,농업]]], [advp, [np, [adnp, [np, [n,천하[[, [np, [n,대본]]], [post,으로]], [pred, [v,삼], [tns,2]]], [dcl,1]]].

The deep structure ===>

[[s, [ss, [advp, [ss, [sjp, [np, [n,조선]],0], [predp, [advp, [np, [n,국초]], [post,부터,6]], [objp, [np, [adnp, [np, [cn, [n,농본], [n,민생]]]], [np, [cn, [n,기본], [n,정책]]]], [pred, [v,내세우], [tns,2]]], [dcl,1]], [aux,3,ㅓ]], [predp, [objp, [np, [n,농업]]], [advp, [np, [adnp, [np, [n,천하]]], [np, [n,대본]]], [post, 으로,10]], [pred, [v,삼], [tns, 2]]], [dcl, 1]]].

Generated English sentence ===>

From the beginning of the nation, Choseon hung out the basic policy of physiocracy and public welfare, and regarded the agriculture as the world basic.

Using the temporal logic programming language Tokio for algorithm description and automatic CMOS gate array synthesis

Masahiro Fujita*, Makoto Ishisone, Hiroshi Nakamura, Hidehiko Tanaka, and Tohru Moto-oka

Faculty of engineering, University of Tokyo
7-3-1 Hongo Bunkyo_ku Tokyo, Japan 113

*: Now at FUJITSU LABORATORIES LTD.

Abstract

To date, simulation has been the primary method used to support hardware logic design. In particular, there has been little that could support such design from the system level, such as a language to describe processing algorithms. In this paper, we will propose a silicon compiler, which is designed to support CMOS gate arrays from the system level. Descriptions from the system level through the state diagram level are done by using the temporal logic programming language called Tokio. Being based on temporal logic, Tokio enables the use of temporal operators. This facilitates the description of concurrent operations that cannot be easily described in Prolog. In addition, because the mathematical models are clearly defined, verification and synthesis can be easily supported. At present, only a simulator coded in Prolog is available to support descriptions of this level in Tokio.

A program that automatically synthesizes logical circuits for CMOS gate array from state diagram level is supported. The core of this program has already been developed in C-Prolog. Synthesis has already been tested at our laboratory. We used the Unify Processor (UP) of PIE (Parallel Inference Machine) which is currently under development, as an example.

This paper introduces the hardware design support strategy based on Tokio, and explains the details of the program that synthesizes CMOS gate arrays from the descriptions of the state diagram level.

1. Introduction

Significant progress in device and implementation technologies has made it possible to create large-scale, complicated hardware systems. However, conventional CAD technology is primarily related to the implementation process. This means that conventional CAD technology is not powerful enough to support hardware logic design at a higher level. A need has developed for a hardware logic design support system, also known as a silicon complier, that can support logic design from the system level, and that can be liked to an implementation design CAD system.

For the language to be used in the hardware logic design support system, we proposed a logic programming language, which has enough mathematical backgrounds. A representable logic programming language is Prolog. The classical predicate calculus on which Prolog is based, however, does not incorporate the "time" concept. In other words, it does not allow descriptions of concurrent operations, and it requires special techniques for hardware descriptions. Temporal logic (Manna and Pnueli 1981, Moszkowski 1983) includes the "time" concept, and Tokio (Aoyagi et al. 1985, Kono et al. 1985) - a programming language based on temporal logic - was selected to describe hardware. The proposed design support system will provide the verification and synthesis capabilities for design descriptions written in Tokio, based on the theory of temporal logic.

The proposed system, also known as a silicon complier, will receive algorithm descriptions written in Tokio, execute the design process, and finally generate the CMOS gate circuit. CMOS gate arrays are selected, because they are provided with a relatively high degree of integration and a sophisticated CAD system for implementation.

2. Temporal logic programming language Tokio (Aoyagi et al. 1985, Kono et al. 1985)

Temporal logic is considered an ordinary classical logic that is additionally supplied with several temporal operators to enable time-related description. Such logic is defined in terms of discrete time, and temporal operators can be used to specify a value for each variable at each time. Temporal logic such as Linear Time Temporal Logic (LTTL) (Manna and Pnueli 1981) and Interval Temporal Logic (ITL) (Moszkowski 1983) are available, depending on the operators provided. Tokio is an extended version of LTTL, uses the easy-to-describe characteristics of ITL, and can be easily converted into LTTL. LTTL is decidable in the range of propositional logic, and research into this logic has made substantial progress (Manna and Pnueli 1981).

Just as Prolog is a logic programming language based on classical logic, Tokio is a temporal logic programming language based on temporal logic. Because temporal logic includes classical logic, Tokio includes Prolog. That is, Tokio is a version of Prolog that has been extended to describe concurrent processing. The use of Tokio, therefore, contributes to simplifying hardware descriptions at different levels, from the system level through the gate level. The following discusses the configuration of the proposed hardware design support system in which Tokio serves as the nucleus.

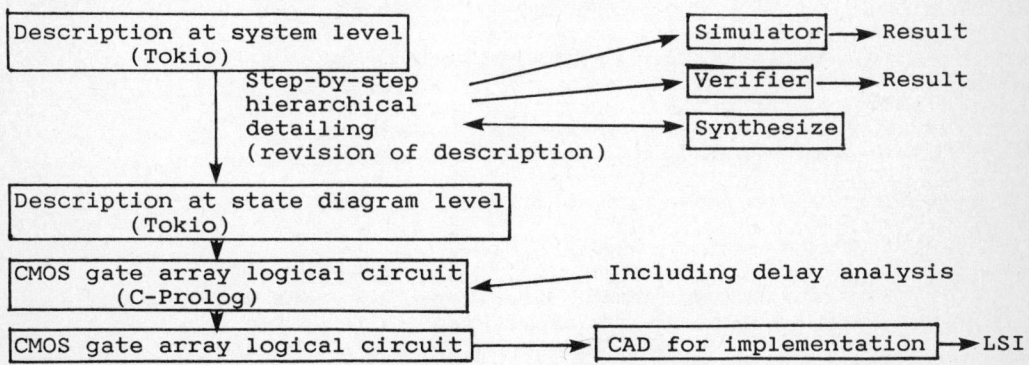

Fig. 1 Configuration of hardware design support system based on temporal logic programming language Tokio

3. Hardware design support system based on Tokio

Figure 1 shows the configuration of the proposed hardware design support system. First, the designer must determine the processing algorithm. Specifically, the designer must describe the algorithm in Tokio, and verify it by using a simulator and a verifier.

This algorithm description may not physically match the hardware.

Therefore, the designer must continue to revise the design description until it conforms to the actual hardware environment. During this process, the design si detailed step-by-step to match the processing image. In other words, it is described in a hierarchical manner. The following functions support this design description detailing procedure:

(1) Simulation
(2) Verifying whether the two given Tokio descriptions are identical
(3) Synthesizing a Tokio description with physical entity (data path) information to generate a more detailed Tokio description

This design detailing procedure is carried out up to the state diagram level (i.e., the same level as hardware description language DDL (Juley and Dietmeyer 1968)). When the state diagram level is reached, the Tokio description is expanded into a state transition table. Then, it is processed by the CMOS gate array logical circuit synthesis program. This program has been completed for the most part, and is discussed in the next chapter. This program outputs a logical circuit description for CMOS gate arrays. This output is forwarded to the implementation design CAD, where it is used to design an LSI gate array.

## 4. CMOS gate array logical circuit synthesis program

The system configuration shown in fig. 1 indicates that the CMOS gate array logical circuit synthesis program receives the Tokio description at the state transition diagram level. However, because Tokio is not yet fully supported, the program currently receives DDL (Juley and Dietmeyer 1968). Tokio, as explained in chapter 2, describes intervals that consists of several consecutive time series each. DDL is considered to consist of such intervals whose lengths are all 1. In other words, DDL can be considered the result of detailing a Tokio description down to the state diagram level.

The CMOS gate array logical circuit synthesis program has the DDL translator (Juley and Dietmeyer 1969) to process the received DDL description. The program then receives the translator output. The DDL translator output includes the following:

- Terminal transfer table
- Register (including memory) transfer table
- State transition table
- Table of logical expressions for dummy terminal (generated by the translator and composed of conditional expressions for transfer and transition)
- Cross-reference table

The transfer table shows the transfer range for each destination terminal register (bits to be transferred or, for memory, addresses), source of transfer, and transfer conditions. The state transition table indicates the current state, next state, and transition conditions. Fig. 2 is an example of the register transfer table.

| MAR (0 : 9) | | 10 BIT REGISTER |
|---|---|---|
| SINK RANGE | SOURCE | TRANSFER CONDITION |
| (0 : 9) | IAR (0 : 9)<br>ADR (0 : 9) | ADS<br>DEC |

Fig.2 DDL translator output example (register transfer table)

## 4.1 Logic design of CMOS gate arrays

In a CMOS gate array, basic gates called "basic cells" are arranged on the chip. Each basic cell consists of several n-MOS and p-MOS transistors. Fig. 3 shows equivalent circuit of two n-MOS and two p-MOS transistors. The desired circuit can be obtained by connecting these basic gates by aluminum wires.

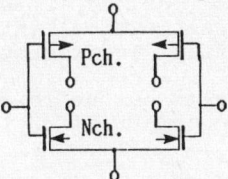

Fig. 3 Basic cell equivalent circuit

Basic cells do not function as logical elements until they are wire-connected. The manufacturer, therefore, first determines the basic logical element wiring modes to be used in logical circuit design. These modes include NOT, NAND, flip-flop, etc., which are registered in a library. The collection of logical elements registered in this library is called the unit cell family, and the user designs their logical circuit by using elements in the family.

## 4.2 Flow of circuit synthesis process

The CMOS gate array logical circuit synthesis program is expected to input DDL translator output (terminal and register transfer table, state transition table, etc.), and generate a logical circuit at the unit cell level for CMOS gate arrays. At this time, the program must perform the following three operations:

(1) Simplifying the circuit
DDL translator output such as transfer table, has a relatively large redundancy. This means that, if such output is expanded into unit cell circuit as is, the number of required gates and delay time will both be significantly increased. In addition, the circuit to be generated through the synthesis process should match the characteristics (based on NAND and NOR) of the CMOS gate array logical circuit by considering the number of gates and the delay time. Therefore, the circuit must be simplified during the circuit synthesis process.

(2) Fan-in/fan-out considerations
The maximum fan-in for unit cells is limited, meaning that an element with a fan-in value exceeding the maximum must be divided into several unit cells. The maximum fan-out is also limited by the manufacturer, and the circuit to be generated must satisfy the maximum fan-out value.

(3) Analyzing the number of gates and delay time
The maximum number of gates is determined by the gate array to be used. The delay time determined by the clock speed. If the generated circuit exceeds these maximum values, logic separation or design modification is necessary.

For such complicated processing, it is not efficient to directly synthesize circuits at the unit cell level. To solve this problem, the synthesis program uses virtual units called "macro units". In other words, the circuits are first synthesized at macro unit level. Macro units, as virtual logical elements, have the following characteristics:

(1) Unlimited fan-in
(2) Infinite fan-out
(3) Input N bits and output N bits
(4) Functionally more advanced (more abstract) than unit cells

For example, in addition to macro units that perform basic operations such as AND and OR, there are those that process more advanced function like addition/subtraction, comparison, and register handling.

When compared to unit-cell-level circuit, the use of macro-unit-cell circuit for simplification or gate count and delay analysis will result in the following advantages:

(1) Less data needs to be manipulated, which simplifies and speeds up processing.
(2) Because its functions are more abstract, it can be technology independent to some extent. This means that this system can also be logically applied to TTL circuits by modifying the operations following the macro unit level.

We decided, therefore, that the synthesis program should read the DDL translator output, expand it into macro units, and execute the various operations for expansion into unit cells.

4.3 Outline of processing

The synthesis process is divided into six phases according to the decisions described above (see table 1).

Phase1: Converts the DDL translator output to Prolog description
Phase2: Expands Prolog description into macro units, performs simplification 1, and generates a cross-reference table
Phase3: Performs simplification 2
Phase4: Analyzez the number of gates and delay time, and modifies the design according to the analysis results
Phase5: Expands macro units into unit cells and performs simplification 3
Phase6: Converts expansion result data for tools

Table 1 Process phases

In phase 1, the program receives the DDL translator output including terminal and register transfer tables, a state transition table, and a table containing logical expressions for transition and transfer conditions. The program converts this output into Prolog description format.

In phase 2, the program expands the data obtained in phase 1 into a circuit for which macro unit are used. At the same time, it performs simplification 1 and generates a cross-reference table. Simplification will be explained in detail in the next section. The result of the expansion in this phase include such general function as AND, OR, and REGISTER, and are not dependent on any specific technology.

In phase 3, simplification 2 is performed at the macro unit level. The circuit is converted into one suitable for CMOS gate arrays. Details on this conversion will be given later.

In phase 4, the program analyzes the number of gates and the delay time. Macro units are considered to have an infinite fan-out as previously explained. During this process, however, fan-out analysis and buffer insertion are also done by taking into account the operation used to expand macro units into unit cells. The values obtained in phase 4 are not fully accurate because the precise delay time cannot be determined until the cells are mounted on the chip. In addition, the number of gates will be changed by the simplification to be performed in phase 5.

In phase 5, the program expands the macro units into unit cells. Simplification 3 is performed at the same time.

In phase 6, the program converts the obtained unit cell circuit data so that it can be input to various tools, such as the simulator, for more precise delay analysis.

Simplification

As described above, there are three levels of simplification; number 1, 2, and 3, corresponding to the logical expression, macro unit, and unit cell levels, respectively. The following operations are done during there three simplification procedures:

- Simplification 1: Fetches common parts from similar logical expressions (see (a) in fig. 4).
- Simplification 2: Primary simplification. Eliminates duplicated units (see (b) in fig. 4) and performs replacement according to the specific rules for optimization (see (c) in fig. 4). At this time, simplification according to the CMOS gate array characteristics, i.e., using NAND/NOR for basic gates, is performed.
- Simplification 3: Optimizes the constant and data calculator (see (d) in fig. 4).

```
T1 = A & B & C & D            COM = A & B & C
T2 = A & B & C & E    =>      T1 = COM & D
                              T2 = COM & E
```
(a) Combining common parts ( & represents AND)

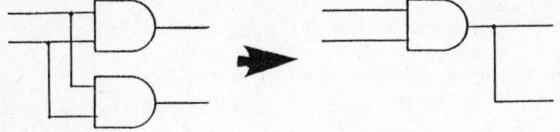

(b) Eliminating duplicate gates

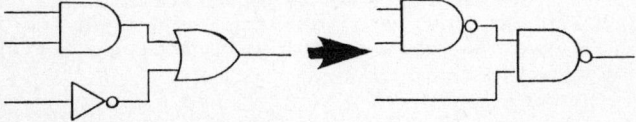

(c) Replacement by rules

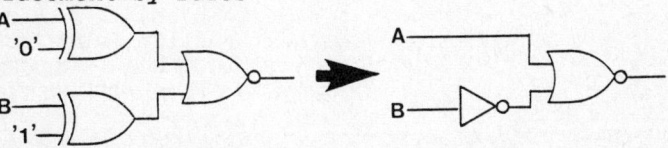

(d) Optimizing constants

Fig. 4 Implementation by Prolog

## 4.4 Implementation by Prolog

The system proposed in this paper is written in C-Prolog [9], which is developed at Edinburgh university. The simplification operations, which are important factors in implementations, are discussed below.

### Simplification 1

During simplification 1, which is performed at the logical expression level, common portions of similar logical expressions are unified. The algorithm is as follows.

- Reads one logical expression
- Fetches the common part of previous expressions, which is stored in a separate area, and merges it with the newly obtained expression to generates a new common part.

IF a common part does not exist,
THEN
- Expands the previous common part into a macro unit
- Stores the newly obtained expression as the new initial value of the common part

ELSE
- Stores the new common part and obtained expression as data

ENDIF
- Repeats the above operation for all expressions. When there are no more expressions:
  IF any common part and expression are still stored
  THEN
  - Expands them into macro units.

### Simplification 2

This is the primary simplification of the three simplification steps. IT is further divided into four as follows:
(1) Unification of units that have the same functions, same inputs, but different nets (see figure 5)
(2) Simplification of AND or OR gates that have several identical inputs (see figure 6)
(3) Simplification of multiplexer gates containing sets that have the same source under different conditions (see figure 7)
(4) Simplification according to the replacement rules

Fig. 5 Simplifying gates with different outputs

Fig. 6 Simplifying gates with identical inputs

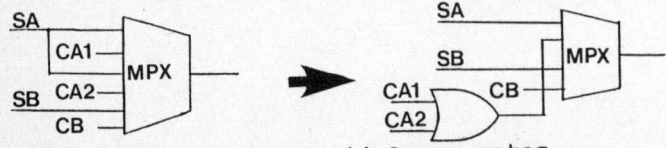

Fig. 7 Simplifying multiplexer gates

Fig. 7 Simplifying multiplexer gates

In stage (4), the program finds circuit patterns to which the replacement rules are applicable, and replaces the units following the rules. This results in:
- Dividing multi-input AND and OR gates
- Optimizing NOT-NOT and AND-OR gates

Thus, the stage 4 procedure consists of two major operations:
- Finding circuit patterns to which replacement rules apply
- Replacing them according to the rules

The following shows the definition of predicate "optimize" generated for the above.

```
optimize(macro(F,ID,B,IO)):-
        match(N,STAT,ID),
        substitution(N,ID,Info),
        (
                STAT == opt,
                count_info(Info,M),
                M < 0
        ;
                STAT == opt
        ),
        exec_info(Info),
        !.
```

The following explains the predicates used in this definition.

match(N,STAT,ID)
If the unit with the specified identification number (ID) matches the pattern determined by a rule, this returns the rule number (N) and rule type (STAT).

substitution(N,ID,Info)
This applies the rule with the specified number (N) to the unit with the specified identification number (ID), and returns the replacement data (Info). Note that it does not perform any actual replacement.

count_info(Info,M)
This returns the amount by which the number of gates will change (M) when the specified data (Info) is executed.

exec_info(Info)
This actually replaces the unit according to the specified data (Info).

In other words, the "optimize" operation can be expressed as "Find a unit that matches the pattern of a rule. If the rule is not of the optimization type (STAT=/=opt), then replace the unit; if the rule is of the optimization type, then only replace the unit if the number of gates will descrease (M<0)."

4.5 Example of synthesis: Unify Processor (UP)

For an example of this synthesis system, we used the Unify Processor (UP) of the highly parallel inference engine PIE (Goto et al. 1983), which is currently being developed, for conversion into CMOS gate array circuits.

The UP currently used in PIE was designed manually. It consists of approximately 500 TTL IC circuits and 17 internal registers (356 bits in total), and is controlled by a microprogram. For this example, we described the UP in DDL, converted it through the DDL translator as the data to be processed. The source UP description written in DDL was approximately 1000 lines long.

Result of synthesis

Process times

Table 2 lists the process times required for individual phases. These values are CPU times measured on a VAX11/730.

```
Phase1................  5 h 30 m
Phase2
  Expansion...........       40 m
  Cross-reference.....11 h 30 m
Phase3................74 h 30 m
Phase4
  Fan-out analysis....  3 h 30 m
  Gate count analysis.       10 m
  Delay time analysis. 2 h
Total.................92 h
```

Table 2 Process time

Results of expansion into macro units

Table 3 shows the results of expression into the macro units at the end of phase 2.

|  | Macro unit count | Basic cell count |
|---|---|---|
| State transition | 43 | 124 |
| Registers | 19 | 4752 |
| Memory | 8 | 0 |
| Memory address | 23 | 1380 |
| Register transfer | 344 | 7646 |
| Terminal transfer | 122 | 5041 |
| Dummy terminal | 1796 | 7600 |
| Total | 2355 | 26543 |

Table 3 Result of expansion into macro units

Effect of simplification (Table 4)

|  | Gate count | Change | Required time |
|---|---|---|---|
| Initial | 26543 |  |  |
| Simp 1 | 19666 | -6877 | 6 h 30 m |
| Simp 2 | 17467 | -2199 | 1 h |
| Simp 3 | 16604 | -863 | 17 h 40 m |
| Simp 3 | 16405 | -199 | 8 h |

Table 5 Effects of simplification

As shown above, the number of gates has been reduced by 10,000, which is approximately 40 % of the total. Simplification 3 (Simp 3) was preformed twice because there may be remaining circuit patterns to which the rules of replacement apply to at the end of first Simp 3. Simp 3 was not executed more than twice because the number of gates did not significantly change, and because the execution time should be minimized.

## 5. Conclusion

In this paper, we described the hardware logic design support system based on temporal logic programming language Tokio and the automatic CMOS gate array synthesis system. At present, Tokio can only be supported by the interpreter written in C-Prolog, but we are now creating a high-speed processing system based on the C language. We are also discussing a new verification/synthesis system.

The nucleus of the automatic CMOS gate array synthesis system has been completed using C-Prolog. We have shown that the system can synthesize approximately 20,000 gates, and the execution time can be reduced to several hours by using a large-scale computer.

We are now working to facilitate greater support of Tokio to create a real silicon compiler.

## References

Manna Z, Pnueli A (1981) Verification of concurrent programs part I: the temporal framework, Stanford univ. rep. STAN-C81-836

Moszkowski B (1983) Reasoning about digital circuits, Stanford univ. rep. STAN-CS-83-970

Aoyagi T, Kono S, Fujita M, Moto-oka T (1985) Logic Programming Conference '85, Tokyo Japan

Kono S, Aoyagi T, Fujita M, Tanaka H (1985) Logic Programming Conference '85, Tokyo Japan

Fujita M (1984) Logic design assistance with temporal logic, phD dissertation, Univ. of Tokyo

Juley JR, Dietmeyer DL (1968) A digital system design language (DDL), IEEE trans. computer, vol. C-17, no. 9

Juley JR, Dietmeyer DL (1969) Translation of a DDL digital system specification to equation, IEEE trans. computer, vol. C-18, no. 4

Pereira F (1984) C-Prolog users manual version 1.5, EdCAD, Edinburgh univ.

Goto A, Aida A, Tanaka H, Moto-oka T (1983) Highly parallel inference engine PIE, Logic Programming Conference '83, Tokyo Japan

# A PARALLEL LOGIC SIMULATOR BASED ON CONCURRENT PROLOG

Yasunori Noda[*], Tetsuo Kinoshita[**], Akira Okumura[**], Tatsuro Hirano[*], and Tadashi Hiruta[*]

[*] Design Automation Center
Engineering Administration Division
OKI Electric Industry Co. Ltd.
4-10-3 Shibaura, Minato-ku, Tokyo 108, Japan

## ABSTRACT

Using the framework of the parallel logical language, Concurrent Prolog, the concepts and the strategies for the parallel logic simulation are defined. Some types of a prototypical parallel logic simulator are implemented by Concurrent Prolog, and they are used for logic simulations of some sample objects. The performance and the applicability of Concurrent Prolog in the parallel logic simulation will be discussed.

## 1. Introduction

Many requirements for high performance CAD systems are urged because the amount of the information utilized in the design process and the degree of the complexity of the digital systems to be designed have increased recently. It has been expected that the parallel processing improves the performance of CAD systems. From the parallel processing point of view, the concepts and the structure of a parallel logic simulator based on the parallel logical language, Concurrent Prolog (CP), are described in this paper. In chapter 2, the concepts of parallel processing in the CAD system are mentioned briefly. The fundamental strategies for a parallel logic simulator based on the parallel processing model are categorized in chapter 3. The precise structure and results of the prototypical system of this parallel logic simulator are described in chapter 4. And, chapter 5 are general discussions about the parallel logic simulation on CP in the CAD framework.

## 2. Parallel Processing in CAD systems

In the design of digital systems, the intrinsic properties of their behavior indicate so high parallelism that designers of such digital systems are able to describe the behavior model of them according to the concept of the parallel processing model formally. There are twos way for implementing such parallelism, i.e. one is by hardware model and another is by software model. The many interests of recent studies on CAD systems have been devoted to the parallel processing by the hardware model. The flexibility is one of the important factors of the CAD systems. Although the CAD tools based on the parallel processing by software model might be slower than the special purpose CAD engine, in this sense, some algorithms or conceptual models by software model are proposed. For the design and the verification of digital circuits, a high performance logic simulator is one of the most important tools in CAD systems. It is easy to introduce the concept of the parallel processing into the framework of a logic simulator because the behavior of digital systems are parallel inherently. The authors (Noda 1984) designed a logic

---

[**] Artificial Intelligence Sect., Knowledge Information Processing R&D Dept., Systems Laboratory.

simulator by the object oriented programming language on Prolog. Mandala(Furukawa 1984). Utilizing the basic ideas of the previous work, a parallel logic simulator (PLS/CP) is designed and implemented on Concurrent Prolog (CP). Concurrent Prolog is one of the parallel logical languages (Shapiro 1983), and a fundamental structure of a parallel processing of PLS/CP is based on the facilities of CP.

## 3. Strategies for Parallel Logic Simulation

Concerning the physical behavior of the digital systems, each component is operating in parallel independently. Those features give many metaphors to the design of the strategies of the parallel logic simulation.

Components of the digital systems can be modelled as mutually connected processes which exchange event_information and take action independently. In such modelling, each event has to be generated according to the timing constraint regulated by the simulation_clock. This constraint is solved in the conventional sequential simulation by the event_list mechanism which manages events altogether. However, in the parallel logic simulation, it is not only inefficient to manage all events intensively in the event_list manager but also unreasonable to increase the burden of the processing in the event_list manager. In this reason, the management of events have to be distributed into the processes in some way, and each process has to treat events concurrently. So that, the treatment of the timing (synchronization) of the behavior of the processes and the strategy for exchanging the behavioral information such as events between processes are key factors in the parallel logic simulation.

EVENT_TYPE vs. NON_EVENT_TYPE

There are two ways to transmit the information of the output (internal_state) of each process to other processes. One way is to send information only when the output of each process changes. Another way is to send the information of the output even if the change of output does not occur. The former is called EVENT_TYPE simulation and the latter is called NON_EVENT_TYPE simulation. In the EVENT_TYPE, the total amount of the messages between processes can be reduced more than in the NON_EVENT_TYPE. On the other hand, each process of NON_EVENT_TYPE is able to behave like the real hardware component, because each process always receives its own input all the time so that it isn't necessary to wait and to synchronize arriving events.

GLOBAL_TYPE vs. LOCAL_TYPE

For the treatment of the timing, it is also able to consider two strategies. One is to centralize the control of the simulation clock, and another is to distribute it. The former is called GLOBAL_TYPE and the latter is called LOCAL_TYPE. In the GLOBAL_TYPE simulator, all processes are synchronized with the centralized simulation clock (master clock) therefore each process sends only the information of the output (change of the internal_state).

While, the processes of a LOCAL_TYPE simulator have to send the timing information with the output because each process of a LOCAL_TYPE contains the local_clock (internal_clock) within it and behaves asynchronously. In a LOCAL_TYPE simulator, it is the problem to avoid the deadlock in the looped circuits, and some strategies are known to solve this problem (Chandy 1979). According to the above considerations, the strategy of a parallel logic simulator is categorized as follows.

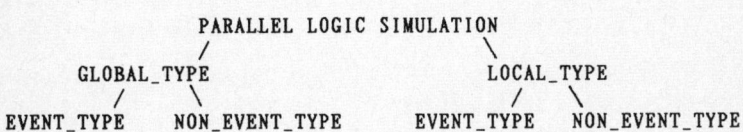

## 4. Implementation of a Parallel Logic Simulator on Concurrent Prolog (PLS/CP)

### 4.1 Global_Type Simulator

#### (a) Process Configuration

The process structure of a GLOBAL_TYPE simulator is shown in Fig. 4.1. The TIMER_PROCESS sends the message of the current_time (simulation clock) to all processes so as to synchronize them. Concluding the whole processing of all processes at the current time, the TIMER_PROCESS renews the value of current_time.

Receiving at the current_time message, the EVALUATOR_PROCESS calculates the output value according to the internal states of each process. And, if the event (change of the output) is occurred then send this value to the DELAY_PROCESS. Simultaneously, the EVALUATOR_PROCESS takes in the current input values (those were sent out from preceding processes through the process streams of CP), and renews the internal states. The DELAY_PROCESS holds the output event during its own delay time, and after this duration, returns the output event to the EVALUATOR_PROCESS. The EVALUATOR_PROCESS sends this output event to the next processes of another component.

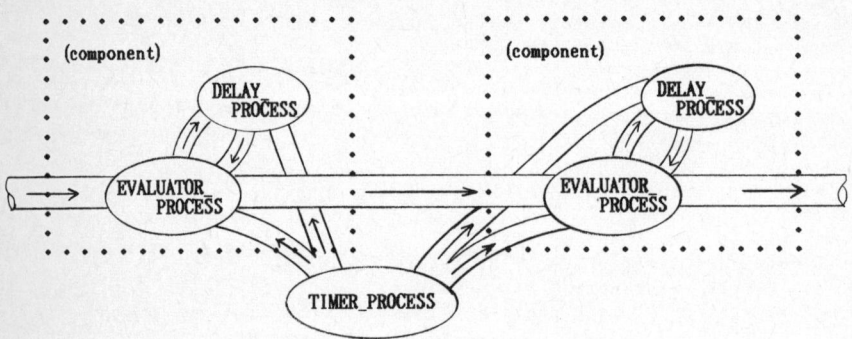

Fig. 4.1 Process Configuration of a GLOBAL_TYPE simulator

#### (b) Representation of the components

The representation of the components of the digital systems is categorized into two types. One is the behavior_description_module (BDM), and another is the structure_description_module (SDM).

The behavior_description_module (BDM) represents the component of the logical element in terms of their inputs, outputs and internal states. The simulation is executed by the cooperative behavior of those BDM processes.

The structure_description_module (SDM) represents the structure of the component in terms of the connections between internal subcomponents. Each subcomponent is also represented as SDM or BDM. Using these framework, the structure of the component is represented hierarchcally. The connections between those SDMs define the input-output streams between the processes of the BDM. In the execution of the simulation, those SDMs are reduced into the set of BDMs according to the structure of those input-output streams. In this sense, SDM gives the definitions of the structure of the digital systems, in terms of the set of the functional building blocks, and BDM gives the definition of the behavior of each functional building block, respectively.

The example of the description of SDM of a 2_to_1_MULTIPLEXER is shown in Fig. 4.2. In this description, each predicate in the body of "mpx" clause corresponds to the

```
mpx(Name.T.Inx.Iny.Ctr.Out.F1-F8):-
    nand_2in(Name-na1.T.M2?.M3?.M4.F1-F2).
    nand_2in(name-na2.T.Ctr.M1?.M5.F2-F3).
    nand_2in(name-na3.T.M4?.M5?.M6.F3-F4).
    inv(Name-inv1.T.Ctr.M2.F4-F5),
    inv(Name-inv2.T.Inx.M3.F5-F6).
    inv(Name-inv3.T.Iny.M1.F6-F7).
    inv(Name-inv4.T.M6?.Out.F7-F8).
```

Fig. 4.2 SDM description of a 2_to_1_NULTIPLEXER (GLOBAL_TYPE)

```
and_2in(Name.T.I0.I1.O.Chain):-
    gata_2in(and.Name.T.I0-x.I1-x.O-x.null.Chain).

delay_time(and._.1).

evaluator(and.1.1.1).
evaluator(and.0._.0).
evaluator(and._.0.0).
evaluator(and.1.x.x).
evaluator(and.x.1.x).
evaluator(and.x.x.x).

gate_2in(Ty.N.[end|Ts].I0.I1.end-O._.[F|F1]-[F|F2]).
gate_2in(Ty.N.[T|Ts].I0-I0t.I1-I1t.New-Ot.fetch.[A|F1]-[B-F2]):-
    T/--end |
    evaluator(Ty?.I0t.I1t.Out).
    event_check(Ty.N.[T|Ts].(Out?)-New.Os.Ot.[A|F1]-[B|FF]).
    fetch2(Ty.N.Ts?.I0-I0t.I1-I1t.Os-(Out?).FF-F2).
gate_2in(Ty.N.Ts?.I0-I0t.I1-I1t.O.null.[F|F1]-[F|F2]):-
    T/--end |
    fetch2(Ty.N.Ts?.I0-I0t.I1-I1t.O.F1-F2).

fetch2(Ty.N.[f|T].[I0|I0s]-I0t.[I1|I1s]-I1t.O.[F|F1]-[F|F2]):-
    gate_2in(Ty.N.T?.(I0s?)-I0.(I1s?)-I1.O.fetch.F1-F2).
fetch2(Ty.N.[f|T][I0|I0s]-I0t.I1-I1t.O.[F|F1]-[F|F2]):-
    prolog(var(I1)) |
    gate_2in(Ty.N.T?.(I0s?)-I0.I1-I1t.O.fetch.F1-F2).
fetch2(Ty.N.[f|T].I0-I0t.[I1|I1s]-I1t.O.[F|F1]-[F|F2]):-
    prolog(var(I0)) |
    gate_2in(Ty.N.T?.I0-I0t.(I1s?)-I1.O.fetch.F1-F2).
fetch2(Ty.N.[f|T].I0-I0t.I1-I1t.O.[F|F1]-[F|F2]):-
    prolog((var(I0).var(I1))) |
    gate_2in(Ty.N.T?.I0-I0t.I1-I1t.O.null.F1-F2).
```

Fig. 4.3 BDM description of a 2_input_AND gate (GLOBAL_TYPE)

SDM. i.e. "nand_2in" and "inv" represents a 2_input_NAND gate and an INVERTOR respectively. The variable "T" of the "mpx" receives the current_time from the TIMER_PROCESS and distributes the current_time message to each "nand_2in" SDM respectively. Variables with ?_annotation represent the input-output streams between CP clauses. Variables "F1". "F2". "F3". "F4". "F5". "F6". "F7" and "F8" are used for chaining processes so as to synchronize each SDM.

In Fig. 4.3. the descriptions of BDMs of a 2_input_AND gate are illustrated. These BDMs becomes the processes of CP in the execution of the simulation. Each BDM is constructed from the control description of the BDM and the functional description of the component. Predicate "nand_2in" has the instance name of the real component "Name". the clock port "T". input ports "I0". "I1". output port "O". and variable for chaining the stream "Chain". The predicate "gate_2in" receives the input events from "fetch2" and calculates its output by "evaluator". Here. "gate_2in" and "fetch2" are control descriptions. and "evaluator" and "delay_time" are functional descriptions.

## 4.2 Local_Type Simulator

### (a) Process Configuration

Each process of the digital systems in the LOCAL_TYPE simulator does not behave synchronously as the one of a GLOBAL_TYPE simulator. The occurrence time of the event in each component is defined independently as the sum of the value of the current_time and the value of the delay_time of each component. In Fig. 4.4. the process structure of a LOCAL_TYPE simulator is depicted.

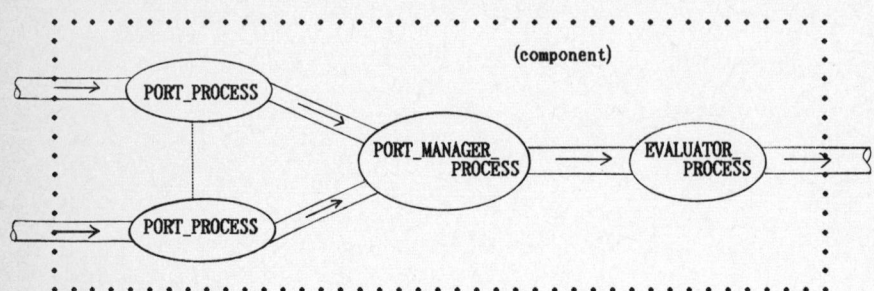

Fig. 4.4 Process Configuration of a LOCAL_TYPE simulator

Each event from preceding component arrives at each input port asynchronously. so that in a LOCAL_TYPE simulator. the detection of the arrival of asynchronous events become more difficult than the GLOBAL_TYPE. To handle those asynchronous events. PORT_PROCESS is defined for each input port. Each PORT_PROCESS accepts the arriving events and sends these events one by one according to the the request of the PORT_MANAGER_PROCESS. The simulator which has the event handling process for each input port. is called PORT_TYPE. On the contrary. like a GLOBAL_TYPE simulator. a simulator which does not have any input port and receives all input events simultaneously. is called NON_PORT_TYPE.

PORT_MANAGER_PROCESS gets events from each PORT_PROCESS. sorts them according to the event_occurrence_time of each event. updates the internal_current_time. accepts current value of inputs, and sends those inputs to EVALUATOR_PROCESS. EVALUATOR_PROCESS calculates the current output according to the current inputs sending from PORT_MANAGER_PROCESS. This output is sent to the next components with the event_occurrence_time which is the sum of the internal_time and delay_time of this component. When the circuits have the loop structure. EVALUATOR_PROCESS generates the null_event until the arrival of the first event in order to avoid the deadlock.

### (b) Representation of the elements

Similar to a GLOBAL_TYPE simulator. the descriptions of BDM and SDM are used for the representation of the logical components. BDM and SDM of a LOCAL_TYPE simulator are represented as same as of a GLOBAL_TYPE except the description of the simulation clock and the variable for chaining the stream. These information can be omitted in a LOCAL_TYPE because every processes of this type behave independently according to the asynchronous events and the internal_current_time information.

The example of BDM of a 2_input_AND gate is illustrated in Fig. 4.5. The procedural meaning of each predicate is the same of Fig. 4.3. The predicate "eval2" represents the function of this element. "gate2" corresponds to the process of the PORT_PROCESS and the PORT_MANAGER_PROCESS and "evaluator2" corresponds to the EVALUATOR_PROCESS. The predicate "evaluator2" calculates the output of this component. decides the occurrence of the output event by the "event_manager" process. updates the internal_current_time and sends the output to the next components.

```
and_2in(Name. I0. I1. Out) :-
    delay_time(and_2in. Td).
    gate2(and_2in-Name. Tc. I0. I0c-x. I1. I1c-x. F).
    evaluator2(and_2in-Name. Tc?. I0c-x. I1c-x. Out-x. Td. stat. F?).

delay_time(nand_2in. 1).

eval2(and_2in-_. stat. 1. 1. 1).
eval2(and_2in-_. stat. 0. X. 0).
eval2(and_2in-_. stat. X. 0. 0).
eval2(and_2in-_. stat. x. 1. x).
eval2(and_2in-_. stat. 1. x. x).
eval2(and_2in-_. stat. x. x. x).
eval2(and_2in-_. end. _. _. end).

gate2(N. Tmin. I1. I1c-A. I2. I2c-B. Flag) :-
    port(N-p1. I1c-A. I1. T1. Tmin?. [stat|Flag]).
    port(N-p2. I2c-B. I2. T2. Tmin?. [stat|Flag]).
    port_manager(N. [I1c?. I2c?]. [T1?. T2?]. Tmin. [stat|Flag]).

evaluator2(N. [Tc|Ts]. [I0|I0s]-I0c. [I1|I1s]-I1c. 0-0e. Td. stat. [F|Fs]) :-
    eval2(N. F. I0. I1. OUT_T).
    event_manager(N. 0_T?. 0e?. Tc?. Td?. 0. 0s).
    evaluator2(N. Ts?. I0s?-I0. I1s?-I1. 0s-0_T. Td. F?. Fs?).
evaluator2(N. _. _. _. _. _. end. _).
```

Fig. 4.5 BDM description of a 2_input_AND gate (LOCAL_TYPE)


## 4.3 Experimental Results

Using Concurrent Prolog Compiler (CPC) developed in ICOT, the prototypical parallel logic simulator is implemented. CPC is a translator which reads clauses written in CP and translates them into the sequential Prolog. Unfortunately, the parallel machine (sequential machine) which executes the CP system in parallel does not exist yet, so that CPC is used to emulate the behavior of the CP program in the sequential Prolog environment.

```
mpx(Name. T. Inx. Iny. Ctr. Out. F1-F8) :-
    nand_2in(Name-na1. T. M2?. M3?. M4. F1-F2).
    nand_2in(Name-na2. T. Ctr. M1?. M5. F2-F3).
    nand_2in(Name-na3. T. M4?. M5?. M6. F3-F4).
    inv(Name-inv1. T. Ctr. M2. F4-F5).
    inv(Name-inv2. T. Inx. M3. F5-F6).
    inv(Name-inv3. T. Iny. M1. F6-F7) ,
    inv(Name-inv4. T. M6?. Out. F7-F8) .

fadd(Name. T. Inx. Iny. Cin. Carry. Sum. F1-F6) :-
    inv(Name-inv1. T. Inx. M1. F1-F2).
    inv(Name-inv2. T. M2?. M3. F2-F3).
    mpx(Name-mpx1. T. Inx. M1?. Cin. M2. F3-F4).
    mpx(Name-mpx2. T. Inx. Iny. M2?. Carry. F4-F5).
    mpx(Name-mpx3. T. M2?. M3?. Iny. Sum. F5-F6) .

add_3(T. Ix0. Ix1. Ix2. Iy0. Iy1. Iy2. S0. S1. S2. C. F1-F4) :-
    fadd(fa1. T. Ix0. Iy0. G?. C0. S0. F1-F2).
    fadd(fa2. T. Ix1. Iy1. C0?. C1. S1. F2-F3).
    fadd(fa3. T. Ix2. Iy2. C1?. C. S2. F3-F4).
    fix(G. 0).
```

Fig. 4.6 SDM description of a 3_bit_adder (GLOBAL_TYPE)


A 3_bit_adder and an 8_bit_CPU model are used as the sample objects to be designed. The summary of some performance parameters of the prototypical simulator are shown in Table 4.1. Fig. 4.6 shows the description of SDM of a 3_bit_adder for a GLOBAL_TYPE simulator.

The functional sturcture of an 8_bit_CPU model is shown in Fig. 4.7. and the description of SDM of an 8_bit_CPU module is also shown in Fig. 4.8. Fig. 4.9 is a simple program of an 8_bit_CPU used as a test data of the simulation. In the case of an 8_bit_CPU model, the total size of the CP program of simulation system is about 1100 lines. About 30% of the program is for the descriptions of the kernel of the prototypical simulator, and about 70% is for SDM/BDM descriptions of an 8_bit_CPU model. Part of the output of a LOCAL_TYPE parallel simulator for an 8_bit_CPU model, is shown in Fig. 4.10.

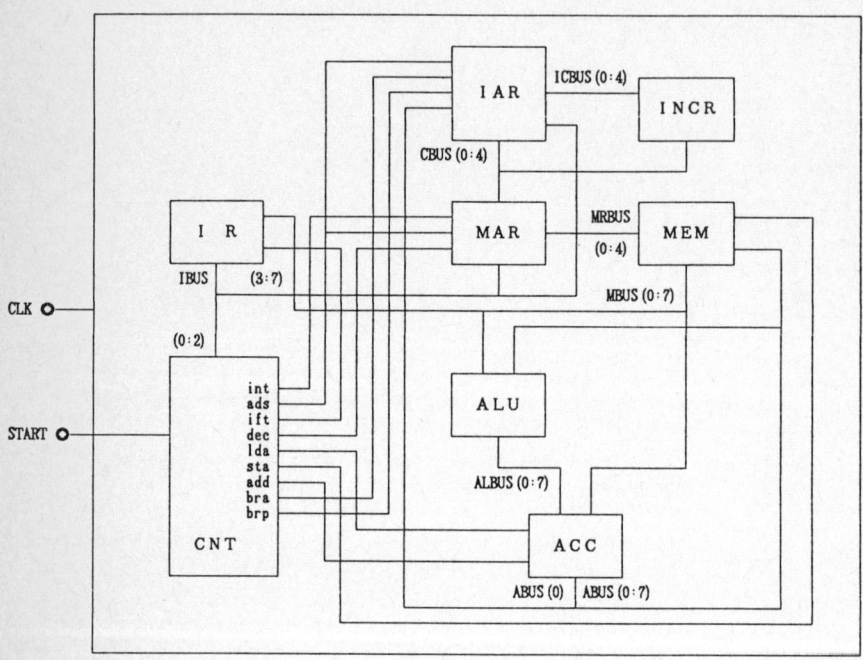

Fig. 4.7 Functional structure of an 8_bit_CPU model

```
cpu_8bit(Start,Clk):-
    ir(Mbus_L?,Mbus_H?,Ift,Clk,Ibus_0to2,Ibus_3to7),
    cnt(Start?,Clk?,Ibus_0to2,Int,Ads,Ift,Dec,Lda,Sta,Add,Bra,Brp),
    car(Abus_0?,Brp,Bra,Ads,Icbus?,Ibus_3to7,Clk?,Cbus),
    incr(Cbus?,Clk?,Icbus),
    mar(Int?,Ads?,Dec?,Ibus_3to7?,Cbus?,Clk?,Mrbus),
    mem(Mrbus,[Abus_0?|Abus_1to7?],Sta?,Mbus_L,Mbus_H),
    alu(Mbus_L?,Mbus_H?,[Abus_0?|Abus_1to7?],Albus_L,Albus_H),
    acc(Add?,Lda?,Albus_H?,Albus_L?,Mbus_L?,Mbus_H?,Clk?,[Abus_0|Abus_1to7?]).
```

Fig. 4.8 SDM description of an 8_bit_CPU model (LOCAL_TYPE)

| Address | Mnemonic | Operand |
|---------|----------|---------|
| 0 0 0 0 0 | B R A | 0 1 0 0 0 |
| 0 1 0 0 0 | L D A | 1 0 0 0 0 |
| 0 1 0 0 1 | A D D | 0 0 0 0 1 |
| 0 1 0 1 0 | S T A | 1 1 0 0 0 |

Fig. 4.9 Sample program for an 8_bit_CPU model

```
  0 : CNT_clock = 0
  2 : CNT_ads = 0
  2 : CNT_dec = 0
  2 : CNT_ift = 0
  3 :                          IR_mbus_H_I -0 = 0
  3 :                          IR_mbus_H_I -1 = 0
  3 :                          IR_mbus_H_I -2 = 0
  3 :                          IR_mbus_H_I -3 = 0
  3 :                          IR_mbus_L_I -0 = 0
  3 :                          IR_mbus_L_I -1 = 0
  3 :                          IR_mbus_L_I -2 = 0
  3 :                          IR_mbus_L_I -3 = 0
  5 : CNT_add = 0
  5 : CNT_bra = 0
  5 : CNT_brp = 0
  5 : CNT_lda = 0
  5 : CNT_sta = 0
 10 : CNT_clock = 1
 20 : CNT_clock = 0
 22 : CNT_int = 1
 30 : CNT_clock = 1
 32 : CNT_ads = 1
 40 : CNT_clock = 0
 50 : CNT_clock = 1
 52 :                                              MEM_mrbus_I -0 = 0
 52 :                                              MEM_mrbus_I -1 = 0
 52 :                                              MEM_mrbus_I -2 = 0
 52 :                                              MEM_mrbus_I -3 = 0
 52 :                                              MEM_mrbus_I -4 = 0

472 : CNT_dec = 1
472 : CNT_ibus_0to2_I-1 = 0
472 : CNT_ift = 0
480 : CNT_clock = 0
490 : CNT_clock = 1
492 :                                              MEM_mrbus_I -1 = 0
492 :                                              MEM_mrbus_I -3 = 0
492 :                                              MEM_mrbus_I -4 = 0
492 : CNT_dec = 0
495 :                          IR_mbus_H_I -0 = 1
495 :                          IR_mbus_L_I -0 = 1
500 : CNT_clock = 0

m1 :    [[[[[1,1,1,0],[0,0,0,0]],[[0,0,0,0],[0,0,0,0]]]
        ,[[[0,0,0,0],[0,0,0,0]],[[0,0,0,0],[0,0,0,0]]]
        ,[[[x,x,x,x],[0,0,0,0]],[[0,0,0,0],[0,0,0,0]]]
        ,[[[0,0,0,0],[0,0,0,0]],[[0,0,0,0],[0,0,0,0]]]]
m2 :    [[[[0,0,0,1],[0,0,0,0]],[[0,0,0,0],[0,0,0,0]]]
        ,[[[0,0,0,0],[0,0,0,0]],[[0,0,0,0],[0,0,0,0]]]
        ,[[[x,x,x,x],[0,0,0,0]],[[0,0,0,0],[0,0,0,0]]]
        ,[[[0,0,0,0],[0,0,0,0]],[[0,0,0,0],[0,0,0,0]]]]
m3 :    [[[[1,0,0,0],[0,0,0,0]],[[0,0,0,0],[0,0,0,0]]]
        ,[[[0,0,0,0],[0,0,0,0]],[[0,0,0,0],[0,0,0,0]]]
        ,[[[0,0,1,1],[0,1,1,0]],[[0,1,0,1],[0,0,0,0]]]
        ,[[[0,0,0,0],[0,0,0,0]],[[0,0,0,0],[0,0,0,0]]]]
m4 :    [[[[1,0,0,0],[0,0,0,1]],[[0,0,0,0],[0,0,0,0]]]
        ,[[[0,0,0,0],[0,0,0,0]],[[0,0,0,0],[0,0,0,0]]]
        ,[[[0,0,0,0],[0,0,0,1]],[[1,0,0,0],[0,0,0,0]]]
        ,[[[0,0,0,0],[0,0,0,0]],[[0,0,0,0],[0,0,0,0]]]]
```

-87634 reductions and 22675 suspensions in 589 cycles and xwd(2,79154) msec.
(-77904 rps.)
Degree of parallelism is 113360/1000.


Fig. 4.10 Part of the output of a LOCAL_TYPE simulator for the simulation of an 8_bit_CPU model

Table 4.1 Summary of the performance parameters of parallel logic simulators

| Simulation Strategy / Performance | GLOBAL_TYPE | | LOCAL_TYPE | | | |
|---|---|---|---|---|---|---|
| | EVENT_TYPE | NON_EVENT_TYPE | EVENT_TYPE | | | NON_EVENT_TYPE |
| | NON_PORT_TYPE | NON_PORT_TYPE | NON_PORT | PORT_TYPE | PORT_TYPE | |
| No. of events | 152 | 152 | 152 | 152 | 41 | 369 |
| No. of reductions | 17165 | 36972 | 12415 | 16379 | 123499 | 25449 |
| No. of suspentions | 5139 | 16039 | 4170 | 31384 | 785895 | 18542 |
| No. of cycles | 272 | 40 | 134 | 323 | 674 | 422 |
| run_time (msec) | 37424 | 434 | 27599 | 44414 | 619955 | 311269 |
| circuit | 3_bit_adder | | | | 8_bit_CPU | |

## 5. Discussions

### 5.1 Comparison of the parallel logic simulation strategies

GLOBAL_TYPE vs. LOCAL_TYPE

It is complicated to synchronize the messages of all processes in a GLOBAL_TYPE. As shown in Table 4.1, the amount of the reductions of a GLOBAL_TYPE simulator is greater than that of a LOCAL_TYPE simulator. This result means that the GLOBAL_TYPE simulator has much burden of the processing than a LOCAL_TYPE because a GLOBAL_TYPE has to manage the large amount of the messages of all processes.

In a LOCAL_TYPE simulator, each process behaves independently and it isn't necessary to consider the synchronization of the processes. Therefore, it is easy to describe the control structure of the simulator and the object to be simulated. From those considerations, a LOCAL_TYPE parallel logic simulator is more superior to a GLOBAL_TYPE one in the sense of the design productivity and the performance of the parallel logic simulation.

EVENT_TYPE vs. NON_EVENT_TYPE

The amount of the messages to be transmitted in the NON_EVENT_TYPE simulator is greater than the EVENT_TYPE. In the EVENT_TYPE simulator applied to the circuit with the loop structure, the amout of the messages increases and the performance of the simulation goes down. In the NON_EVENT_TYPE simulator, the average of the amount of the messsages is greater than the EVENT_TYPE in any objects, but it is easy to manage the messages and to describe the simulator even in the case of the object with loop structure.

PORT_TYPE vs. NON_PORT_TYPE

In order to improve the readability of the program, the number of processes is increased in the PORT_TYPE, while the number of the clauses is increased in the NON_PORT_TYPE. It is necessary to describe the large amout of the modules in order to define the functional modules in the logic simulation so that the PORT_TYPE is more preferable than the NON_PORT_TYPE in order to reduce the burden of the programmer.

### 5.2 Applicability of CP in the parallel logic simulator

The mechanism of the process stream in CP is similar to the physical structure of the digital systems. Therefore it is easy to describe the structure and the functions of components by CP.

The component which has the state statically like a PROM_component, is not able to be represented in CP because the process of CP only exists dynamically.

The direction of the stream by the read_only_annotation is fixed as an one-way traffic stream so that the stream like a bidirectional_bus can not be represented. Futher, it is easy to detect an arrival of messages by the read_only_annotation of CP, on the contrary, it is hard to recognize that any messages have not been arrived by the stream mechanism of current CP.

There are some problems of the facilities of CP now, and it is difficult to say that CP is appropriate as a system description language of the CAD system. However, many studies on the parallel logical language are performed, and it is expected that the parallel logical language will be utilized for the implementation of the CAD system in the future.

6. Conclusion

In order to study the applicability of the parallel processing within the CAD system frameworks, the sturcture of some types of parallel logic simulator have been proposed and implemented on the parallel logical language Concurrent Prolog. These simulators have been applied to some simple circuits such as a 3_bit_adder and an 8_bit_CPU model, and the performance of those prototypical parallel logic simulators has been estimated. As a result, the parallel processing is easily embedded into the framework of the logic simulation by the operational model of Concurrent Prolog. And using the representation scheme of Concurrent Prolog, the structure of the parallel logic simulator can be designed as an unified structure constructed from the descriptions of the kernel of the simulator and the descriptions of the digital systems. From a logic simulation's point of view, using the local_type (asynchronous) non_event_type simulation on the parallel machine, the parallel logic simulation will be performed more effective than a global_type (synchronous) event_type simulation on the conventional sequential machine.

Acknowledgement

This work was supported by the Fifth Generation Computer Project, MITI, Japan. The authors thank to Dr. Kouichi Furukawa, the chief of the first laboratory of institute for new generation computer technology (ICOT), for his helpfull discussions.

Reference

Chandy K, Misra J (1979): Distributed Simulation: A Case Study in Design and Verification of Distributed Program, IEEE Trans. on Software Engineering, No.5, SE-5.

Furukawa K, Takeuchi A, Kunifuji S (1984): Mandala:Knowledge Programming System on the Logic Programming Language, ICOT Technical Report, TR-043, (in Japanese).

Koekawa I, Nakagawa H (1981): On the evaluation of the parallel type logical simulator, Reseach Memo 10-9, JIPS, (in Japanese).

Noda Y, Kinoshita T, Okumura A, Hirano T (1984): On the structure of the CAD system, Logic Programming Conference 84, 14-5, (in Japanese).

Shapiro Y (1983): A Subset of Concurrent Prolog and its Interpreter, ICOT Technical Report, TR-003.

A Method of Representing Processes in a Constraint Solver

I. Nagasawa

Computation Center, Kyushu University,
6-10-1 Hakozaki Higashiku, Fukuoka 812 Japan

ABSTRACT

Constraints solving theory is a practical approach to the knowledge based CAD/CAM systems. Previously we presented a computation model, the **Method of Constraint Reduction** based on the logic programming notion. As an application of the model to the design problem in time domain such as timing design or verification of a sequence controller, a method of representing a system of cooperating processes is introduced. This method is characterized as follows. The idea of process reduction is borrowed from Concurrent Prolog but the process reduction is performed nondeterministically. The method treats a system of processes with state variables and constraints between them.

INTRODUCTION

Constraints solving theory (Sussman 1980; Okino 1983) is a practical approach to the knowledge based CAD/CAM systems. Previously we presented a computation model, the Method of Constraint Reduction (Nagasawa 1984, 1986), based on the logic programming notion. As an application of the computation model, a machine design calculation support system (Nagasawa 1986) was also developed. We present here, another application of the model to the design problem in time domain such as timing design or verification of a sequence controller. A method of representing a system of cooperating processes, which is a model of mechanical systems such as machine tools is introduced. This method is characterized as follows.

(1) The idea of process reduction is borrowed from Concurrent Prolog (Shapiro 1983) but the process reduction is performed nondeterministically.
(2) The method treats a system of processes with state variables and constraints between them. In the reduction procedure, two reduction process, the process reduction and the constraint reduction are combined to use.

After a brief introduction to the Method of Constraint Reduction, the basic notion of process is presented by two examples.

Constraint Reduction System

In the constraint solving approach, a design problem is presented in the form of a set of constraints, which is solved by the Constraint Reduction System(CRS). We describe here the basic notion of the CRS.

### Syntax:

The CRS is an extention of Prolog, and so many parts of its syntax are borrowed from Prolog. However, in this paper we use Lisp like syntax summarized as follows.

The data objects of the language are called terms. A term is a constant, a variable or a compound term. The symbols for a constant or a variable can be any sequence of characters. The constants include integers, floating point numbers and symbols for constants. Variables are distinguished from constants by an initial capital letter. A compound term is represented in a form of Lisp's S-expression.

### Constraints:

Constraints are represented as terms. To distinguish them from ordinary Prolog terms, we call them again "constraints".

### Invoking CRS:

To invoking CRS, We have:

$$:- \quad // \quad C_1, C_2, \ldots, C_n.$$

Where $C_1, C_2, \ldots, C_n$ are constraints. The order in which the constraints are presented is not important.

### Reduction Rules:

A reduction rule is a Prolog procedure, which comprises one or more clauses of the form:

(1) $A \; :- \; G_1, G_2, \ldots, G_m.$
(2) $A \; :- \; G_1, G_2, \ldots, G_m \; !! \; T_1, T_2, \ldots, T_n.$ $\quad (m \geq 0, n > 0)$
(3) $A \; :- \; G_1, G_2, \ldots, G_m \; // \; C_1, C_2, \ldots, C_n.$

Where $G_1, G_2, \ldots, G_m, T_1, T_2, \ldots, T_n$ are goals and $C_1, C_2, \ldots, C_n$ are constraints. To realize the constraints reduction function, we introduce two operators, the test operator "!!" and the reduction operator "//". The effect of "!!" is similar to the Prolog cut operator. However it also modifies the reduction process of the CRS. The function of these two operators are detailed later.

### Annotation of Variables:

To restrict dataflow under evaluation of constraints, two annotations of variables are introduced. We call "?" prefixed (postfixed) to a variable as the input(output) annotation, and also a variable annotated as the input(output) variable. The unification of terms containing annotated variables is an extention to normal unification. An input(output) variable is unifiable only with a nonvariable(variable) term. If X is a variable, then the unification of X and Y? succeeds, and the result is an output variable Y?. Input(Output) variables appear only within the head(body) of reduction rules.

**Reduction Procedure**

First we assume to try to reduce a constraint C, which is evaluated by the CRS as an ordinary Prolog goal. The result is classified into three cases.

(1) **Fail**: Fail is the case where the result of evaluation of C fails in Prolog semantics and "!!" has been evaluated. In this case the constraint C is regarded as having no solution.
(2) **Success**: Success is the case where the result of evaluation of C is successful in Prolog semantics. If the reduction operator "//" which is followed by a set of constraints $C_1, C_2, \ldots, C_n$ is evaluated under the evaluation of C, then C will be reduced to a set of constraints $\{C_1, C_2, \ldots, C_n\} \Theta$. Where $\Theta$ is a composition of substitutions being done under the evaluation of C. Otherwise, C will be reduced to an empty set.
(3) **Suspended**: Suspended is the case where the result of evaluation of C fails in Prolog semantics and the test operator "!!" has not been evaluated. In this case, the system obtains no information about C.

<u>Reduction Procedure:</u>

The execution of the CRS, solving a set of constraints S, using a set of reduction rules R, can be described informally as follows. Each constraint C in S is evaluated in an arbitrary order to reduce itself to other constraints using the rules in R. If the evaluation of C fails, backtracking occurs. The system terminates if any constraints in S are not reducible. The outline of the reduction procedure is given in Fig. 1(a). The predicate reduce takes two arguments, and it tries to reduce the constraint C in the first argument. If the constraint C is proved to be suspended, using (suspendp C) as the test, then it is merged to the suspended constraints, which is also given as the second argument of reduce. When the constraint C can be reduced to constraints Ds, using (exec C Ds), it returns the updated constraints to the first argument. In other cases, the failure of evaluation of (exec C Ds) causes backtracking.

```
(solve Cs) :- (reduce Cs nil).

(reduce nil Ws) :- (monitor Ws).        (monitor Ws):-
(reduce (C | Cs) Ws) :-                      (pick_equ Ws Equs Rest),
    (exec C Ds),                             (solve_equ Equs),!,
    (append Cs Ds Cs1),                      (reduce Rest nil).
    (append Ws Cs1 Cs2),                 (monitor Ws).
    (reduce Cs2 nil).
(reduce (C | Cs) Ws) :-                 (b) A deadlock monitor.
    (suspendp C),
    (reduce Cs (C | Ws)).
```

(a) The reduction procedure.

Fig. 1. The reduction procedure of the CRS.

<u>To resolve dead lock:</u>

In the reduction procedure presented above, each constraint is evaluated independently from each other to reduce itself to other constraints. But this is not sufficient for a case such as multi-nonlinear equations, so the reduction procedure must be extended to resolve deadlock. Figure 1(b) shows an example of deadlock monitor which can solve multi-equations.

Implementation:
Using a intelligent backtracking technique and a priority controll, a reasonably efficient system with small overhead was obtained. More detailed explanation of the implementation techniques (Nagasawa 1986) is omitted here.

## REPRESENTING PROCESSES IN THE CRS.

A process is a time varing model of system components such as machine tools or electronic circuits. In order to represent processes in the CRS, the notion of process reduction is borrowed from Concurrent Prolog. In the CRS, processes are presented as terms in much the same way as constraints and are not distinguished from constraints as far as computation model is concerned. However, the intended model of the process is not the same as constraint. A process is characterized as follows.

(1) A process takes local state as arguments, each of which is composed of a set of state variables. The state variables may be constrained each other by "constraints".
(2) Processes communicate with each other by sending and receiving messages. If a process receives messages from other processes then it changes its local state and may send a message to other processes. The behavior of a process is presented in the form of reduction rule.
(3) In the reduction procedure, two reduction processes, the process reduction and the constraint reduction cooperate each other. The process reduction and the constraint reduction correspond to the event driven simulation and the constraints solving of state variables respectively.

### Timing Design of a Simple Transfer Robot.

Figure 2 shows a model of a simple transfer robot. The robot takes four states *pause*, *accel*, *full* and *brake*. *Pause* is the state where robot arm is stopped. In the state, when the robot receives an "on" message, it turn on the switch of the motor to accelerate its arm and change its state to *accel*. *Accel* is the state where the robot arm speeds up to maximum. *Full* is the state where the robot arm being drived at maximum speed. In the *accel* or *full* state, when the robot receives an "off" message it turns off the switch of the motor, applies the brake of the arm and changes its state to *brake*. *Brake* is the state where robot arm decreases in speed down to zero. When the speed of the robot arm becomes zero, the robot falls in *pause* state again.

The reduction rule of the robot is shown in Fig. 3. The predicate *robot* takes two arguments, and it receives a message at the first argument. The state of the robot is the value of its 2nd argument of the form: (<name> <time> <position> <speed>). Where <name> is a state name selected from *pause*, *accel*, *full* and *brake*, <time> is the time when the robot falls in the state, <position> is the position of the arm at the time and <speed> is the speed of the arm at the time. The $GD^2$ (inertia moment), the brake torque, the driving torque, the friction torque and the maximum speed of arm is assumed to be $315.3 kgfm^2$, $200 kgfm$, $2.0 kgfm$, $0.35 kgfm$, $1/6 rad/sec$ respectively.

Now we trace the execution of the CRS, which solves a simple problem such as: At first the robot pauses at home position. When the robot receives an "on" message and an "off" message subsequently, it shifts its arm to a position 165 deg(6.88 rad) distant from home position. What time does the robot receive the message?

The problem is presented as (1) in Fig. 4. First, the robot in (1) receives "on" message, and is reduced itself to the robot in (2), using the reduction rule (R1). This simulates the state change of the robot from *pause* to *accel*. Then the robot in each of the steps (3a),(4a) and (5a) is also reduced itself to the robot and a set of constraints of state variables in the next step. After executing some steps, the evaluation of the constraint (7.76 <= 5) in (6a) however results in failure, and causes backtracking. Now the robot in (2) is reduced to the robot and two equations in (3b), using the reduction rule (R3). In the same manner, the system repeats reduction and terminates at step (7b).

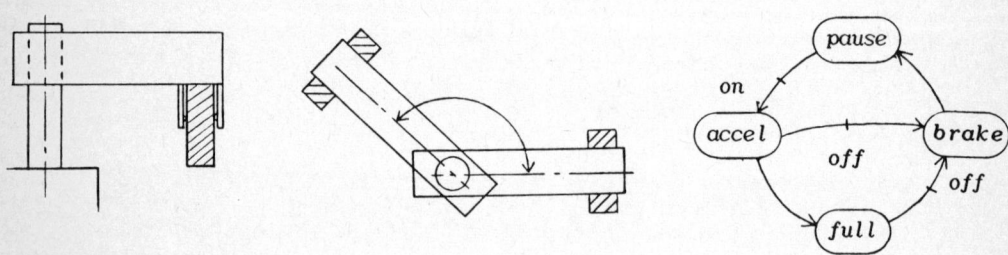

Fig. 2  A model of simple transfer robot and it's state diagram.

```
(R1) (robot ?Mi (pause Ts Rs 0)) :-
        (Mi = ((on Ta)|Ms))
        //(robot Ms (accel Ta Rs 0)).

(R2) (robot ?Mi (accel Ta Ra 0)):-
        (Mi = ((off Tb)|Ms))
        //(robot Ms (brake Tb Rb Nb)),
        (Rb - Ra == 315 / 7160 * Mb / 1.65),
        (Tb - Ta == 315 / 375 * Nb / 1.65),
        (Mb = Nb ** 2),
        (Nb <= 5).

(R3) (robot Ms (accel Ta Ra 0)):-
        //(robot Ms (full Tf Rf 5)),
        (Rf - Ra == 315 / 7160 * 25 / 1.65),
        (Tf - Ta == 315 / 375 * 5 / 1.65).

(R4) (robot ?Mi (full Tf Rf 5)):-
        (Mi = ((off Tb)|Ms))
```

```
            //(robot Ms (brake Tb Rb 5)),
            (Rb - Rf == (Tb - Tf) * 1 / 6),
            (Tf < Tb).

(R5) (robot Ms (brake Tb Rb Nb)):-
        //(robot Ms (pause Ts Rs 0)),
        (Rs - Rb == 315 / 7160 * Mb / 2.35),
        (Ts - Tb == 315 / 375 * Nb / 2.35),
        (Mb == Nb ** 2).

(R6) (robot ?Mi (pause T R N)):-
        (Mi = ((fget (r R))|Ms))
        //(robot Ms (pause T R N)).
```

Fig. 3. Reduction rule of the robot.

full brake
Tf   Tb

brake  pause
Tb  Ts

Change of the arm in speed.

```
(1) :- // (robot ((on 0)(off Tb)(fget (r 2.88))|Ms)
         (pause _ 0 0)).
                    (R1)

(2) :- // (robot ((off Tb)(fget (r 2.88))|Ms)
         (accel 0 0 0)).
                    (R2)

(3a) :- // (robot ((fget (r 2.88))|Ms)
         (brake Tb Rb Nb)),
         (Rb - 0 == 315 / 7160 * Mb / 1.65),
         (Tb - 0 == 315 / 375 * Nb / 1.65),
         (Mb == Nb ** 2),
         (Nb <= 5).
                    (R5)

(4a) :- // (robot ((fget (r 2.88))|Ms)
         (pause Ts Rs 0)),
         (Rs - Rb == 315 / 7160 * Mb / 2.35),
         (Ts - Tb == 315 / 375 * Nb / 2.35),
         (Mb = Nb ** 2),
         (Rb - 0 == 315 / 7160 * Mb / 1.65),
         (Tb - 0 == 315 / 375 * Nb / 1.65),
         (Nb <= 5).
                    (R6)

(5a) :- // (robot Ms? (pause Ts 2.88 0)),
         (2.88 - Rb == 315 / 7160 * Mb / 2.35),
         (Ts - Tb == 315 / 375 * Nb / 2.35),
         (Mb = Nb ** 2),
         (Rb - 0 == 315 / 7160 * Mb / 1.65),
         (Tb - 0 == 315 / 375 * Nb / 1.65),
         (Tqb >= T1),
         (Nb <= 5).
                  :
                omitted
                  :
(6a) :- // (7.96 <= 5).

           fail & backtrack !!
```

```
                    (R3)
(3b) :- // (robot ((fget (r 2.88))|Ms)
         (full Tf Rf 5)),
         (Rf - 0 == 315 / 7160 * 25 / 1.65),
         (Tf - 0 == 315 / 375 * 5 / 1.65).
                    (R4)
(4b) :- // (robot ((fget (r 2.88))|Ms)
         (brake Tb Rb 5)),
         (Rb - Rf == (Tb - Tf) / 6),
         (Tf < Tb),
         (Rf - 0 == 315 / 7160 * 25 / 1.65),
         (Tf - 0 == 315 / 375 * 5 / 1.65).
                    (R5)
(5b) :- // (robot ((fget (r 2.88))|Ms)
         (pause Ts Rs 0)),
         (Rs - Rb == 315 / 7160 * Mb / 2.35),
         (Ts - Tb == 315 / 375 * 5 / 2.35),
         (Mb == Nb ** 2),
         (Rb - Rf == (Tb - Tf) / 6),
         (Tf < Tb),
         (Rf - 0 == 315 / 7160 * 25 / 1.65),
         (Tf - 0 == 315 / 375 * 5 / 1.65).
                    (R6)
(6b) :- // (robot Ms? (pause Ts 2.88 0)),
         (2.88 - Rb == 315 / 7160 * Mb / 2.35),
         (Ts - Tb == 315 / 375 * 5 / 2.35),
         (Mb == Nb ** 2),
         (Rb - Rf == (Tb - Tf) / 6),
         (Tf < Tb),
         (Rf - 0 == 315 / 7160 * 25 / 1.65),
         (Tf - 0 == 315 / 375 * 5 / 1.65).
                  :
                omitted
                  :
(7b)              nil

       solution
          Rf == 0.667 rad == 38.25 deg
          Tf == 2.55 sec
          Rb == 2.41 rad == 138.1 deg
          Tb == 6.38 sec
          Ts == 7.67 sec
```

Fig. 4. Trace of the reduction process.

## Verification of Timing of a Simple Relay Circuit.

### Relay:
A relay has some timing constraints as illustrated in Fig. 5 to guarantee correct action. The action of the relay is presented in the form of reduction rule shown in Fig. 7. A relay takes three arguments, input port, output port and state. It sends and receives a message of the form (<1 or 0> <time>). Where <1 or 0> denotes turn_on or turn_off of input current and <time> is the time when the change occurs. The meaning of the reduction rule (Ron) is as follows. When a relay receives a turn_on message (1 T) at input port, it sends a turn_on message (1 Ty) at output port, with some time delay d. However to guarantee correct action, it is required that the relay receives the next turn_off message till after Ty + don. On the contrary, the reduction rule (Rer1) shows undesirable behavior of the relay, and simply stops the simulation. The meaning of the reduction rule (Roff) and (Rer2) are similar to those.

### Wired or connection:
A model of wired or connection of two contacts is shown in Fig. 8. The change of input current directly emerges the changes of output current. A wor takes four arguments, first two arguments are input ports, 3rd is output port and 4th are the states of two contact and output current.

### Simulation of a simple relay circuit:
Figure 6 shows a self-holding circuit. We trace the execution of the CRS and enumerate the possible action of the circuit.

At first, two contact P, Q are open and no current flows through the coil X of the relay. When the contact P turns on and turns off subsequently, what is the behavior of the circuit?

The initial state of the circuit is shown in (1) of Fig.9. First, the wor in (1) receives an "on" message and reduces itself to the wor and two timing constraints (after Qs T1) and (T2 >= T1), using the reduction rule (P1). Then the wor in (2) and the relay in (3a) are also reduced to themselves in the same manner. However the timing constraints in (4a) contradict each other as shown in Fig. 10(a) and causes backtracking. Now the relay in (3a) reduced to the constraint (before (0 T2) T1+d+don), using the reduction rule (Rer1) and then the one solution in (5b) is obtained. This solution shows the case when the input current changes too rapidly to guarantee the correct action of the relay. By applying the forced backtracking to the system, another solution which shows the correct action of the circuit is also obtained in (6b).

### Solving the timing constraints:
Timing constraints are presented in the form of simple inequalities such as:

(1) Variable $\geq$ Variable + Constant
(2) Variable $\leq$ Variable + Constant
(3) Variable = Variable + Constant

Cook (1984) presented a method to solve them in which the maximum and minimum values of the variables were propagated. This method is implemented by the deadlock monitor.

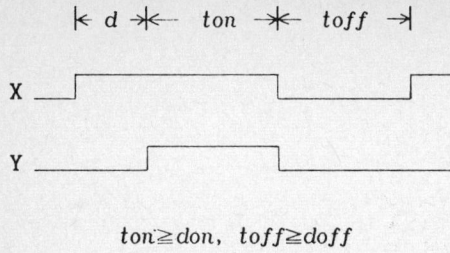

$ton \geq don, \; toff \geq doff$

Fig. 5. Timing constraints of a relay.

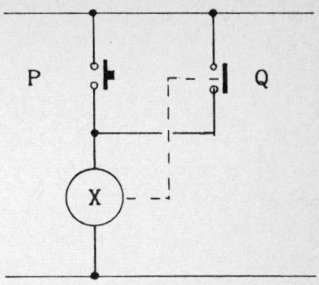

Fig. 6. A simple relay circuit.

```
(Ron)    (relay ?Xi ((1 Ty)|Ys) 0):-
             (Xi = ((1 T)|Xs))
         // (relay Xs Ys 1),
             (Ty == T + d),
             (after Xs (Ty + don)).

(Roff)   (relay ?Xi ((0 T)|Ys) 1):-
             (Xi = ((0 T)|Xs))
         // (relay Xs Ys 0),
             (after Xs (T + doff)).

(Rer1)   (relay ?Xi _ 0):-
             (Xi = ((1 T)|Xs))
         // (before Xs (T + d + don)).

(Rer2)   (relay ?Xi _ 1):-
             (Xi = ((1 T)|Xs))
         // (before Xs (T + doff)).
```

Fig. 7. Reduction rule of the relay.

```
(P1) (wor ?Pi Qs Xs (Po Qo Xo)):-        (Aft) (after ?Xs T):-
         (Pi = ((P T)| Ps)),                     (Xs = ((_ Ta)| _))
         (or P Qo Xo)                         // (Ta >= T).
     // (wor Ps Qs Xs (P Qo Xo)),
         (after Qs T),                   (Bef) (before ?Xs T):-
         (after Ps T).                           (Xs = ((_ Tb)| _))
                                              // (Tb <= T).
(P2) (wor ?Pi Qs ((X T)| Xs) (Po Qo Xo)):-
         (Pi = ((P T)| Ps)),             (OR)  (or 0 0 0).
         (or P Qo X),                          (or 0 1 1).
         ( X =/= Xo)                           (or 1 0 1).
     // (wor Ps Qs Xs (P Qo X)),                (or 1 1 1).
         (after Qs T),
         (after Ps T).
```

(Q1) (wor Ps ?Qi Xs (Po Qo Xo)):-
      (Qi = ((Q T)| Qs)),
      (or Po Q Xo)
      // (wor Ps Qs Xs (Po Q Xo)),
      (after Qs T),
      (after Ps T).

(Q2) (wor Ps ?Qi ((X T)| Xs) (Po Qo Xo)):-
      (Qi = ((Q T)| Qs)),
      (or Po Q X),
      ( X =/= Xo)
      // (wor Ps Qs Xs (Po Q X)),
      (after Qs T),
      (after Ps T).

**Fig. 8. Reduction rule of the wired OR connection of two contacts.**

(1) :- // (wor ((1 T1)(0 T2)| Ps) Qs Xs (0 0 0)),
        (relay Xs Qs 0).

                              (P2)

(2) :- // (wor ((0 T2)| Ps) Qs Xsa (1 0 1)),
       (after Qs T1),
       (T2 >= T1),
       (relay ((1 T1)| Xsa) Qs 0).

                              (P2)

(3a) :- // (wor Ps Qs Xsb (0 0 0)),
        (after Ps T2),
        (after Qs T2),
        (after Qs T1),
        (T2 >= T1),
        (relay ((1 T1)(0 T2)| Xsb) Qs 0).

                              (Ron)

(4a) :- // (wor Ps ((1 Tqc)|Qsc) Xsb (0 0 0)),
        (after Ps T2),
        (Tqc >= T2),
        (Tqc >= T1),
        (T2 >= T1),
        (relay ((0 T2)| Xsb) Qsc 1),
        (Tqc == T1 + d),
        (T2 >= Tqc + don).

                fail & backtrack !!

                              from (3a)
                              (Rer1)

(4b) :- // (wor Ps Qs Xsb (0 0 0)),
        (after Ps T2),
        (after Qs T2),
        (after Qs T1),
        (T2 >= T1),
        (T2 <= T1 + d + don).

(5b) one solution

         T1 <= T2 <= T1 + d + don

                forced backtrack

                              from (2)
                              (Ron)

(3c) :- // (wor ((0 T2)| Ps) ((1 Tqb)| Qsb) Xsa (1 0 1)),
        (Tqb >= T1),
        (T2 >= T1),
        (relay Xsa Qsb 1),
        (Tqb == T1 + d),
        (after Xsa (Tqb + don)).

                              (P2)

(4c) :- // (wor ((1 Tqb)| Qsb) Xsc (0 0 0)),
        (after Ps T2),
        (Tqb >= T2),
        (Tqb >= T1),
        (T2 >= T1),
        (relay ((0 T2)| Xsc) Qsb 1),
        (Tqb == T1 + d),
        (after Xsa (Tqb + don)).

                fail & backtrack !!

                              from (3c)
                              (Q1)

(4d) :- // (wor ((0 T2)| Ps) Qsb Xsa (1 1 1)),
        (T2 >= Tqb),
        (after Qsb Tqb),
        (Tqb >= T1),
        (T2 >= T1),
        (relay Xsa Qsb 1),
        (Tqb == T1 + d),
        (after Xsa (Tqb + don)).

                              (P1)

(5d) :- // (wor Ps Qsb Xsa (1 1 1)),
        (after Ps T2),
        (after Qsb T2),
        (T2 >= Tqb),
        (after Qsb Tqb),
        (Tqb >= T1),
        (T2 >= T1),
        (relay Xsa Qsb 1),
        (Tqb == T1 + d),
        (after Xsa (Tqb + don)).

(6d) another solution

         T1 + d = Tqb <= T2

**Fig. 9. Trace of the reduction process.**

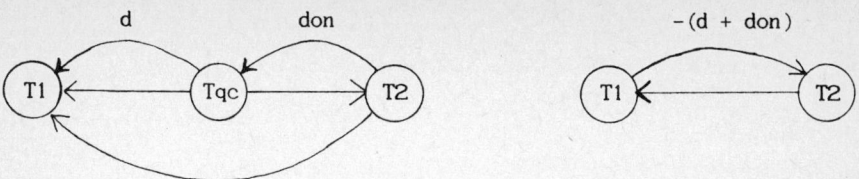

(a) Inconsistent timing relation at (4a)   (b) Consistent timing relation at (4b)

Fig. 10 Timing relations.

CONCLUSION

As an application of the computation model, the Method of Constraint Reduction, we presented a method of representing a system of processes with constraints. It is proved that the expressing power of the method is also enough to the design problem in time domain such as timing design or verification. An experimental design system in time domain is under development now.

REFERENCES

Cook,P.W.(1984) Constraint Solver for Generalized IC Layout, IBM J.Res.Develop. vol 28/5: 581-589

Nagasawa,I., Furukawa,Y., Aramaki,S.(1984) ADL - A Designer's Language Based on Logic Programming (in Japanese), trans. IPS Japan, vol. 25/2: 606-613

Nagasawa,I., Furukawa,Y.(1986) A machine design calculation support system, using the Method of Constraints Reduction (in Japanese), trans. IPS Japan, vol. 27/1: 112-120.

Nagasawa,I.(1986) A Machine Design System with Logic Programming, In: Kitakawa,T.(ed) JARECT Computer Science & Technologies, vol.18 OHMSHA and North-Holland, to appear.

Okino,N., Kakazu,Y., Kubo,H.(1983) TIPS - Technical Information Processing System for CAD/CAM, In: Kitakawa,T.(ed) JARECT Computer Science & Technologies, vol.7: 204-224, OHMSHA and North-Holland

Shapiro,E.Y.(1983) A Subset of Concurrent Prolog and Its Interpreter, Technical Report TR-003 ,ICOT

Sussman,G.J., Steele Jr,G.L.(1980) CONSTRAINTS - A Language for Expressing Almost- Hierarchical Descriptions, Artif. Intell. vol. 14: 1-39, North-Holland

# KRIP: a Knowledge Representation System for Laws relating to Industrial Property

Katsumi Nitta,

Electrotechnical Laboratory
Umezono, Sakura-mura,
Niihari-gun, Ibaraki,
Japan 305

Juntaro Nagao

Nihon Business Consultant Co.
1-6-3, Dogenzaka,
Shibuya-ku, Tokyo,
Japan 150

## ABSTRACT

To develop an expert system which solves the legal problem, the predicate logic and the frame structure are not always appropriate, because they lack in the ability to describe temporal information. KRIP is an expert system of the Patent Law. The knowledge base of this system is built in the language KRIP/L that is integration of the frame structure and the interval logic and that is implemented in Prolog. In this paper, the specification of KRIP/L and the organization of KRIP system are reported.

## 1. INTRODUCTION

In the field of law, consultation systems have been developed and various methods to represent the knowledge of the law have been proposed. However, each law has its own features and problems, so the unified treatment of laws is impossible. To represent the knowledge of law, a logic or a frame structure or network structure have been employed by some research groups. However, the laws relating to Industrial Property have the following features, and the knowledge representation methods that have been proposed so far are insufficient for these laws.

i) Various kind of provisions are involved. Therefore, the Patent Law cannot be translated into a predicate calculus. For example, provisions are classified into a public law and a private law, or a procedural law and a substantive law. Therefore, to represent provisions, the role of each provision must be considered.

ii) There are lots of provisions about time and period, and temporal representation is necessary.

iii) Not only an applicant, but the President of the Patent Office and an examiner must obey the provisions, and sometimes they judge differently about the interpretation of events.

Most systems proposed so far didn't recognize the difference between a procedural law and a substantive law, and didn't have enough function to represent temporal knowledge.

In section 2, we point out some features of laws relating to industrial property in detail. In section 3, the organization of KRIP is explained briefly. In section 4, the provision description language KRIP/L is introduced. KRIP/L is the integration of the frame structure and the interval logic, and has convenient functions to describe the relation between a procedural law and a substantive one. In section 5, the Japanese interface is explained. The user of this system can consult using a natural language. In section 6, an inference engine of KRIP is explained.

## 2. PROBLEMS OF LAWS RELATING TO INDUSTRIAL PROPERTY

The laws relating to industrial property are composed of Patent Law, Utility Model Law, Design Law, Trade Mark Law, and some international treaties. These laws have similar provisions and the same features. Therefore, we deal with only the Patent Law. There are more than 200 sections, and more than 50 procedures are prescribed in the Patent Law.

### 2.1 A Substantive Law and a Procedural Law

A 'Substantive' law is the norm of people, and a 'procedural' law are procedures to realize the norm. In the Patent Law, both types of laws are involved. Some substantive provisions are used to decide whether an application should be refused or not. These provisions are used during an examination, and they are referred to explicitly by procedural provisions. In the Patent Law, most procedural provisions are considered as meta-knowledge of such substantive provisions (Fig. 1).

The first chapter of the Patent Law provides general provisions. General provisions prescribe the definitions of concepts, the way to compute terms, amendments of procedures, the capacity of taking procedures, and the capacity of enjoying rights. These provisions are referred to when procedural provisions or substative provisions are applied. The general provisions can be regarded as meta-knowledge of another provisions.

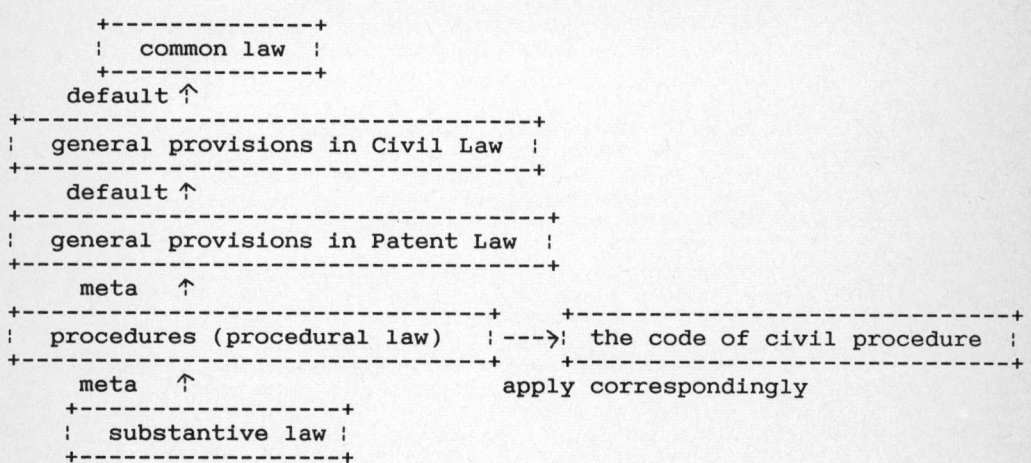

Fig. 1 Relation among Provisions

### 2.2 Period

In Patent Law, there are a lot of provisions concerning time and period as follows.

i) The term of the patent right shall be 15 years.
  ii) The examination of patent applications shall be carried out upon a request for examination. The request should be made within seven years from the date of patent application.
  iii) If a patent application is withdrawn or invalidated, such application is deemed never to have been made.

## 2.3 Interpretation of Laws

Provisions are written in natural language. Generally speaking, these provisions are written more logically than ordinary sentences. However, to interpret the provisions correctly, the implicit knowledge which a patent attorney has is still needed. Let us consider the following cases.
  i) Patent Law is a particular law of the Civil Law, and provisions of the Civil Law are regarded as default knowledge of the patent law.
  ii) The relation between concepts is needed to apply provisions correctly.

## 3. KRIP: Knowledge Representation System of Laws Relating to Industrial Property

The expert system which is under development is called KRIP. The purpose of this system is to help the applicant of the patent to take proper proceedings before the Patent Office. The applicant can consult with KRIP to investigate if the proceedings that have been taken are legal or not, to get the proper proceedings that have to be taken in the future, and to refer to the provisions concerning some key word.

### 3.1 Function of Legality Checking

KRIP has the function to check the legality of each procedure and to advise the proper treatment for the real problem.

At first, the user of KRIP inputs the procedures (called events) that have been taken before the Patent Office. User can input events in natural language (Japanese), and if there isn't enough information, KRIP shows the lacking information and asks the user to input more sentences.

The legality check of a procedure X is treated in three points.
  i) Whether X is taken legally and satisfies the premises of provisions or not.
  ii) Whether there is any procedure left untaken or not.
  iii) Whether the person who took X satisfies the premises of capacity or not.

i) and ii) are called 'a procedure check' and iii) is called 'a type check'.

### 3.2 Organization of KRIP

KRIP is implemented in DEC-10 Prolog (on DEC2060) and Prolog/KABA (on personal computer NEC PC9801) and is composed of following subsystems (Fig. 2).

        Japanese Interface
            input of natural language (definitive clause grammer)
            output of result

```
            frame editor
        knowledge base
            concepts of law ... frame
            provisions      ... interval logic
            control
        Inference Engine
            Type Check
            Legality Check
            Reference of Provisions


DEC2060 (DEC10 Prolog)
+----------------------------------------------------------------+
|  <Inference Engine>              <Knowledge Base>              |
|     type check                      concepts (frame)           |
|     legality check                  provisions (logic)         |
|     reference of provisions         control                    |
|                                                                |
|                                  <Short Term Memory>           |
|                                     objects                    |
|                       TRANS         working memory             |
+----------------------------------------------------------------+
NEC9801 (Prolog/KABA)        |
+----------------------------------------------------------------+
|                       TRANS                                    |
|                                                                |
|                       menu                                     |
|  <Interface>                     <Editor>                      |
|     event input                     display objects            |
|     syntax analysis                 modification               |
|     display result                  file                       |
+----------------------------------------------------------------+
```

Fig. 2 Organization of KRIP

## 4. KNOWLEDGE BASE

Provisions are described in the language KRIP/L. KRIP/L is proposed to build the knowledge base of KRIP. It employed integration of the interval logic and the frame structure.

### 4.1 Concept of Provisions

Each concept which occurs in Patent Law is described using a frame structure called 'class'. The 'is_a' relation between classes composes a tree-like taxonomy, and the lower class inherit the information from the upper class (Fig. 3). The syntax of a class is as follows.

```
        class < class name >
            super: <upper class>
            <slot name>: <value> OR {<class name>}
                .
                .
            action: [Prolog program].
        end_class.
```

If the value of each slot is undefined, the class name is described in the value part. This information works as constraint of types of value.

The slot 'action' contains information concerning the effect of the procedure. It is a goal sequence of Prolog, and is activated after the procedure is proved to be taken legally.

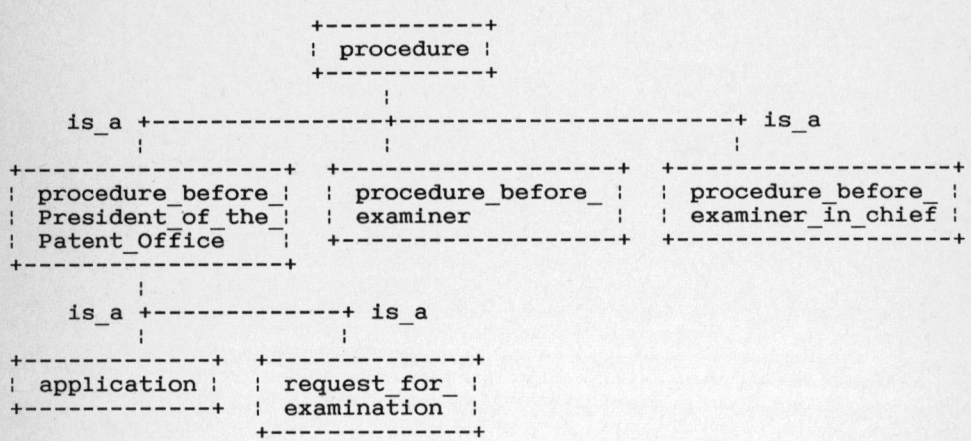

Fig. 3 Taxonomy of class

When the user inputs the events, objects are created in the short term memory. An object is the instance of a class. If the time of the event is defined by a user, the object is bound to a time-chain (Fig. 4).

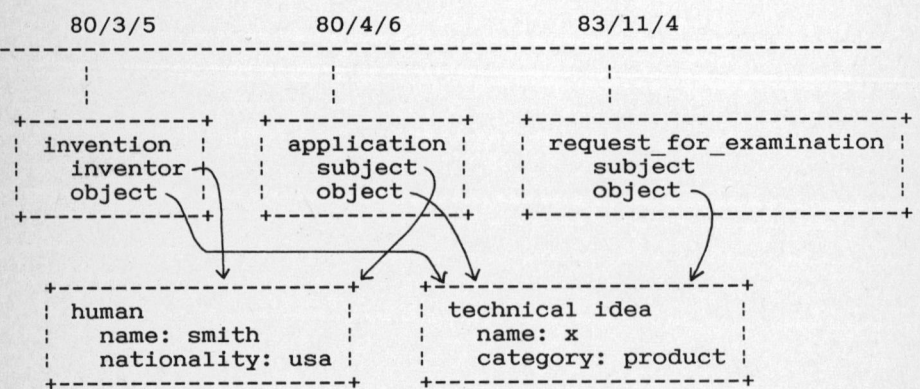

Fig. 4 Data Objects

## 4.2 Provisions

Provisions of the Patent Law are not described in a uniform manner. For example, sometimes one procedure is provided in more than one section, and sometimes more than one procedure is described in one section. Therefore, ignoring chapter and section and editing the provisions into a uniform representation is an effective way of building the knowledge base. However, we selected the way to represent the provisions per every section, because we want to simulate the reference of sections as done by the patent attorney, and to show the user the process of referring to a section concerning the judgement. The section is described in the following syntax.

```
        section No.
          provision clause.
             .
             .
```

The definition of a provision clause is as follows.

1) a provision clause

A provision clause(PCL) is a kind of temporal logic.

```
        provision clause ::=
          Prolog clause ¦
          [interval_form]=>right_term ¦
          [interval_form]=>~right_term ¦
          [interval_form]-->L proceeding_term ¦
          [interval_form]-->M proceeding_term ¦
          [interval_form]-->~ proceeding_term ¦
          [interval_form]proceeding_term ---> provision clause ¦
          [interval_form]~proceeding_term ---> provision clause ¦
          [interval_form]*right_term -->L proceeding_term ¦
          [interval_form]*right_term -->M proceeding_term ¦
          [interval_form]*right_term -->~ proceeding_term ¦
```

'[interval_form]=>P' means that predicate P stands during the interval defined by interval_form.
'[interval_form]=>~P' means that predicate P does not stand during the interval defined by interval_form.
'[interval_form]-->L Q' means that procedure Q may be taken during the interval defined by interval_form.
'[interval_form]-->M Q' means that procedure Q must be taken during the interval defined by interval_form.
'[interval_form]-->~ Q' means that procedure Q must not be taken during the interval defined by interval_form.
'[interval_form]Q ---> PCL' means that PCL is evaluated if procedure Q is taken during the interval defined by interval_form.
'[interval_form]~Q ---> PCL' means that PCL is evaluated if procedure Q is not taken during the interval defined by interval_form.
'[interval_form]*P -->L Q' means that procedure Q may be taken if P stands during the interval defined by interval_form.
'[interval_form]*P -->M Q' means that procedure Q must be taken if P stands during the interval defined by interval_form.
'[interval_form]*P -->~ Q' means that procedure Q must not be taken if P stands during the interval defined by interval_form.

Clauses containing '=>' are used to describe the substantive law, and clauses containing '-->' are used to describe the procedural law.

2) interval form

    interval form::=    point_form:point_form

An interval form is defined as a pair of point_forms. The point_form defines an event or a combination of events. When a point_form is evaluated, the value is the date when the event occurred. A date is described as a triple of integers (year/month/day). Because each point_form of interval_form defines the date, if interval_form is evaluated, the value is a time interval defined by two dates.

3) point form

    point_form::= point_term ¦ point_term & point_form ¦
                  point_form & generic_term ¦
                  point_form ; point_form ¦
                  point_form <* point_form

    point_form::= event ¦ shift
    generic_term::= apply ¦ a term of Prolog


'event(ID,CL,CD,INT)' means that the occurrence of the event ID whose class name is CL and whose slots satisfies CD is recognized in the interval of INT (Fig. 5). Here, ID is an integer that identifies an object, CL is a class name, CD is the condition that slots of ID should satisfy, and INT is a pair of dates.

'shift(INT1,PR,INT2)' means that the interval INT2 is the moving down of the interval INT1 by the period of PR. Here, INT1 and INT2 are a pair of dates and PR is defined as follows.
              5 years,      [3 years, 4 months],    40 days

'apply(ID,NO,RT)' means that if the provision of section NO is applied to the object ID, the result is RT. Here, ID and NO are integers, and RT is a term.

'A & B' means that A and B stand. In other words, the occurrence of A and B is recognized.
'A ; B' means that either A or B stands.
'A <* B' means that A occurs before B occurs.

[ ] is used as the operator to get the interval. For example, the value of '[event(ID,CL,CD,INT)]' is INT. The value of '[A & B]' is the intersection of [A] and [B].

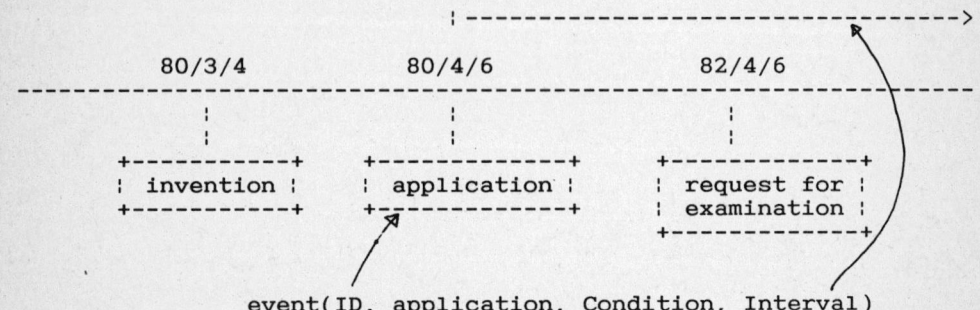

event(ID, application, Condition, Interval)

Fig. 5 System Predicate 'event'

## 4.3 Information of Control

The provisions of the Patent Law are not described in a uniform manner, and the relations between provisions are difficult to represent in the form of a clause. To make up for these difficulties, the control information is introduced. The control information is useful in representing not only the relation between provisions, but the order of reference of provisions. The control information is not always given literally in the Patent Law. However, a patent attorney uses control information as the meta-knowledge to refer to sections effectively.

Let us consider the following provisions.

```
section a.
    [A:B]-->P.
section b.
    [C:D]-->P.
```

In this case, procedure P is provided in two sections, and without the control information we cannot find the relation between these sections--whether the relation of these sections is an AND-relation or an OR-relation.

To express the relation between provisions, control information is used. The sysntax of this information is as follows.

```
control No.
    if_success: [...].
    if_failure: [...].
```

'No' is a section number, and this information provides the next section to be referred to.

## 4.4 Example for Description of Provisions

As examples for the description in KRIP/L, sections 29 and 48 (ter) are shown.

Section 29.
(1) Any person who has made an invention which is industrially applicable may obtain a patent therefor, except in the case of the following inventions:
    (i) inventions which were publicly known in Japan prior to the filing of the patent application;
    (ii) inventions which were publicly worked in Japan prior to the filing of the patent application;
    (iii) inventions which were described in a publication distributed in Japan or elsewhere prior to the filing of the patent application.

Section 48 (ter).
(1) When a patent application has been filed, any person may, within seven years from the date thereof, make a request for examination to the President of the Patent Office.

The description of these provisions is as follows.

```
section 29.
  [ fact(ID, invention, [], _ ) &
        industrially_applicable(ID#object)
     :
```

```
  ( effect(_, publicly_known,  [object:ID#object,country:japan],_);
    effect(_, publicly_worked, [object:ID#object,country:japan],_);
    effect(_, publication    , [object:ID#object],_)
  ) <* effect(_, application, [object:ID#object],_)
] => right_to_obtain_Patent([subject:ID#inventor,
                             object:ID#object]).

section 48-3.
[ effect(ID, application, [], _) : shift(ID#date, 7 years, _) ]
         --> m request_for_examination([object:ID]).


class invention.
    inventor:  {human}.
    object:    {technical_idea}.
    date:      {time}.
    reference: [29,32].
end_class.

class request_for_examination.
    super:     proceedings_before_the_President.
    subject:   {party}.
    object:    {application}.
    reference:[48,48-2,48-3].
    action:    [get_time(T), assert(register(request,T))].
end_class.
```

## 5. USER INTERFACE

The user can interact with this system in his natural language (Japanese). If the user inputs an event by a Japanese sentence, the sentence is analysed, and the data objects corresponding to the event are created in a working area. If the information of the sentence is not sufficient, the system asks the user some supplementary questions.

The interface subsystem is implemented in DCG. By the key word of the sentence, the type of the sentence is fixed. The following is an example for the interface.

```
           menu of commands
        registration of events.........1
        legality check.................2
        editor.........................3
        save/load of events............4
        reference of sections..........5
        clear the working area.........6
        end............................7
```

Please select the next command.    : 1.

Please input events.

```
    smith is a human.
Is the nationality of smith japanese?
    y.
Is smith an adult?
    y.
Is smith an interdict?
    n.
smith is registered.
```

```
Please input events.

    smith filed an application on 2 november in 1980.

What is the object of the application?
    x.
please input facts about x.
    x is the technical idea of a product.

            .
            .
```

## 6. INFERENCE ENGINE

When the user of this system finishes the input of events, the data objects are created in the working area. As the next step, the user can confirm the events by an editor (command 3). After confirmation, if the user selects command 2, the legality checking starts.

### 6.1 The Organization of the Inference Engine

In the long-term memory, provisions and concepts and control information are included. In the short-term memory, data objects and temporary information are included. The inference engine is composed of control part and two parts --- type check part and legality check part.

### 6.2 Type Check

The type checking is done as follows. From the working area, an object which corresponds to a procedure is selected. For each slot of the data object, the value of the slot must satisfy the constraint given in the definition of classes.

### 6.3 Legality Check

After type checking is finished, each object corresponding to a procedure is checked whether it is legally effective or not. A procedure P is provided by three kinds of clauses.

```
            [...] --> L P.
            [...] --> M P.
            [...] --> ~ P.
```

The condition that a procedure P must satisfy is defined as the left side of the arrow '-->'. Therefore, the system evaluates the left side and computes the interval <T1,T2>. If P is taken during this interval, P is judged as legal (In the case that the right side is ~P, if P isn't taken during this interval, P is legal).

As the second step, the system searches for the procedures left untaken. If there is a clause

```
            [...] --> L P.
```

and P is not taken during the interval evaluated by the left side, the system warns about it.

An example for the result of the legality check is shown as follows.

```
        The procedure 'application(77/11/2)' is checked.
            The procedure is provided in Section 36.
                The result of the check is legal.
                    (There  is  no  constraint   concerning  the  date   of
                    application)
        The procedure 'request_for_the_examination(85/4/5)' is checked.
            The procedure is provided in Section 48-3.
                The result of the check is illegal.
                    (Request_for_the_examination should  be  taken  between
                    77/11/2 and 84/11/2)
          .
          .
          .
        The legality check ends.

        The illegal procedure is ---- request_for_the_examination(85/4/5).
```

A procedure taken illegally in the past isn't always invalid. If its defect isn't so serious and if it is removed by an amendment, it is deemed as taken legally. Therefore, when the system finds a procedure taken illegally, the only process that it takes is warning.


7. DISCUSSION

In this paper, we presented the function of legality checking of the expert system KRIP. The description language KRIP/L is the integration of the frame structure and the interval logic. KRIP/L is proposed to describe the procedural law. The retroactive effect and the limitation of a procedure are described easily by KRIP/L.

Sections described in KRIP/L are 3,6,7,8,17,17-2,17-3,18,29,32, 33,36,39,48-2,48-3,49,50,51,52,55,57,58,60,62,64,65-2. The description of these sections is more difficult than expected. There is ambiguity in interpreting provisions, and sometimes temporal provisions should be created. When the interpretation of a provision is controversial, we selected an opinion which is supported by many law scholars. We are sure that if procedural laws are provided in KRIP/L, the will be more understandable than that in natural language.

The new version of KRIP/L and the tool for building a legal expert system which is available on a personal computer are under development.


REFERENCES

[1] J.F.Allen, et al., "Maintaining Knowledge about Temporal Intervals", CACM Vol.26, No.11, 1983.
[2] R.J.Brachman, et al., "Krypton: A Functional Approach to Knowledge Representation", Computer Vol.16, No.10, 1983.
[3] R.L.Schwartz, et al., "An Interval Logic for Higher-Level Temporal Reasoning".
[4] N.Yonezaki, "Templog: A Tempral Logic Programming Language", Proc. Conference of Japan Society of Software Science and Technology, 1984 (in Japanese).
[5] R.Kowalski, et al., "A Logic-based Calculus of Events", Research Memo, Imperial College, 1985.
[6] M.J.Sergot, et al., "The British Nationality Act as a Logic Program", Research Memo, Imperial College, 1985.

CONSULTATION SYSTEM FOR DIAGNOSIS OF HEADACHE AND FACIAL PAIN :
"RHINOS"

Yasushi MATSUMURA, Takashi MATSUNAGA, Yusuke MAEDA*,
Shusaku TSUMOTO*, Hiroshi MATSUMURA**, and Michio KIMURA*

Osaka University Hospital 1st Internal Department
1-1-50 Fukushima Fukushima-ku
Osaka JAPAN

*Osaka University Medical School
**Kansai Medical College, Department of Neurosurgery


ABSTRACT

How do doctors make diagnoses based on their medical knowledge? In this paper a hypothesis is proposed concerning a diagnostic method used by doctors in specialized areas of the medical field. The knowledge for the hypothesis has been provided by an authority in the field of medicine, and a diagnostic system for headache and facial pain, named RHINOS, has been implemented using the programming language Prolog, which is operative on a microcomputer with reasonable CPU time. Because it is operative on a microcomputer, RHINOS is portable and readily available.

RHINOS has four kinds of rules. Some perform as forward links from manifestations to diseases. Others perform as backward links from diseases to manifestations. Through harmonious use of this knowledge, RHINOS makes not only single diagnosis also makes differential-diagnosis. It also diagnoses cases of complication of two or more diseases.

RHINOS was used to diagnose 50 patients and 82% of its diagnostic results were equal to those made by a specialist. 16% were close to those. This shows that RHINOS is capable of diagnosing patients in almost the same way as a specialist.


INTRODUCTION

Man is able to compute, only his computing speed has the limitation. Computers today can make up for his slow computing. Man is able to memorize but there is a limitation in his memory capacity. A machine that can make up for the difficiency of man's memory capacity would bring man to be in full activity.

Such machines are required in the medical field. Physicians have to memorize a tremendous amount of knowledge which is renewed and increasing from time to time. All this knowledge cannot be memorized by one physician. They have coped with this preblem by dividing the knowledge to memorize. In other words, each physician becomes specialized and examines only the patients he can cope with. However, this plenty amount of divided knowledge unintegrated does not mean the real time knowledge. Integrated knowledge is required mostly by the physician who examines the patient first. He has to tell precisely whether he is able to cope with the disease by himself, and if not, he will send the patient to what specialist. Screening is important in medicine. Suppose a patient with malignant tumor visits a physician. If he is not in doubt about tumor, the machine that can find out a very small tumor, if it has already been invented, would be of no use. Examining every patient with a high-power machine would cost a lot. However, the knowledge required for screening is abundant and hard to memorize. A machine that memorizes this knowledge for a physician would be very meaningful in medicine.

In order to answer this, the author clarified medical diagnosis and what kind of knowledge physicians need for diagnosis, and developed a system called RHINOS (Rule-based Headache and facial pain INformations Organising System) which assists physicians to diagnose the patients whose chief complaints are headache and/or facial pain.

## DIAGNOSIS BY PHYSICIAN

Diagnosis by physician is done step by step, that is, history taking, physical examinations, routine (laboratory and imaging) examinations, specific examinations and so on. With the impressions gained in these manners, physicians select a most appropriate one out of many diseases. Unlike expert systems that use causal network such as CASNET[Weiss 1978] and CADUCEUS[Pople 1982], RHINOS has two processes of different directions. One is to ascertain a suspected disease, another is to exclude neglectable diseases. The two kinds of knowledge are required in order to diagnose in the two ways mentioned above. One is the knowledge such as "If the symptom A is observed, then the patient's disease is X." And the other one is such that "If the patient's disease is X, then the symptom A will be observed." Using this knowledge, one (or more) disease is affirmed and the rest are neglected finally, and this is the end of diagnosing process.

## THE MODEL OF DIAGNOSIS

Following is a formarized model for the diagnosing process described above. Each patient with disease $di$ ($i=1,2,...$) may have some symptoms $r$. These are called his/her <u>symptom set</u>, and the set of symptom sets of all patients in the world, who suffered/suffer/will-suffer from $di$, is called $Si$ for short. A certain subset of $Si$ is named $Si$. All elements of $Si$ must be known. the author assumes that diagnosis is to estimate $Si$ including $r$, using the information of $Si$. Now the author can define the following two coefficients.

```
             Number of patients who have symptom set r and disease di
    SI=-----------------------------------------------------------
    (%)          Number of patients who have symptom set r
```

SI should be read as <u>Satisfactory Index</u> of $r$ for $di$.

$$CI = \frac{\text{Number of patients who have symptom set } r \text{ and disease } di}{\text{Number of patients who suffer from } di}$$
(%)

CI should be read as <u>Covering Index</u> of symptom set $r$ for disease $di$.

One <u>rule</u> is formed by symptom set $r$, disease $di$, SI and CI. Symptom set $r$ in a rule is the <u>condition part</u> of the rule. If symptoms of a patient satisfies the condition part, the author calls the rule <u>matches</u> him/her. SI indicates degree of suspicion, and CI indicates degree of negation. the author can assert a patient to suffer from $di$ when a rule for $di$ matches him/her and its SI=100. Moreover, the author can assert a patient not to suffer from a disease $di$ when a rule for $di$ with CI=100 does not match him/her. If SI and CI are defined in $Si$, the above assertions must be true. However, in fact, the author cannot get the SI nor CI. Practically, the author may use SI and CI defined in $S$, instead of them when $Si$ is large enough. Suppose each disease $di$ has a rule with SI=100 and CI=100, a patient with only one disease must match only one of above rules. This means only one disease is affirmed and other diseases are all negated. Even if a disease $di$ does not have rules with SI=100 and CI=100, the author can get the same conclusion when the sum of CI's of rules for $di$ with SI=100 is 100.

The author can get to this situation at the end stage of diagnosing process. However, in intermediate steps, the author cannot always find rules like this. Then how the rules should be stated? What is important in each step is to negate what should be negated, and to determine what is most suspicious among diseases that were not negated. To fulfill above objectives, the author defined rules to be as follows.

For a disease $di$, the author looks for a rule whose SI is the largest. If there are more than one rules that have same SI's, adopt one with larger CI. If CI (or the sum of CI's) is not 100, the author looks for another rule. This rule is with the largest SI among the rest rules. The sum of CI's reaches to 100. The author repeats this procedure of introducing new rules until the sum of CI's becomes 100.

In this way, rules for each disease are defined. Then the author can try to match the rules with patient's symptoms. The result tells us that; 1) When any rule for disease $di$ does not match, the patient does not suffer from $di$. 2) When a rule for disease $di$ matched, his/her probability of suffering $di$ is greater than the SI of the rule. Generally, some diseases have their symptom sets match with a patient. Matched rules are ordered by its SI, and the author assumes higher SI implies higher possibility. Note that the highest disease isn't always same as the result of the final diagnosis. From the above definition, the author can suppose that intermediate stages do not negate the disease of the final diagnosis.

## DESIGNING USEFUL DIAGNOSING SYSTEM

1. Informations Required To Be Provided

Even if a system produces diagnoses or therapies for patients from their history and findings, physicians will not use it when the answers have any possibility of errors. What physicians need is such systems that supply exact information useful for diagnoses. Then what kind of information is useful for diagnoses? Then above rules tell us; a) What kind of diseases are negated. b) Possibility of affirmed disease. Even non-expert doctors in the field are able to diagnose using such information.

2. Selection Of Application Field

It is difficult to build a system that covers all diseases. The author must select fields where such systems are useful and easy to use. The first information from a patient is his/her chief complaints. Classification of diseases by chief complaints make the system easy to use. The first stage of diagnosis is important and difficult. Hence systems that support this stage is very useful.

3. Environment

Micro-computers are the most easily accessible computers for doctors, especially for general practitioners. Those systems that work on micro-computers are better for prevalence. Satisfying the above requirements, Thw author implemented a system called RHINOS (Rule-based Headache and facial pain INformation Organizing System).


RHINOS

1. Outline

This system manages the patients who complain of headache and/or facial pain chiefly. It helps the physicians to diagnose the disease from which the patients suffer only by history taking and physical findings.

2. Diseases To Be Considered

To implement the system easily on computers, the author have further categorized into 39 types of the diseases which give rise to headache and/or facial pains, according to Classification of headache[Friedman 1962] which was established by six American experts chaired by A. P. Friedman. First depth classifications are following 15.

1. Intracranial disease
2. Muscle contraction headache
3. Vascular headache
4. Neuralgic headache or facial pain
5. Psycogenic headache
6. Inflamatory disease of the eye
7. Ear disease
8. Geniculate neuralgia
9. Nasal sinus disease
10. Jaw joint disease

11. Teeth disease
12. Nose disease
13. Invasive disease to the skull
14. Craniocervical anomary
15. Arteriosclerotic headache

## 3. Environment

The author employed Prolog-KABA[Sakuragawa 1984] as a programming language. Horn clauses of Prolog are convenient for knowledge representation. Also, Prolog-KABA executes fastest in Prolog processors which operates on microcomputers. the author employed NEC's PC-9801 (CPU 8086, main memory 384 KB) on which Prolog-KABA can operate. On this environment, user of RHINOS never waits more than 10 seconds at any situation. A bench-mark test[Mizoguchi 1984] shows that Prolog-KABA on PC-9801 is faster than DEC-10 Prolog on DEC-2020.

## 4. Main Operation Of The System

The author has contrived to enter all the necessary information and not to enter unnecessary information as possible;

a) Enter the answers to basic (routine) questions about headache and facial pain.
b) Delete diseases which can be denied, and put the rest in order of frequency.
c) Put further questions about diseases which fall in the range of 95 % of most frquent ones.
d) If a rule whose SI is over 80 matches, go to e), otherwise put further questions about the rest 5 %.
e) Display the name and SI of the disease which a rule has matched, and display CI's of all the memorized rules of the diseases which any rule has not matched.
f) Check if the disease which a rule has matched explains all the symptoms so far entered.
g) If there exists any symptom which can not be explained, display those whose cause should be identified. If the symptom indicates combination of some diseases, display them.

The above mentioned method is close to that which physicians employ in practice.

## 5. Knowledge

In order to implement systems as mentioned above, the following four types of rules are required.

### a) Exclusive Rule (EX-rule)

A rule whose CI=100 and whose SI is set to be as large as possible, as concerning as the first basic questions. One rule is established for each disease. After having put basic questions, these rules will be applied to negate deniable disease hypothesis.

Example) If one has arteriosclerotic headache, one must have following symptoms;
Age: over 51
Pain location: any of whole, half-side, frontal part, temporal part, parietal part, occipital part, and suboccipital part
Degree of pain: to the degree of being laid up
Jolt headache: +

b) Inclusive Rule (IN-rule)

A rule in which SI is set to be as large as possible from information with history and physical examinations. For each disease, there exists in general more than one IN-rules in which CI are set to be as large as possible. An IN-rule will be applied to the disease which has not been denied by an EX-rule. The condition part of an IN-rule includes those which do not included in the first basic questions. These are also applied by putting further questions.

Example) If one has a restless headache which is serious in the morning, and jolty in its character, and the arteriosclerotic change on the eye fundi, and no tenderness on the cervical spine, suspect that it would be arteriosclerotic headache. ...SI=90

c) Associate Rule (AS-rule)

This rule is constructed from manifestations which are characteristic of the disease, although it is not included in the conditional part of an IN-rule. When as IN-rule matches, the system applies AS-rules of the disease.

Example) That it is a throbbing pain confirms that the disease is an arteriosclerotic headache.

d) Disease Image

The system classifies entered diseases into two classes, i.e., ones whose causes should be found and others. Disease image is a set of rules of each disease's possible symptoms whose causes should be found. (Note that EX-rules are for each disease's <u>necessary</u> symptoms.) The system applies disease image to the disease matched by an IN-rule. If so far entered information whose cause should be identified is not included in disease image, the system considers combination of other diseases.

6. Input

First of all, the system puts basic questions (fig.1) to all the patients. Questions are as follows:

Name, Age, and Sex of the patient
First period when the headache occured
Process
Location of the pain
Character of the pain

Degree of the pain
Neurological findings accompanied with the headache
Sleeping situations
Past history
Family history
Jolt headache

There are two ways of answering, one in which data such as name, age, sex and first occurence of headache is entered directly, and the other in which one will choose answers. The author has contrived the following to avoid input errors.

a) Display the entered part of pain by graph.
b) If one enters 'acute', 'subacute' or 'chronic' answering the question of 'Process,' the system requires the user to enter the periods of maximum pain and check by the difference if the answer was correct.
c) If the choices of question are difficult to be understood, one can refer to explanation by entering HELP key.

After entering basic questions, the system puts further additional questions (fig.2). User answers additional questions by yes or no. Questions about tenderness spot are put by displaying locations of these pains in color graph.

To the question about location of pain, which are contained in basic question, patients tend to answer only the location of maximum pain. Therefore, the system applies rules without identifying unentered positions to be ones of pain, and confirms the locations of pain by further questions.

User may answer both basic and additional questions by 'unknown.' If 'unknown' has been entered, it is interpreted so that EX-rule and IN-rule match, and AS-rule and Disease image disregard.

7. Output

The diseases which were not negated with their with their percent frequencies are listed in frequential order when the basic questions are over. (fig.3) The diseases are listed by priority of SI at the moment when the additional questions are over, with SI if the IN-rule matches, otherwise with CI. (fig.4) User can have the matched symptoms for rule-matched diseases, or the non-matched symptoms for the diseases for which the rule does not match. (fig.5) Futhermore, the explanation of the concept of a disease, required examinations and the therapy will be displayed.

8. Other Related Functions

In addition, there are functions as follows:

a) The system can write out a hospital chart. This is made out from the input data to the form of natural language representation. (fig.6)
b) The system can store and search for patient data. The input data can be stored and

referred to by the patient's name, diseases, etc.
   c) The system can answer following questions:
      The reason to deny a certain disease.
      The condition to admit a certain disease.
      The concept of a diseases, examinations and therapy.
   User can utilize the functions described above as CAI.

KNOWLEDGE REPRESENTATION

The four kinds of rules described above are represented as follows in Horn clause of Prolog.

1. Exclusive Rule

   ex-rule(disease-code):-R1,R2,.. Rn.

where, Ri=sym()@sym()@...@sym(). sym() represents a symptom and stands for sym(location,half,right,severe) etc.
('There is a severe pain on right half part of the head.' is the meaning.) (Definition of @ is to come later.)

2. Inclusive Rule

   in-rule(disease-code, SI, rule-number):-R1,R2,...Rn.

3. Associate Rule

   as-rule(disease-code, rule-number):-R1,R2, ..Rn.

4. Disease Image

   disease-image(disease-code):-sym();sym();...sym().

@ is the operator defined as follows: A@B evaluates A and B. If the value of either A or B is true, then its value is true. The difference from A;B is that it evaluates B independently of the result of the evaluation of A. Physicians would like to evaluate both symptoms A and B, knowing that the patient has the disease D if the symptom A or B is observed. One reason for this is that the observation of both symptoms A and B may make a degree of certainty a little greater than that of the case with only symptom A. Another reason is that the symptom A and B are equivalently recognized by physicians so that it seems no operative difference exists between 'symptom A or B' and 'symptom B or A.'

KNOWLEDGE ACQUISITION

To obtain the rules mentioned above, knowledge has been acquired from an expert of the headache and facial pain, using the following question table.

QUESTION 1    Name of disease_____

1. The liable age of the disease onset. from___to___
2. The location of pain which is always present on this disease.
3. The possible character of pain of this disease.
4. The degree of pain which is out of the range about this disease.
5. The onset form that this disease cannot cause.
6. Jolt headache. Present or absent?
7. The occurence frequency of this disease among all the diseases which cause headache or facial pain.

QUESTION 2

The symptoms are based on history-taking and physical examinations. The numerical value is supposed on the basis of the presence of the headache or facial pain.

1. Which set of symptoms(Y) is needed on assuming this disease strongly?
2. How many percentage(SI) is the rate of existence of this disease among patients with symptom Y?
3. How many percentage(CI) is the rate of patients with symptom Y among the patients suffering from this disease?
4. Is CI greater than 90%? If yes, exit QUESTION 2 and proceed QUESTION 3, otherwise proceed to 5.
5. What kind of the set of symptoms(Y') do the patients have who are actually suffering from this disease but don't have any set of the symptoms mentioned before?
6. How many percentage(SI') is the rate of existence of this disease among the patients with symptom Y'?
7. How many percentage(CI') is the rate of patients who are suffering from this disease and have any set of the symptoms mentioned before?
8. Is CI' greater than 90%? If so, exit QUESTION 2 and proceed QUESTION 3, otherwise go back to 5.

Remarks 1) The symptom Y and Y' are selected to let the SI and SI' maximum, and to let also the CI and CI' maximum if the values of SI and SI' stopped increasing.
Remarks 2) QUESTION 2 ends when CI' stopped increasing even though not exceeded 90%.

QUESTION 3

List characteristic symptoms of the disease except for the ones mentioned in the QUESTION 2.

QUESTION 4

List all of the other symptoms which this disease provokes possibly.

Question 1-4 is for making EX-rule, IN-rule, AS-rule and Disease Image, respectively. Before asking QUESTION 4, the list of the symptoms are made through the QUESTION 1,2,3 and are separated into ones the causes of which must be sought and the others.

It needs rather many questions, but each step is easy to reply. As the values of SI and CI are made objectively, it is easier for the experts to reply than using certainty factor of the MYCIN.[Shortliffe 1976]

ASSESSMENTS AND PROBLEMS

The informations provided by RHINOS are correct, so long as the knowledge acquired by the experts contains no mistakes. If there is some mistakes of the informations of RHINOS, the author can find easily which rule causes the mistakes. However, the disease with the highest SI does not necessarily match with the final diagnosis. Thinking of the fact that RHINOS diagnoses only from the history and physical examinations, that is quite natural. The purpose of RHINOS is to produce the informations which are required for the doctors to diagnose from the history and the physical examinations. On this point, RHINOS is effective efficiently. Incidentally, the result of the evaluation[Matsumura 1984] of the system for the actual 50 cases of patients is as follows:

82% :The diagnosis matched with the ones of experts.
16% :The diagnosis was suitable ones.
(Only one case was not coincided because it was a rare disease which is worth for case report.)

The system is still improving, and the new version (already developed) can be expected to result more precisely.

The most important problem of RHINOS is the errors on inputing. As for the results above, no error was present on inputing, because the author himself had operated. However, if physicians use this system actually, inappropriate answers may be produced frequently because of the input errors. It is necessary to pay close attention and to make the effort to use the objective words, graphics, re-assuring system, more explanatory functions, and to provide good manuals, in order to decrease the input errors.

RHINOS is a system made for the purpose of actual utilization. After evaluated strictly and judged to be able to be used actually, the author is planning to make this system open to the users who are intended to give the assessment.

fig.1 Question about the character of the pain

CHARACTER OF THE PAIN
1) Throbbing pain
2) Continuous pain
3) Bursting pain
4) Radiation pain
5) Others
Enter a number : 1

fig.2 Additional question

Is the following symptom observed?
SCLEROSIS OF RETINAL ARTERY
Enter Y or N : Y

fig.3 List after screening

Followings are diseases that must be considered after screening process.

| | |
|---|---|
| COMMON MIGRAINE | 38% |
| TENSION VASCULAR HEADACHE | 19% |
| CLASSIC MIGRAINE | 19% |
| CLUSTER HEADACHE | 10% |
| INTRACRANIAL MASS LESION | 6% |
| SYMPTOMS OF OTHER DISEASES | 6% |
| ----------------------------------------- | --- |
| HEMIPLEGIC OR OPHTHALMOPLEGIC MIGRAINE | 2% |
| INTRACRANIAL ARTERIAL DISEASE | 1% |

fig.4 Diagnostic conclusions

RHINOS diagnostic conclusions

| | | |
|---|---|---|
| 1 COMMON MIGRAINE | POSITIVE | SI=100 |
| 2 INTRACRANIAL MASS LESION | POSITIVE | SI=20 |
| ---- | ---- | ---- |
| 3 SYMPTOMS OF OTHER DISEASE | NEGATIVE | CI=90 |
| 4 CLASSIC MIGRAINE | NEGATIVE | CI=95 |
| 5 CLUSTER HEADACHE | NEGATIVE | CI=95 |
| 6 TENSION VASCULAR HEADACHE | NEGATIVE | CI=90 |

fig.5 Explanation table

COMMON MIGRAINE is suspected. SI=75
Because of following symptoms:
Character of pain: throbbing pain
Process: paroxysmal repetative

Pain on eye: no
Symptom inbetween paroxysm: none
Jolt headache: yes
But following symptom can not be caused by the disease, maybe combination with other diseases.
Vomitting: yes


fig.6 Patient record in natural language

Name: Takashi Matsunaga, male, 26years old
Since 1985-01-01, paroxysmal repetative headache began.
Duration of the paroxysmal is 6 hours. There is no Prodromal syndrome. Pain location is whole head. Character of the pain is continuous pain. The pain is too severe to continue work. There is no concurrent neurological sign during paroxysm.
Nothing in paticular in past history.
Nothing in paticular in family history.
There is a severe jolt headache.


REFERENCES

Freidman, A. P.,(1962) Classification of Headache, Acheivements of Neurology, 6:173.
Pople, H. E. Jr.,(1982) Heuristic Methods for Imposing Structure on Ill-Structured Problems: The Structuring of Medical Diagnosis, in Szolovits, E. (ed.), Artificial Intelligence in Medicine, Westview Press, Colorado.
Matsumura, Y., et. al.,(1984) Consultation System for Diagnoses of Headache and Facial Pain: RHINOS, Proceedings of 4th Joint Conference on Medical Informatics, pp.766-771,(in Japanese).
Mizoguchi, F., et. al.,(1984) Comparison of Prolog Processors, Proceedings of 3rd Logic Programming Coference in Japan.
Sakuragawa, T.,(1984) Prolog-KABA Manual, Iwasaki Giken, Kyoto,(in Japanese).
Shortliffe, E. H.,(1976) Computer-based Medical Consultations: MYCIN, American Elsevier, New York.
Weiss, S, M., Kulikowski, C. A., Safir, A.,(1978) Glaucoma Consultation by Computer, Computers in Biology and Medicine, 8:25-40.

# KNOWLEDGE REALIZATION AND TRANSFORMATION IN KRISP

Isao Sugiyai, Keiko Ishikawa
Heavy Apparatus Engineering Laboratory
TOSHIBA Corporation
1,Toshiba-cho, Fuchu, Tokyo 183   Japan

## ABSTRACT

KRISP is a system written in Prolog for the representation and inference of complex and ill-structured knowledge. Its logic programming approach makes knowledge transformation from experts' knowledge to a executable knowledge base easier. It also helps a process called knowledge realization which is the integration of fragmented knowledge into meaningful rules at each transformation stage. KRISP was applied to electric power system diagnosis and it was found that it performed a little better than domain experts and it was also effective in the problem domains where physical data structure can be mapped onto logical data structure directly.

## 1. INTRODUCTION

KRISP (Knowledge Representation and Inference System in Prolog) is a Prolog based expert system which is effective for problem domains where a simple classification method does not work and knowledge is complex and ill-structured. The knowledge is represented in a logic programming style using Horn clauses in place of conventional IF-THEN rules. The expert knowledge can be easily transformed from intangible concepts in the expert's mind to an executable knowledge base coded in Prolog[1] without forming a physical program model of the target system. This semantic transformation is composed of several transformations and is one of the distinctive characteristics of our system.

In each transformation, knowledge is first divided into several components and then fragmented knowledge is grouped into several abstract concepts according to the experts' model of the real world. These concepts are transformed into Prolog predicates in a one-to-one correspondence to form executable knowledge. This integration process is called realization and it is a major force of knowledge transformation.

We apply KRISP to the domain of electric power system diagnosis where conditions mentioned above for suitability of the system -- complex and ill-structured knowledge -- are met. It especially fits to the problem domain where the physical data structure can directly map onto the logical data structure. In our example, the power system facilities are collections of devices which are connected by power lines. This data structure can be interpreted as objects and relations among them.

To increase the performance of our system, we extracted two kinds of knowledge from experts:  one from veteran operators,  and another from system designers with highly specialized knowledge of power systems. As a result of this combined knowledge base, our expert system performed better than a single domain expert. All the case studies conducted showed that KRISP diagnosis told the user the correct answer together with all possibilities which it was difficult for a human operator to figure out at the instance of the emergency such as power failure.

As for the inference mechanism, the system depends on the knowledge which represents human thoughts directly in the logic programming language. The semantics is always kept during knowledge transformations. Therefore, the behavior of the inference resembles human thinking process quite well and gives reliable results.

In this way, we confirmed the effectiveness of Prolog in applying knowledge acquisition, representation and utilization. In this paper, a practical expert system is introduced and considerations are given to the KRISP style of knowledge processing, focusing on knowledge realization and transformation in Prolog.

## 2. CONCEPTS OF KRISP

### 2.1. WHAT IS KRISP

There are many expert systems and expert system building tools available today. These systems are mostly written in LISP and based on IF-THEN type rules with a very few exceptions. KRISP is one of these exceptions and written in Prolog. It provides facilities such as knowledge editing, knowledge verification, and inference. It was originally developed for the specific domain - electric power system failure diagnosis, and written in C-Prolog[2] on VAX-11. KRISP offers an environment for knowledge processings in logic programming.

### 2.2. DEVELOPMENT OF KRISP

The objectives of the development of KRISP are as follows:

(1) To provide solutions to problem domains where conventional production systems can not.
(2) To make a prototype in a short period of time in order to shorten the knowledge acquisition and verification cycle time.
(3) To build a practical expert system which really "works".
(4) To confirm the effectiveness of logic programming as applied to knowledge transformation.

The use of Prolog as indicated in the last objective was an important factor in realizing the other objectives. The specific reasons for choosing Prolog for implementing the whole system as well as for knowledge representation are listed below:
(1) Logic representation is necessary for and effective in describing domain knowledge. The system behaves quite similarly to human experts in the diagnosis of the target system.
(2) Knowledge acquisition in Prolog is very straightforward and does not require any physical modeling of the problem(i.e. program design). As a result, it takes relatively short time to make an executable knowledge base.The verification and modification of knowledge can also be done effectively in a short time.

### 2.3. THE STRUCTURE OF KRISP

The system is composed of five units. They are Knowledge base unit, Knowledge management unit, System management unit, Consultation unit, and Communication unit. As shown in Figure 1, there is no independent inference engine or working memory although knowledge can be treated independently from the controlling mechanisms. The system management unit includes the user interface.

### 2.4. APPLICATION OF KRISP

KRISP was applied to power system failure diagnosis. In power systems, as soon as power failure occurs, protective relays are activated (implying that CB was tripped) and necessary circuit breakers (CB) disconnect a power lines so that the damaged area may be minimized. After the failure, the system must be restored to its pre-accident condition based on the operator's justification and previous experiences. An operator must find the locations and causes of the failure and plan the restoration processes. This diagnosis, however, always involves the possibility of human errors such as mis-judgement or mis-operation in case of emergency. Therefore, the expert system's assistance in finding out the cause and location are very useful to eliminate human errors and make a good diagnosis.

KRISP finds the cause and the location of the failure according to its knowledge base, which contains rules of relays, CBs, system configurations, and system operation. Names of activated relays and CB's are given to the system, then KRISP starts inference in the forward direction. Data used during this process are summarized below:
    INPUT DATA  : Accident device list (CB, Relay)
    OUTPUT DATA : Accident region list, Accident kind list, Occurence rate
    DATA BASE   : Facility database, Rule base
In Figure 2, an example of accident and diagnosis by KRISP is shown. There are actually six intermediate possibilities according to the trace of this program. They were boiled down to one final decision with 100% credibility using rules about devices which have some probability of failure.

## 2.5. RESULTS OF KRISP

The performance of the system in the example above met the requirement on the expert system in this problem domain.
(1) Correctness of diagnosis
    More than ten case studies were conducted with no bias on selecting the problem. All problems were the cases which actually happened previously and the causes and locations were determined by operators with great difficulty at the moment of accident. All KRISP diagnosis on these cases found the right decisions with the highest occurence rate. The KRISP diagnose actually reflected real cases and the way it reached the conclusions was very similar to that of human experts.
(2) The trace of inference
    The trace function of KRISP shows inference paths one by one so that the user can be informed of rules used and reasons of diagnosis. In several cases, the trace of inference exactly matched the human expert's way of thinking. This is considered to be a major contribution of straight knowledge transformations in Prolog with semantics being kept.
(3) The execution time
    Although the time necessary to draw conclusions varies depending on the nature of problem, it usually takes from several to thirty seconds. This response time was permissible in this application. The program was run on a VAX-11/780 and implemented in C-Prolog. It was not necessary to use other low level languages for speeding up the execution.

From the above results, KRISP showed quite satisfactory results in this particular application. As long as responsiveness is within the required time range, using Prolog gives more merits than shortcomings and opens up the door to another dimension of knowledge processing.

## 3. THE DEVELOPMENT OF KRISP

### 3.1. DEVELOPMENT STEPS

Building expert systems generally requires several steps to take. These steps are as follows:

(1) Determine problem domains
(2) Choose the development methods
(3) Collect experts' knowledge
(4) Build the knowledge base
(5) Verify and modify knowledge base

In building KRISP, steps (3) through (5) in the development cycle were shortened because of the logic programming approach. In step (1), the selection was based on the fact that there existed explicit needs for expert system diagnosis and the problems were well-studied, complex and ill-structured enough to apply knowledge engineering methodology.

### 3.2. THE CHOICE OF DEVELOPMENT METHODS

As stated in 2.2, the development of KRISP was based on knowledge acquisition and inference in Prolog. The compatibility of Prolog with the selected domain knowledge is good due to the similarity of physical data structure and logical data structure. The static knowledge such as information of facilities of power system are stored in the facility database in the form of devices and their relationships, whereas the procedural knowledge represents device-to-device relationships logically in Prolog's Horn clauses. Prolog was found to be well suited to represent such a problem domain where the physical patterns can easily be transformed to logical relationships.

The selection of C-Prolog on the VAX-11/780 was based on the following reasons:
(1) Execution speed is relatively fast enough to process large knowledge database.
(2) Japanese characters including Kanji can be used for predicate names and messages. Communicability of the expert system with users is essential for practical system making. The user is able to read the Prolog predicate names indicating the semantics, without having had previous Prolog experience, and traces of reasonings in Japanese.

## 3.3. KNOWLEDGE ACQUISITION

The first thing to be done is the selection of experts who provide domain specific knowledge. We chose experts with deep domain knowledge and a wide view of the problem. In our application, knowledge of expert operators combined with that of system designers to get both practical and theoretical aspects of knowledge. As a result of this fusion of more than one kind of knowledge, the expert system outperformed a single human operator. In the next step, the knowledge was transfered to a knowledge engineer via many interview sessions. The knowledge engineers then translated it to Prolog expressions. This process involved the conceptualization of experts' knowledge and expressing it in Prolog predicates. Necessary predicates were written accordingly, forming a hierarchy of knowledge representations. The example of knowledge representation is shown in Figure 8.

For the specific application area, once all necessary concepts were collected and written in Prolog, predicates, which are on the top level of hierarchy representing the chunk of knowledge, were defined as knowledge primitives to be used in writing new rules. Predicates at lower levels were black-boxed and hidden from the users. The user interface facility hereby enables users to write new rules by selecting these primitives according to the user interface guidances. Knowledge acquisition becomes much easier in this stage.

Since knowledge were grouped together in several chunks according to the diagnosis steps, or were highly modularized, incremental knowledge base building was possible. Diagnosis results were narrowed down as knowledge acquisition approaches to the final step of analysis of the failure. The rules were basically grouped into four kinds of rules (chunks). They are relay principle, multiple accidents, mis-trip, and mis-non-trip. The structure of the knowledge base is shown in Figure 3.

The acquisition process takes four months with several experts and a knowledge engineer. There are 72 rules of relay, multiple-accident, and mal-operation. The number of primitives defined is 48 where the number of predicates is 185. The area of power system covered by the facility database is about a half of one prefecture in this particular application.

## 3.4. Knowledge base of KRISP

As shown in Figure 1, the knowledge base are composed of two kinds of knowledge; one is static data of the problem domain(both fixed and variable ones), and another is the dynamic knowledge in the form of rules written in the horn clause of Prolog. They are called data base and rule base respectively.

The data base stores the data in Prolog predicates and represents, for example, the properties of the diagnosis objects and relationships between objects. The physical structure of the data base is flat in a sense that it is a collection of predicates with the name tag and its attributes. However, this data base becomes logically structured when Prolog interpreter access the data. This mechanism is called 'virtual schema data interpretation mechanism(VSDIM)'. The pattern matcher constructs logical hierarchy dynamcally when data are retrieved or accessed. The user can define his/her own data format or schema as meta-knowledge and can choose any schema during executions for the same data base of the flat structure. This schema is called virtual data schema or VDS.

As for the rule base, knowledge are grouped into several chunks called knowledge modules which contained a collection of rules used for the same purpose or the related area. In our application, there are four knowledge modules shown in Figure 3. They are used in the inference system in sequence. The order of knowledge modules applied is determined by the user definable meta-knowledge table with default setting. The order of inference within the knowledge module can also be controlled by inference control knowledge on the meta-knowledge tables. The control of inference has three modes to be chosen accordingly; 'once only', 'search all', and 'priority base', to be specified as control knowledge. They are also contained in the meta-knowledge tables.

## 3.5. Knowledge base editor

The knowledge acquisition process is supported by the intelligent knowledge editor. It provides three kinds of edittig functions; one for rule knowledge editor. It provides three kinds of edittig functions; one for rule base editing and another for data base editing and the other for meta-knowledge editing. Figure 9 shows the structure and functions of this editor.

The rule editor has user defined templates called virtual rule schemata(VRS). The VRS has information on the syntax of rules and knowledge primitives used. The knowledge primitives are meaningful rule sets which are composed of smaller or lower level primitives. The lowest level primitives contain Prolog codes which interface with data base or the real world. The VRS gives the user guidances of writing rules which are the collection of knowledge primitives by means of the dialogue between the user and the expert system. When the rule is created, the user can attach the message which will be shown as trace informations or used to dialogue with the user. The rules in VRS are used by the virtual schema rule interpretation mechanism(VSRIM). The Figure 9 diagrammed knowledge editor configuration.

The knowledge editor provides the facilities for editing meta-knowledge. The meta-knowledge is composed of rule firing priority, inference mode and knowledge module firing order. These meta-knowledge are used to control inference process during the expert system executions.

As for the data base editing, The user can define the data format called virtual data schemata(VDS) which is used dynamically for data handlings. The user can see the data only through the VDS during the editing. The VDS gives the foundation of data base access to the virtual schema data interpretation mechanism(VSDIM). Both VSRIM and VSDIM are included in the knowledge management unit. The examples of editing are shown in Figure 10.

Flexibilty and transparency of knowledge representation of KRISP are realized by these virtual schemata, VRS and VDS. The editor knows both systax and semantics and enable the knowledge transformation of knowledge with semantics being kept throughout the acquisition phase. This knowldege editor keeps the track of semantics during knowledge transformation process and makes transfomation as logically as possible.

### 3.6. REPRESENTATION AND CODING

There are usually two kinds of knowledge, static and procedual , in the problem domain. The procedual knowledge is a rule for dynamic inference and static knowledge is data used by procedual knowledge. In our example, the former is relay rule and the latter is a facility database.

As for the procedual knowledge, The acquired knowledge was first organized into hierarchical abstract concepts and then mapped onto corresponding Prolog predicates. The chunking of knowledge according to the concept structure resulted in several knowledge classes. For each class, input/output interfaces are defined and reorganized for the efficient handling of knowledge. Then these knowledge were interpreted into logic programming expressions in Prolog with some additions of cut operators and list operation routines. This process was easy because each concept is directly transformed into Prolog predicate with the name indicating its semantics. For example, the predicate which find the multiple accident possibility was named "FIND_MULTIPLE_ACCIDENTS". The representation of each knowledge was not restricted to a IF-THEN type rule. It rather allows any kinds of expressions of Prolog as long as they observe the syntax of the language. This capability of writing Prolog codes directly gave the representation depth and power in the inference process.

The structure of Horn clause knowledge is as shown in Figure 4. the header labels the knowledge with meaningful name followed by condition predicates and action predicates. Header usually has several variables to communicate with its body.

As for the data representation in KRISP, data are highly structured in conventional representations and to access a particular data in a lower level, the long path must be followed. While data structure in Prolog can be very flat, meaning that the data are accessed directly by pattern matching and unification processes of Prolog. Therefore, the design of data structure in Prolog is straightforward, and data handlings are easily done. This difference between data access of conventional language and that of Prolog is shown in Figure 5. The example of facility data representations is shown in Figure 6.

In the problem domain we chose - electric power system, the physical data structure of electric power system has almost one-to-one correspondence to its logical representation. The device corresponds to the object in logical model and a power line connecting devices is equivalent to a relation. Therefore, logic programming approach fits very well to this kind of domain.

### 3.7. COMPILATION AND INFERENCE

For the sake of accuracy and efficiency, the acquired knowledge is compiled and new prolog codes are generated. The compiler does the following tasks:

(1) Prolog syntax check
    Check the Prolog codes for its syntax.
(2) Knowledge redundancy check
    Check if knowledge is proved by other clauses.
(3) Contradiction check
    Static contradictions are sought out.
(4) Implicit knowledge interpretation

If the order of clause is specified, then rearrange the order accordingly.

Compiled knowledge is then used for the diagnosis. Inference is performed on the compiled knowledge. There is no independent inference mechanism. KRISP makes use of Prolog's own pattern matching mechanism for the inference. The control of inference on the system coded in Prolog is possible by means of meta knowledge and understandings of Prolog behavior of proving predicates. The meta knowledge here means the indication of order of clauses which is usually implicitly stated. The order of clause is important knowledge and KRISP gives the user to express this meta knowledge explicitly. The compiler does the rest. The order of inference follows the path shown below:

-> relay principle -> mis-trip -> multiple accidents -> mis-non-trip -> result

Final results are mostly obtained by applying elimination method in each step.

### 3.8. VERIFICATION

The verification of collected knowledge were done simultaneously as well as modifications of the knowledge base. Knowledge verification was done using real cases of power failures which were difficult for even experts to find the causes and locations in the past ( One of cases tested is shown in Figure 2 ). After executing the diagnosis, KRISP's answers were compared with real cases. The causes and locations of the failure of all fifteen cases were matched with the answers with the highest credibility from KRISP.

The path of reasonings is very important in verification step. It is shown by the trace function of KRISP. The reasoning procedures are traced step by step in readable sentences. An example of trace is shown in Figure 7. The contents of trace output was found to be very similar to the human experts' logical analysis steps.

### 3.9. USER INTERFACE

The user interface of KRISP is included in the system management unit. It is conversation oriented, and communicates with user in understandable Japanese language and mostly the guiding fill-in-the-blank style. There are four kinds of user interface functions:
(1) System operation
(2) Knowledge editor for facility database and rule base
(3) Input/output during inference process
(4) Input/output during verification process

The knowledge editor provides the functions of addition, deletion, modification of knowledge base in conversational mode. Since there are two kinds of knowldege base, the facility database and rule base, the user interface gives two kinds of formats for each kind.

The user interface for facility database knows all formats of facilty data types. It is possible to retrieve current values based on selected keys as well as adding new data by filling the blank.

The rule base editor shows primitives as components of a rule. It guide the user by showing only feasible selections at each step. The user needs merely to choose desired primitives from the selection menu. The flow of user interface operation is shown in Figure 8 and the screen images of knowledge editing are shown in Figure 10.

The user interface for inference and verification is for getting necessary information from the user and giving back appropreate messages in a conversational mode. It is a mixture of menu selection and question answering style.

Since knowledge representation in Prolog is different from production rule type representation, the user interface helps the user to think in the familiar knowledge description format, while being free from particular knowledge of logic programming.

## 4. CONSIDERATIONS

### 4.1. KNOWLEDGE REALIZATION AND TRANSFORMATION IN PROLOG

In the development of expert system, the knowledge acquisition-verification-modification cycle is necessary to obtain a reliable knowledge base. This cycle as shown in Figure 11 may be regarded as knowledge transformation processes which convert vague experts' knowledge into usable knowledge for expert system users in several transformations. The basis of each transformation lies in knowledge realization process. Realization involves three steps. First, identification of knowledge is done, and then, abstraction of identified knowledge follows. Finally, the integration of knowledge makes concretion of abstract concepts possible. This identification-abstraction-integration process is called realization because at the end of this process, there exists knowledge which is substantialized in some form and usable for next transformation step. In other words, realization of knowledge transforms knowledge into another kind of knowledge. As transformations progress, knowledge is becoming more usable and more concrete. Suppose that a transformation connects problem space with solution space, the realization step looks like the diagram shown in Figure 12. It basically works to connect the real world or the problem space with solution space.

KRISP was implemented in Prolog and made transformation within the logic model possible by describing each concept in Horn clause. Hence transformations become very natural and 'crisp'.

In mapping solution space to problem domain, conventional method needs physical models to map to the real world, while logic programming method needs only logical model. This fact made the transformation in the conventional programming difficult. As shown in Figure 13, the logical transformation path works for both formalization and coding processes in KRISP and provides a shortcut.

To make knowledge usable in a expert system, Knowledge must be first divided into small concepts with some groupings. The inference process uses these components to draw some conclusions by integration of knowledge. Knowledge realization and transformation supports this knowledge division-integration process and logic programming provides the means to realize this flow without entering physical model. Naturally, all works are done in logical world in logic programming.

### 4.2. PROGRAM TRANSFORMATION IN LOGIC PROGRAMMING

In the system design of large scale programs, the following developmental steps, called software life cycle, must be followed.
(1) Requirement specification
(2) Logical design
(3) Physical design
(4) Verification
(5) Operation and Maintenance

Among these steps, requirement specification defines requirements on software and is analogous to knowledge acquisition process in the expert system building. The logical and physical design means functional design and program design or 'what' and 'how' of software, respectively. There is always a gap between these two phases because the transformation cannot be formal and must be done manually in conventional language.

On the other hand, the transformation in Prolog makes direct logical concepts to program conversion possible. Figure 13 shows the this difference in transformations. In both ways, the problem is first divided into sub-problems or concepts which form a logical model. In a conventional method, these functional modules are reorganized manually in terms of program modules, while in logic programming, the concept structure is directly mapped to logical model written in Prolog. This transformation between concepts is one-to-one correspondent and keeps the semantics of the model. At this stage, each concept is converted into Prolog's predicates. This transformation between concepts is one-to-one correspondent and keeps the semantics of the model. At this stage, each concept is converted into Prolog's predicates. Prolog program is executable without designing the physical model and gives a solution to the problem in shorter time.

## 5. CONCLUSION

KRISP is intended to treat the problem to which conventional expert system cannot be applied. It is implemented in Prolog to provide the mean to transform experts' knowledge into executable knowledge base without designing physical model of the system. Logic programming contributed to straightforward knowledge acquisition and representation. The resulted knowledge base is very usable and crisp.

KRISP was applied to the electric power system diagnosis and its diagnosis has been 100% accurate so far. The reasoning path showed much similarity with human experts' way of thinking. It has been considered to be a practical expert system by experts in the application domain.

The capability of KRISP is characterized by its good ability of knowledge realization and transformation supports. These concepts may not be new, but we confirmed, from the experiences of building not a toy program but a practical large scale expert system in Prolog, that logic programming was really effective in a certain application and that knowledge realization and transformation of complex and ill-structured knowledge could be done effectively. We will enhance the KRISP functions and user interface and expand its problem domain for the future use.

## ACKNOWLEDGEMENT

Authors would like to acknowledge all experts who gave us their knowledge, which made this system possible and our colleagues who supports us all the time.

## REFERENCES

1. Clocksin,W.f. and Mellish,C.S., Programming in Prolog, Springer-Verlag, 1981.
2. DEC, C-Prolog User's guide, Degital Equipment Corporation, 1984.

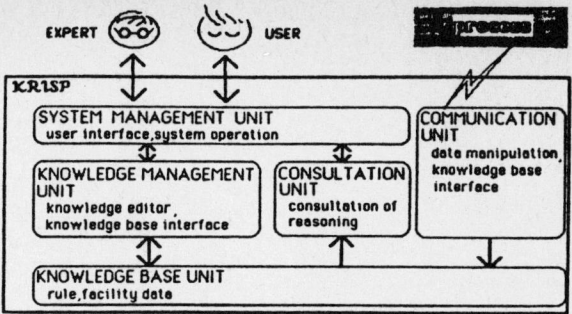

Fig.1 Structure of **KRISP**

Names of tripped CB's ? = (cb4,cb5,cb6).
Names of tripped relays? = (s87_cb4,s211_cb5,s211_cb6).

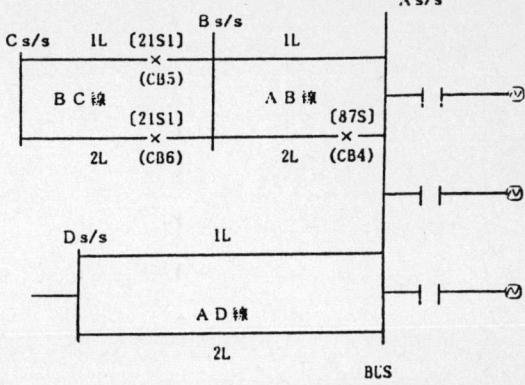

⟹ (probability=100.00%)
multiple accidents at
line-B C-1 (within 80% of the line from tripped end) an
line-B C-2 (within 80% f the line from tripped end),
and the kind of both accidents is "SHORT" covering 2LG,
with mis-tripped relay 's87_cb4'

Fig.2 Example of accident and diagnosis by **KRISP**

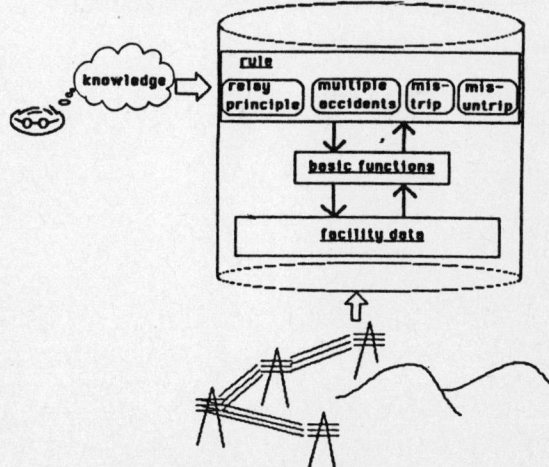

Fig.3 Structure of knowledge base

PREDICATE_NAME(X1,X2,....,Xn):-CONDITION1(X1,X2),
                               CONDITION2(X1,X4),
                               ACTION1(X2),
                               CONDITION3(X5),
                                  :
                               ACTION5(X1).

**Fig.4 Basic format of horn clause knowledge**

basic format of data base
"RELATION(F1,F2,......,Fn).  1≤n<∞"

example

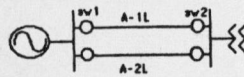

● sw1 is power-source-end of A-1L.
⟹ power-source-end(A-1L,sw1).

● A-1L and A-2L are parallel.
⟹ parallel(A-1L,A-2L).

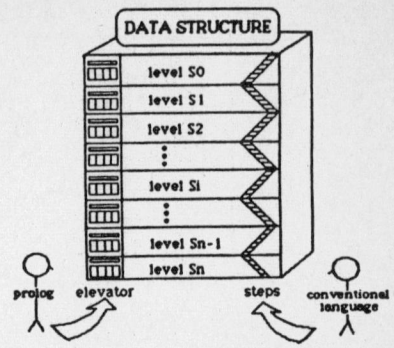

**Fig.5 Difference of data access method between prolog and conventional language**

**Fig.6 Knowledge representation in database**

    Names of tripped CB's ? = (cb4,cb5,cb6).
    Names of tripped relays? = [s87_cb4,s211_cb5,s211_cb6].

   ☆The list of relays tripped by this accidents is:
     s87_cb4, s211_cb5, s211_cb6

   ☆Based on the relay trip principle, possible regions of accidents
   will be identified.
     ★The protection coverage of s87_cb4 is
      line-A B-2
     and the kind of accident is "SHORT" on 2LG

     ★The protection coverage of s211_cb5 is
      line-B C-1 (within 80% of the line from the tripped end)
     and the kind of accident is "SHORT" on 2LG

     ★The protection coverage of s211_cb6 is
      line-B C-2 (within 80% of the line from the tripped end)
     and the kind of accident is "SHORT" on 2LG

   ···from the reasonings above, the possible accident regions are:
     line-B C-1, line-B C-2, line-A B-2

   ☆Next, check mis-untripped CB's

    ···There are no possibilities

   ☆Multiple accidents will be checked in this step
     ★line-A B-2 and line-B C-2 are covered more than one relay
     which has different directions of coverage, therefore multiple
     accidents are highly suspected ···3

        :

   ☞ from all reasonings above,we made a diagnosis below :

 ---)

    (1) (probability=100.00%)
      multiple accidents at
      line-B C-1 (within 80% of the line from tripped end) and
      line-B C-2 (within 80% f the line from tripped end),
      and the kind of both accidents is "SHORT" covering 2LG,
      with mis-tripped relay 's87_cb4'

**Fig.7 Example of trace**

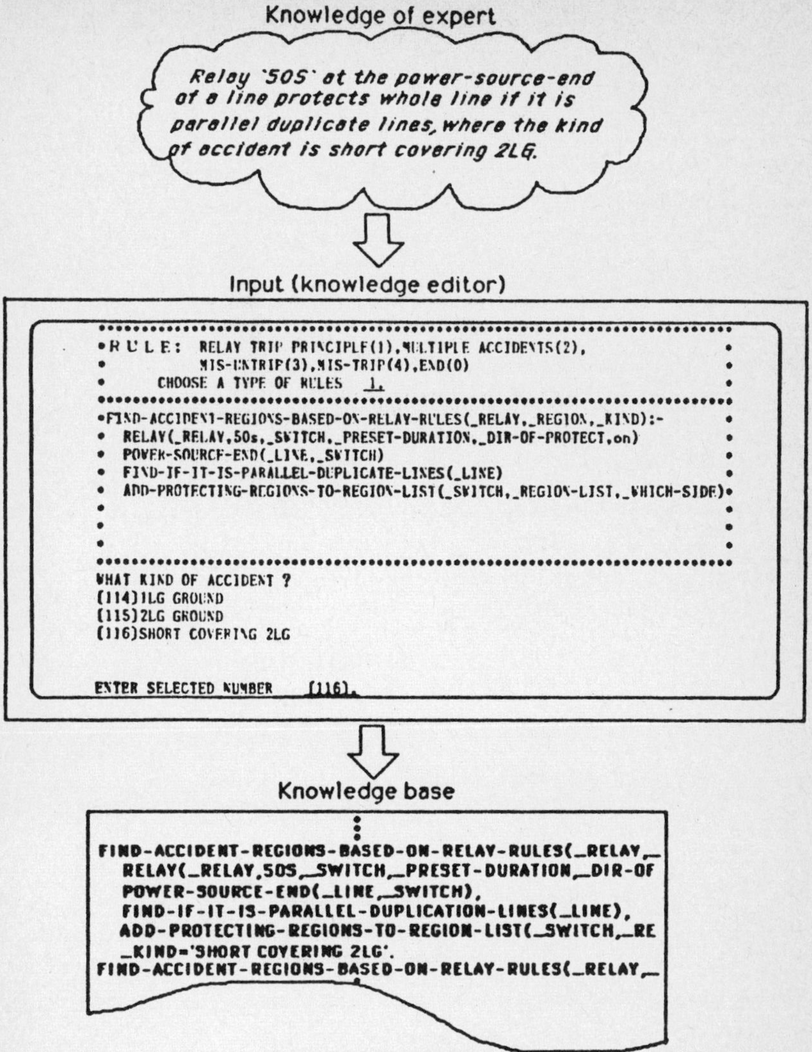

## Knowledge of expert

*Relay `50S` at the power-source-end of a line protects whole line if it is parallel duplicate lines, where the kind of accident is short covering 2LG.*

⇩

### Input (knowledge editor)

```
••••••••••••••••••••••••••••••••••••••••••••••••••••••••••••••••••••
• R U L E :  RELAY TRIP PRINCIPLE(1),MULTIPLE ACCIDENTS(2),         •
•            MIS-UNTRIP(3),MIS-TRIP(4),END(0)                        •
•       CHOOSE A TYPE OF RULES   1.                                  •
••••••••••••••••••••••••••••••••••••••••••••••••••••••••••••••••••••
•FIND-ACCIDENT-REGIONS-BASED-ON-RELAY-RULES(_RELAY,_REGION,_KIND):-  •
• RELAY(_RELAY,50s,_SWITCH,_PRESET-DURATION,_DIR-OF-PROTECT,on)      •
• POWER-SOURCE-END(_LINE,_SWITCH)                                    •
• FIND-IF-IT-IS-PARALLEL-DUPLICATE-LINES(_LINE)                      •
• ADD-PROTECTING-REGIONS-TO-REGION-LIST(_SWITCH,_REGION-LIST,_WHICH-SIDE)•
•                                                                    •
•                                                                    •
••••••••••••••••••••••••••••••••••••••••••••••••••••••••••••••••••••
WHAT KIND OF ACCIDENT ?
(114)1LG GROUND
(115)2LG GROUND
(116)SHORT COVERING 2LG

ENTER SELECTED NUMBER     [116].
```

⇩

### Knowledge base

```
                             :
FIND-ACCIDENT-REGIONS-BASED-ON-RELAY-RULES(_RELAY,_
 RELAY(_RELAY,50S,_SWITCH,_PRESET-DURATION,_DIR-OF
 POWER-SOURCE-END(_LINE,_SWITCH),
 FIND-IF-IT-IS-PARALLEL-DUPLICATION-LINES(_LINE),
 ADD-PROTECTING-REGIONS-TO-REGION-LIST(_SWITCH,_RE
 _KIND='SHORT COVERING 2LG'.
FIND-ACCIDENT-REGIONS-BASED-ON-RELAY-RULES(_RELAY,_
```

Fig.8 Knowledge flow

(1) Menu of **KRISP**

```
                    K R I S P
            - For Electric Dispatching System -
                  TOSHIBA Corporation

    This system will determine the accident locations in the
    power dispatching system by using information of tripped
    CB's and tripped RELAYs. It performs following functions.

        [0] END
        [1] FIND ACCIDENT LOCATIONS
        [2] EDIT FACILITY DATABASE
        [3] EDIT RULE BASE
        [4] VERIFY KNOWLEDGE BASE

    Choose one of above functions  &
```

(2) User interface of data

```
    FACILITY DATA

    TYPE : LINE(1),UNIT BUS(2),MULTI-BUS(3) → 1.
           TRANS(4),SWITCH(5),END(0)

    NAME → LINE-A B-1.

    POWER SOURCE END → s24

    DISTRIBUTION END → s41

    DISTRIBUTION SIDE → (s53)

    PARALLEL LINES → (LINE-A B-1,LINE-A B-2)
```

(3) User interface of rule

```
    R U L E :  RELAY TRIP PRINCIPLE(1),MULTIPLE ACCIDENTS(2),
               MIS-UNTRIP(3),MIS-TRIP(4),END(0)
          CHOOSE A TYPE OF RULES   1.

    FIND-ACCIDENT-REGIONS-BASED-ON-RELAY-RULES(_RELAY,_REGION,_KIND):-
      RELAY(_RELAY,50n,_SWITCH,_PRESET-DURATION,_DIR-OF-PROTECT,on)
      POWER-SOURCE-END(_LINE,_SWITCH)
      FIND-IF-IT-IS-PARALLEL-DUPLICATE-LINES(_LINE)
      ADD-PROTECTING-REGIONS-TO-REGION-LIST(_SWITCH,_REGION-LIST,_WHICH-SIDE)
```

```
WHAT KIND OF ACCIDENT ?
(114)1LG GROUND
(115)2LG GROUND
(116)SHORT COVERING 2LG

ENTER SELECTED NUMBER   (116).
```

Fig 9 Screen image of **KRISP**

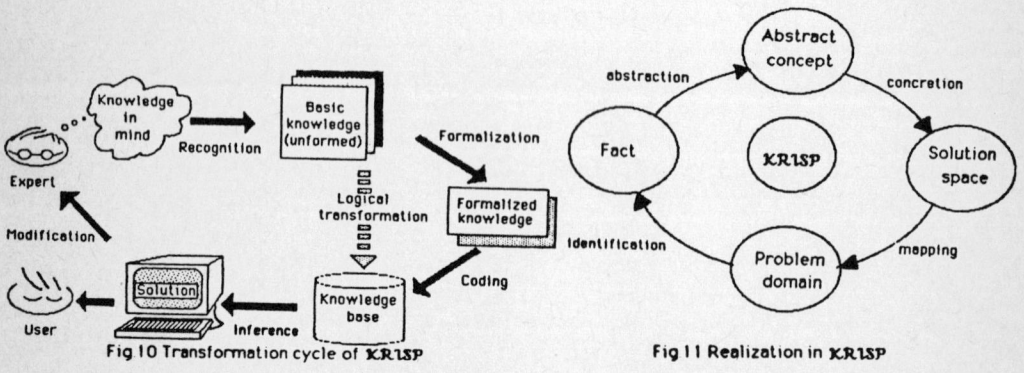

Fig 10 Transformation cycle of **KRISP**

Fig 11 Realization in **KRISP**

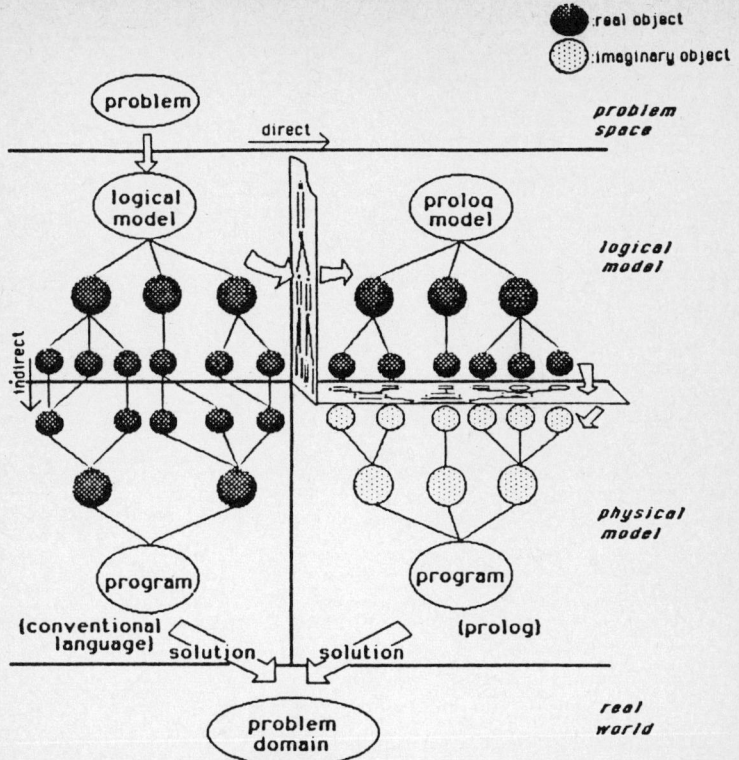

Fig.12 Comparison between prolog and conventional languages in program transformation

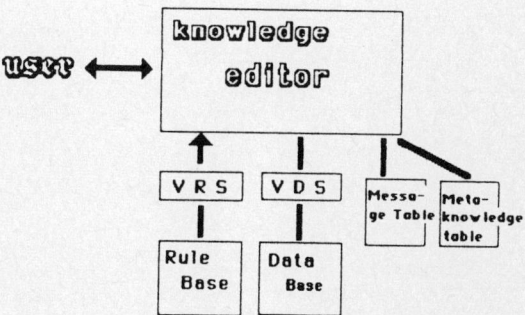

Fig.13   The structure of knowledge editor

JUL 3 0 1986